The Correctness-by-Construction Approach to Programming

Derrick G. Kourie • Bruce W. Watson

The
Correctness-by-Construction
Approach to Programming

 Springer

Derrick G. Kourie
University of Pretoria
Department of Computer Science
Pretoria
South Africa

Bruce W. Watson
Stellenbosch University
FASTAR Group, Information Science
Stellenbosch
South Africa

ISBN 978-3-642-44854-6   ISBN 978-3-642-27919-5 (eBook)
DOI 10.1007/978-3-642-27919-5
Springer Heidelberg Dordrecht London New York

ACM Codes: D.2, F.3, F.4

Printed on acid-free paper

Springer is part of Springer Science+Business Media (www.springer.com)

Preface

Software correctness is a perennial concern. It can and should be addressed as well as possible at various levels and in various complimentary ways. This book is devoted to software correctness at the programming-in-the-small level—down at the point where the developer is in the process of giving birth, so to speak, to an algorithm or part of an algorithm. Its concern lies with that which Brooks [15] calls the *essentials*:

> Those aspects of the programming task which are inescapably error-prone; which confound and confuse our minds, even though individual programming commands in isolation seem quite simple; those uncomfortable points in the code where we are inclined to behave intuitively, guessing at or making little leaps in logic—just tiny little leaps—in an effort to speed up the coding effort. And when we are done with coding and everything compiles nicely, then we hold our breath and live in faith and hope that if there were small misjudgments, they will be exposed during testing.

The book advocates a development style known as *correctness by construction*. The idea is to start with a succinct specification of the problem, which is progressively evolved into code in small, tractable refinement steps. Experience has shown that the resulting algorithms are invariably simpler and more efficient than solutions that have been hacked into correctness. Furthermore, such solutions are guaranteed to be correct (i.e. they are guaranteed to comply with their specifications) in the same sense that the proof of a mathematical theorem is guaranteed to be correct.

The idea is not new. It emerged from earlier attempts in computer science to prove programs to be correct *after* the code had been written. By the mid-eighties, hopes that such ex post facto correctness proofs could contribute practically to software correctness more or less reached a dead end. Without imposing some restraint on how code is to be produced, proofs rapidly become too complex—both for the human mind, and for computers. Instead, a tradition built up, starting with some of the most prominent founding personalities in computer science (Dijkstra, Hoare, Knuth, Wirth) of methodically evolving correct code from specifications in a disciplined step-wise fashion.

Dijkstra was arguably the most vociferous proponent of these ideas. He positioned himself as a prophetic voice crying out in the wilderness that the only path to creating enlightened software developers was through "the cruelty of really teaching computer science" [13]. He contrasted this approach with software engineering, whose charter he disparagingly characterised as "How to program if you cannot." This kind of polarising language has led to unfortunate caricatures around two computer science stereotypes: industry-based developers who supposedly hack around in the real world producing lots of flakey code; and head-in-the-clouds academia engaging in impractical esoteric scientific research. In this caricatured world, the former call themselves software engineers and the latter call their research "formal methods".

We vigourously contest these polarised stereotypes and we hope that this book will contribute to their erosion. We aim to convince the reader that the kind of methodical formal approach that Dijkstra and others have advocated is well within the reach of the average computer scientist and software engineer. Not only that: we hope that the reader will discover that, when confronted with algorithmic problems whose logic is unusually complicated or confusing, it is both satisfying and profitable to develop the code by engaging in a correctness by construction style of programming. We have therefore pitched this text at those who actually develop code, rather than at the formal method purists. At the risk of being accused of being insufficiently formal, we have avoided the kind of presentation style which has given formal methods the reputation of being the domain of an elite few.

The way in which we set about achieving our purpose is by a series of graded examples, rather than by an over-emphasis on the theory that drives the correctness by construction development method. However, a modicum of theoretical and notational background is unavoidable, and this we provide in Chap. 2. After rapidly reviewing first-order predicate logic in this chapter, we relate it to the idea of (total) correctness of Hoare pre-post formulae. This allows us to define the notion of the weakest precondition which, in turn, allows for precisely defining the semantics of the commands used in Dijkstra's Guarded Command Language (GCL)—the notation used throughout the book. Initially we rely on Hoare pre-post notation for expressing the refinement laws of Morgan's refinement calculus [32], but later also introduce Morgan's somewhat more concise notation. We restrict ourselves to a small but useful set of the refinement laws, thus shielding the average computer scientist from the more obscure refinement rules which will only interest theoretical computer scientists.

Chapter 3 illustrates the correctness by construction development method on a number of simple algorithms, many of which might have already been seen in the first or second year of study. Chapter 4 looks at a variety of intermediate range algorithms across a broad spectrum of application domains: analysing array properties (such as finding the longest segment of different elements); raster graphics applications; computational geometry; the majority voting problem; etc. Chapter 5 considers the development method in the context of procedure calls, including recursive procedure calls.

Chapters 6 and 7 are intended as *case studies*. Chapter 6 shows how the correctness by construction method was used to derive an elegant recursive algorithm for constructing the cover graph of a so-called set intersection closed lattice. The formal concept analysis (FCA) research community are discovering how variants of these lattices can be used in a numerous applications such as machine learning and data clustering. The derived algorithm turns out to be significantly superior to many other competing algorithms in the domain. Although a version of the algorithm had been intuitively discovered in the nineties, its articulation was so obscure that even domain specialists found it difficult to understand and verify. As a result, there were niggling doubts about its correctness, despite thorough testing. The case study highlights the fact that the correctness by construction derivation leads to a clear, comprehensible version of the algorithm. Its correctness can thus be readily apprehended and accepted by the user community.

The Chap. 7 case study illustrates yet another useful feature of correctness by construction: it offers a rational basis for articulating algorithm taxonomies. The chapter shows how, when a number of *related* algorithms are developed in this style, their commonalities are clearly exposed, thus offering a basis for taxonomising the related algorithms. The resulting taxonomies are not only useful from a pedagogical perspective; they also tend to expose algorithmic "gaps" in the derived taxonomy, thus suggesting further areas of algorithmic research. In this text we have chosen to illustrate the idea in respect of algorithms to construct minimal acyclic finite automata. Such automata are widely used for in domains such as natural language processing, voice recognition and intrusion detection. This is but one of several other studies which have relied on correctness by construction as a basis for taxonomising.

Although these last two chapter are specialist in nature, we consider them important in that they dispel the myth that correctness by construction should be positioned in the domain of dilettante formal methods theoreticians. On the contrary, we think that any respectable computer science/software engineering university curriculum ought to cover the basic material to be found in this book and that every well-educated computer scientist/software engineering graduate should know something about its major themes. It is becoming increasingly apparent that in universities where such material is casually bypassed under the pretext of focussing the curriculum on industry needs, the better-informed students feel cheated by what they perceive as a dumbing down of courses—and they would be right! Such a viewpoint directly contradicts IEEE's Guide to the Software Engineering Body of Knowledge (SWEBOK)[1] which identifies themes covered in this book as part of the software engineer's armory of tools and methods. Similarly, this book's material will be seen to be consonant with the aspirations of the Software Engineering Method and Theory (SEMAT) initiative which, in its call to action[2], somewhat controversially aims to "refound software engineering based on a solid theory".

The first four chapters of the book, as well as Chap. 6 has formed the core of a fourth year course (involving about 30 contact hours) that we have presented for more than a decade. More of the book can be covered in this time if the instructor

---

[1] See Chap. 10 of the SWEBOK specifications available from http://www.computer.org/portal/web/swebok/home.

[2] See http://www.semat.org/bin/view.

selectively omits and/or assigns as self-study, some of the material in Chaps. 3, 4 and 6. We have found that students are well-able to cope with self-studying many of the examples in Chaps. 3 and 4, provided that the instructor has initiated them into the approach by walking through a representative number of examples. Such self-study-based fast tracking through Chaps. 3, 4 and 6 enables one to cover the main ideas in Chap. 7 as well—something that is well worth doing.

Students who wish to take the course are advised that they should have a basic background in logic. Subject to this proviso, we believe that much of the material can be taught at third year level and probably even earlier. Indeed, because of Dijkstra's influence, this approach to programming was taught at an introductory level at Eindhoven University of Technology.

Many people have contributed to this book in many different ways. They all deserve our sincerest thanks:

- Numerous students whose feedback over the years has helped improve the quality of text.
- Loek Cleophas, who has read and critiqued earlier drafts of the book.
- Alexander Skelton, who wrote the first draft of Chap. 5 as a student project.
- Our many colleagues and friends who have constantly inspired and encouraged us in various ways to produce this book.
- Last, but not least, our respective families who have been a constant source of support and encouragement to us.

Pretoria, South Africa   *Derrick G. Kourie*
Eindhoven, Netherlands   *Bruce W. Watson*

Contents

Chapter 1
Introduction

There are many debates amongst software engineers about the extent to which one should engage in so-called upfront design. But the focus of the debate relates mostly to programming-in-the-large: how to approach the problem of designing a large system of interacting objects or components. The "Big Upfront Design" (BUD) adherents believe that energy should go into developing an initial overall architectural outline of the system; the adherents of the more recent agile software development movement are inclined to let a system architecture evolve from the bottom up, so to speak. Their energy goes into identifying small components of the overall system, developing test cases and writing code that handles these test cases.

But whatever view one takes, it seems that—as a matter of fact—by the time people get down to programming-in-the-small (i.e. actually writing code), there is rapid recourse to the keyboard:

> Try a little bit of this and a little bit of that; put in an if-command here and a loop there; two int variables would seem to do the trick; let us try to compile; oops—forgot about the else part of the if-command; compile again; oh dear—a syntax error; fix and recompile; run the test cases; darn—test case 3 fails; desperately resort to pen and paper to scratch out a couple of exploratory diagrams; ah—perhaps a separate method is needed to deal with a newly-discovered boundary condition . . .

Those who do not recognise this kind of scenario are truly blessed. To most real programmers, it will be painfully, if not embarrassingly, familiar. The purpose of these notes is to change the way that readers think when coding at this programming-in-the-small level.

Now we are not so naïve as to believe that we will persuade all and sundry to derive paper solutions to problems before entering code at a keyboard. It is just as vain to hope that the multitudes will take time to sit cross-legged in Zen-like meditation to clearly think through the problem at hand before taking to a keyboard, desirable as such a practice may be! However, we do cherish a fond hope that this book will change thought processes: that they will foster the kind of mentality that, almost as a matter of second nature, asks: what should the pre- and postconditions be for this method; what holds at the end of this piece of code; what might be the

D.G. Kourie and B.W. Watson, *The Correctness-by-Construction Approach to Programming*, DOI 10.1007/978-3-642-27919-5_1,
© Springer-Verlag Berlin Heidelberg 2012

loop's invariant, etc. And we will not be disappointed if a few individuals discover that it is sometimes actually both intellectually pleasing and time-wise profitable to derive a paper solution to critical problems in the code, before hitting the keyboard.

The underlying problem solving strategy that we advocate is to refine progressively an abstract description of a problem—its specification in terms of pre- and postconditions—to its ever-more concrete realisation, culminating in the concrete solution specified in Guarded Command Language (GCL). A very particular kind of abstract specification is one in which the pre- and postcondition is "invariant"— by which we roughly mean that they are the same, barring certain variations in the variable values that describe them. It will be seen that such "invariance" is an extremely powerful aid to solving iterative problems. Invariance lies at the heart of the solution to practically all the example problems that we will later be considering. Because of its importance, and to sharpen intuition, we now present two example problems that are easily solved by identifying invariants.

1.1   Invariance Examples

An invariant of a sequence of steps to solve a problem, is a condition that is true before carrying out those steps, and that remains true after executing the entire sequence of steps. If the problem solution is somehow made easier as a result of executing the sequence once, then one would hope that by repeatedly executing the sequence of steps (i.e. by looping) the problem can eventually be solved. It is important to note that the invariant is not required to hold after each step; rather, it should hold after executing the entire sequence.

The following two problems serve as a foretaste of the kind of thinking that will be promoted in the remainder of this text. They show that the notion of an invariant *of a sequence of steps* can be a powerful aid to solving problems.[1]

1.1.1   A Chess Board Problem

Consider an 8×8 chess board from which the squares in the upper left and lower right corners have been removed, as shown in Fig. 1.1. Also available is a large number of domino tiles such as the two shown to the right of the board in the figure, each of which covers exactly two squares of the chess board. Assume that tiles may not lie on top of one another. Nor may they hang over the edge of the chess board.

---

[1]How one finds an invariant for a sequence of steps cannot be prescribed. It is very much dependent on the problem to be solved. It is an art that comes with practice.

Fig. 1.1 Chessboard and squares

Is it possible to lay tiles on the chess board in such a way so that all squares are covered?

If you try an exhaustive approach to laying all combinations of domino tiles on the board, you *might* eventually arrive at an answer. This is the equivalent of trying to hack out an answer to a coding problem on a trial-and-error basis at a keyboard. However, there is a more subtle and elegant way to tackle the problem. Consider the following assertions:

- A regular chess board contains the same number of black and white squares.
- The modified chess board in this problem has had two white squares removed— therefore it has two more black than white squares.
- Every tile placement reduces by one the number of uncovered black squares and the number of uncovered white squares.
- Thus, no matter how one lays a tile, there will always be more black squares than white squares.

  One could express this by saying that the following relationship is invariant with respect to the tile laying operation:[2]

$$number(white) \neq number(black)$$

- As a consequence, there is no way of laying the tiles so that

$$number(white) = number(black) = 0$$

Becoming aware of an invariant in this problem space not only rapidly leads to an answer to the problem; it also indicates solutions to a whole class of similar problems. The chess board did not have to be the standard 8×8 size: it could

---

[2]Actually, we could make the invariant even more precise, namely number(white) $+ 2 =$ number(black). However, this increased precision does not help us any further in solving the problem.

Fig. 1.2 20 black and 17 white balls

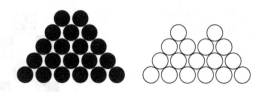

have had an arbitrary number of columns and rows. Neither was it necessary to couch the problem in terms of removing two squares from opposite corners: any number of squares could have been removed from anywhere on the board. The answer to the problem would have been the same, for any starting position such that number(white) $\neq$ number(black).

1.1.2 A Black and White Balls Game

Another problem that can be solved using an invariant is the following. Suppose we take the pile of 20 black balls and 17 white balls shown in Fig. 1.2 and mix them together in a bag.

A step consists of randomly drawing two balls from the bag, examining their colours, and then returning one ball back into the bag according to the rules below. (Assume that a sufficient stock of additional balls is available to allow for more than 20 black or more than 17 white balls in the bag, if required by the rules.) The following rules are to be applied.

1. If 2 *white* balls are drawn, return 1 *white* ball.
2. If 1 *white* and 1 *black* ball is drawn, return 1 *black* ball.
3. If 2 *black* balls were drawn, return a *white* ball.

Clearly, the number of balls in the bag decreases by one after each "draw 2 return 1" step. Eventually there will only be one ball left in the bag. At that point, the game terminates.

> What colour ball remains at the end of the game?

Once more, the natural instinct of most people is to "hack out" a solution.

> How many white balls remain after the first move if rule 1 applies? And how many white balls remain after the second move? What if rule 2 or 3 applies in the second move? etc.

If you were to forge ahead meticulously and systematically with such an approach, you will eventually arrive at the correct answer—provided you do not make mistakes. To reduce the chances of an error, you will undoubtedly need to jot down the state of the bag after each step. You might reasonably hope that it will not be necessary to examine exhaustively every possible trace of steps—perhaps a pattern in the evolution of the bag's state will eventually emerge and will expose the answer.

In fact, that instinctive quest for a *pattern* corresponds to the search for an invariant. Without denying the need for some initial thought-probing into the bag's state-by-state evolution as steps are executed, we encourage re-focussing ones intellectual energy to deliberately aim at discovering an invariant pattern. This is a matter of practice and habit. Often an invariant emerges very rapidly, without needing to rely on pen and paper.

Instead of focussing on the state of the bag after one or two or three moves, perhaps it is worth first considering the nature of the rules themselves—independently of the concrete state of the bag (initially having 20 black and 17 white balls). A moment's thought will convince you that the rules imply the following invariant property of the bag's state before and after each step:

The parity of the number of *black* balls in the bag remains the same.

Thus, if the game started with an even (or uneven) number of black balls, then an even (or uneven) number of black balls remains after each step. Furthermore, the number of balls decreases by one after each step.[3] Eventually, after the second last step, there will be only two balls left; and a single ball will remain after the last step has been executed.

Clearly, the invariant informs us that the last ball will be white if the game started with an even number of black balls—which was indeed the case for the starting position specified above. However, the invariant gives us a general solution to the entire class of similar problems. The last ball will be:

- Black if the starting position was, say, 17 white balls and 21 black balls;
- White if the starting position was 78,140 white balls and 24,276 black balls;
- Black if there were initially 1,000 white balls and 1 black ball;
- White if there were initially 0 white balls and 520 black balls; etc.

1.2 The Way Ahead

In each of the above two examples, the solution to a seemingly complex problem involving a sequence of steps became obvious as soon as we discovered a relevant invariant—a property about the state of the problem space that remained constant after each step. In the forthcoming chapters, we shall see that similar thinking can be powerfully employed in developing loops.

The essence of our quest in the remainder of this book will be to derive code from specifications. Once a problem has been specified, a number of refinement laws can be deployed to refine incrementally the specification. Each refinement step adds more algorithmic information to the specification and can be proven to be a correct

---

[3] As will be seen later, this is an example of a so-called variant—a function that strictly decreases towards a fixed minimum value. It guarantees that the problem can be solved in a finite number of steps.

refinement—one that is consistent with the previous specification. Eventually a fully algorithmic specification of the original problem is attainted. The algorithm is guaranteed to be correct in the same sense that the proof of a mathematical theorem is guaranteed to be correct.

Chapter 2 introduces the notation to be used, as well as the theoretical underpinning upon which we rely for the step-wise refinement from specification to code. Subsequent chapters provide a series of example problems to illustrate this so-called *correctness by construction* approach. The examples range from several well-known simple problems in Chap. 3, to somewhat more complex problems in Chap. 4. It will be seen that the approach inevitably involves the construction of loops, and that loop invariants play a fundamental role in arriving at correct and elegant loops. Chapter 5 extends these ideas to allow for function calls in general, placing the emphasis on solutions that entail recursive function calls.

The last two chapters shift gear. Their purpose is to support the view that the correctness-by-construction approach to software development is not merely a theoretical computer science theme. On the contrary, it can be used as a research and development instrument for

- Discovering and illuminating the correctness of new and better algorithms—as will be illustrated in Chap. 6, and
- Taxonomising algorithmic solutions to problem domains and thereby illuminating the interrelationship between algorithms—as demonstrated in Chap. 7.

Chapter 2
Background

The correctness by construction methodology advocated by this book starts off with a predicate-based specification of the problem at hand, and then incrementally refines that specification to code. However, to be able to do this, several preliminary notational and theoretical matters have to be in place. This chapter provides that background.

- Firstly, we need a very precise "language" to specify and reason about the current or intended states of a computer. Section 2.1 briefly reviews just such a language—the well-known first order predicates calculus. The section draws attention to the fact that predicates can be deemed to be strong or weak in as much as they more specifically or more generally characterise a set of computer states.
- Section 2.2 then shows how such predicates (about computer states) can be used as the basis for specifying the pre- and postconditions of code that is to be developed to address some problem. However, if the code is to be meaningfully described by such pre- and postconditions, then the individual programming language commands that constitute that code must themselves be describable in terms of pre- and postconditions. The section therefore also introduces the notion of pre- and postconditions as a way of specifying the meaning (semantics) of commands of a programming language.
- Section 2.3 relies on this approach to language specification to define commands in Dijkstra's well-known GCL. This small, simple but very elegant set of commands is used in the remainder of the text as the vehicle for describing algorithms.
- The foregoing provides a basis for defining when one specification, given in terms of a pre- and postcondition, may be regarded as a refinement another. In fact, Sect. 2.4 gives various refinement rules that can be used to transform a high-level pre- postcondition-based specification into equivalent GCL code. Exactly how to do this will be amply illustrated in the remainder of the text.
- Object orientation (OO) is widely used as a paradigm for driving software development. It therefore behoves us to discuss whether and how the correctness-by-construction approach to developing software relates to OO. Section 2.5

D.G. Kourie and B.W. Watson, *The Correctness-by-Construction Approach*
to Programming, DOI 10.1007/978-3-642-27919-5_2,
© Springer-Verlag Berlin Heidelberg 2012

briefly addresses these questions. We show how to connect inheritance in OO to procedure refinement as described in the previous section, and we use this to define class refinement.

- Finally, Sect. 2.6 records several notational conventions that are to be used henceforth.

2.1 Predicates

In order to describe a problem in terms of pre- and postconditions, we need a notation in which to express and reason about these conditions. For this, we will use first order predicate calculus. There are numerous texts which deal extensively with predicate calculus. Here we briefly outline the main elements that will be needed.

2.1.1 Propositional Calculus

First order predicate calculus extends on propositional calculus. Propositional expressions (or simply *propositions*) are built up from well-known logical operators. They also arise when so-called relational operators are used, usually in the context of arithmetic or real number types. They also occur in the presence of the $\in$ symbol used in the context of sets. A proposition may thus be defined as follows:

- The Boolean values true and false are propositions.
- If x and y are variables that denote propositions, then $x \vee y$, $x \wedge y$, $x \Longrightarrow y$, $x \Longleftrightarrow y$ and $\neg x$ are propositions.
- If E_1 and E_2 denote expressions whose respective values are of a type that is ordered by the relational operator $<$, then $E_1 < E_2$ is a proposition that evaluates to true if and only if the value of E_1 is less than the value of E_2. Similarly propositions can also be formed from the other relational operators ($\leq$, $>$, $\geq$, $=$ and $\neq$).
- $x \in S$ is a proposition whose value is true if x is an element of the set S, and false otherwise.
- If x is a proposition, then (x) is a proposition with the same truth value.

The truth values of these propositions for different evaluations of x and y are given in the following table:

x	y	$x \vee y$	$x \wedge y$	$x \Longrightarrow y$	$x \Longleftrightarrow y$	$\neg x$
true	true	true	true	true	true	false
true	false	true	false	false	false	false
false	true	true	false	true	false	true
false	false	false	false	true	true	true

Of course, this table will be familiar to all who have had an introductory courses in logic and/or programming. Nevertheless, the interpretation of $x \implies y$ is counter-intuitive for many, and is a frequent cause of confusion. Recall that x is termed the antecedent and y, the consequent of this proposition. It is well to remember the following

$(x \implies y)$ is false only when x is true and y is false.
In all other cases, $(x \implies y)$ is true.

It is also useful to remember that the proposition $(x \implies y)$ is equivalent to the proposition $(\neg x \vee y)$, by which we mean that for all true or false allocations to the variables x and y, the two propositions evaluate to the same truth-value. This can expressed by stating that $(x \implies y) \iff (\neg x \vee y)$ is a tautology, or alternatively by writing:

$$(x \implies y) \equiv (\neg x \vee y)$$

Note that the foregoing definition of a proposition allows for two types of variables: proposition variables, and variables of some type. The latter may appear in the context of typed expressions joined by relational operators (as stated in the third bullet above). These variables are *unbounded* (or *uninstantiated*). In general, it is not possible to assign a truth value to a proposition that contains uninstantiated variables.

For example, x and y are unbounded in the proposition $(x > 5) \wedge (y < 10)$. It is not possible, without further information, to assign a truth value to this proposition. A truth value is evident only when the variables x and y have each been assigned particular values in a particular context.

Paradoxically, however, we do not *always* have to assign values to unbound variables in order to ascertain the truth value of a proposition containing unbounded variables. For example, the proposition $(x > 0) \vee \neg(x > 0)$ contains the unbounded variable, x, (assume it is of type integer) but clearly has value true. Similarly, the proposition $\neg(p \wedge \neg p)$ contains the variable p that represents some unspecified proposition. Nevertheless, a little thought will also confirm that the truth value of this compound expression is always true, no matter what truth value is assigned to the variable p. These latter two propositions are examples of *tautologies*. A tautology is a proposition which is always true, no matter what values are assigned to its variables.

When mixing programs and predicates, as will be done later, a predicate method[1] in the program will also be regarded as a proposition. We could therefore have a proposition such as $isCircle(x) \wedge y > 10$ where $isCircle()$ is assumed to be predicate method that returns true if its argument is a circle object and false otherwise. Again, the proposition only acquires a truth value when the unbounded variables, x and y are instantiated to specific values of an appropriate type.

---

[1] i.e. a method that returns a Boolean value.

2.1.2   Predicate Calculus

In first order predicate calculus, all propositions are regarded as predicate formulae (simply referred to as predicates). Additionally, predicate calculus includes the *quantified* predicate formulae, as next described.

Let x be a *list* of variables (called the bound variables) and let R be a set of values (called the range) that x may take on. Suppose $f : R \rightarrow \mathbb{B}$ is a function that maps each element in the set R to an element in the set of Boolean values, i.e. $\mathbb{B} = \{\text{true}, \text{false}\}$. Then:

- $\forall x \in R : f(x)$ is a predicate that evaluates to true if and only if $f(x) = \text{true}$ for each x in R. If $R = \varnothing$ then $\forall x \in R : f(x)$ evaluates to true.
- $\exists x \in R : f(x)$ is a predicate that evaluates to false if and only if $f(x) = \text{false}$ for each x in R. If $R = \varnothing$ then $\exists x \in R : f(x)$ evaluates to false.

There are several variations of the syntax of quantified predicates. For example, there may be multiple bound variables of different types, as in the following example: $\forall (x_1, x_2, y) \in \mathbb{N} \times \mathbb{N} \times \mathbb{R} : (f(x_1, y) \vee g(x_2))$. Here, x_1 and x_2 are elements of the set of natural numbers (denoted by $\mathbb{N}$), y is an element of the set of real numbers (denoted by $\mathbb{R}$).

In other instances, the range may be implied, in which case we simply leave it out, as in $\exists x : f(x)$.

2.1.3   Predicates Define Sets of States

A precondition of a code segment, S, is simply a predicate formula that asserts something about the state of the computer on which S is to be executed, just prior to that execution taking place. Likewise, a postcondition is a predicate asserting what is supposed to be true after S has executed. The state of the computer is described by the value of the variables relevant to S.

Thus $(x > 5)$ could be a precondition or postcondition of S, asserting that the particular variable, x, is greater than 5—an assertion that may or may not be true; and an assertion that makes no claim about the values of other variables used by S.

We will normally treat a variable as if it was a mathematical entity. However, to be completely accurate, we might need to relate the variable x to the way it is stored in memory: is it stored as an integer or real number? how many bytes does it occupy? etc. In correctness arguments, these issues could be important, in as much as they indicate limitations on the variables in relation to precision and the range of values (maximum and minimum) that may be assumed. When necessary, we will explicitly relate x to its computer representation by indicating its type. Thus, $x : T$ will be used to indicate that variable x is of type T.

In fact, if we assume that each variable in a program is uniquely associated with certain bytes in memory, then a predicate such as $(x > 5)$ has a one-to-one

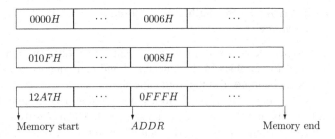

Fig. 2.1 Examples of elements in the set $States_{(x>5)}$

correspondence with *a set* of memory states. Suppose p is an arbitrary predicate that contains unbound variables referring to program variables. There will be some memory states, say $t_1, \ldots t_n$, in which p evaluates to true and other states, say $f_1, \ldots, f_m$ in which p evaluates to false.

Notation 2.1.1 ($States_p$). *The set of states in which the predicate p evaluates to* true *is denoted by $States_p$.*

Thus if we assume that x in the predicate $(x > 5)$ is a variable that is stored as a 16-bit integer in memory at a byte-address $ADDR$, then $States_{(x>5)}$ corresponds to the set of all states of memory, each of whose elements has a hexadecimal value in byte-address $ADDR$ that is in the range 0006H to 7FFFH (assuming a sign bit in the most significant digit), and any arbitrary bit values stored in the remainder of the memory. Figure 2.1 illustrates three of the many possible states in $States_{(x>5)}$.

2.1.4 Strong and Weak Predicates

As with any other predicate formulae, pre- and postconditions may rely on logical connectives such as $\vee$ and $\wedge$ to join simpler predicates together; they may be quantified; and we may reason about their truth or falsity. We will be particularly concerned to compare predicates with one another in relation to whether one is *weaker* or *stronger* than another.

Suppose W and S are predicates. As an intuitive, but slightly incomplete definition, we might say that S is stronger than W (or, equivalently, W is weaker than S) if and only if $S \implies W$.

Although this is quite a simple notion, it sometimes causes confusion. It is therefore worth elaborating a little on the matter, especially because it is intimately bound up with the rules of refinement discussed in Sect. 2.4 of this chapter—rules which form the core of the software construction method that we are advocating.

Our above definition actually takes liberties in the use of language. Strictly speaking, we should have said:

Definition 2.1.2 (Predicate Strength). S is stronger than W if and only if $(S \Longrightarrow W)$ *is a tautology.*[2]

Now, a tautological relationship may never evaluate to false (no matter what values are assigned to variables in the antecedent and consequent) and therefore $S \Longrightarrow W$ may never be false. But the truth table shows that $S \Longrightarrow W$ can only be false when S is true and W is false. So to test a claim that S is stronger than W, it is sufficient to verify that there are *no* circumstances in which S is true and W is false. Put positively, we may merely verify that whenever S is true then W is also true.

For example, we can easily test the claim that $(x > 5)$ is stronger than $(x > 0)$, by noting that every instantiation of x that renders $(x > 5)$ to be true, also renders $(x > 0)$ as true—it is just not possible to choose a value of x which renders $(x > 5)$ to be true and $(x > 0)$ to be false.

What apparently confuses many is the fact that there may be instantiations of variables in S and W that render S to be false but W to be true. For example, suppose x is 3 in our example. Then $(3 > 5)$ is false but $(3 > 0)$ is true. It is a mistake to conclude at this point that $(x > 5) \Longrightarrow (x > 0)$ is consequently false, and therefore that $(x > 5)$ is not stronger than $(x > 0)$. Refer back to the truth table for propositional expressions, and it will be clear that the truth value of false $\Longrightarrow$ true is true!

There are several other perspectives of what it means to say that one predicate is stronger or weaker than another. One of these views relies on the notion of substitution.

Definition 2.1.3 (Single Substitution). $P[x \backslash a]$ denotes the predicate that results by substituting each and every occurrence of the variable x that occurs in predicate P with the symbol a.

Note that we do not insist that the substituting symbol, a, should be a constant—it might also be another variable. For simplicity, the notation assumes that x is a single variable and a is a single substituting symbol. However, as indicated later in Notation 2.3.3, the same notation also allows that x may be a list of variables, and a a list of substituting symbols. In such a case, the nth variable in the variable list is to be substituted by the nth substituting symbol. Some subtleties to be considered in such a case of multiple variable substitution are pointed out later.

Stated in terms of this substitution notation, what we have just argued above is that

$$((x > 5) \Longrightarrow (x > 0))[x \backslash 3] \equiv \text{true}$$

Also relying on this notation, we may base the claim that $(x > 5)$ is stronger than $(x > 0)$ on the fact that

$$\forall X : ((x > 5) \Longrightarrow (x > 0))[x \backslash X] \equiv \text{true}$$

---

[2]Note that by this definition S is stronger than itself, since $(S \Longrightarrow S)$ is a tautology—i.e. $(S \Longrightarrow S) \equiv \text{true}$.

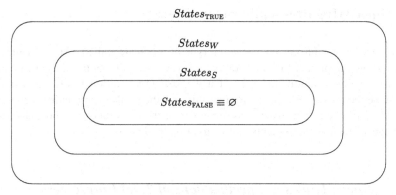

$$States_{FALSE} \subseteq States_S \subseteq States_W \subseteq States_{TRUE}$$
$$FALSE \Rightarrow S \Rightarrow W \Rightarrow TRUE.$$

Fig. 2.2 Outer oval represents all possible machine states

Note that even if the antecedent and the consequent in the predicate $(x > 5)$ $\implies$ $(x > 0)$ both evaluate to false, as would be the case when $(X = -100)$ then, since the predicate (false $\implies$ false) evaluates to true, the predicate is true.

It is instructive to relate the idea of strong and weak predicates back to the notion of the set of states associated with true instances of the predicates concerned. It is easy to see that $States_{(x>5)} \subseteq States_{(x>0)}$. It therefore turns out that the following are equivalent ways of stating the same thing:

- S is stronger than W.
- $S \implies W$ is a tautology.
- $\forall V : (S \implies W)[v \backslash V] =$ true, where v indicates the list of variables that are referred to in S and W, and V is a list of values that these variables may assume.
- $States_S \subseteq States_W$.

Notation 2.1.4 ($\Rightarrow$). $S \Rightarrow W$ *is used to indicate that S is stronger than W. $\Rightarrow$ is the "implied everywhere" symbol and indicates that "everywhere S implies W".*

Also note that the set consisting of *all possible memory states* corresponds to the predicate true, and can be denoted by S_{true}. true is thus the weakest possible predicate and every other predicate is stronger than it. Conversely, false is the strongest possible predicate, $States_{false} = \varnothing$, and every other predicate is weaker than false. The matter is visually illustrated in Fig. 2.2.

We could summarise this by noting that if P represents the set of all possible predicates, then $\forall p : P : States_{false} \subseteq States_p \subseteq States_{true}$. Alternatively, we could say: $\forall p : P :$ false $\Rightarrow p \Rightarrow$ true.

In general, therefore, a weaker predicate is less strict about the values that variables may assume, compared to its stronger counterpart. One might associate with the notion of a weak predicate, words such as: more abstract, more liberal, less strict, etc.

2.2   Specifying Pre- and Postconditions

In this section, we introduce a particular type of predicate, called a Hoare triple, as a well-known approach to specifying pre- and postconditions in relation to code. Relying on this notation, the idea of a weakest precondition is then explained. As will be seen in the section that follows this one, the weakest precondition concept is an elegant way of specifying the semantics of the constructs of a programming language, as well as the semantics of a larger body of code.

2.2.1   Hoare Triples as Specifications of Total Correctness

Suppose that S is some code, and that P and Q are two predicate formulae. Then $\{P\} \, S \, \{Q\}$ is itself a predicate formula that asserts the following:

> If P is true just before S executes then S *will terminate* and then Q will be true.

This is a so-called Hoare triple in which P is a precondition of S and Q is the resulting postcondition. Because it is a predicate formula, such a Hoare triple is either true or false, provided its variables are appropriately bound, as discussed below.

Note carefully that in order for the predicate to evaluate to true S *has to terminate* if started in an arbitrary state of $States_P$. In this case, we speak of "total correctness"—i.e. if the predicate is true then S is said to be "totally" correct with respect to the precondition P and postcondition Q.[3] We shall interpret all triples to be assertions about total correctness.

However, as already stated, if the variables in $\{P\} \, S \, \{Q\}$ are not bound, then it may not be possible to assign a truth-value to the predicate—just as it is not possible to decide whether or not $(x > 5)$ is true without knowing the value of x. However, sometimes a truth value can indeed be assigned to $\{P\} \, S \, \{Q\}$, even if some or all of the variables are not bound to any value.

This happens, for example, if the Hoare triple constitutes a tautology. To give a concrete example, suppose we denote by *skip* the do-nothing, or empty command in some programming language. Then the triple $\{P\} \, skip \, \{P\}$ is true for *any* predicate P. In fact, the triple defines the meaning (or semantics) of the *skip* command. This is an example of how Hoare triples can be used to provide the so-called axiomatic semantics of programming constructs.

The objective in this text is slightly different. It is to start with the pre- and postconditions that describe a problem, where the symbol S initially describes the code in an entirely symbolic and non-specific manner. In this case, we can think of a Hoare triple as a *specification* of a problem. It tells us the pre- and postconditions

---

[3]In some texts, $P \, \{S\} \, Q$ is interpreted as a statement of *partial correctness*, by which is meant the assertion that if P is true and S executes then Q will be true *if* S terminates.

of the problem, and we then have to find an explicit solution to the problem—an instantiation of S to code which renders $\{P\}\ S\ \{Q\}$ to be true.

We will rely on various rules of refinement, rules of inference and axioms associated with Hoare triples incrementally to change S into an increasingly specific form that corresponds to commands of a program. These various rules will be provided in Sect. 2.4. However, at this point it is useful to enrich our notation in anticipation of some of the refinement rules. Specifically, we allow for the specifier to indicate which list of variables in S may be changed in order to arrive at the postconditions. Thus $\{P\}\ s : S\ \{Q\}$ specifies that in order to ensure that postcondition Q is met, the code in S may only change the value of one or more variables in the list s. The variables whose values may change, i.e. those in the list s above, are called the *frame variables* (or, more concisely, simply the *frame*) of the specification.

As an example, consider the specification

$$\{x \geq 0\}\ y : S\ \{y^2 = x\}$$

For this predicate to be true the code represented abstractly by S should assign a value to y that corresponds to the square root of some x, where x is guaranteed to be non-negative at the start of the code. If we assumed the existence of a *sqrt* method, then a legitimate elaboration of the specification into a program would be

$$\{x \geq 0\}\ y := sqrt(x)\ \{y^2 = x\}$$

On the other hand, if the starting problem was (somewhat obscurely) stated as:

$$\{x \geq 0\}\ x, y : S\ \{x = y \wedge y^2 = x\}$$

then a program that complies with this specification could be:

$$\{x \geq 0\}\ x := 1; y := 1\ \{x = y \wedge y^2 = x\}$$

Note that this is *one* program that complies with the specification. In general, many programs can comply with a given specification. (Can you think of another way of assigning values to x and y that would meet the specification in this particular instance?)

As a final example, if the problem was (somewhat perversely) stated as

$$\{true\}\ y : S\ \{y^2 = x\}$$

then we would have to throw up our hands in despair—the precondition does not place any limit on the initial value of x, and the frame requires that we only change values of y in order to meet the postcondition. Because this specification allows that x could possibly be negative, there is no version of S that can guarantee to always derive a y that is the square root of x. We are being asked to derive an infeasible program!

2.2.2   Weakest Preconditions and Semantics

To explain what a programming language command does, means to indicate the *semantics* of the command. Normally, this is done informally, i.e. in natural language, and sometimes an illustrative example may be given. However, in Sect. 2.3, it is our intention to introduce the GCL specification language by defining the semantics of the core GCL commands in an alternative and very precise way, namely by specifying, for each command, the so-called *weakest precondition* required for that command to produce a given postcondition.

To gain some insight into the idea of a weakest precondition, consider two predicates P and P' such that $P \Rightarrow P'$—i.e. P' is weaker than P.

Now suppose it has been shown that $\{P\}\ S\ \{Q\}$ is true for some fixed and given program S and for some fixed and given P and Q. Suppose, too, that another analysis reveals that $\{P'\}\ S\ \{Q\}$ is also true. This means that after S terminates, the postcondition Q will be attained, even if initial conditions comply with a predicate that is weaker than P, namely with P'. Perhaps it will be possible to find an even weaker predicate than P', say P'', such that $\{P''\}\ S\ \{Q\}$ is true, etc.

Eventually, for a given S and Q, there will always be exactly one precondition, say W, that is the very weakest possible of all possible preconditions that render $\{W\}\ S\ \{Q\}$ to be true. Not surprisingly, we call this predicate the *the weakest precondition* of S with respect to Q and denote it by $wp(S, Q)$. It can be defined formally as follows:

Definition 2.2.1 (Weakest Precondition). Let S be a program and Q be a predicate. Then the predicate $wp(S, Q)$ is the weakest precondition of S with respect to Q, if and only if

$$\{wp(S, Q)\}\ S\ \{Q\}$$

and

$$\forall P \cdot (\{P\}\ S\ \{Q\}) \Longrightarrow (P \Rightarrow wp(S, Q))$$

There are a few points about the weakest precondition that may seem obvious, but are nevertheless worth emphasising.

- It should be emphasised that, per definition of the weakest precondition, it will always be the case that:

$$\{wp(S, Q)\}\ S\ \{Q\}$$

- If, for a *given* S and some for predicate variable Q (by which we mean that Q is not given an explicit form such as $(x > 5)$), we can find an expression for $wp(S, Q)$ in terms of Q, then we would have very specifically—uniquely, in fact—characterised the behaviour (or meaning, or semantics) of S.

Thus, $wp(S, Q)$ is one very neat way of defining the semantics of a program or statement S.[4]

- Also noted that for a *given* Q, say $(x > 5)$, and for some given S, the precondition of S with respect to Q will be some predicate that typically depends on x. Its exact form will of course depend on S. If we have already determined an explicit general expression for $wp(S, Q)$, then finding $wp(S, (x > 5))$ is a straightforward matter of substituting $(x > 5)$ for Q.

In the next section, various commands of the so-called GCL will be described in terms of their precondition semantics.

2.3 Guarded Command Language

Dijkstra proposed and used a very simple yet powerful language in which to specify algorithms. It is known as the GCL,[5] and abbreviated to GCL. Although GCL has very precise semantics, it is not normally implemented on a computer. Nevertheless, it is a simple matter to translate a GCL program into one of the commonly implemented languages: Java, C++, C#, etc. GCL relies on the following constructs:

Construct	Symbol
Empty command	*skip*
Assignment	:=
Composition	;
Selection	**if**
Repetition	**do**

Each of these commands will now be discussed. The discussion will not only focus on the syntax and semantics of the respective commands, but will also touch on various other matters of interest. We shall postpone until Sect. 2.4, a discussion about how a program made up of these commands can be refined out of a Hoare triple specification.

---

[4]There are at least four different approaches to defining the semantics of S: operationally; translationally; denotationally; and axiomatically. Details are beyond the scope of this text. However, it may be of interest to note that the precondition approach is generally classified as an axiomatic approach to defining semantics, and we usually speak of the "precondition semantics" in this context.

[5]Although program constructs are commonly referred to as *statements*, Dijkstra preferred the term *command*. For this reason, the term shall be used consistently throughout this text.

2.3.1 Empty Command

We have already encountered the *skip* command. It is a command which "does nothing". Curiously, however, the command is both theoretically interesting, and operationally necessary in GCL. From an operational point of view, we shall see below that it is sometimes mandatory to use a *skip* command as part of a selection command. From a theoretical point of view, the *skip* command very simply illustrates the notion of a weakest precondition.

Since the *skip* command does nothing, if we want postcondition Q to hold after executing it, then clearly this postcondition will be attained if Q holds before executing *skip*. Thus, as we have already indicated, $\{Q\}$ *skip* $\{Q\}$ is true for any arbitrary predicate, Q. We may then enquire: can the precondition Q be weakened in some or other fashion, and still guarantee the attainment of Q after executing *skip*? Clearly, the answer is "no". Just to drive home the point, while the specification

$$\{x > 5\} \; skip \; \{x > 5\}$$

is always true, the specification with a slightly weaker precondition, say

$$\{x > 0\} \; skip \; \{x > 5\}$$

is false. The latter is easily seen by considering some value of x that satisfies the precondition but not the postcondition (e.g. $x = 3$). Clearly if $x = 3$ before executing the *skip* command, the resulting state (namely one in which x still equals 3) does not satisfy the postcondition. We thus conclude that *skip* may be precisely and formally defined as follows:

Definition 2.3.1 (Empty Command). The instruction, *skip*, is a command such that for any predicate Q, $wp(skip, Q) = Q$.

It is important to note that the definition insists that Q may assume *any* value. There may well be some command(s), S, such that $\{Q\}$ S $\{Q\}$ is true for *some* values of Q, but *skip* is the only command in the entire universe that not only guarantees $\{Q\}$ S $\{Q\}$ to be true for *any* value of Q, but also guarantees that $\{P\}$ S $\{Q\}$ is false if P is strictly weaker than Q.

2.3.2 Diversion: Some Extreme Cases

The material presented in this section diverts from the main discussion about GCL semantics. We believe that the material covered gives an interesting theoretical insight into the meaning and nature of both Hoare triples precondition semantics. Nevertheless, it is not essential background for understanding the rest of this text, and some readers may wish to skip it—at least on first reading.

Delving into the meaning of a few "extreme" Hoare triples will sharpen the understanding of the theory developed to date, and will show its overall consistency and elegance.

Let us start by asking the question: What kind of instruction or program S would comply with each of the following specifications? We then consider each case in turn.

1. {true} S {true}
2. {false} S {true}
3. {false} S {false}
4. {true} S {false}

2.3.2.1 Case 1: For What Values of S Does {true} S {true} Hold?

In this case, the answer certainly includes $S = skip$, since we have just seen that $\{Q\}$ $skip$ $\{Q\}$ holds for all values of Q, and thus specifically for $Q = $ true. The questions is, does {true} S {true} hold for any other instances of S?

We can get a sense of how to interpret this question by recasting the meaning of the Hoare triple in terms of its initial definition—i.e. {true} S {true} is actually just an abbreviated way of asserting the following predicate:

If the computer is in a state belonging to the set $States_{true}$ just before S executes,
then S will terminate and the computer will end up in a state belonging to the set $States_{true}$.

We are obviously dealing here with a predicate of the form: *antecedant* $\Longrightarrow$ *consequent*.

The *antecedent* is the predicate "the computer is in some arbitrary state (i.e. any element of $States_{true}$) just before S executes". This predicate clearly always has the truth value true.

The *consequent* is the predicate "S terminates and ends up in a state belonging to the set $States_{true}$"—which is a rather complicated way of saying "S terminates".

It seems, therefore, that the predicate {true} S {true} is only rendered false by programs which loop forever when started in some state. Note carefully that S is not required to loop forever when started from *every* state. If there is only one state from which to launch S which will cause it to loop forever, then {true} S {true} must be judged to be **false**. The overall conclusion therefore is as follows.

{true} S {true} is true for any S that always terminates, no matter from which state it is started.

2.3.2.2 Case 2: For What Values of S Does {false} S {true} Hold?

To get a handle on the kind of S that might be involved in such a specification, let us reason once again from first principles about the weakest precondition.

While $\{wp(S, Q)\}$ S $\{Q\}$ is always true, the precondition indicates a "boundary" at which other Hoare triples of the form $\{P\}$ S $\{Q\}$ are also true. Specifically $\{P\}$ S $\{Q\}$ is true if and only if P is stronger than $wp(S, Q)$, i.e. $P \Rightarrow wp(S, Q)$. The logical conclusion flowing from this observation is quite astonishing:

We have already noted that false is the strongest of all predicates;
therefore false $\Rightarrow wp(S, Q)$, whatever S and Q may be; and
therefore $\{false\}$ S $\{Q\}$ is true whatever S and Q may be!

This rather counter-intuitive result means that the answer to the question posed in the heading is as follows:

Any program, S, satisfies the predicate $\{false\}$ S $\{true\}$.

You might be tempted to object: what happens if S is a non-terminating loop? You may vaguely sense that a non-terminating loop "does not have" a weakest precondition. We shall probe this matter in a little more detail below. Suffice it to say that the precondition of a non-terminating S with respect to Q does indeed exist—it is a predicate. Whatever it is, it must be the case that false $\Rightarrow wp(S, Q)$, and so our above argument is entirely general: $\{false\}$ S $\{Q\}$ and $\{false\}$ S $\{true\}$ are predicates that are always true, even if S is non-terminating!

2.3.2.3 Case 3: For What Values of S Does {false} S {false} Hold?

The reasoning that led to the answer to the previous question was entirely general:
$\{false\}$ S $\{Q\}$ is true whatever S and Q may be!
Therefore, again the question posed in the heading is to be answered as follows:

Any program, S, satisfies the predicate $\{false\}$ S $\{false\}$.

Again, this holds, even if S is non-terminating.

2.3.2.4 Case 4: For What Values of S Does {true} S {false} Hold?

We illuminate this question by expanding the Hoare triple $\{true\}$ S $\{false\}$ in terms of its initial definition, as we did before:

If the computer is in a state belonging to the set $States_{true}$ just before S executes,
then S will terminate and the computer will end up in a state belonging to the set $States_{false}$.

Here, the *antecedent* is the predicate "the computer is in some arbitrary state (i.e. any element of $States_{true}$) just before S executes". This predicate clearly always has the truth value true.

The *consequent* is a predicate that asserts that "S terminates **and** the computer does not end up in any state at all (i.e. a state that is an element of $States_{false} = \varnothing$)". Put differently, the *consequent* asserts that:

(S terminates) **and** ($\exists s : \varnothing \cdot$ (the computer ends up in state s)).

We see immediately that the *consequent* is false, whether or not S terminates, because the predicate $(\exists s : \varnothing \cdot (\text{the computer ends up in state } s))$ always has truth-value false.

{true} S {false} is therefore logically equivalent to the predicate true $\Longrightarrow$ false which, in terms of the truth tables, evaluates to false. It does not matter what form S assumes, the predicate remains false. Therefore, no program S can satisfy {true} S {false}. The answer to the question "For what values of S does {true} S {false} hold?" is therefore

There is no S whatsoever for which {true} S {false} has value true.

The foregoing discussion is summarised in the table below.

$\{P\}\, S\, \{Q\}$	true for which S?
{true} S {true}	Any S that terminates irrespective of start state
{false} S {true}	Any S
{false} S {false}	Any S
{true} S {false}	No S whatsoever

Having regard to properties that relate to extreme Hoare triple contexts strengthens insight into the meaning of the notation. Similarly, it is interesting and relevant to consider weakest preconditions in limiting situations. The following questions are of interest.

2.3.2.5 How Can the Expression $wp(S, \text{false})$ Be Interpreted?

The last two rows of the above table point to two extremes of the triple: $\{P\}\, S\, \{\text{false}\}$. In the third row, we see that the expression is true for any S when $P = \text{false}$. The fourth row, however, informs us that the expression is false for any S when $P = \text{true}$. The question thus arises: is there a P that is weaker than false such that for some S, $\{P\}\, S\, \{\text{false}\}$ is true. If this were to be the case, then $States_P \supset States_{\text{false}} = \varnothing$. Hence there would be some state, $x \in States_P$, such that S, when launched from state x, would terminate in some state $\in States_{\text{false}} = \varnothing$. Clearly, this is never possible, irrespective of S. We therefore conclude as follows:

$wp(S, \text{false}) = \text{false}$ for all S.

The dual of this question is addressed next.

2.3.2.6 How Can the Expression $wp(S, \text{true})$ Be Interpreted?

We already know that $wp(skip, Q) = Q$ for any Q, because that is precisely the definition of *skip*. Thus, $wp(skip, \text{true}) = \text{true}$ is one instance of a possibly more general response to the question posed above.

In probing the meaning of $wp(S, \text{true})$ when S is something other than *skip*, let us again return to our basic definitions of the precondition and of a Hoare triple. Since $wp(S, \text{true})$ is the precondition predicate such that $\{wp(S, \text{true})\}$ S $\{\text{true}\}$ is true, the following must hold:

> **If** the computer is in a state belonging to the set $States_{wp(S,\text{true})}$ just before S executes,
> **then** S will terminate and the computer will end up in a state belonging to the set $States_{\text{true}}$.

Again, we are dealing here with an assertion of the form: *antecedant* $\Longrightarrow$ *consequent*. The *consequent* amounts to an assertion that we really do not care about the final state in which we end; for the *consequent* to be true it is sufficient that S should terminate. If it does not terminate, then the consequent is false. Taking this all together, and abusing notation somewhat by assuming that $(x \in States_{wp(S,\text{true})})$ asserts that execution of S starts in a state of $States_{wp(S,\text{true})}$, the following predicates may be regarded as equivalent:

$$\{wp(S, \text{true})\} \ S \ \{\text{true}\}$$

$$(x \in States_{wp(S,\text{true})}) \Longrightarrow (S \text{ terminates})$$

The second predicate is of the form (*antecedent* $\Longrightarrow$ *consequent*) which, in terms of the truth table entries, is true under the following circumstances:

- Both $(x \in States_{wp(S,\text{true})})$ and $(S \text{ terminates})$ are true
  (since $(\text{true} \Longrightarrow \text{true}) = \text{true}$)
- $(x \in States_{wp(S,\text{true})})$ is false but $(S \text{ terminates})$ is true
  (since $(\text{false} \Longrightarrow \text{true}) = \text{true}$)
- Both $(x \in States_{wp(S,\text{true})})$ and $(S \text{ terminates})$ are false
  (since $(\text{false} \Longrightarrow \text{false}) = \text{true}$)

However, since $States_{wp(S,\text{true})}$ is, per definition, the *largest* set of states which leads to the realisation of the postcondition, the scenario reflected in the second bullet cannot arise. (We make this claim for all normal commands, S, that are in common use, but return to it later.) In other words, $wp(S, \text{true})$ is the weakest predicate that guarantees the termination of S—the bullets assure us that if S is commenced in a state that satisfies the $wp(S, \text{true})$ then S will terminate, and that S will not terminate otherwise.

> $wp(S, \text{true})$ is the set of states from which S may be started, that guarantees the termination of S.

But, you may object, what if S is inherently an infinite loop? What if there is no state in which S may be started which will guarantee its termination? Well, in that case $wp(S, \text{true}) = \text{false}$ and thus $States_{wp(S,\text{true})} = \varnothing$. As a result, only the third bullet above can ever be realised.

The conclusion therefore holds, whether or not S terminates under some circumstances, or always loops forever: $wp(S, \text{true})$ is a predicate representing the set of all states from which S may be started, that guarantees the termination of S.

2.3.2.7 The Meaning of *abort*

Recall, that we arrived at the conclusion that $wp(S, \text{true})$ represents the set of states guaranteeing the termination of S, based on the assumption that S is one of the "normal" computer commands in common use. We argued that for such commands, the scenario represented by the second bullet above could never arise. What we avoided saying, however, is what we mean by a "normal" command.

For the purposes of the present text, a normal command is one whose behaviour is predictable. Even an infinite loop can be regarded as a normal command, since we know what it does—it loops forever.

However, as we know, sometimes a program behaves unpredictably. We wash our hands here of the need to speculate why this happens: whether because of stray pointers, division by zero, or whatever. We simply decide, for theoretical purposes, to equate such behaviour to the execution of a special command called *abort*.

abort is a completely chaotic command. We can think of it as having a weakest precondition that cannot be determined with respect to any postcondition, including the postcondition true. Note that this is not a claim that *abort* does not have a weakest precondition with respect to some postcondition. It is merely a claim that this weakest precondition cannot be known. Nevertheless, although unknown, $States_{wp(abort,\text{true})}$ represents some real (possibly empty) set of machine states. The predicate $\{wp(abort, \text{true})\}$ *abort* $\{\text{true}\}$ remains true, because the same three scenarios that we displayed previously also hold for *abort*, namely:

- If $x \in States_{wp(abort,\text{true})}$ and *abort* executes, then *abort* terminates in some arbitrary state (since $(\text{true} \implies \text{true}) = \text{true}$).
- If $x \notin States_{wp(abort,\text{true})}$ and *abort* executes, then *abort* terminates in some arbitrary state (since $(\text{false} \implies \text{true}) = \text{true}$).
- If $x \notin States_{wp(abort,\text{true})}$ and *abort* executes, then *abort* does not terminate (since $(\text{false} \implies \text{false}) = \text{true}$).

This means that if *abort* is launched in some states not in $States_{wp(abort,\text{true})}$, then it terminates in some arbitrary state, while if launched in other states not in $States_{wp(abort,\text{true})}$, it loops forever. However, it is so chaotic that we do not know how to characterise start states that cause it to stop, and start states that cause it to loop forever; and neither do we have any information about what the final state might possibly be, in those cases where *abort* perchance terminates.

Of course, one should never purposefully execute *abort*. However, sometimes *abort* is used to describe what happens when we accidently execute unacceptable code. Indeed, Dijkstra uses *abort* to describe what happens if you commence the execution of a "normal" instruction in a state that does not comply with the instruction's precondition with respect to some specified postcondition. Anything could happen: the machine could either loop forever, or end up in some non-predictable final state. Under such conditions, the instruction to be executed behaves in a way that is indistinguishable from *abort*.

2.3.3   Assignment

GCL allows for both single and multiple assignment. For the moment, we consider single assignment only. In both cases assignment is denoted by :=, thus sensibly not overloading the = symbol, which is the relational operator for equality.

We will define the precise semantics of single assignment in terms of its weakest precondition. This entirely general definition applies to assignment in any programming language.

Definition 2.3.2 (Single Assignment). If x is a variable (of some type T), and E some expression (of the same type T), then the assignment instruction $x := E$ is such that, for any predicate Q, $wp(x := E, Q) = Q[x \backslash E]$.

We assume that E is a legitimate expression in GCL, without defining what this is—i.e. it is assumed that the normal rules apply.

In terms of this definition, the following is always true:

$$\{Q[x \backslash E]\}\ x := E\ \{Q\}$$

Many, upon first encountering this claim, are somewhat taken aback. It seems slightly counter-intuitive. We are inclined to say: Surely if Q is true just before E is assigned to x, then Q with all occurrences of x replaced by E will be true afterwards! But a little thought will convince otherwise.

Consider, for example, the triple:

$$\{P\}\ x := x + 1\ \{x > 5\}$$

Clearly, if x is to be greater than 5 after being incremented by 1, then prior to that assignment the predicate $(x + 1 > 5)$ should hold. Note however that this is the same as $(x > 5)[x \backslash x + 1]$. Moreover, it is the very weakest assertion that should hold before executing $x := x + 1$ that will guarantee the postcondition of $(x > 5)$, i.e.

$$wp(x := x + 1, x > 5) \equiv (x > 5)[x \backslash x + 1] \equiv (x + 1 > 5) = (x > 4)$$

Thus, the following predicates are true:

- $\{x > 4\}\ x := x + 1\ \{x > 5\}$, since $(x > 4)$ is the weakest precondition
- $\{x > 5\}\ x := x + 1\ \{x > 5\}$, since $(x > 5) \Rightarrow (x > 4)$, the weakest precondition.
- $\{x > 1,000\}\ x := x + 1\ \{x > 5\}$, since $x > 1,000 \Rightarrow (x > 4)$, the weakest precondition, etc.

while the following is false:

- $\{x > 3\}\ x := x + 1\ \{x > 5\}$, since $(x > 3)$ is weaker than the weakest precondition, $(x > 4)$.

So, counter-intuitive as it may initially be, the precondition given above for assignment does indeed make sense. Readers who are not fully convinced should verify this for a variety of other scenarios. This will confirm that assignment's precondition is as stated.

Here we have started off with a notion of what assignment means, and proposed and verified its weakest precondition. However, as before, we may turn the matter on its head. Suppose we came from a universe where we did not know what assignment meant, but we understood the idea of the weakest precondition. Then by stating the precondition for assignment, we fully state what assignment means—we state its semantics.

Before defining multiple assignment in terms of its weakest precondition, we first need to extend the single substitution Definition 2.1.3 to multiple substitution.

Definition 2.3.3 (General Substitution).   Assume that P is a predicate, that $x_1 \ldots x_n$ is a list of distinct variables, and that $a_1 \ldots a_n$ is a list of expressions. Then $P[x_1, x_2 \ldots x_n \backslash a_1, a_2 \ldots a_n]$ denotes the predicate that results after simultaneously substituting each and every occurrence of x_i in predicate P with a_i. By simultaneous substitution is meant that a_i only replaces occurrences of x_i that were in P at the start of the substitution process; occurrences of x_i that might result from other substitutions are ignored.

To illustrate the meaning of "simultaneous" substitution, consider the multiple substitution:

$$(x > y)[x, y \backslash y, z]$$

The result of this substitution is

$$(y > z)$$

and not

$$(z > z)$$

In other words, we do not say:

substituting x with y in the expression yields $(y > y)$; and
substituting y with z yields $(z > z)$.

Instead, the substitutions of x and y with y and z, respectively, in the expression $(x > y)$ takes place "simultaneously", yielding $(y > z)$.

We can now define multiple assignment as follows:

Definition 2.3.4 (Multiple Assignment).   If $x_1, \ldots x_n$ is a list of distinct variables (of types $T_1, \ldots T_n$), and $E_1, \ldots E_n$ is a list of expressions (of corresponding types, namely $T_1, \ldots T_n$), then the precondition of $x_1, x_2, \ldots x_n := E_1, E_2, \ldots E_n$ with respect to predicate Q is given by

$$wp(x_1, \ldots x_n := E_1, \ldots E_n, Q) = Q[x_1, \ldots x_n \backslash E_1, \ldots E_n].$$

The multiple assignment command is not a necessary construct. It does not exist in most real computer programming languages, and it is not difficult to translate any multiple assignment back to a sequence of single assignment commands. However, it often aids in shortening the specification of code. The common example is that of swapping two variables. This is easily specified as the multiple assignment

$$x, y := y, x.$$

Relating this back to the precondition for multiple assignment, the question arises: what does a postcondition look like that says that the variables x and y have been swapped. It does not work to say:

$$(x = y) \land (y = x)$$

Why not? Because this postcondition is equivalent to $(x = y)$, and this postcondition state is attained, not by swapping x and y, but either by assigning x to y, or vice versa. Moreover, such a postcondition is attained from any starting state—it is easy to verify that $wp(x := y, (x = y \land y = x)) = \text{true}$.

To indicate in the postcondition Q of some specification $\{P\}\ S\ \{Q\}$ that two variables have been swapped, we need to be able to refer in Q to the value of the variables as they were in P, before they were changed in S. There are various notational conventions for doing this. In this text, we shall use a subscript 0 for a variable, to indicate its value before some code has been executed. For example in $\{P\}\ S\ \{y = x_0\}$ the postcondition should be interpreted to mean that y must be the same as the value that variable x had before the code S was executed. Generally this convention will not cause any problems. Although subscript integer values are also in other contexts, the meaning of the 0 subscript will be obvious from the particular context, and should not cause confusion.

Equipped with this notation, we can express the fact that x and y have been swapped as follows: $(x = y_0) \land (y = x_0)$. The precondition that ensures this postcondition after executing the multiple assignment $x, y := y, x$ is computed as follows:

$$wp((x, y := y, x), (x = y_0) \land (y = x_0))$$

$\equiv$ $\{$ Definition of multiple assignment weakest precondition $\}$

$$((x = y_0) \land (y = x_0))[x, y, \backslash y, x]$$

$\equiv$ $\{$ Apply substitution$\}$

$$(y = y_0) \land (x = x_0)$$

$\equiv$ $\{$ Holds trivially in the precondition $\}$

true

Note the following two points:

- In this text, we shall often use the above style of presenting formal arguments or derivations—i.e. write down an expression; give a hint or brief explanation (in parenthesis) of why the next step is justified; give the next step in the argument; give a hint to justify the next step; give the next expression; etc.

- Note that, when applying the substitution, x_0 and y_0 are not candidates for substitution. They are to be regarded as constant values, not as variables.

The foregoing precondition derivation tells us that the multiple assignment swap will achieve its objective (the postcondition) from *any* starting condition. Thus, for example, the following Hoare triple is true

$$\{x > 0 \wedge y \le 0\}\, x, y := y, x\, \{x = y_0 \wedge y = x_0\}$$

since $\{x > 0 \wedge y \le 0\} \Rightarrow$ true.

2.3.4 Composition

The notion of composing commands is simple but powerful. We may define the composition of two code segments $S1$ and $S2$ in terms of precondition semantics as follows:

Definition 2.3.5 (Composition). The composition of code segments $S1$ and $S2$ is denoted by $S1; S2$. $wp(S1; S2, Q) = wp(S1, wp(S2, Q))$.

From one perspective, this definition tells us *exactly* what the composition command means: the precondition to ensure that Q is attained after executing $S1; S2$ is the same as the precondition to ensure that $wp(S2, Q)$ holds after executing $S1$.

However, as will be seen later, the precondition semantics is a little constraining if the need is to refine S to, say, $S1; S2$. Instead, it is more convenient to take note of the following more general statement:

Property 2.3.6. *If a predicate, say M can be found such that*

$$(\{P\}\, S1\, \{M\}) \wedge (\{M\}\, S2\, \{Q\})$$

then

$$\{P\}\, S1; S2\, \{Q\}$$

In many texts, the above is expressed by the following notation:

$$\frac{(\{P\}\, S1\, \{M\}) \wedge (\{M\}\, S2\, \{Q\})}{\{P\}\, S1; S2\, \{Q\}}$$

Composition assists in breaking up a coding task into smaller, more manageable sections. For example, suppose we need to write code that complies with the following specification:

$$\{\text{true}\}\, x, y : S\, \{x = y \wedge y^2 = x\}$$

Thus, from any arbitrary initial state, we wish change x and y so as to arrive at the postcondition, which at first sight seems rather constrained: not only must x and y be equal, but $y^2 = x$. Although a code solution to this specification is not too difficult think up directly, it is of interest to see how we can "derive" a solution by the following a measured reasoning process.

It would seem reasonable to achieve the postcondition's two conjuncts in two steps, suggesting that S could be seen as the composition of two commands, i.e. as $S1; S2$. Suppose that after executing $S1$ some predicate M becomes true. Thus, we seek $S1$ and $S2$ such that:

$$\{\text{true}\}\, x, y : S1\, \{M\} \wedge \{M\}\, x, y : S2\, \{x = y \wedge y^2 = x\} \qquad (2.1)$$

Rather than trying to establish $S1$ that achieves some yet unclear M, it is often more profitable to work "backwards"—i.e. to fill in code for $S2$ that achieves at least part of the postcondition. Several possibilities suggest themselves: we could assign x to y; or y to x; or the square of y to x; or the square root of x to y.

Let us opt for the first course of action—i.e. $S2$ becomes the assignment $x := y$. (This choice may seem rather arbitrary. Nevertheless, it is easy to verify that any choice could be made. A different but accurate solution to the problem would then be found.)

Having decided on $S2$, and knowing the required postcondition, means that we are able to compute the associated weakest precondition:

$\quad wp(x := y, (x = y \wedge y^2 = x))$

$\equiv \quad$ {Definition of assignment weakest precondition}

$\quad (x = y \wedge y^2 = x)[x\backslash y]$

$\equiv \quad$ {Apply substitution}

$\quad y = y \wedge y^2 = y$

$\equiv \quad$ {$(y = y) \equiv$ true}

$\quad$ true $\wedge\, y^2 = y$

$\equiv \quad$ {Absorbtion rule: true $\wedge\, P \equiv P$}

$\quad y^2 = y$

This precondition seems to be a reasonable choice for M in (2.1). Thus, we now need to find $S1$ so that the following is true.

$$\{\text{true}\}\, x, y : S1\, \{y^2 = y\} \wedge \{y^2 = y\}\, x := y\, \{x = y \wedge y^2 = x\} \qquad (2.2)$$

We see that the predicate $y^2 = y$ could actually be written as $y = 0 \vee y = 1$ (since 0 and 1 are the two roots of the equation $y^2 - y = 0$). This suggests that we could change $S1$ either into a command that assigns 0 to y, or into a command that assigns 1 to y. Choosing (again arbitrarily) to assign 1 to y, the logical expression in (2.2) can be re-written as:

$$\{\text{true}\}\, x, y : y := 1\, \{y^2 = y\} \,\wedge\, \{y^2 = y\}\, x := y\, \{x = y \wedge y^2 = x\} \qquad (2.3)$$

Note that this logical expression (of the form $A \wedge B$ where A and B are Hoare triples) may either be true or false. The second conjunct (i.e. the B part) clearly has value true, because it corresponds to the form $\{wp(S, Q)\}\, S\, \{Q\}$ where S is $x := y$ and Q is $x = y \wedge y^2 = x$.

To show that the first conjunct is true, we need to prove that

$$\text{true} \Rightarrow wp(y := 1, (y = 0 \vee y = 1))$$

This is because, in the general case, we can only be sure that $\{P\}\, S\, \{Q\}$ is true if P is stronger than $wp(S, Q)$ (i.e. $P \Rightarrow wp(S, Q)$). In the case of expression (2.3), P corresponds to true. We thus derive the precondition as follows:

$wp(y := 1, (y = 0 \vee y = 1))$

$\equiv$ {Definition of assignment weakest precondition}

$(y = 0 \vee y = 1)[y \backslash 1]$

$\equiv$ {Apply substitution}

$1 = 0 \vee 1 = 1$

$\equiv$ {Common sense}

false $\vee$ true

$\equiv$ {Truth tables}

true

Since true $\Rightarrow$ true we can confidently affirm that the following is a valid specification—i.e. a specification (actually in this case, already a program) consisting of the conjunct of two Hoare triples, which is such that if the precondition of each triple is fulfilled, the code will achieve the corresponding postcondition:

$$\{\text{true}\}\, y := 1\, \{y^2 = y\} \wedge \{y^2 = y\}\, x := y\, \{x = y \wedge y^2 = x\}$$

It will be convenient to abbreviate the conjunction of Hoare triples as above into the following:

$$\{\text{true}\}\, y := 1\, \{y^2 = y\} \,;\, x := y\, \{x = y \wedge y^2 = x\}$$

We could also write this out in a form that corresponds to the way in which code is laid out, where predicates in parenthesis serve in the role of code comments:

$\{\,\text{true}\,\}$

$y := 1$

$\{y^2 = y\}$

$$; x := y$$
$$\{x = y \land y^2 = x\}$$

Note that in this text, we will generally follow the convention of placing the semicolon on the same line as the next command to be executed, rather than at the end of the last statement that preceded the "execution" of this composition command.

Generalising from these conventions, the predicate on the left hand side below, may be written out in abbreviated form as on the right hand side:

$$\{P\} \ S_1 \ \{R\} \land \{R\} \ S_2 \ \{P\} \equiv \{P\} \ S_1 \ \{R\} \ ; S_2 \ \{P\}$$

Where convenient, this abbreviated form will be written out on separate lines, resulting in the more conventional line-by-line style for writing code.

$$\{P\}$$
$$S_1$$
$$\{R\}$$
$$; S_2$$
$$\{Q\}$$

2.3.5 Selection

At first sight, the GCL command for selection might seem similar to a switch-command, a case-command or sequence of nested if-else commands in some conventional language, but the similarities are superficial—the GCL command has a number of significant semantic differences.[6] The syntax is as follows:

if $G_1 \rightarrow S_1$
$\ \ \parallel \ \ G_2 \rightarrow S_2$
$\ \ \ \ \cdots$
$\ \ \parallel \ \ G_n \rightarrow S_n$
fi

The G_i are predicates, called guards, and the S_i are GCL commands (possibly the composition of a number of commands). Hence each $G_i \rightarrow S_i$ constitutes a so-called guarded command—which is where the GCL language gets its name.

---

[6]In fact, the ADA select command is inspired by the GCL command, as is the choice operation in CSP (and subsequent CSP variants such as FSP as a specification language and Occam as an implementation language).

The semantics of the select command require that, as a first step in executing the command, all the guards are evaluated. If one or more evaluates to true, then one of the corresponding commands is non-deterministically selected for execution. If no guard evaluates to true then the select command executes *abort* !

Now this latter semantic requirement is unusual for those who are used to the if-command in common programming languages. However, Dijkstra's requirement that the GCL select command should function in this way was quite deliberate. He strongly believed that one ought to consciously establish and make explicit what has to happen under *every* circumstance. There is thus no provision for a default *skip*. If there are circumstances in which nothing ought to happen, then GCL still requires of one to make those circumstances explicit, articulate them as a guard, and then indicate that a *skip* command should be executed whenever that guard fires.

The non-determinism that results when more than one guard evaluates to true, means that the associated commands should, in each case, do what is required. The classically quoted mini-example is the use of the select command to set the variable *max* to the maximum of two values, x and y. This could be specified in GCL as follows:

$$\textbf{if } x \geq y \rightarrow max := x \parallel x \leq y \rightarrow max := y \textbf{ fi}$$

If $x = y$, then both guards are true and the assignment command associated with either one of them can be selected for execution. In this particular example, the outcome will be the same—the value of *max* will indeed be the maximum of the two other variables.

The example illustrates that GCL is a *specification* language, as opposed to an *implementation* language such as Java. From a specification perspective, it is not important which guard is selected: either will do. In implementing a GCL specification, one has to make a choice about how the non-deterministically specified options will be deterministically implemented. If one needs to implement the *max* example specified above, (say in Java) a particular choice of a condition has to be made, and particular assignment statements have to be used, both in the context of an if-else command.

But it need not be the case that non-determinism represents alternative paths to the same outcome, as was the case in this *max* example. Sometimes, a non-deterministic GCL specification can be used to specify conditions under which random outcomes occur. Although GCL will not be used in this fashion here, for completeness the following artificial example is provided to illustrate the idea. The example specifies that the outcome of tossing a coin might either be heads or tails. Which specific outcome eventuates from a given toss is, of course, unpredictable:

$$\textbf{if } toss \rightarrow outcome := heads$$
$$\parallel \quad toss \rightarrow outcome := tails$$
$$\textbf{fi}$$

The precondition of the select command with respect to postcondition Q, in its general form, is slightly more complicated than those given for previous commands.

Definition 2.3.7 (Selection). Let $IF \equiv$ **if** $G_1 \rightarrow S_1 \parallel \ \ldots \ \parallel \ G_n \rightarrow S_n$ **fi**. Then

$$wp(IF, Q) = \bigvee_{i=1}^{n}(G_i) \wedge \bigwedge_{i=1}^{n}(G_i \implies wp(S_i, Q))$$

Recall that this tells us what the weakest predicate is that should hold if we wish to have a guarantee that predicate Q holds after executing the select statement that has guards $G_i \rightarrow S_i, i = 1 \ldots n$. It is a precise, albeit rather complicated, statement of the semantics of the select command.

$\bigvee_{i=1}^{n}(G_i)$ means that any state that falls within the set of states associated with weakest precondition, will be such that at least one of the guards will be true.

On the other hand, if the select command is initiated from a state that does *not* fall within its precondition with respect to postcondition Q (thus, if the select statement is initiated from a state where every guard evaluates to false), then the semantics does not pronounce on what will happen. Put differently, under such circumstances, anything may happen—whatever happens will not contradict the select statement's semantics.

But semantics that tolerates *any* behaviour, is reminiscent of the semantics of the *abort* command. It is for this reason that Dijkstra declared that to execute the select command from a state that does not satisfy any guard, is to execute the *abort* command. The semantics of the select command in this respect are neither arbitrary nor flippant; it is consistent with the body of theory around the notion of weakest precondition!

Nevertheless, this precondition does not provide any immediate insight about how to arrive at a particular select command, if our starting information is that we have to comply with a more general specification $\{P\} \ S \ \{Q\}$. To take such a *constructive* step, we will have to rely on a refinement rule relating to the select command, which will be given in Sect. 2.4.

2.3.6 Repetition

The final GCL command to be considered is repetition. In its general forms, it looks a lot like the select command, in that it has several guarded commands.

$$
\begin{aligned}
&\textbf{do} \ \ G_1 \rightarrow S_1 \\
&\parallel \ \ \ G_2 \rightarrow S_2 \\
&\qquad \ldots \\
&\parallel \ \ \ G_n \rightarrow S_n \\
&\textbf{od}
\end{aligned}
$$

The repetition command (or loop) iterates zero or more times. At the start of each iteration, all guards are evaluated. As with the select command, a command associated with a true guard is non-deterministically selected for execution. The loop iterates until all guards evaluate to false. In that case—unlike the select command—it does not behave as *abort*. Instead, it terminates successfully and control is passed to the next command in the sequence of program commands.

Note that the above form can also be seen as a loop with one guard only, i.e. as:

$$\textbf{do } GG \rightarrow S \textbf{ od}$$

where $GG = G_1 \vee G_2 \ldots \vee G_n$ and S is the select command:

$$\begin{aligned}
&\textbf{if } G_1 \rightarrow S_1 \\
&\textbf{\char"0007 } \ G_2 \rightarrow S_2 \\
&\quad \ldots \\
&\textbf{\char"0007 } \ G_n \rightarrow S_n \\
&\textbf{fi}
\end{aligned}$$

This form is also used quite frequently, both in this text and elsewhere.

Of all the constructs mentioned to date, the repeat command's precondition is the most complicated. For this reason, and because it does not significantly illuminate the way towards constructively refining loops from specifications, we will not state it here. Instead, we turn the discussion to loop invariants.

For most examples in this text, we will be interested in finding *an invariant* of some loop: a predicate that holds just before the loop is entered, that holds at the end of every iteration of the loop, and that therefore also holds immediately after the loop has terminated.

Definition 2.3.8 (Loop Invariant). Predicate P is an invariant of the loop **do** $G \rightarrow S$ **od** if and only if $\{P\}\, G \rightarrow S\, \{P\}$.

Thus, a loop invariant is a predicate that is true at the end of each iteration of the loop, provided that it was true at the start of the loop's body, and provided that the loop's body terminates.

If we view the loop as having the form **do** $G_1 \rightarrow S_1 \, \| \ \ldots \ \| \ G_n \rightarrow S_n$ **od**, then for P to qualify as a loop invariant, it should hold whenever control reaches the points indicated by $\triangledown$ below, provided P holds before the loop commences:

$$\begin{aligned}
&\textbf{do } {}_{\triangledown} G_1 \rightarrow S_1 \, {}_{\triangledown} \\
&\textbf{\char"0007 } \quad {}_{\triangledown} \cdots \\
&\textbf{\char"0007 } \quad {}_{\triangledown} G_n \rightarrow S_n \, {}_{\triangledown} \\
&\textbf{od } {}_{\triangledown}
\end{aligned}$$

Note the following:

- A loop can have any number of invariants. In fact, true is an invariant of any loop: in any loop, there is always some state in the universal set of states, $States_{\text{true}}$, that holds at the indicated points above.

- The fact that a loop has an invariant does not mean that the loop will terminate. In fact, in any non-terminating loop, its condition, $G = G_1 \lor G_2 \lor \ldots \lor G_n$, is quite obviously an invariant.

- If P is an invariant of a terminating loop, not only will P be true at the end of the loop, but so will $\neg G = \neg(G_1 \lor G_2 \lor \ldots \lor G_n)$, the loop's condition. Thus, letting DO represents the loop in Definition 2.3.8 and given that P is an invariant of the loop, we can be sure that the loop will terminate if and only if $\{P\}\ DO\ \{P \land \neg G\}$ is true.

- Similarly, the loop **do** $G_1 \rightarrow S_1\ \|\ \ldots\ \|\ G_n \rightarrow S_n$ **od** is guaranteed to terminate if each of the commands in the guarded commands is guaranteed to terminate. In fact, the following should evaluate to true for $i = 1, \ldots n$:

$$\{P \land G_i\}\ S_i\ \{P\}$$

If for some j, $\{P \land G_j\}\ S_j\ \{P\}$ is false, then it may be the case that the loop will never terminate: the triple may be false precisely because, under starting conditions allowed by the precondition, S_j might itself never terminate.

2.4   Refinement Rules

We are now in a position to relate the foregoing information to a set of rules or heuristics, to be used in refining an abstract specification of a problem into a more concrete one. As the refinement proceeds, more and more code is incorporated into the specification, so that the final concrete specification is, in fact, a program in GCL.

Let $Spec(P, S, Q)$ be an alternative notation for $\{P\}\ S\ \{Q\}$. If S is merely a variable standing "abstractly" in the place of a GCL program, and P and Q are given, then it is not possible to know a priori whether $Spec(P, S, Q)$ is true or not—just as it is not possible to say whether $(x > 10)$ is true or not without knowing something about the value of x—its precise value, or even some range of values which it may assume. We can only decide on the truth-value of $Spec(P, S, Q)$ once S has been instantiated with some concrete GCL code.

We could, in principle, substitute S with *any* concrete GCL program. Some subset of these substitutions will render the specification $Spec(P, S, Q)$ true and the remainder will render it false.

A concrete GCL program that renders $Spec(P, S, Q)$ to be true is said to *satisfy* the specification.

Notation 2.4.1. *Sat*$(C, Spec(P, S, Q))$ *is a predicate that asserts that the GCL program C satisfies the specification Spec*(P, S, Q).

Refinement is based on the idea of deriving from $Spec(P, S, Q)$ a new refined specification which is such that any GCL program that satisfies the refined specification will also satisfy the original specification.

To make this idea more formal, let us denote by *GCL* the universal set of GCL programs, and let $X \sqsubseteq Y$ denote the assertion that X is refined by Y (or, equivalently, Y is a refinement of X). The meaning of this assertion is given in the following definition.

Definition 2.4.2 (Refinement). $Spec(P, S, Q) \sqsubseteq Spec(P', S', Q')$ if and only if

$$\forall C : GCL \cdot Sat(C, Spec(P', S', Q')) \implies (Sat(C, Spec(P, S, Q)))$$

Thus $Spec(P, S, Q)$ is refined by $Spec(P', S', Q')$ if every GCL program that satisfies the specification $Spec(P', S', Q')$ also satisfies the specification $Spec(P, S, Q)$

Note, firstly, that the definition does not exclude the possibility that $S = S'$, i.e. that a specification can be refined simply by changing its pre- and/or its postcondition.

Note, secondly, that we do not include an 'only if' in the definition. This means that, even if $Spec(P, S, Q) \sqsubseteq Spec(P', S, Q')$, it might nevertheless be possible to find a concrete GCL program, say C, that satisfies $Spec(P, S, Q)$ but that does not satisfy $Spec(P', S, Q')$. This is simply a round-about way of saying that there could be many refinement paths for a given specification $Spec(P, S, Q)$, each leading to different concrete GCL programs that all satisfy $Spec(P, S, Q)$ but that do not necessarily satisfy all possible refinements of $Spec(P, S, Q)$.

Consider, for example, the specification $Spec(\text{true}, S, x < 5)$ and the specification $Spec(\text{true}, S, x < 2)$. Clearly $Spec(\text{true}, S, x < 5) \sqsubseteq Spec(\text{true}, S, x < 2)$. (Why? Because any concrete program that starts in an arbitrary state and terminates with $x < 2$, by definition also terminates with $x < 5$.) However the program $x := 4$ satisfies $Spec(\text{true}, S, x < 5)$ but it does not satisfy $Spec(\text{true}, S, x < 2)$.

At first sight, how one is supposed to arrive at a refined specification of some given specification might seem something of a mystery. Fortunately, there are a large number of refinement *rules* to assist one in doing so. In fact, Morgan [32] lists more than 70 such rules in the appendix to his book. Being confronted by such a volume can be quite overwhelming, especially when a large proportion of those rules turn out to be more of theoretical than of practical interest. Since our it is not our objective to present a full theory of refinement, we list below a very small selection of all the possible refinement rules—ones that we have found to be helpful in constructing algorithms.

2.4.1 Strengthen Postcondition Rule

Suppose you are asked to write a program that complies with the specification $Spec(P, S, x > 0)$. Instead of doing this, you actually write code that complies with the specification $Spec(P, S, x > 5 \land y = 2)$. What have you done? You have provided a program that complies not only with the original specifications, but also with a specification where the postcondition has been strengthened—you have refined the original specification to a concrete program that guarantees a stronger postcondition. This generalises to the following refinement rule:

Rule 1. *If $Q' \Rightarrow Q$ then $Spec(P, S, Q) \sqsubseteq Spec(P, S, Q')$*

2.4.2 Weaken Precondition Rule

In contrast to the previous scenario, suppose that you are asked to write a program that complies with the specification $Spec(y > 0, S, x > 0)$. Instead of doing this, you write code (call it C) that complies with the specification $Spec(\text{true}, S, x > 0)$. This time, you have refined the original specification to a concrete program that guarantees the required postcondition, even if the precondition is *weaker* than originally required.

Put into the familiar Hoare triple notation, if the code, C, renders true the predicate:

$\{\text{true}\} \, C \, \{x > 0\}$

then it must surely be the case that C also renders true the predicate:

$\{y > 0\} \, C \, \{x > 0\}$

Since this applies generally for any C, the definition of refinement can be referenced, namely:

$$\forall C : GCL \cdot (Sat(C, Spec(\text{true}, S, x > 0))) \Longrightarrow (Sat(C, Spec(y > 0, S, x > 0)))$$

and we thus conclude that $Spec(y > 0, S, x > 0) \sqsubseteq Spec(\text{true}, C, x > 0)$.

This specific example generalises to the following refinement rule:

Rule 2. *If $P \Rightarrow P'$ then $Spec(P, S, Q) \sqsubseteq Spec(P', S, Q)$*

2.4.3 Skip Rule

Suppose that you wish to attain postcondition $x > 0$, but you know a priori that the precondition $5 < x < 100$ must hold before executing the code. In this case, you need not do anything to ensure that $x > 0$ will hold—the precondition implies everywhere (is stronger than) the postcondition, so the postcondition holds without further action. This is an instance of the more general *skip* refinement rule. It is the first rule that we encounter where GCL code (albeit the humble *skip* command) results from applying a refinement rule to a specification that may not yet contain GCL code:

Rule 3. *If $P \Rightarrow Q$ then $Spec(P, S, Q) \sqsubseteq Spec(P, skip, Q)$*

2.4.4 Sequences of Refinements

It is not difficult to prove that refinement is transitive—i.e. that

if $X \sqsubseteq Y$ and $Y \sqsubseteq Z$ then $X \sqsubseteq Z$.

For the sake of brevity, we omit a formal proof of this claim.

The consequences of the claim, however, is that a sequence of refinement rules can be applied to some specification, arriving at ever more refined specifications, each of which is a refinement of all specifications preceding it in the sequence (including the original specification). In other words, the definition of refinement given above supports the notion of refining a specification in a stepwise or incremental fashion.

The following briefly illustrates this idea. It is based on the assumption that $P \Rrightarrow Q$. Note the suggested layout for such refinement reasoning. At each refinement step, a hint is given in braces, briefly indicating the justification for that refinement step:

$Spec(P, S, Q)$

$\sqsubseteq$ {Skip rule since $P \Rrightarrow Q$ is given}

     $Spec(P, skip, Q)$

$\sqsubseteq$ {Weaken Precondition rule}

     $Spec(Q, skip, Q)$

2.4.5 Refinement and Weakest Preconditions

A special case of rule 2 is when a precondition P is maximally weakened, namely to the precondition of the specification with respect to the given postcondition.

Rule 4. *If $P \Rrightarrow wp(S, Q)$ then $Spec(P, S, Q) \sqsubseteq Spec(wp(S, Q), S, Q)$*

2.4.6 Assignment Rule

We will not use this general precondition rule directly. However, we will rely on it to state specific rules for specific GCL constructs.

We can use rule 4 to derive a refinement rule for the assignment command. Suppose that we are given that $P \Rrightarrow Q[x \backslash E]$ where E is some expression. Then the following holds:

     $Spec(P, x : S, Q)$

$\sqsubseteq$ {By rule 4}

     $Spec(Q[x \backslash E], S, Q)$

$\sqsubseteq$ {By the definition of refinement}

$Spec(Q[x \backslash E], x := E, Q)$

$\sqsubseteq$ {Explanation below}

$Spec(P, x := E, Q)$

The last step in this sequence of refinements looks wrong. We do not have a *strengthen precondition* refinement rule, but we have done precisely that: strengthened the precondition. However, on closer consideration, you will discover that the refinement step is indeed legitimate, but we have to consider the original definition of refinement to perceive this.

For this last step to be a legitimate refinement, the original refinement definition requires that any concrete specification that satisfies $Spec(P, x := E, Q)$ should also satisfy $Spec(Q[x \backslash E], x := E, Q)$. Fortunately there is only one concrete specification that can be considered here, namely the given specification itself, which already has GCL code $x := E$ as the concrete code for the specification. It is indeed the case that this GCL code also satisfies $Spec(Q[x \backslash E], x := E, Q)$, and hence, the refinement step is a valid one.

This leads to the following rule for assignment:

Rule 5. *If* $P \Rightarrow Q[x \backslash E]: Spec(P, x : S, Q) \sqsubseteq Spec(P, x := E, Q)$

Thus, for example, suppose that $P = (y > 100)$ and $Q = (x > 10)$. Since $(x > 10)$ $[x \backslash y + 5] \equiv y > 5$ and since $y > 100 \Rightarrow y > 5$, the assignment rule allows the following refinement:

$$\{y > 100\} \, x : S \, \{x > 10\} \sqsubseteq \{y > 100\} \, x := y + 5 \, \{x > 10\}$$

We have reverted to the conventional notation for Hoare triples, merely to emphasise that the alternative notation used above (such as, for example, $Spec(y > 100, x : S, x > 10)$) is just that—no more than an alternative that is arguably a little more concise.

Note that the x in the assignment refinement rule 5 can be viewed as a list of variables, and E as a list of expressions, so that the rule can also be applied in the case of multiple assignment. Also note that the rule only holds if P is stronger than $Q[x \backslash E]$. If this is not the case, the rule may not be invoked!

2.4.7 Composition Rule

The sequential composition rule is based on the idea that if we wish to refine $Spec(P, S, Q)$, then we should seek out some intermediate predicate M that we believe to be more easily attainable from the precondition state, P. This intermediate state then serves as a sort of half-way house from which to find some other code that will enable us to arrive at the required postcondition, Q.

The rule is best stated in Hoare triple notation, but relying on the extended notation previously introduced. It is merely a restatement of the definition of the composition operator:

Rule 6. $\{P\}\, S\, \{Q\} \sqsubseteq \{P\}\, S_1\, \{M\}\, ; S_2\, \{Q\}$

Consider a very simple example. Suppose that our purpose is to attain a postcondition $x = 1 \wedge y = 0$, and that we start with the most generous precondition possible, true. The specification of the program, S, that we wish to derive is $\{\text{true}\}\, S\, \{x = 1 \wedge y = 0\}$.

A fairly obvious thing to do to achieve this objective, is to attain the two conjuncts of the postconditions sequentially: first the one and then the other. Suppose we decide to attain the conjunct $x = 1$ first. Then we can apply the composition refinement rule as indicated in the first step below:

$\{\text{true}\}\, S\, \{x = 1 \wedge y = 0\}$

$\sqsubseteq \quad \{\text{Composition rule}\}$

$\{\text{true}\}\, S_1\, \{x = 1\}\, ; S_2\, \{x = 1 \wedge y = 0\}$

$\sqsubseteq \quad \{\text{Assignment rule: } (x = 1) \Rightarrow (x = 1 \wedge y = 0)[y \backslash 0]\}$

$\{\text{true}\}\, S_1\, \{x = 1\}\, ; y := 0\, \{x = 1 \wedge y = 0\}$

$\sqsubseteq \quad \{\text{Assignment rule: } \text{true} \Rightarrow (x = 1)[x \backslash 1]\}$

$\{\text{true}\}\, x := 1\, \{x = 1\}\, ; y := 0\, \{x = 1 \wedge y = 0\}$

2.4.7.1   A Brief Digression

Note that our justification for using the assignment rules in steps 2 and 3 above might not be very convincing. In each case, several reasoning steps have been skipped. Here is a fuller justification for step 2. Start by noting that:

$(x = 1 \wedge y = 0)[y \backslash 0]$

$\equiv \quad \{\text{Substitution}\}$

$(x = 1 \wedge 0 = 0)$

$\equiv \quad \{\text{Tautology}\}$

$(x = 1 \wedge \text{true})$

$\equiv \quad \{\text{Truth table for } \wedge\}$

$(x = 1)$

Thus $(x = 1 \wedge y = 0)[y \backslash 0] \equiv (x = 1)$ and since $(x = 1) \Rightarrow (x = 1)$ (because an identical predicate everywhere implies itself), it follows that the assignment rule may be applied, in terms of which S_2 is replaced by $y := 0$.

Similarly, a more complete justification for the third refinement step could also have been given. The question this raises is the following: how much formal reasoning is necessary? There is no unambiguous answer to such a question. The inclination of novices might be to dismiss such slow incremental reasoning as we have given above as a waste of time. Those with more experience realise that it is precisely in skipping such seemingly tiresome reasoning steps that errors tend to occur.

In fact, we will blushingly admit that in an earlier draft of this text there was an error, albeit an insignificant one, in each of these steps. The error was that in each case, the antecedent and consequent of the "implies everywhere" symbol had been incorrectly swapped. For example, step 2 was justified by the claim that

$$(x = 1 \wedge y = 0)[y \backslash 0] \Rightarrow (x = 1)$$

held, instead of

$$(x = 1) \Rightarrow (x = 1 \wedge y = 0)[y \backslash 0]$$

Fortuitously, in this particular instance it this did not lead to a erroneous conclusion.

In general, then, it is better to err on the side of too much rather than too little justification. Errors tend to occur precisely at the point where hand-waving and over-confidence step in.

2.4.7.2   How to Choose the Mid-Predicate

Note that the composition refinement rule 6 does not demand that M has to be in any particular relationship to P and/or Q—the rule is valid for an arbitrarily chosen M. However, just as it would normally be wiser to go from Cape Town to London via Johannesburg rather than via Delhi, so too, in practice M should be chosen to be, in some sense, en route from P to Q. Loosely speaking, this would mean that M should be chosen to be stronger than P but weaker than Q. The code, S_1 can be seen as shrinking the original precondition set of states, $States_P$ down to a smaller set, $States_M$, which then gets further shrunk by S_2 down to $States_Q$.

In practice, it might be too idealistic to hope that an M can reasonably be found such that $States_Q \subseteq States_M \subseteq States_P$. Just as the most comfortable route between two cities may not be along a perfectly straight line, so too, it might be necessary to make some compromises in choosing M. However, if you find that you have chosen an M such that $States_P \cap States_M = \emptyset$ and/or that $States_M \cap States_Q = \emptyset$, then that would be good reason to suspect that you are headed 180 degrees away from your intended destination.

2.4.8   Following Assignment Rule

The next rule is a special case that combines the composition rule and the assignment rule. The intermediate state needed in the composition rule, M, is chosen so that the assignment rule can be applied to the S_2 part of the composition rule. We could derive it as follows:

$\{P\}\, x, y : S\, \{Q\}$

$\sqsubseteq$ {Use composition refinement rule}

$\{P\}\, x, y : S_1\, \{M\}\,;\, x, y : S_2\, \{Q\}$

$\equiv$ {Choose M as $Q[x \backslash E]$}

$\{P\}\, x, y : S_1\, \{Q[x \backslash E]\}\,;\, x, y : S_2\, \{Q\}$

$\sqsubseteq$ {Use assignment refinement rule}

$\{P\}\, x, y : S_1\, \{Q[x \backslash E]\}\,;\, x := E\, \{Q\}$

Note, once again, that the assignment refinement rule can only be applied if $Q[x \backslash E] \Rightarrow Q[x \backslash E]$, which holds trivially. Whenever the assignment rule is invoked in a sequence of refinements as above, it should be assumed that this "implied everywhere" requirement has been verified.

The foregoing derivation leads to the "Following Assignment Rule":

Rule 7. $\{P\}\, S\, \{Q\} \sqsubseteq \{P\}\, S_1\, \{Q[x \backslash E]\}\,;\, x := E\, \{Q\}$

We can use this rule to refine the same starting specification that we had before, as follows:

$\{\mathsf{true}\}\, S\, \{x = 1 \wedge y = 0\}$

$\sqsubseteq$ {Use following assignment rule}

$\{\mathsf{true}\}\, S_2\, \{x = 1 \wedge 0 = 0\}\,;\, y := 0\, \{x = 1 \wedge y = 0\}$

$\equiv$ {Simplify using rules of logic}

$\{\mathsf{true}\}\, S_2\, \{x = 1\}\,;\, y := 0\, \{x = 1 \wedge y = 0\}$

$\sqsubseteq$ {Use assignment rule, since $\mathsf{true} \Rightarrow \{1 = 1\}$}

$\{\mathsf{true}\}\, x := 1\, \{x = 1\}\,;\, y := 0\, \{x = 1 \wedge y = 0\}$

2.4.9 Selection Rule

Suppose that we are provided with the specification $\{P\}\, S\, \{Q\}$, where P and Q are explicitly known, but not S. We wish to construct some explicit form of S that complies with this specification. We might discover that a disjunction of predicates, $G_1 \vee G_2 \vee \ldots \vee G_n$, naturally suggest itself as a weaker form of P (i.e. $P \Rightarrow G_1 \vee G_2 \vee \ldots \vee G_n$). This is often an indicator that a select command should be used to refine the specification. The shape of the select command that may be used is indicated in the following selection refinement rule.

Rule 8. *If* $P \Rightarrow G_1 \vee G_2 \vee \ldots \vee G_n$ *then:*

$$\{P\} \, S \, \{Q\} \sqsubseteq \{P\}$$

> **if** $G_1 \rightarrow \{G_1 \wedge P\} \, S_1 \, \{Q\}$
>
> ▯ $G_2 \rightarrow \{G_2 \wedge P\} \, S_2 \, \{Q\}$
>
> ▯ $\ldots$
>
> ▯ $G_n \rightarrow \{G_n \wedge P\} \, S_n \, \{Q\}$
>
> **fi**
>
> $\{Q\}$

This rule slightly extends the notation used to date. It contains predicates in braces ({ and }) before and after each command, S_i, of a guarded command. These may either be regarded as assertions embedded into the code that serve as comments to indicate what is true at that point in the code, or they may be construed as pre- and postconditions in Hoare triples, one such triple replacing each command of the relevant guarded command. In the latter case, $\{G_i \wedge P\} \, S_i \, \{Q\}$ is to be interpreted as any code which satisfies that particular specification.

Consequently the above refinement is usually the first in a sequence of refinement steps in which subsequent refinements relate to one or more triples of the form $\{G_i \wedge P\} \, S_i \, \{Q\}$ within the select statement, eventually leading to explicit forms for all these specifications.

It is not difficult to recognise that this rule articulates a true refinement as defined in Definition 2.4.2: any concrete code that satisfies the refining specification (on the right hand side) also satisfies the refined specification (on the left hand side). The requirement that $P \Rightarrow G_1 \vee G_2 \vee \ldots \vee G_n$ is, however, crucial. If P was weaker than this requirement, then the precondition would allow for the select statement to be initiated from a state that did not render any of the guards to be true. As previously noted, this would result in *abort*, which is obviously not a refinement of $\{P\} \, S \, \{Q\}$.

2.4.10   Repetition Rule

We have already suggested that a loop invariant is often useful in constructing the loop. But, as has also already been noted, a loop invariant does not guarantee loop termination—something more is needed. We therefore seek a refinement rule for a repetition command that not only relates to an invariant of the loop, but that also guarantees loop termination. This additional characterization of a terminating loop is called a *variant*.

Definition 2.4.3 (Variant of a Loop). A variant of a loop is an *integer expression* in one or more of the variables that are used in the loop, whose value decreases in each iteration of the loop, and whose value is considered to bounded from below by some value.

Being bounded from below, means that the variant cannot decrease beneath some fixed value.[7] This means that if a loop has a variant, then the loop will definitely terminate eventually. As an example, consider the following (rather trivial) loop.

$$i := 10; \text{ do } (i > 0) \to i := i - 1 \text{ od}$$

A variant for this loop is the expression i. This is an expression in one of the variables in the loop; it starts with value 10; and it always decreases (by 1) in every iteration. Because of the loop's guard, it is also bounded below by 0—the value of the variant can never legitimately be less than 0 in the loop. As a result, we can confidently state that the loop will terminate.

This does note mean, of course, that every loop that terminates will inevitably have an variant. Rather, it means that if we a priori determine a variant for a loop that is to be constructed, and ensure that the loop in fact has that variant, then we may be assured that it will terminate eventually.

In this text, we are concerned with designing terminating loops only. We therefore regard it as imperative to specify a variant, V, for every loop that is to be designed. In addition, we will also always identify an invariant, P, for each loop that we design. Our objective is to have loops that are characterised by the following specification:

$$\{P\} \text{ do } G \to \{P \wedge G \wedge (V = V_0)\} \, S \, \{P \wedge (0 \leq V < V_0)\} \text{ od } \{P \wedge \neg G\}$$

Here, V_0 is the value of the variant before the loop's body is executed. Note, also, that the above form extends the notation in a similar way to the select command's refinement rule, rule 8. Recall that in that case, a predicate in braces can either be seen as part of a Hoare triple, or as an assertion in code.

Of course, only one guard has been used in the repeat command above, but the same idea applies if multiple guards are used. Let DO be a repeat command with multiple guards, i.e.:

$$DO \triangleq \text{do}$$

$$G_1 \to \{P \wedge G_1 \wedge V = V_0\} \, S_1 \, \{P \wedge (0 \leq V < V_0)\}$$

$$\| \quad \cdots$$

$$\| \quad G_n \to \{P \wedge G_n \wedge V = V_0\} \, S_n \, \{P \wedge (0 \leq V < V_0)\}$$

$$\text{od}$$

Note that we are assuming here that each S_i satisfies the predicate

$$\{P \wedge G_i \wedge V = V_0\} \, S_i \, \{P \wedge (0 \leq V < V_0)\}$$

---

[7]As a matter of convention, an integer expression rather than a real-valued expression is used, and normally the variant is scaled so that it is bounded from below by 0.

Based on this definition of DO, the following refinement rule for constructing a repetition command can be used:

Rule 9. *If $GG = G_1 \vee G_2 \ldots \vee G_n$ and V is a variant, then:*

$$\{P\} \, S \, \{P \wedge \neg GG\} \sqsubseteq \{P\} \, DO \, \{P \wedge \neg GG\}$$

This rule suggests a general strategy for developing a loop—a strategy that will be followed in the remainder of this text. It involves the following steps:

1. Determine what is required of the loop (the postcondition, Q) and what is to be regarded as the starting condition of the problem (the precondition, P). The problem is therefore to determine S such that $\{P\} \, S \, \{Q\}$.
2. Find a meaningful way to write down Q, or some stronger predicate than Q as the conjunction of two other predicates: $I \wedge \neg G$. The first, I, will serve as the loop invariant. The negation of the second, G, will serve as the loop's condition.
3. Determine what is to be done to ensure that the predicate I is reached from state P. Perhaps nothing needs to happen, but in general it is necessary to perform some sort of initialization of variables. At this stage, then, the following is required to hold, where the details of B, the loop's body, are still to be worked out:
   $\{P\} \, Init \, \{I\} \, ; \mathbf{do} \, G \rightarrow \, \{I \wedge G\} \, B \, \{I\} \, \mathbf{od} \, \{I \wedge \neg G \Rightarrow Q\}$
4. Determine a variant, V, for the loop. This further characterises the B needed for the loop to work, in that the following should hold:
   $\{P\}$
   Init
   $\{I\}$
   $; \mathbf{do} \, G \rightarrow \{I \wedge G \wedge V = V_0\} \, B \, \{I \wedge 0 \leq V < V_0\} \, \mathbf{od}$
   $\{P \wedge \neg G \Rightarrow Q\}$
5. Now refine B into code that will ensure that
   $\{I \wedge G \wedge V = V_0\} \, B \, \{I \wedge 0 \leq V < V_0\}$ holds.

The strategy involves a number of refinement steps, each employing one of the refinement rules given earlier. In outline, the refinement steps are as follows:

$\quad \{P\} \, S \, \{Q\}$

$\sqsubseteq \quad$ {Strengthen postcondition rule: $I \wedge \neg G \Rightarrow Q$}

$\quad \{P\} \, S \, \{I \wedge \neg G\}$

$\sqsubseteq \quad$ {Composition rule using I as intermediate predicate}

$\quad \{P\} \, Init \, \{I\}; \, S_2 \, \{I \wedge \neg G\}$

$\sqsubseteq \quad$ {First refine *Init* as needed, then apply repetition rule}

$\quad \{P\} \, RefinedInit \, \{I\}; \, \mathbf{do} \, G \rightarrow B \, \mathbf{od} \, \{I \wedge \neg G\}$

$\sqsubseteq \quad$ {...Use refinement rules to refine B further...}

This broad strategy needs to be suitably adapted if a repeat command with multiple guarded commands is to be constructed.

2.4.11 Procedures and Procedure Calls

We shall defer to Chap. 5 a full discussion about refinement in the context of procedures. Here we briefly touch on a few relevant concepts, the intention being to provide a setting for the discussion on OO that follows in the next section.

Loosely speaking, a procedure can be thought of as a block of commands that is associated with both a name and zero or more parameters. The name allows for the procedure to be invoked (or called), each call assigning specified values to the parameters. From the perspective of this text, such an invocation serves in the place of a GCL command, or rather, it replaces a sequence of GCL commands. The precise form of the commands to be replaced depend on the values assigned to parameters that may form part of the procedure call.

The circumstances will be discussed under which a refinement such as $\{P'\}\,S\,\{Q'\} \sqsubseteq \{P\}\,\mathcal{P}\,\{Q\}$ is permitted, where $\mathcal{P}$ represents in a general fashion an invocation of some procedure.

What complicates the matter considerably is that there are different kinds of parameters, each with its own semantics. Chapter 5 will discuss the various kinds of parameters, and the rules 10 to 13 given in that chapter will show how each parameter kind affects refinement. The rules will specifically be concerned with the pre- and postconditions of procedures.

For the moment we simplistically ignore all issues around parameters. We also assume that a pre- and postcondition has been articulated for each procedure to specify its behaviour. Thus, in general we may designate the specification of procedure $\mathcal{P}$ as $Spec(P, \mathcal{P}, Q)$.

Suppose that $Spec(P1, \mathcal{P}1, Q1)$ and $Spec(P2, \mathcal{P}2, Q2)$ are the specifications for procedures $\mathcal{P}1$ and $\mathcal{P}2$ respectively. The strengthen postcondition and weaken precondition refinement rules (rules 1 and 2 above) may be applied to determine whether or not $Spec(P1, \mathcal{P}1, Q1) \sqsubseteq Spec(P2, \mathcal{P}2, Q2)$. As a matter of notational convenience, if we assume that the respective pre- and postconditions are known, we will simply write $\mathcal{P}1 \sqsubseteq \mathcal{P}2$ instead of $Spec(P1, \mathcal{P}1, Q1) \sqsubseteq Spec(P2, \mathcal{P}2, Q2)$.

Thus, by Rule 1, $\mathcal{P}1 \sqsubseteq \mathcal{P}2$ if $(Q2 \Rightarrow Q1) \wedge (P1 = P2)$. Similarly, by Rule 2, $\mathcal{P}1 \sqsubseteq \mathcal{P}2$ if $(P1 \Rightarrow P2) \wedge (Q1 = Q2)$.

This means that procedure $\mathcal{P}1$ may be refined by writing a new procedure $\mathcal{P}2$ that requires the same precondition as $\mathcal{P}1$ but delivers a stronger postcondition; or that delivers the same postcondition, but requires a weaker precondition. Of course, if both rules can be applied, we also arrive at a refined procedure. We will rely on these general ideas in discussing OO in the next section.

2.5 Object Orientation

Object orientation is well entrenched as a software development paradigm. Its principal strength is that it facilitates the mapping of real-world entities to the software (classes). In the jargon of OO advocates, OO narrows the gap between the problem space and solution space. Unsurprisingly, issues of algorithmic correctness do not disappear when one develops code within the OO paradigm—the correctness by construction approach to software development as discussed in the rest of this text remains both useful and valid within the OO context.

However, because of the notion of inheritance in OO, pre- and postconditions of *procedures* merit special consideration. In order to understand why this is so, let us briefly overview key concepts as developed under the *classical understanding* of OO. In doing so, we note that there are numerous variants of this classical understanding, and that nomenclature and conventions vary considerably across different programming languages. Nevertheless, the core ideas in OO for the purposes of our discussion are as follows.

A class may be thought of as a type that has members: i.e. variables (called instance variables), and procedures. Multiple instances (or objects) of a class can be created. An object's state is determined by the value of its instance variables. These variables *encapsulate* the object's state in the sense that only the object's procedures are allowed to change its state—i.e. to change an object's state, one has to invoke a procedure of the object.

A class may have subclasses. In such a case, the members of the superclass are *inherited* by the subclasses. This means that the objects of a subclass not only have members defined in the subclass itself, but also have the members defined in the superclass. It is also possible to *override* inherited members in the subclass. This is achieved by using the same name for a subclass instance variable as superclass instance variable; and/or by defining a procedure in the subclass that has the same signature as a superclass procedure.

Most programming languages place no constraint on the way in which a procedure is overridden: the overriding procedure in the subclass may conform to any specification, without reference to the specification of the superclass procedure. *This is in violation of the original intention in OO.* In the classical view, a superclass's objects are meant to be more abstract (or less refined or more general) than objects of its subclass. For the most part, precisely what is meant by abstraction/refinement/generalisation/specialisation has been left a little vague, OO authors generally illustrating these notions by way of example. Typical examples given are of a Vehicle superclass that specialises to a Car subclass; an abstract Shape superclass that is specialised to a Rectangle subclass; a BankAccount class that specialises to both SavingsAccount and ChequeAccount subclasses; etc.

A procedure that is inherited and not overridden in a subclass obviously retains its original specification—i.e. it inherits the pre- and postconditions of the procedure in the superclass. To override the superclass procedure means (except in a trivial case) to change not only its internal code, but also its specifications—its pre- and postconditions.

Clearly, the notion of refinement has no relationship to haphazard overriding where code and pre- and postconditions are arbitrarily changed. Instead, we will consider one class to be a refinement of another exclusively under the following circumstances.

Definition 2.5.1 (Class Refinement).   Suppose $\mathcal{R}$ is subclass of class $\mathcal{A}$. Then $\mathcal{A} \sqsubseteq \mathcal{R}$, if and only if $\mathcal{R}$ does not introduce new procedures as members and $\mathcal{A}.P \sqsubseteq \mathcal{R}.P$ for every procedure $\mathcal{A}.P$ in class $\mathcal{A}$ that is overridden by procedure $\mathcal{R}.P$ in class $\mathcal{R}$.

It would be pleasing if real world OO programming languages supported class refinement. Unfortunately, few do so. Eiffel is a notable exception. It allows one to specify explicitly the pre- and postconditions of a procedure. These are automatically carried over to inherited procedures. In addition, when overriding a procedure one can optionally weaken the carried over precondition and/or optionally strengthen the carried over postcondition. These procedure pre- and postconditions are treated as assertions that can be evaluated at runtime.

If it happens that the postconditions of all procedures in class have a set of conjuncts in common, these conjuncts may be thought of as the class's *invariant*. No matter which procedure is invoked on the object of a class, once the procedure has completed, the invariant continues to characterise the state of the relevant object. Eiffel also provides explicit support for the articulation of class invariants. See [31] for a full discussion of Eiffel.

The foregoing definition of class refinement allows us to retain the conventional notion of a superclass being more abstract/general than a refined subclass, which is in turn appropriately described as more specialised. How are we then to characterise a subclass which has not overridden any superclass procedures, but which has simply added new procedures to those that are inherited? Because we have not refined any procedure, it does not seem appropriate to call the subclass a refinement of the superclass. Nevertheless, it seems appropriate to speak of the subclass as being a specialisation of the abstract superclass. Following [27], we offer the following definition:

Definition 2.5.2 (Class Enrichment).   Suppose $\mathcal{E}$ is subclass of class $\mathcal{A}$. Then $\mathcal{E}$ is an *enrichment* of A, written as $\mathcal{A} \sqsubseteq_e \mathcal{E}$, if and only if $\mathcal{E}$ introduces new members but does not override any inherited members of $\mathcal{A}$.

In terms of this definition, an abstract class can be specialised in a stepwise fashion in one of two complementary directions at each step: either by refinement or by enrichment. The application at hand will dictate precisely which classes and subclasses are necessary in the final design. Starting from abstract class $\mathcal{A}$, we can thus envisage a sequence of refinements and enrichments to arrive at a subclass S. Because refinement and enrichment as defined above are mutually independent, one could arrive at S by first carrying out all the necessary enrichments and then carrying out the required refinements. In principle, this could happen in the following three steps: $\mathcal{A} \sqsubseteq_e \mathcal{E} \sqsubseteq S$. In [27], $\mathcal{E}$ is called the *base abstraction* of S and is characterised by the fact that none of its members are refinements. Such a base abstraction, $\mathcal{E}$, is conceptually useful in that all subclass of $\mathcal{E}$ refine it, even subclasses that are more than one hierarchical level removed from $\mathcal{E}$. Note that in terms of our above definitions, such subclasses cannot be said to refine more abstract classes such as $\mathcal{A}$.

Also depending on the needs of the application, $\mathcal{A}$ may have other subclasses that serve as base abstractions of a different subset of subclasses.

The base abstraction therefore contains all unrefined members needed by $\mathcal{S}$, all its children, and any of its siblings. The various sibling and deeper descendent classes are derived by refining, according to the dictates of the application at hand, different sets of members of $\mathcal{E}$.

We end this brief overview of OO by commending "Design by Contract" (DbC), advocated by Meyer [31], as an approach to developing OO software. In terms of this paradigm, the procedure's pre- and postconditions are conceived of as constituting a *contract* between procedure developer and procedure user. The contract states that if the user ensures that a procedure call adheres to the precondition, then the developer *guarantees* that the result will conform to the postcondition. DbC meshes perfectly with the correctness-by-construction approach to software development that is advocated in this text. The latter addresses programming-in-the-small, emphasising correctness at the lowest level of coding and algorithmic design. The former extends these ideas one level higher, into the realm of classes and their associated procedures. One might say that DbC emphasises *what* must be achieved at the level of procedures, whereas correctness-by-construction focusses on *how* to achieve this within a procedure.

2.6   Supplementary Notation

We close this chapter with various notational conventions that will be used as and when convenient.

2.6.1   Morgan's Refinement Calculus

A calculus for refinement of specifications was formalized by Morgan [32], in an alternative notation to Hoare triples. The rules that have been presented above are the most frequently used refinement rules enunciated by Morgan, but adapted for Hoare triples. Morgan's notation is a little more concise, and will be used later when convenient.

In Morgan's notation $w : [P, Q]$ is a specification of a program with frame w, precondition P, and postcondition Q. The notation allows that such a specification can, where appropriate, be refined to code, instead of to another specification of this form. It also allows that such a specification can be embedded in part of a code structure (e.g. within the command part of a guarded command). It is precisely for this reason that the notation is quite concise.

Morgan calls the condition governing a rule's applicability (the *if* part in the rule's statement) its proviso. The provisos and rules enunciated above are given in Morgan's notation in Table 2.1. It is left to the reader to make the mapping between the two sets of rules. This table ought to serve as a handy reference point for the rest of the text.

2.6.2 Arrays and Sequences

It will be assumed that arrays start at index 0 and that $A.len$ denotes the length of the array A. We shall refer to the ith element of array A as A_{i-1}.

As far as possible, we shall open intervals such as $[i, j)$ when referencing a subarray of an array. For example $A_{[i,j)}$ denotes the subarray $A_i, A_{i+1} \ldots A_{j-1}$.

The advantage of using an open interval such as $[i, j]$ is that the length of the subarray is readily apparent, namely $(j - i)$. For this reason, we will avoid using intervals such as $[i, j]$, whose length is $(j - i + 1)$, unless other considerations apply.

In a few isolated examples, instead of arrays, we will rely on sequence notation used in some texts. Suppose that s is some sequence. Then:

- s_i represents the $(i+1)^{\text{st}}$ element in the sequence s. (The first element is thus s_0.)
- $s.q$ represents the number of times that element q appears in the sequence s.

Table 2.1 Refinement rules in Morgan's notation

Rule #	Rule name	Proviso and rule
1	Strengthen postcondition	If $Q' \Rrightarrow Q$ then $w : [P, Q] \sqsubseteq w : [P, Q']$
2	Weaken precondition	If $P \Rrightarrow P'$ then $w : [P, Q] \sqsubseteq w : [P', Q]$
3	Skip	If $P \Rrightarrow Q$ then $w : [P, Q] \sqsubseteq skip$
5	Assignment	If $P \Rrightarrow Q[\backslash E]$ then $w : [P, Q] \sqsubseteq w := E$
6	Sequential composition	$w : [P, Q] \sqsubseteq w : [P, R]; w : [R, Q]$
7	Following assignment	$w, x[P, Q] \sqsubseteq w, x[P, Q[x \backslash E]]; x := E$
8	Selection	If $P \Rrightarrow G_1 \vee G_2 \ldots G_n$ then $w : [P, Q] \sqsubseteq$ **if** $G_1 \rightarrow w : [G_1 \wedge P, Q]$ ▌ $\ldots$ ▌ $G_n \rightarrow w : [G_n \wedge P, Q]$ **fi**
9	Repetition	If $GG = G_1 \vee G_2 \ldots G_n$ and V is a variant, then: $w : [P, P \wedge \neg GG] \sqsubseteq$ **do** $G_1 \rightarrow w : [P \wedge G_1, P \wedge (0 \leq V < V_0)]$ ▌ $\ldots$ ▌ $G_n \rightarrow w : [P \wedge G_n, P \wedge (0 \leq V < V_0)]$ **od**

- $s \uparrow r$ represents the prefix of s consisting of the first r elements (at index positions 0 to $r - 1$).
- Combining this notation, we can also use $s \uparrow r.q$ to represent the number of times that q appears in the first r elements of the sequence s.

2.6.3 Additional GCL Commands

Occasionally, it will be convenient to augment the classical GCL commands by more convenient commands whose semantics are fairly obvious.

- For example, it will sometimes be handy to write a loop as:

$$\textbf{for} \ \ i : I \rightarrow S \ \ \textbf{rof}$$

This describes a loop in which i is a loop variable that assumes a different value from some set, I, in each iteration, and iteration terminates when all values have been assumed. If this command is used, then the contents of the set I should of course not be changed by S. Furthermore, if I is ordered in some way, then it will be assumed that the elements of I will be selected in some order. If I is simply a set with no known ordering on the elements, then no assumption may be made about the order in which I's elements are selected.
- When a select command has the form

$$\textbf{if} \ G \rightarrow S \ \| \ \ \neg G \rightarrow skip \ \textbf{fi}$$

some authors are wont to abbreviated it to

$$\textbf{as} \ G \rightarrow S \ \textbf{sa}$$

This extends on Dijkstra's original notation, using "as" which is the Dutch translation of "if". Whether this subsequent addition to GCL appropriately honours the memory of Dijkstra is an open question.
- Occasionally, it will be useful to gather a sequence of commands into a unit that is treated as a single block. This is indicated as follows: $\|[S_1; S_2; \dots; S_n]\|$.
- Variables may be declared at the beginning of a specification or block using the keyword **var**. For example, we could declare x to be a natural number as follows: **var** $x : \mathbb{N}$.
- Sequences of code may be encapsulated into a procedure or function with a given name. Parameters of these procedures or functions are usually defined as part of the enclosing text in which the specification is being described. In the case of functions, the returned value should also be specified. The following skeletal outlines illustrate the relevant requirements. Note the keywords that are used to start and end procedures and functions. Also note that in the skeleton below, parameters x and y are used in the procedure and function, and a tuple,

$\langle w, z \rangle$ is returned by the function. This tuple notation is not necessary, but may be useful if you want to return more than one item from a function.

> **proc** $P(x, y)$
> $\quad \ldots$
> **corp**

> **func** $F(x, y) : \langle w, z \rangle$
> $\quad \ldots$
> $\quad w, z := \ldots$
> $\quad \ldots$
> $\quad$ **return** $\langle w, z \rangle$
> **cnuf**

Note, however, that in Chap. 5 a fuller discussion of the semantics of procedures and functions will be provided, as well as refinement approaches that are relevant in such a context

2.7 Revision Exercises

1. When is the boolean expression $x \Rightarrow y$ false?
2. To what does $\exists x : R \cdot f(x)$ evaluate if $R = \phi$?
3. Consider the following assertion:

   "Either you do not love me, or you will do what I command."

   With which assertion(s) below is this assertion logically equivalent? Assume that there could be zero, one or more equivalent assertions.

   (a) If you love me, you will do what I command.
   (b) If you do not love me, you will do what I command.
   (c) If you love me, you will not do what I command.
   (d) If you do not love me, you will not do what I command.

4. Consider the array A. Suppose that predicate $Exists(A, i, j, r)$ represents the assertion that there is some element, say k, in the interval $[i, j)$ such that $A_k = r$. Similarly, suppose that predicate $All(A, i, j, r)$ represents the assertion that for every element, k, in the interval $[i, j)$, $A_k = r$.

   (a) Write down formal definitions of $Exists(A, i, j, r)$ and $All(A, i, j, r)$, using universal and/or existential quantifiers.
   (b) What is the truth-value of the following predicates. Briefly justify your answers.

    i. $Exists(A, 0, 0, r)$

    ii. $All(A, 0, 0, r)$

    iii. $Exists(A, 0, 5, 2) \Rightarrow \neg All(A, 0, 5, 1)$

5. Explain what $X \Rightarrow Y$ means in terms of $State_X$ and $State_Y$.

6. Consider each of the following predicates and indicate whether it is stronger than $x > 0$, weaker than $x > 0$, equivalent to $x > 0$, or none of the foregoing. NB: equivalence may be interpreted as both stronger and as weaker.

    (a) $(x > 0) \wedge (x \leq 0)$

    (b) $(x > 0) \wedge (y \leq 0)$

    (c) $(x > 0) \vee (x \leq 0)$

    (d) $(x > 0) \vee (y \leq 0)$

    (e) $(x > 0) \Rightarrow (x \leq 0)$

    (f) $(x \leq 0) \Rightarrow (x > 0)$

7. Indicate whether the following is true, false, or whether the truth value cannot be determined from the data.

    (a) $\{wp(S, Q)\} \, S \, \{Q\}$

    (b) $\{false\} \, S \, \{x > 5\}$

    (c) $\{x < 6\} \, x := x + 1 \, \{x > 5\}$

    (d) $\{true\} \, \text{if } x > 0 \rightarrow y := 10 \, \text{fi} \, \{true\}$

    (e) $\{x = 6\} \, \text{if } x > 0 \rightarrow y := 10 \, \text{fi} \, \{x > 0 \wedge y > 0\}$

    (f) $\{P\} \, S \, \{Q\} \sqsubseteq \{P\} \, S_1 \, \{Q[x \backslash E]\}; x := E \, \{Q\}$

    (g) $wp(x, y := y, x, (x > y \wedge x > z)) = x > z \wedge y > z$

    (h) $\{x > 0\} \, skip \, \{x > 5\}$

    (i) $\{true\} \, \text{if } x > 0 \rightarrow y := 10 \, \text{fi} \, \{true\}$

    (j) $\{P\} \, S \, \{wp(S, P)\}$

    (k) $\forall x : \varnothing \cdot ((x > 0) \wedge (x < 0))$

    (l) $\{(x < 7) \wedge (z = 5) \wedge (y < 7)\} \, skip \, \{(z < x) \wedge (y < 7)\}$

    (m) $\{true\} \, x := 1; \text{do } (x = 1) \rightarrow skip \, \text{od} \, \{true\}$

    (n) $\{false\} \, x := 1; \text{do } (x = 1) \rightarrow skip \, \text{od} \, \{false\}$

    (o) $\{false\} \, x := 1; \text{do } (x = 1) \rightarrow skip \, \text{od} \, \{x \neq 1\}$

    (p) $\{true\} \, x := 1; \text{do } (x = 1) \rightarrow skip \, \text{od} \, \{false\}$

    (q) $\{wp(S, Q)\} \, S \, \{Q\}$ where S is given by $x := 1; \text{do } (x = 1) \rightarrow skip \, \text{od}$

8. State and derive the "following assignment" refinement rule.

9. After reviewing the meaning of the "implies everywhere" relationship, determine which of the following instances the "implies everywhere" relationship holds?

    (a) $(x > y) \Rightarrow (x \geq y)$

    (b) $(x \Rightarrow y) \Rightarrow (y \Rightarrow x)$

    (c) $(x \Leftrightarrow y) \Rightarrow (y \Rightarrow x)$

    (d) $(xy > x) \Rightarrow (y > 1)$

    (e) $(xy > x) \wedge (x > 0) \Rightarrow (y \geq 1)$

    (f) $(x > 0) \vee (y > 1) \Rightarrow (xy > x)$

10. How should the integer ranges $R1$ and $R2$ be defined, respectively, so that the following first order predicates evaluate to true.

$\forall x : \quad R1 \cdot (A \Rightarrow B)$
$\forall x : \quad R2 \cdot (A \Leftrightarrow B)$

where A and B are as defined below. Also indicate in each case whether it could be claimed that $A \Rightarrow B$.

(a) $A \triangleq 3 < 0$ and $B \triangleq 3 \le 0$
(b) $A \triangleq 3 < 0$ and $B \triangleq x \le 0$
(c) $A \triangleq x < 0$ and $B \triangleq x \le 0$
(d) $A \triangleq 3 \ge 0$ and $B \triangleq x \le 0$

11. Give a refinement of $\{P\}\ S\ \{Q\}$ if $R \Rightarrow Q$.
12. Prove that $\{y > 25\}\ x : S\ \{x > 5\} \sqsubseteq \{y > 5\}\ x := y + 5\ \{x > 5\}$.
13. Determine an expression for the weakest precondition of each of the items of code in the following Hoare triples with respect to the indicated postcondition. Use your result to argue either that the Hoare triple is a true predicate, or a false predicate, or that there is not enough information to determine its truth-value.

(a) $\{y < 10\}$ **if** $((x > 0) \wedge (y < 10)) \to y := 10$ **fi** $\{$true$\}$
(b) $\{P\}\ x := x + y\ \{P[x \backslash (x + y)]\}$

14. Are the following legitimate refinements?

(a) $\{x > 1\}\ S\ \{x \ge 0\} \sqsubseteq skip$
(b) $\{x > 1\}\ S\ \{x \ge 0\} \sqsubseteq x := 1$
(c) $\{x > 1\}\ S\ \{x \ge 0\} \sqsubseteq y := 1$
(d) $\{$true$\}\ S\ \{x \ge 0\} \sqsubseteq y := 1$

15. In a series of steps refine $\{y < 10\}\ S\ \{y > 0\}$ to:
    if $((x > 0) \vee (y < 10)) \to y := 10$ **fi**
    Why is it not possible to refine this same specification **if** $((x > 0) \wedge (y < 10)) \to y := 10$ **fi**

16. A student wishes to show that $A_1 \wedge A_2 \Rightarrow B_1 \wedge B_2$. Under which of the following circumstances has she achieved her purpose?

(a) She shows that $A_1 \Rightarrow B_1 \wedge B_2$
(b) She shows that $A_1 \Rightarrow B_1$ and then shows that $A_2 \Rightarrow B_2$
(c) She shows that $A_1 \Rightarrow B_1$ and then shows that $A_2 \Rightarrow B_1$

17. Let C represent the concrete program:

do (true) $\to$ **skip od**

Which one or more of the following predicates about C are true:

(a) $\{$true$\}\ C\ \{$true$\}$
(b) $\{$false$\}\ C\ \{$false$\}$
(c) $\{$true$\}\ C\ \{$false$\}$

    (d) $wp(C, \text{false}) = \text{false}$
    (e) $wp(C, \text{true}) = \text{false}$

18. Consider the specification $Spec(P, S, Q)$. Suppose that, because of the structure of the specific problem confronting you, you know that S involves doing
something (still to be worked out) and then decrementing x by 1. Show how the
following assignment refinement rule can be used to refine the specification.

19. You need to refine the following specification:

    $x, y, z : [P \wedge (x = a),\ Q \wedge (x = yz)]$,

where P and Q are predicates. Show how the *following assignment* rule could
be used as a first step of your refinement.

20. Sue claims that $wp(S, Q) \equiv (x > max(0, -y))$, where

    S is $x, y := x + y, x$
    Q is $((x > 0) \wedge (y > 0))$ and
    $max(p, q)$ returns the maximum of p and q.

    Do you agree with Sue?

21. Show that $wp(IF, (y > 0)) \equiv (x > min(0, y))$ where IF is given by:

    $IF \equiv \textbf{if } (x > 0) \rightarrow y := 10 \ \| \ (x \leq 0) \rightarrow y := x - y \ \textbf{fi}$

Will this IF command will abort if executed from a state in which $x = -10$
and $y = -3$?

22. Indicate whether the following relationships are true or false:

    (a) If $Spec(P, S, Q) \sqsubseteq Spec(P', S', Q')$ and $Spec(P', S', Q') \sqsubseteq Spec(P'', S'', Q'')$ then $Spec(P, S, Q) \sqsubseteq Spec(P'', S'', Q'')$
    (b) If $Spec(P, S, Q) \sqsubseteq Spec(P', S', Q')$ and $Spec(P, S, Q) \sqsubseteq Spec(P'', S'', Q'')$ then $Spec(P', S', Q') \sqsubseteq Spec(P'', S'', Q'')$
    (c) If $P \Rightarrow wp(S, Q)$ then $Spec(P, S, Q) \sqsubseteq Spec(wp(S, Q), S, Q)$
    (d) If $P \Rightarrow Q$ then $Spec(P, S, Q) \sqsubseteq Spec(P, \text{skip}, Q)$

23. For the purposes of this question, make a reasonable assumption about the
relationship between $(INV \wedge \neg G)$ and Q. Also assume that $P \Rightarrow INV$.

    (a) Consider the following two refinement steps. State the refinement rules that
have been applied in each case.

        $\{P\} \, S \, \{Q\}$
    $\sqsubseteq$ $\{\text{Refinement 1}\}$
        $\{P\} \, S \, \{INV \wedge \neg G\}$
    $\sqsubseteq$ $\{\text{Refinement 2}\}$
        $\{P\} \, S1 \, \{INV\}; S2 \, \{INV \wedge \neg G\}$

    (b) Show the refinements that would typically be next applied to $S1$ and $S2$
respectively?

Chapter 3
Simple Examples

In this chapter, a number of fairly elementary algorithms are developed. They are, namely: linear search; finding the maximal element in an array; a version of binary search; a simple pattern matching algorithm; raising a number to a specific integer power; and finding the integer approximation of a logarithm to the base 2.

It is probable that the reader will already have encountered at least some of these algorithms—if not all of them. Our purpose is to use these fairly simple algorithm to introduce a particular style of programming-in-the-small. In considering an algorithmic problem, the approach starts off by focussing on the context of the problem: what may be regarded as true before the algorithm is to execute? How can this context be described more exactly as a predicate. This becomes the precondition. Then one considers in more precise terms what the algorithm is to achieve, also seeking to express this as a predicate. These pre- and postconditions constitute the problem's specifications.

The resulting specification is then refined in a systematic fashion, relying on the refinement rules mentioned in the previous chapter. Eventually a GCL coded solution to the problem is derived. The coded solution is guaranteed to be correct— i.e. to be a refinement of the problem's specification. This claim is, of course, subject to the accuracy of our reasoning which is indeed fallible. However, it will be seen that the *kind* of reasoning deployed is different from the conventional thought processes in deriving algorithms: it is more systematic, and it is closer to mathematical reasoning. As such, it is somewhat less error-prone, and it is inclined to point us towards error sources that are often ignored in conventional approaches to writing code.

This is what has been termed the software *correctness by construction* approach to developing software. Of course, in saying this, we do not for a moment wish to denigrate development approaches which emphasise testing. In fact, we would strongly advocate thorough testing of any software that is developed—the two approaches are entirely complimentary.

D.G. Kourie and B.W. Watson, *The Correctness-by-Construction Approach*   55
to Programming, DOI 10.1007/978-3-642-27919-5_3,
© Springer-Verlag Berlin Heidelberg 2012

3.1 Linear Search

Consider the array A of some type (say, integer), and let x be a variable of the same type. Under the assumption that the value of x occurs as an element of A, find an index i at which it appears. (Note that we say *an* index instead of *the* index, since x can appear in more than one place in A.)

3.1.1 Formulating the Problem

To make it all easier, define a predicate $app(A, x, l, h)$ to mean that the value of x appears somewhere in $A_{[l,h)}$. Now we could express this in predicate logic order formula as follows:

$$app(A, x, l, h) \triangleq \exists i : [l, h) \cdot (A_i = x)$$

However, often—as in this example—this level of detail in expressing predicates is not strictly necessary, since it does not significantly contribute to the reasoning process. In this example, then, we will never need to refer to the quantified formula, although it does no harm to bear it in mind when thinking about the problem

Recall that the range $[l, h)$ includes the l, but not the h—*it is closed at the lower end and open at the upper end*. Also, recall from Sect. 2.6.2 that we will assume throughout that indexing of arrays begins at 0. Given that, the problem to be solved can be specified as: determine code, S such that $\{app(A, x, 0, A.len)\}\ i : S$ $\{(A_i = x)\}$.

However, it will be convenient to restrict ourselves to the slightly more compact notation of Morgan:

$$i : [app(A, x, 0, A.len), (A_i = x)]$$

It should be noted that this is actually a rather imprecise specification in the sense that $app(A, x, 0, A.len)$ continues to hold at all times. It is global invariant. Consequently, it could have been inserted as a conjunct in the postcondition, and it should be regarded as true under all conditions, no matter how we refine this initial specification. This fact will become relevant later on in our reasoning.

3.1.2 Choosing the Invariant

Next come the steps of choosing the invariant. In order to do this, we need some intuition: if we are to find such an element of A (which is not even sorted), we pretty much have to look at every element of the array. We could do this randomly, or from left to right or from right to left, or in some other pattern.

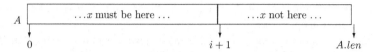

Fig. 3.1 Linear search before x has been found

For the purpose of this example, we try *right to left*. The invariant is chosen to express something that is holds (is **true**) at the top and bottom of every iteration (execution) of the loop, and therefore also holds before and after the loop. It should, in some sense, also express the progress that we have been making towards our end-goal (computationally). Assume that the loop has progressed to a stage where everything from the top of the array (whose index value is $A.len - 1$) down to index $i + 1$ has been examined and found not to contain the sought-after value, x. Figure 3.1 depicts this schematically.

We can then express the invariant, *inv*, as follows:

$$inv \triangleq \neg app(A, x, i + 1, A.len)$$

In other words, our invariant says that we know that x *does not appear* as an element of the subarray $A_{[i+1,A.len)}$.

We can now refine our specification, by strengthening the postcondition:

$$i : [app(A, x, 0, A.len), inv \wedge (A_i = x)] \tag{3.1}$$

Clearly, this is a strengthening, since we simply added a conjunct, *inv*, to the postcondition, $(A_i = x)$, and, in general $X \wedge Y$ is always stronger than both X and Y. (This can be verified easily by thinking in terms of predicates as being represented by sets of states, and by noting that predicate conjunction corresponds to state set intersection.)

3.1.3 Establishing the Invariant

We already know that the general pattern for a specification before we can refine it to a loop should be something like $i : [inv, inv \wedge \neg G]$. To get our refined specification into this shape, we notice that the current precondition $app(A, x, 0, A.len)$, has only a vague resemblance to our *inv*. So, we refine using sequential composition, with the aim of transforming the precondition to become *inv* after executing some code. The refined specification of the problem is then:

$$i : [app(A, x, 0, A.len), inv]; i : [inv, inv \wedge (A_i = x)] \tag{3.2}$$

We can now work separately on the two parts of the specification to the left and right of the composition operator.

The first part of our specification (3.2) can be viewed as nothing more than some actions needed to establish the invariant (which must hold before the iteration can start). Starting with

$$i : [app(A, x, 0, A.len), inv]$$

if we fill in the definition of *inv*, we get

$$i : [app(A, x, 0, A.len), \neg app(A, x, i + 1, A.len)]$$

It should not be that difficult to see that the assignment $i := A.len - 1$ will be a suitable refinement.

Let us go through the formal steps to verify that this is indeed an appropriate assignment. What is needed, is a confirmation that the conditions for applying the assignment rule indeed hold. These conditions are that the precondition must everywhere imply the postcondition, in which appropriate substitutions have been made. Specifically in this case, the following must apply:

$$app(A, x, 0, A.len) \Rrightarrow \neg app(A, x, i + 1, A.len)[i \backslash A.len - 1]$$

or

$$app(A, x, 0, A.len) \Rrightarrow \neg app(A, x, A.len, A.len)$$

The right hand side of the "implies everywhere" asserts that the value of x does not appear in the range $A_{[A.len, A.len)}$. This is, of course, a **true** assertion, since nothing can appear in an empty range.[1] Since **true** is implied everywhere by *any* predicate, it is therefore also implied everywhere by $app(A, x, 0, A.len)$. This confirms that the proposed assignment is a valid refinement according to our assignment rule. The specification in (3.2) therefore refines to the following:

$$i := A.len - 1; \; i : [inv, inv \wedge (A_i = x)] \tag{3.3}$$

Having refined the first part of specification (3.2) down to a simple assignment statement in specification (3.3), we now continue to refine the loop.

3.1.4   Refining to Create a Loop

The second part of our sequential composition in (3.3) is

$$i : [inv, inv \wedge (A_i = x)]$$

---

[1] One can easily prove this assertion rigorously by referring to the definitions for existential and/or universal quantification in Sect. 2.1.2 in the context of the predicate formula version of $app(A, x, A.len, A.len)$.

We see immediately that this fits the pattern needed for loop refinement, where $(A_i = x)$ is construed as the negation of the guard. The guard of the loop will therefore be taken as $A_i \neq x$.

We now need to choose a variant—some expression that expresses the fact that we are making progress through every iteration of the loop. For this example, we will choose i as our variant V. This is a good choice since we are moving through A from right to left (i is decreasing) and i will never go negative (due to the precondition of this entire problem, which says that the value of x appears *somewhere* in A).

According to the repetition refinement rule, we can refine the second part of (3.1) into

$$\textbf{do } A_i \neq x \rightarrow$$
$$i : [inv \wedge A_i \neq x, inv \wedge (0 \leq i < i_0)]$$
$$\textbf{od}$$

All that remains is to refine the body of the loop into code. Intuitively (it is not always that easy), we can see that $i := i - 1$ is a good choice. We can confirm that this assignment is a legitimate refinement by doing the necessary substitution as required by the assignment rule, to show that

$$inv \wedge A_i \neq x \Rightarrow (inv \wedge (0 \leq i < i_0))[i \setminus i - 1]$$

Substituting *inv* by its definition and substituting $i - 1$ for i gives:

$$\neg app(A, x, i + 1, A.len) \wedge A_i \neq x \Rightarrow \neg app(A, x, i, A.len) \wedge (0 \leq i - 1 < i_0)$$

Clearly, the two conjuncts to the left of the $\Rightarrow$ symbol can be simplified to the same predicate as the first conjunct to the right of the symbol, namely $\neg app(A, x, i, A.len)$. We thus need to show that something of the following form holds: $P \Rightarrow P \wedge Q$. At first sight, this seems unlikely to be the case—intuitively, by adding the conjunct Q to P, one would imagine that the predicate P has been strengthened, and P cannot imply everywhere something that is stronger than itself, $P \wedge Q$! Indeed, this would generally be the case, but in this particular situation, it is not so. We argue as follows.

Consider what has to be shown if we want to prove that $P \Rightarrow P \wedge Q$ does *not* hold. We would have to find an instance where P is true but Q is false, for then the left hand side, P, would be true but the right hand side, $P \wedge Q$, would be false. In this particular situation, we need to find an i that falsifies the $(0 \leq i - 1 < i_0)$ but retains $P \equiv \neg app(A, x, i, A.len)$ as true.

In actual fact, $(0 \leq i - 1 < i_0)$, is made up of *two* conjuncts: $(0 \leq i - 1) \wedge (i - 1 < i_0)$. Now $(i - 1 < i_0)$ simply asserts that the decremented value of i is less than its unchanged value, which is obviously true. Thus, the only way in which $(0 \leq i - 1) \wedge (i - 1 < i_0)$ can be falsified is if $(0 \leq i - 1)$ is false, i.e. if $(0 > i - 1)$. Put differently, $(0 \leq i - 1) \wedge (i - 1 < i_0)$ is false if and only if $(i \leq 0)$ is true.

But any such choice of i means that the P parts of the "implies everywhere" argument are also falsified. Recall that the P parts assert that $\neg app(A, x, i, A.len)$, but if i is zero or less, then this is simply another way of asserting that x does not appear at all in array A. Now by the data given for the problem, such an assertion is false.[2]

Hence, there is no i for which the left hand side of the "implies everywhere" is true while the right hand side is false. The "implies everywhere" thus holds, and the assignment is consequently justified.

3.1.5 Putting it All Together

We can now glue all of the pieces together to get the following code as a refinement of specification (3.3):

$$
\begin{aligned}
& i := A.len - 1; \\
& \textbf{do}\ A_i \neq x \rightarrow \\
& \qquad i := i - 1 \\
& \textbf{od}
\end{aligned}
$$

3.2 Finding the Maximal Element

For the second example, we take a look at the maximal element problem. We assume that A is an array of integers (or reals—it does not really matter) and that A contains at least one element. The problem is to determine the index, i, that specifies a maximum element of A. (Again, we say *a* maximum element instead of *the* maximum element, because there may be many entries corresponding to the largest value.)

3.2.1 Formulating the Problem

There are, of course, many ways in which to solve this problem, some sensible, and some not. A feasible but silly thing to do would be to sample random elements of A, somehow keeping track of which element had been tested, and stopping when we had some assurance that each element had been sampled. Clearly, it is far more orderly to sample a contiguous area of the array, keeping track of the index of the maximum element in the contiguous area sampled to date.

---

[2]Recall that we noted at the start of this discussion, in Sect. 3.1.1, that $app(A, x, 0, A.len)$ holds invariantly throughout—i.e. x was assumed to appear *somewhere* in A.

For the moment, let us keep the start and end indices (*l* and *h* respectively) of such a contiguous area general, and simply decide to use $max(A, l, h, i)$ as a predicate which asserts that i is the index of a largest element in the subarray $A_{[l,h)}$.

Although it is not to absolutely necessary to express max explicitly as a predicate formula, nothing is lost by doing so:

$$max(A, l, h, i) \triangleq \forall j : [l, h) \cdot (A_j \leq A_i) \land (l \leq i < h)$$

The idea is therefore to find the i such that $max(A, 0, A.len, i)$ is true. Part of the problem statement was that the array A is not empty, so this is expressed in our specification's precondition:

$$i : [A.len > 0, max(A, 0, A.len, i)]$$

Note that, once more, we may not assume anything about the array's internal structure (for example, that it is sorted). In the absence of any relationship between array elements, clearly some kind of linear traversal of the array is about the only reasonable strategy for solving the problem.

In this case, let us (arbitrarily) elect to traverse the array from left to right. This means that we will need a variable, j, to indicate the index range explored to date. Consequently, the specification could more accurately be written with j as an additional frame variable.

$$i, j : [A.len > 0, max(A, 0, A.len, i)]$$

3.2.2 Choosing the Invariant

As we traverse A from left to right, we will use i to keep track of the index of a maximum found so far. The situation after searching the subarray $[0, j)$ is depicted in Fig. 3.2.
That means that an invariant, inv, can be defined in terms of i and j as follows:

$$inv \triangleq max(A, 0, j, i)$$

Note carefully that inv provides information about $A_{[0,j)}$; it says nothing about whether $A_j > A_i$ or not.

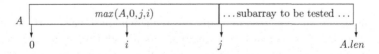

Fig. 3.2 Maximal element search in subarray $[0, j)$

The postcondition of the problem's specification can be written in terms of this invariant, by virtue of the following equivalence:

$$max(A, 0, A.len, i) \equiv (inv \land j = A.len)$$

Since equivalence can be regarded as strengthening (or weakening), the strengthening postcondition rule can be invoked to claim that the following is a refinement of the original specification:

$$i, j : [A.len > 0, inv \land j = A.len]$$

3.2.3   Establishing the Invariant

As in the linear search example in Sect. 3.1, we should use a sequential composition to refine our current specification into the right form for creating a loop. Recall that this is the third step in the overall strategy for loop development that we articulated at the end of Sect. 2.4.10.

From the above specification, we choose *inv* as our *mid* predicate for the composition, giving the following as our refined specification:

$$i, j : [A.len > 0, inv]; i, j : [inv, inv \land j = A.len]$$

We can now refine these two specifications separately, before putting their resulting refinements all together.

The first specification is directed at establishing the invariant. It suggests that something needs to be assigned to variables i and j: not only are they explicitly mentioned as frame variables, but they also appear as variables in the invariant's definition.

Assigning 0 to j leaves us in the position of not knowing quite what to assign to i—after all, what is the index of the maximal element in $A_{[0,0)}$ (which is an empty range)? Should it be some special value such as ∞, or perhaps -1?

An alternative is to assign 0 to i. In that case, what should the value of j be? Well, 0 (for i) is certainly the index of the largest element in the range $A_{[0,1)}$, so $j = 1$ would be a good value. This suggests that the following would be an appropriate refinement step in regard to the first piece of the overall specification that we are refining:

$$i, j : [A.len > 0, inv]; \sqsubseteq i, j := 0, 1;$$

Of course, the arguments given to justify this refinement have been fairly informal (though careful and systematic). To formally justify the refinement step (i.e. the use of the assignment rule), we would have to show that $A.len > 0 \Rightarrow inv[i, j \backslash 0, 1]$. The details are left as an exercise for the reader. It will be seen easily that the choice of values to assign to i and j makes the right hand side of the implies everywhere symbol true, so that the implies everywhere is indeed valid, and hence that the use of the assignment rule is justified.

3.2.4 Refining to Create a Loop

The part of the specification which is destined to become a loop is as follows:

$$i, j : [inv, inv \land j = A.len]$$

It is already in the right form to apply the refinement rule for repetition. In the context of that rule, $j = A.len$ is the negation of the guard. Applying the rule gives:

$$\textbf{do } j \neq A.len \rightarrow$$
$$i, j : [inv \land j \neq A.len, inv \land (0 \leq V < V_0)]$$
$$\textbf{od}$$

To proceed, we need to determine which expression to use as a variant, V. Since j is moving through A from left to right, the choice that suggests itself is $V \triangleq A.len - j$. V decreases every time j moves closer to $A.len$ and V will not go below 0. This means that the last conjunct of the postcondition can be simplified as follows:

$$0 \leq V < V_0$$
$$\equiv \quad \{\text{definition of the variant}\}$$
$$0 \leq A.len - j < A.len - j_0$$
$$\equiv \quad \{\text{subtract } A.len \text{ all around}\}$$
$$-A.len \leq -j < -j_0$$
$$\equiv \quad \{\text{multiply by } -1\}$$
$$A.len \geq j > j_0$$

We now need to work on the body of this loop. Throughout, it has been clear that we will need to increment j: this is precisely what it means to "move through A from left to right"; it is also the inspiration for the choice of variant (which requires that $j > j_0$ should hold in the postcondition—j_0 being the *previous* value of j). Suppose we decide to increment j at the end of the loop's body. The "following assignment" rule can be used for this purpose:

$$i, j : [inv \land j \neq A.len, inv \land (A.len \geq j > j_0)]$$
$$\sqsubseteq \quad \{\text{Following assignment rule with } j + 1 \text{ as } E\}$$
$$i, j : [inv \land j \neq A.len, (inv \land (A.len \geq j > j_0))[j \setminus j + 1]]; j := j + 1$$

So, having sorted out the update of j, we may now drop it out of the frame of the remaining specification. It may therefore not be changed in that part of the specification. Instead, that part will be directed at appropriately updating i. To achieve that, we now simplify the predicates in the specification that have not yet been refined to code. For illustrative purposes, we shall most scrupulously justify every step we take:

$$i : [inv \wedge j \neq A.len, (inv \wedge A.len \geq j > j_0)[j \setminus j + 1]]$$

$\equiv$ {distributing the substitution over the two postcondition conjuncts}

$$i : [inv \wedge j \neq A.len, inv[j \setminus j + 1] \wedge (A.len \geq j > j_0)[j \setminus j + 1]]$$

$\equiv$ {substituting in the second postcondition conjunct}

$$i : [inv \wedge j \neq A.len, inv[j \setminus j + 1] \wedge (A.len \geq j + 1 > j_0)]$$

$\equiv$ {reasoning given below}

$$i : [inv \wedge j \neq A.len, inv[j \setminus j + 1] \wedge \mathsf{true}]$$

$\equiv$ {since $P \wedge \mathsf{true} \equiv P$ we may drop the conjunct true}

$$i : [inv \wedge j \neq A.len, inv[j \setminus j + 1]]$$

$\equiv$ {substituting inv with $(\forall r : [0, j) \cdot (A_r \leq A_i) \wedge (0 \leq i < j))$}

$$i : [max(A, 0, j, i) \wedge j \neq A.len, max(A, 0, j, i)[j \setminus j + 1]]$$

$\equiv$ {substitution $j + 1$ for j}

$$i : [max(A, 0, j, i) \wedge j \neq A.len, max(A, 0, j + 1, i)]$$

The foregoing regarded the variant conjunct of the postcondition, $(A.len \geq j + 1 > j_0)$, as true. In order to be clear why this is indeed the case, we need to be clear about what j and j_0 stand for, respectively. To repeat, j_0 is the value that variable j held before the specification. It is treated as a constant, unaffected by any code to which the specification is refined. On the other hand, j is a variable, but since it is no longer in the frame of the specification being considered, it too retains its original value. It is therefore undoubtedly the case that $j + 1 > j_0$.

Now in general, since the value of j does not change in the specification under consideration (i.e. it does not appear as a frame variable), we are allowed to use information about its value in the precondition to infer whether or not $A.len \geq j + 1$ holds in the postcondition. Furthermore, if the precondition affirmed that $A.len > j$ holds, then we could certainly affirm that $A.len \geq j + 1$ is true.

Unfortunately, the precondition gives us somewhat weaker information about j, namely that $A.len \neq j$. Merely to consider the specification in isolation from the preceding code derived in Sect. 3.2.3 does not affirm that $A.len \geq j + 1$ is true: the specification may start with a value of j such that $A.len < j + 1$, in which case the postcondition cannot be met without changing the value of j, and no such change is allowed since j is not in the frame. However, in the context of the problem being solved, we know a priori (because of the way in which the loop is initialized in Sect. 3.2.3) that the loop will never be entered unless $A.len < j$ holds. As a consequence, *in this particular context*, we may take the liberty of affirming that $A.len \geq j + 1$ in the postcondition is in fact true.

Essentially, the precondition of the specification that has been derived states that i is the index of a largest element in $A_{[0,j)}$. It also states in the postcondition that we need the index of a largest element in $A_{[0,j+1)}$. Now it is not too difficult to see that:

$$max(A, 0, j, i) \implies \begin{cases} max(A, 0, j+1, j) \text{ if } A_j > A_i \\ max(A, 0, j+1, i) \text{ if } A_j \leq A_i \end{cases}$$

This reasoning suggests that the select ("if") command might be applicable here to deal with the two cases implied above, namely: $A_j > A_i$ and $A_j \leq A_i$. Recall from Sect. 2.4 the proviso of the refinement rule for the select command was that $P \Rightarrow G_1 \vee \cdots \vee G_n$, where P was the precondition of the refined specification, and $G_1 \ldots G_n$ were the intended guards in the select command.

Now fortunately, the disjunction of the two predicates $A_j > A_i$ and $A_j \leq A_i$ is true, which is implied everywhere by any other predicate, including the precondition of our current specification. As a result (i.e. because "implies everywhere" holds) we may use the selection refinement rule, and then get:

if $A_j > A_i \to i : [A_j > A_i \wedge max(A, 0, j, i) \wedge j \neq A.len, max(A, 0, j+1, i)]$
‖ $A_j \leq A_i \to i : [A_j \leq A_i \wedge max(A, 0, j, i) \wedge j \neq A.len, max(A, 0, j+1, i)]$
fi

Based on the reasoning above, we would expect that the first branch of the alternation refines to $i := j$, while the second branch is simply a skip statement. This gives:

if $A_j > A_i \to i := j$
‖ $A_j \leq A_i \to$ **skip**
fi

Of course, the refinement to the first assignment is only allowed by the assignment rule if:

$$A_j > A_i \wedge max(A, 0, j, i) \wedge j \neq A.len \Rightarrow (max(A, 0, j+1, i))[i \backslash j]$$

Likewise, the refinement to the skip statement is only justified by the skip refinement rule if:

$$A_j \leq A_i \wedge max(A, 0, j, i) \wedge j \neq A.len \Rightarrow (max(A, 0, j+1, i))$$

It is easy to show these two "implies everywhere" relationships. Details are left to the reader.

3.2.5 Putting it All Together

We now have all the ingredients for our final algorithm:

$$i, j := 0, 1;$$
$$\textbf{do } \; j \neq A.len \rightarrow$$
$$\quad \textbf{if } \; A_j > A_i \rightarrow i := j$$
$$\quad \textbf{[} \quad A_j \leq A_i \rightarrow \textbf{skip}$$
$$\quad \textbf{fi;}$$
$$\quad \quad j := j + 1$$
$$\textbf{od}$$

3.3 Binary Search

In this example, the well-known binary search algorithm is constructed from specifications. Given a sorted array A (with elements of type integer or real—it does not really matter) and x (of the same type as the elements), we need to specify and refine a binary search program. Upon termination, i must be an integer such that $A_i = x$ if x is present in A, or $i = -1$ if x is not present in A. Note:

- A is *not* guaranteed to contain the value which we are seeking.
- A is *not* guaranteed to be nonempty; i.e., we may have $A.len = 0$.

3.3.1 Formulating the Problem

We know that the sortedness of A is part of the precondition. Abbreviate the sortedness of A as $sorted(A)$. Also reuse the app predicate of Sect. 3.1. Recall that the ranges are closed at the bottom and open at the top—i.e. $app(A, x, 0, A.len)$ means that the value of x appears in the range $A_{[0,A.len)}$.

The postcondition should express two possibilities: either that the sought-after x value appears in A (and therefore $A_i = x$); or else it does not appear in A (and therefore $i = -1$). The postcondition can therefore be defined as:

$$post \triangleq (app(A, x, 0, A.len) \wedge A_i = x) \vee (\neg app(A, x, 0, A.len) \wedge i = -1)$$

The problem to be solved is therefore:

$$i : [sorted(A), post]$$

It is, of course, necessary to have i as a frame variable, since it must be set to an appropriate value in order to achieve the postcondition. The question is, however, whether additional variables are needed in the frame. We proceed from the premise that the reader is familiar with the general binary search strategy—a strategy that involves the use of a low/high pair of variables. These variables, too, should be mentioned in the frame. Calling these variables l and h respectively, the specification can be restated as follows.[3]

$$i, l, h : [sorted(A), post]$$

3.3.2 Decomposing the Problem

At this point, an overall solution strategy has to be selected. There are several. We could, for instance, decide to initialize i to -1 and then reassign a value to it after the binary search, if x was indeed found during the search. In fact, we could decide to include i as one of the variables to be used *during* the binary search, either to point to the mid-point of the search region, or do be the high- or low end of the search region. None of these strategies can be said to be wrong. However, one has the sense that by introducing i into the picture before or during the binary search, we might be violating the well-established software engineering principle of "separating concerns". Consequently, it will be left as an exercise to the reader to evolve a binary search algorithm along any of these lines. Here, we choose to delay the assignment of a value to i until after the binary search has ended.

We thus divide the specification up into two pieces: one which does the binary search and one which sets i on the basis of what was discovered during the binary search. This "dividing up" is done using a sequential composition refinement step, in just a moment. We first need to determine an appropriate choice for the *mid* predicate.

The mid predicate should express the results of the binary search. At the end of the binary search, l and h should be such that either the subarray $A_{[l,h)}$ consists of a single element (which may or may not be equal to x) or $A_{[l,h)}$ is an empty subarray (in which case x definitely does not appear in A). In the first case, h would have to be $= l + 1$, while in the second case, h must be $< l + 1$. Nevertheless, it is not sufficient to express the mid predicate simply as:

$$sorted(A) \wedge h \leq l + 1$$

Why not? Because such a postcondition can easily be achieved without reaching our actual objective. For example, the assignment $h := l + 1$ ensures that *sorted*

---

[3]These variables are not mentioned in the pre- and postconditions, and are, in this sense, local to the inner workings of the code to be constructed "between" the pre- and postconditions, as it were. Morgan has a refinement rule that regards the introduction of local variables into the frame as a refinement.

$(A) \wedge h \leq l+1$ holds, but this is not at all what binary search is supposed to achieve. We need to strengthen the above formula with a conjunct that expresses the fact that, in searching for an index of A where x may be found, l and h have been invariantly selected such that x always lies at an index of A that is in the range $[l, h)$, if indeed it is to be found in the array A at all. This, after all, is the well-known strategy that is used in binary search.

The question is, how should such an invariant be formulated? It is more complicated than merely claiming that $app(A, x, l, h)$ should always hold, since it could be the case that $\neg app(A, x, 0, A.len)$ holds. On the other hand, if x *is* in the array—i.e. if $app(A, x, 0, A.len)$ holds—then binary search indeed ensures that $app(A, x, l, h)$ holds. This conditionality can be expressed in predicate logic as: $app(A, x, 0, A.len) \implies app(A, x, l, h)$. Note that this predicate is only false when $app(A, x, 0, A.len)$ is true but $app(A, x, l, h)$ is false. Based on this, we constitute our required interim predicate as:

$$mid \triangleq sorted(A) \wedge (app(A, x, 0, A.len) \implies app(A, x, l, h)) \wedge (h \leq l + 1)$$

With this in mind, by the refinement rule for composition, the original problem specification refines to:

$$i, l, h : [sorted(A), mid]; i, l, h : [mid, post] \tag{3.4}$$

The two specification components can now be refined further separately: the first to generate the binary search code, and the second to appropriately assign a value to i.

3.3.3   Generating the Binary Search Code

We have already devised the postcondition of the first specification component in (3.4) (namely *mid*) with an invariant in mind. It expressed the fact that l and h are adjusted in such a way that, if x appears in A at all, then it appears in the range $A_{[l,h)}$. Let us also include as part of the invariant, the fact that A will remain sorted. (Nothing happens to change the order of elements.) The invariant is thus:

$$inv \triangleq sorted(A) \wedge (app(A, x, 0, A.len) \implies app(A, x, l, h))$$

Rewriting *mid* as $inv \wedge h \leq l + 1$, the specification to be refined is:

$$i, l, h : [sorted(A), mid]$$
$$= \quad \{\text{substituting the definition of } mid\}$$
$$i, l, h : [sorted(A), inv \wedge h \leq l + 1]$$

This is starting to look a lot like what is needed for refinement into a loop. Another application of the composition refinement rule will get it into the shape we want, using *inv* as our new interim predicate. The result is:

$$i, l, h : [sorted(A), inv \land h \leq l + 1]$$

$$\sqsubseteq \quad \{\text{sequential composition with } mid' \triangleq inv\}$$

$$i, l, h : [sorted(A), inv]; i, l, h : [inv, inv \land h \leq l + 1]$$

The first part will establish the invariant, while the second part will be refined into the loop. It is straightforward to show, using the multiple assignment rule, that the first part can be refined into:

$$l, h := 0, A.len$$

The proof proceeds by showing that after substitution in the postcondition as required per the assignment rule, a predicate is obtained that is identical to the precondition, and that is therefore implied everywhere by the precondition. As a consequence, the proposed assignment is guaranteed to be a legitimate refinement of the specification. Here is the proof that the postcondition after substitution leads to the precondition:

$$inv[l, h \backslash 0, A.len]$$

$$\equiv \quad \{\text{Substituting for the definition of } inv\}$$

$$(sorted(A) \land (app(A, x, 0, A.len) \implies app(A, x, l, h)))[l, h \backslash 0, A.len]$$

$$\equiv \quad \{\text{Substituting the variables } l \text{ and } h\}$$

$$(sorted(A) \land (app(A, x, 0, A.len) \implies app(A, x, 0, A.len)))$$

$$\equiv \quad \{\text{Since } app(A, x, 0, A.len) \implies app(A, x, 0, A.len) \equiv \text{true}\}$$

$$sorted(A) \land \text{true}$$

$$\equiv \quad \{\text{Since since } sorted(A) \land \text{true} \equiv Q\}$$

$$sorted(A)$$

In considering the second specification, let $h \leq l + 1$ be the conjunct of its postcondition that represents the negation of the guard. The guard will thus be $h > l + 1$. For the loop's variant, we will use $h - l$. This is an expression that must decrease with every iteration and may never go below zero. From the repetition refinement rule, we now obtain the loop:

$$\textbf{do } h > l + 1 \rightarrow$$
$$i, l, h : [inv \land h > l + 1, inv \land (0 \leq h - l < h_0 - l_0)]$$
$$\textbf{od}$$

To refine the loop's body, we know that we have to maintain the invariant (which claims that if x is in A then the interval $A_{[l,h)}$ always contains x) and we also have to ensure that the variant, $h - l$, decreases with each iteration. In fact, there are numerous ways in which these two objectives can be achieved, and each way would lead to a solution of the problem.

For example, we could increment l by 1 if $A_l \neq x$ or we could decrement h by 1 if $A_{h-1} \neq x$ (in both cases decreasing the variant by 1). Neither of these strategies capitalize on the sortedness of A, and each amounts to a form of linear search.

Alternatively, we could randomly guess an index j from the range $[l, h)$ and if it turned out that $A_j \neq x$, we could then rely on the sortedness of A to decide whether to set l or h to j. Or j could be chosen to be $\frac{1}{3}$ of the way between l and h, etc. However, it is well-known that binary search, which halves the search interval $h - l$ in each iteration, is on average (and even in the worst case) the best search method. This is the strategy we shall follow. Note that in all these strategies, it is a case of determining some index in the interval, comparing x against the array's value in that index, and adjusting l and/or h accordingly.

We shall distinguish between three cases, according to whether x is less than, greater than, or equal to $A_{(l+h)/2}$. (Note in passing that in this text we will assume that integer division rounds down.) These three cases constitute three guards, whose disjunction is true, and which may therefore be used in a refinement using the selection rule. (The rule's proviso holds, since the precondition everywhere implies true.) We obtain the following:

$$
\begin{aligned}
&\textbf{if } \ (x < A_{(l+h)/2}) \\
&\quad \to l, h : [inv \wedge h > l + 1 \wedge x < A_{(l+h)/2}, inv \wedge (0 \le h - l < h_0 - l_0)] \\
&\textbf{\textbardbl} \ \ (x = A_{(l+h)/2}) \\
&\quad \to l, h : [inv \wedge h > l + 1 \wedge x = A_{(l+h)/2}, inv \wedge (0 \le h - l < h_0 - l_0)] \\
&\textbf{\textbardbl} \ \ (x > A_{(l+h)/2}) \\
&\quad \to l, h : [inv \wedge h > l + 1 \wedge x > A_{(l+h)/2}, inv \wedge (0 \le h - l < h_0 - l_0)] \\
&\textbf{fi}
\end{aligned}
$$

Note at this point that, once again, there are alternative ways in which to choose the guards. In particular, some binary search implementations merge the equality case with either the "less than" or the "greater than" guard. In fact, in GCL, the equality case could be merged with both guards, resulting in a non-deterministic specification. However, instinctively one senses that it would be better to consider equality separately. Again, one could invoke the "separation of concerns" principle, since equality means that the search has been successful and the loop can be immediately terminated, whereas non-equality means that we need to halve the search area. Thus, considering the equality case separately allows us more rapidly to terminate the loop. The trade-off for this efficiency gain is that more cases have to be considered in each iteration.

Let us now verify whether the "less than" case, the first guard, can be refined to the assignment: $h := (l + h)/2$. In terms of the assignment rule's proviso, this is permitted if:

$$inv \land h > l + 1 \land x < A_{(l+h)/2} \Rightarrow (inv \land (0 \le h - l < h_0 - l_0))[h \backslash (l + h)/2]$$

$\equiv$ {substitution in postcondition}

$$inv \land h > l + 1 \land x < A_{(l+h)/2} \Rightarrow (inv[h \backslash (l + h)/2)] \land (0 \le (l + h)/2 - l < h_0 - l_0))$$

$\equiv$ {algebra}

$$inv \land h > l + 1 \land x < A_{(l+h)/2} \Rightarrow (inv[h \backslash (l + h)/2)] \land (0 \le (h - l)/2 < h_0 - l_0))$$

Now one is tempted to summarily conclude that the variant part of the postcondition evaluates to true. This kind of impulsive decision-making has been the source of many an incorrect implementation of binary search, often leading to an infinite loop. One needs to be very aware of the fact that $(h - l)/2$ is only less than $h_0 - l_0$ if $h > l$—something that is thankfully assured in the precondition (since it specifies that $h > l + 1$). Similarly, it seems obvious that half of some positive value, i.e. $(h - l)/2$, is greater or equal to 0. Once again, the fact that $(h - l)/2$ is positive, is assured by the precondition conjunct in which $h > l + 1$ is required to hold.

In regard to the remaining conjuncts in the above implies everywhere relationship, it is easy to see that if $inv \land x < A_{(l+h)/2}$ holds, as required by the precondition, then $inv[h \backslash (l + h)/2)]$ will hold, due to the sortedness of A, which is asserted in both pre- and postcondition.

As a consequence of all the foregoing reasoning, we are justified in refining the first guard to the assignment $h := (l + h)/2$.

We leave it as an exercise for the reader to articulate the reasoning that justifies the assignment $l := (l + h)/2$ for the third guard. Not surprisingly, it parallels the reasoning given in relation to the first guard. Also left as an exercise, is the reasoning to justify the assignment $l, h := (l + h)/2, (l + h)/2 + 1$ in the case of the second guard.

The resulting select command is therefore:

$$\begin{aligned}
&\textbf{if } (x < A_{(l+h)/2}) \rightarrow h := (l + h)/2 \\
&\text{\textbf{|}} \;\; (x = A_{(l+h)/2}) \rightarrow l, h := (l + h)/2, (l + h)/2 + 1 \\
&\text{\textbf{|}} \;\; (x > A_{(l+h)/2}) \rightarrow l := (l + h)/2 \\
&\textbf{fi}
\end{aligned}$$

Note that after the assignment in the second guarded command, the outer loop's guard, $h > l + 1$, no longer holds; thus, the loop will not execute another iteration. Additionally, the loop's guard could (but need not) also be rendered false if either the first or the third guard of the select command executes.

For completeness, the code developed to date is given:

$$l, h := 0, A.len$$
$$\{inv\}$$
$$;\textbf{do} \ (h > l + 1) \rightarrow$$
$$\qquad \textbf{if} \ (x < A_{(l+h)/2}) \rightarrow h := (l + h)/2$$
$$\qquad [\!] \ (x = A_{(l+h)/2}) \rightarrow l, h := (l + h)/2, (l + h)/2 + 1$$
$$\qquad [\!] \ (x > A_{(l+h)/2}) \rightarrow l := (l + h)/2$$
$$\qquad \textbf{fi}$$
$$\textbf{od}$$
$$\{inv \wedge h \leq l + 1\}$$

3.3.4   After the Binary Search

Consider the specification after the loop that still has to be refined, i.e. the second specification in (3.4): $i, l, h : [mid, post]$. Recall that the *mid* predicate was given by $inv \wedge (h \leq l + 1)$ where:

$$inv \triangleq sorted(A) \wedge (app(A, x, 0, A.len) \implies app(A, x, l, h))$$

This *mid* precondition could have been realized in one of three ways:

1. If we started with $app(A, x, 0, A.len) = \text{true}$, then $app(A, x, l, h)$ has to hold (else the implication in *mid* will be false, since true $\implies$ false is false). This in turn means that $h = l + 1$, since if $h < l + 1$ then the subarray $A_{[l,h)}$ would be empty, contradicting the fact that $app(A, x, l, h)$ has to hold. In other words, the subarray $A_{[l,h)}$ is not empty, but consists only of the one element A_l, and this element is equal to x.
2. If we started with $app(A, x, 0, A.len) = \text{false}$, then $app(A, x, l, h)$ will also be false. In this case, from one point of view, it really does not matter whether $h = l + 1$, or $h < l + 1$. In neither case is A_l equal to x.
3. However, from another point of view, if $h < l + 1$ holds, it may be instructive to consider how this could have come about. One possibility is that the logic of the loop is such that h, always larger than $l + 1$ at the start of the loop's body, somehow acquires a value that is less than $l + 1$ at the end of the loop's body. (In fact, deeper investigation of the loop's body will reveal that this cannot actually happen, but this fact is not immediately relevant to the discussion.) Another possibility (actually, the only one) is that the loop was never entered because the array A is empty. This would mean that $l = h = A.len = 0$. In this case, it would be wise not to refer in code to array element A_l, since no such element exists in the array.

One could therefore consider two possibilities separately: $h = l + 1$ or $h < l + 1$. These correspond (respectively) to "narrowed range to one element, perhaps finding x" and "definitely did not find x". This means we could refine into a pair of nested select statements, with conditions $h = l + 1$ and $h < l + 1$ as the two outer guards, and a nested check to verify whether x was indeed found in the case where $h = l + 1$. The result is the following:

$$
\begin{aligned}
&\textbf{if } h = l + 1 \rightarrow \\
&\quad \textbf{if } A_l = x \rightarrow i := l \; \| \; A_l \neq x \rightarrow i := -1 \textbf{ fi} \\
&\quad \| \;\; h < l + 1 \rightarrow i := -1 \\
&\textbf{fi}
\end{aligned}
$$

As might be suspected, detailed justification in terms of the refinement calculus rules to derive this nested select statement would be quite tiresome. For our purposes, the above discussion constitutes a sufficient justification for the select statement and its structure.

Some programmers might be uncomfortable with the foregoing. They might prefer to keep the amount of code to a minimum, for instance by writing it as follows:

$$
\begin{aligned}
&i := -1 \\
&; \textbf{as } (h = l + 1 \wedge A_l = x) \rightarrow i := l \textbf{ sa}
\end{aligned}
$$

Provided the $\wedge$ operation was carried out as a short-circuit evaluation (indicated later in this text by the conditional-and symbol, **cand**) the foregoing would off course work. However, there is a price to pay for the brevity: information is lost about the underlying logic paths that lead us to conclude that x was not found. In general, brevity of this nature is error-prone and should be avoided.

3.3.5 Putting it All Together

Finally, we get

$$
\begin{aligned}
&l, h := 0, A.len; \\
&\textbf{do } h > l + 1 \rightarrow \\
&\quad \textbf{if } (x < A_{(l+h)/2}) \rightarrow h := (l + h)/2 \\
&\quad \| \;\; (x = A_{(l+h)/2}) \rightarrow l, h := (l + h)/2, (l + h)/2 + 1 \\
&\quad \| \;\; (x > A_{(l+h)/2}) \rightarrow l := (l + h)/2 \\
&\quad \textbf{fi} \\
&\textbf{od}; \\
&\textbf{if } h = l + 1 \rightarrow \\
&\quad \textbf{if } A_l = x \rightarrow i := l \; \| \; A_l \neq x \rightarrow i := -1 \textbf{ fi} \\
&\quad \| \;\; h < l + 1 \rightarrow i := -1 \\
&\textbf{fi}
\end{aligned}
$$

Note that the program is correct, even when $A.len = 0$.

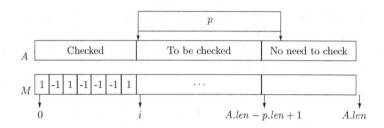

Fig. 3.3 Interim matching scenario

3.4 Pattern Matching

In this section, the constructive approach is outlined to develop an algorithm that does pattern matching. (This is just one of a large number of different pattern matching problems and solutions.) We will dispense with full argumentation to justify each step, rather focussing on the broader flow of reasoning and refinement rules that have to be applied.

We are given a string A, a string p, and an array M, where M stands for "Matched" and where $M.len \geq A.len$). The problem is to set the elements of M to indicate where matches have occurred, based on the following convention:

$$M_i = \begin{cases} 1 \text{ if } p \text{ matches in } A \text{ starting at position } i \\ -1 \text{ if } p \text{ does not match in } A \text{ starting at position } i \end{cases}$$

Note:

- The strings A and p will be treated here as arrays. Thus, for example, p_i denotes element $(i + 1)$ of string p (the first element being p_0); $A.len$ is the length of string A; etc.
- A is not guaranteed to contain an occurrence of p.
- A is not guaranteed to be longer than p.
- The only index values that really matter are $[0, A.len - p.len + 1)$. To fill in the rest of the indices with -1 is not required.
- We assume that $p.len > 0$.

Figure 3.3 schematically depicts the result after matching p against the first i starting positions in A. Starting positions in the range $[i, A.len - p.len + 1)$ still need to be checked, and there is no need to check starting positions in the range $[A.len - p.len + 1, A.len)$

3.4.1 Formulating the Problem

The postcondition should express the fact that every index in the range $[0, A.len - p.len + 1)$ is correctly set as 1 or -1. We call this *post*:

$$\forall k : [0, A.len - p.len + 1) \cdot (M_k = 1 \wedge A_{[k,k+p.len)} = p) \vee (M_k = -1 \wedge A_{[k,k+p.len)} \neq p)$$

All that our precondition states is that the array M is sufficiently large, yielding our specification:

$$M : [M.len \geq A.len, post]$$

Since we eventually want to introduce a loop, we can already keep in mind that we would like to traverse A (and therefore M) from left to right, as depicted in Fig. 3.3. This could mean an invariant like "for all k in $[0, i)$, M_i is set correctly". We can express this as our invariant:

$$inv \triangleq \forall k[0, i) \cdot (M_k = 1 \wedge A_{[k,k+p.len)} = p) \vee (M_k = -1 \wedge A_{[k,k+p.len)} \neq p)$$

The next thing to do, is to add a conjunct G to the invariant, such that $(inv \wedge G)$ is stronger than (or equal to) *post*. Clearly, this is the case if G is chosen as the predicate $i = A.len - p.len + 1$. The specification may now be formulated as follows. Note that i has also been added as an additional frame variable.

$$M, i : [M.len \geq A.len, inv \wedge (i = A.len - p.len + 1)]$$

Using sequential composition, we can do our usual split into the part which will become the loop and the part which will establish the invariant:

$$M, i : [M.len \geq A.len, inv]; M, i : [inv, inv \wedge (i = A.len - p.len + 1)]$$

It is easy to verify a refinement of the first part to $i := 0$. The following argument applies:

> If you substitute 0 for all occurrences of i in *inv*, the "for all" quantification in *inv* is over an empty range, and thus *inv* is true. Since the precondition $M.len \geq A.len$ everywhere implies true the assignment $i := 0$ refines the first part of the specification.

3.4.2 Developing the Loop

We now need to refine the second part of the specification to date, namely:

$$M, i : [inv, inv \wedge (i \geq A.len - p.len + 1)]$$

Here, we can already see that we already have the negation of the guard, namely $(i \geq A.len - p.len + 1)$. For a variant function, we should probably try something like $A.len - p.len - i$, which indicates the number of elements in the array still to be tested. By the refinement rule for repetition, we then have:

$$\textbf{do } i < A.len - p.len + 1 \rightarrow$$
$$M, i : [inv \wedge i < A.len - p.len + 1, inv \wedge (0 \leq V < V_0)]$$
$$\textbf{od}$$

From the variant, we can see that an increment of i is in order, which we can apply using following assignment (or sequential composition followed by simple assignment) to get[4]

$$\textbf{do } i < A.len - p.len + 1 \rightarrow$$
$$M, i : [inv \wedge i < A.len - p.len + 1, inv[i \setminus i + 1]];$$
$$i := i + 1$$
$$\textbf{od}$$

Given the invariant, we would probably like to refine the statement in the body of the loop to something like:

$$\textbf{if } (A_{[i, i+p.len)} = p) \rightarrow M_i := 1$$
$$[\!] \quad (A_{[i, i+p.len)} \neq p) \rightarrow M_i := -1$$
$$\textbf{fi}$$

This is not entirely reasonable, since it requires comparing several characters of A against p all at once. Again, the body of the loop should be split into two pieces, with an eye to refining the first into an inner-loop (which compares the characters) and the second one into an alternation. We will be using j in that inner loop. As a consequence, j becomes a new frame variable as part of the next refinement.

To apply sequential composition, we need another mid'. For that, we should probably state that all of the p characters in interval $[0, j)$ matched (the corresponding characters of A), and either $j = p.len$ (in which case we have matched all of p) or $p_j \neq A_{i+j}$ (j indicates a mismatching character at position j)

$$mid' \triangleq (\forall n : [0, j) \cdot (p_n = A_{i+n})) \wedge (j = p.len \vee p_j \neq A_{i+j})$$

This allows us to make the following refinement

$$M, i, j : [inv \wedge i \neq A.len - p.len + 1, inv[i \setminus i + 1]]$$
$$\sqsubseteq \quad \{\text{sequential composition with } mid' \text{ above}\}$$
$$M, i, j : [inv \wedge i \neq A.len - p.len + 1, mid']; M, i, j : [mid', inv[i \setminus i + 1]]$$

Taking the hint from the disjunction in the mid' predicate, which serves as the precondition to the second part, this second part can be refined into

$$\textbf{if } j = p.len \rightarrow M_i := 1 \; [\!] \; j \neq p.len \rightarrow M_i := -1 \textbf{ fi}$$

---

[4]Here, the part relating to the variant has been omitted, since it will be true under the substitution.

It is easy to show that the refinement to a select command is legitimate. To do this, use the fact that the disjunction of the select command's guards is true, and note that $mid' \Rightarrow$ true.

To refine the first part, we could again introduce an invariant of

$$\forall n : [0, j) \cdot p_n = A_{i+n}$$

and a variant $p.len - j$. After several more steps, it will yield a refinement of:

$$j := 0;$$
$$\textbf{do } j \neq p.len \wedge p_j = A_{i+j} \rightarrow j := j + 1 \textbf{ od}$$

3.4.3 Putting it All Together

When we put all the pieces together, we get

$$i := 0;$$
$$\textbf{do } i < A.len - p.len \rightarrow$$
$$\quad j := 0;$$
$$\quad \textbf{do } j \neq p.len \wedge p_j = A_{i+j} \rightarrow j := j + 1 \textbf{ od};$$
$$\quad \textbf{if } j = p.len \rightarrow M_i := 1 \ [\!] \ j \neq p.len \rightarrow M_i := -1 \textbf{ fi};$$
$$\quad i := i + 1$$
$$\textbf{od}$$

3.5 Exponentiation

Developing algorithms along the lines discussed to date, is of course not as painless as might be suggested by the narrative in previous sections of this chapter. In practice, one's reasoning and instincts often lead up a blind alley, and one has to backtrack and rethink aspects of the approach to the problem. This section illustrates this point.

It discusses a solution for a fairly simple problem but initially takes the reader down a blind alley. However, in taking this walk down a blind alley, sufficient information is obtained to reformulate the problem and to eventually arrive at a good solution. Some discussion about this matter is given at the end. The discussion is based on a real experience—it is not a fictitious example!

The problem is as follows: given a real number a and a positive natural number, n, determine the value of a^n and store the result in the variable z.

3.5.1   Formulating the Problem

The problem can be specified as follows:

$$z : [n > 0, z = a^n]$$

Intuitively, we can start with z at some initial value, and progressively update it to come closer to its intended final value. What invariant condition might apply? Well, perhaps it would make sense to ensure that z always remains a raised to some power such as $a^0, a^1, \ldots a^n$, or in general, to ensure that z is always a^{n-i} for some i. In such a case, z times a^i will always be the same as our desired answer, a^n.

Let us therefore—as a first stab at the problem—define the predicate:

$$p(i) \triangleq (z.a^i = a^n)$$

Now notice that $p(0)$ corresponds to the required postcondition. Hopefully $p(i)$ can serve as a loop invariant. But, if it is to serve in this role, then the program will need to have i as a variable. At this stage, therefore, add i to the specification frame. As previously indicated, such an addition to the frame variables constitutes a true refinement of a specification. We can thus re-write the initial specification as:

$$z, i : [n > 0, p(0)]$$

3.5.2   Establishing the Invariant

Taking $p(i)$ as our invariant, the next step is to apply the sequence rule in order to establish $p(i)$ as the mid predicate.

$$z, i : [n > 0, p(i)]; z, i : [p(i), p(0)]$$

We now clearly need to apply the assignment rule to refine the first part. Noting that $p(i)[i, z \backslash n, 1]$ evaluates to true, we might be tempted to refine to the assignment $i, z := n, 1$. However, z can never end up as 1 in the original problem (unless, of course, $a = 1$, in which case z will always be 1 and nothing else), since n is explicitly forbidden to be 0. It does not therefore seem reasonable to start off with such a value for z—why initialize z to a value that it cannot ever have? If you do that, then you force at least one iteration of the loop, whereas it might be possible to get away with bypassing the loop altogether in some cases.

Instead, we might seek an alternative assignment to refine the first part of our specification. The alternative that suggests itself is to initialize z to a, in which case i has to be initialized to $n - 1$. Once again, $p(i)[i, z \backslash n - 1, a] \equiv (a.a^{n-1} = a^n) \equiv$ true, and since any precondition (including $n > 0$) implies true everywhere, the assignment $i, z := n - 1, a$ is a legitimate refinement of the relevant specification.

3.5.3 Refining to Create a Loop

Consider now the second part of our specification. We can re-write the postcondition as $p(i) \wedge i = 0$. Although this is equivalent to the original form, it may be thought of as "strengthening" the postcondition. We therefore appeal to the strengthening postcondition refinement rule to derive the following specification:

$$z, i : [p(i), p(i) \wedge i = 0]$$

Apply the repetition rule, since the second specification is of the form $w : [inv, inv \wedge \neg GG]$. It seems reasonable to anticipate that i should decline to 0, so we use i as the variant. The result is:

$$\textbf{do } i \neq 0 \rightarrow$$
$$z, i : [(i \neq 0) \wedge p(i), p(i) \wedge 0 \leq i < i_0]$$
$$\textbf{od}$$

Clearly, the way to decrease the variant is by decreasing i. Note that each such change in i in the loop's body must preserve the invariant. One way of preserving the invariant is to multiply z by a and then to decrease i by 1. This would lead to a loop that simply multiplied z by a, n times. (As an exercise, the reader may follow through on this path of reasoning to derive a simple algorithm.)

However, if we think about the invariant, other more creative ideas come to mind. For example, we could also preserve the invariant by multiplying z by a^3 and then decreasing i by 3—provided this did not lead to a z that was a raised to some power greater than n (which would in fact violate the variant part of the postcondition because i would decrement below 0). In fact, we could multiply z by any number of a's in a given iteration and decrease i appropriately, as long as we take care not to overshoot the mark and derive a raised to some power greater than n. The objective should be to decrease i in each iteration by as much as possible, thereby minimizing the number of iterations.

A smart thing to do in this kind of situation is to consider the possibilities when i is odd, and when i is even. There are several advantages in testing on the basis of this "heuristic". On the one hand, to carrying out tests for odd-ness or even-ness can be done very efficiently in bit-arithmetic. Secondly, there are many problems in which this leads to high efficiency in the loop itself. So let us explore this possibility.

Now, the selection rule requires that the precondition—in this case $(i \neq 0) \wedge p(i))$—must imply everywhere the disjunction of the conditions used in the selection. Since $(odd(i) \vee even(i)) = \text{true}$ is everywhere implied by this precondition, the selection rule can be applied to get the following refinement:

$$\textbf{if } odd(i) \rightarrow z, i : [(i \neq 0) \wedge p(i) \wedge odd(i), p(i) \wedge 0 \leq i < i_0]$$
$$\textbf{| } even(i) \rightarrow z, i : [(i \neq 0) \wedge p(i) \wedge even(i), p(i) \wedge 0 \leq i < i_0]$$
$$\textbf{fi}$$

In the present case, if i is even, is there any smart thing to do about z? Well, yes, there might be. A first guess might be to say: we can square z and halve the variable i. On the other hand, if i is odd, we can—as previously suggested—fall back on the simple idea of multiplying z by a and decrementing i by 1, thereby arriving at an even value for i to be used at the next iteration. The refined select command then becomes:

$$\textbf{if } odd(i) \rightarrow z, i := z * a, i - 1$$
$$\textbf{| } even(i) \rightarrow z, i := z * z, i/2$$
$$\textbf{fi}$$

Let us now verify whether this assignment is correct in terms of our refinement rule for assignment. The assignment rule requires that $pre \Rightarrow post[x \backslash E]$ must hold if we are to refine to the assignment $x := E$. In our particular case, the refinement of the first guarded command (when i is odd), requires that the following "everywhere implies" relationship should hold.

$$(i \neq 0) \wedge (z.a^i = a^n) \wedge odd(i) \Rightarrow ((z.a^i = a^n) \wedge 0 \leq i < i_0)[i, z \backslash (i - 1), z.a]$$

Just for absolute clarity, let us rewrite this after the substitution:

$$(i \neq 0) \wedge (z.a^i = a^n) \wedge odd(i) \Rightarrow (z.a.a^{(i-1)} = a^n) \wedge 0 \leq i - 1 < i_0$$

Now, clearly, the variant part on the right hand side is everywhere implied by the left hand side. (If we know that i is not 0 and is odd, then undoubtedly, $i - 1$ is less than its initial value and is not less than 0.) Also, the first conjunct of the right hand side exactly matches a conjunct on the left hand side. Thus, our first guarded command in the select statement, $odd(i) \rightarrow i, z := i - 1, a.z$ is apparently correct.

Consider now, the second of the above cases. Here we need to be convinced that the following holds.

$$(i \neq 0) \wedge (z.a^i = a^n) \wedge even(i) \Rightarrow ((z.a^i = a^n) \wedge 0 \leq i < i_0)[i, z \backslash (i/2), z.z]$$

Again, for absolute clarity, let us rewrite this after the substitution:

$$(i \neq 0) \wedge (z.a^i = a^n) \wedge even(i) \Rightarrow ((z.z.a^{i/2} = a^n) \wedge 0 \leq i/2 < i_0) \qquad (3.5)$$

Again it is easy to reason that variant part is implied everywhere by the left hand side. (If we know that i is not 0 and is even, then $i/2$ is less than its initial value and is not less than 0.) However, no matter how hard one tries: it is not possible to show that the first conjunct of the right hand side somehow follows from the left hand side! Something has gone wrong in our reasoning process!

We are essentially stuck with a predicate of the form $z.z.a^{\frac{i}{2}} = a^n$ on the right hand side, that needs to be implied everywhere by a predicate of the form $z.a^i = a^n$ on the left hand side. Thinking logically and creatively about what the problem may be, we see that things might have worked out somewhat better if one of the z's in the expression $z.z.a^{\frac{i}{2}}$ was in fact $a^{\frac{i}{2}}$, in which case, in (3.5) we would have had as first conjunct on the right hand side:

$$z.a^{\frac{i}{2}}.a^{\frac{i}{2}} = a^n$$

This suggests that we might be able to use an additional variable, say b, to store some product representing a multiplied by itself a number of times, in such a way that the predicate $z.b^i = a^n$ holds invariantly. The idea is that when i is even, then we will square b (and halve i) instead of squaring z, so that the substitution that previously troubled us will instead lead to the right hand side conjunct $(z.(b.b)^{i/2} = a^n)$. Since this would be implied by its counterpart on the left hand side, everything would be in order.

More concretely, let us therefore revise our loop invariant as follows:

$$p'(i) \triangleq (z.b^i = a^n)$$

We now note that $p'(0)$ represents the desired postcondition, as before, provided of course that $b > 0$. We also note that $p'(n-1)$ is a tautology (as before), provided that we initialize both b and z to a. Our refinement could now proceed as follows, where we now no longer repeat all the argumentation:

$z : [n > 0, z = a^n]$

$\sqsubseteq$ {introduce new frame variables}

    $i, b, z : [n > 0, z = a^n]$

$\equiv$ {re-write the postcondition}

    $i, b, z : [n > 0, (i = 0) \land p'(i)]$

$\sqsubseteq$ {apply sequence rule with $p'(i)$ as mid}

    $i, b, z : [n > 0, p'(i)]; i, b, z : [p'(i), (i = 0) \land p'(i)]$

$\sqsubseteq$ {assignment rule}

    $i, b, z := n - 1, a, a; i, b, z : [p'(i), (i = 0) \land p'(i)]$

$\sqsubseteq$ {repetition rule, making use of variant i}

    $i, b, z := n - 1, a, a; \textbf{do } i \neq 0 \rightarrow i, b, z : [p'(i) \land (i \neq 0), p'(i) \land 0 \leq i < i_0] \textbf{ od}$

The body of the loop may be refined, using the selection rule, to:

> **if** $odd(i) \to i, b, z : [(i \neq 0) \land p'(i) \land odd(i), p'(i) \land 0 \leq i < i_0]$
> [] $even(i) \to i, b, z : [(i \neq 0) \land p(i) \land even(i), p'(i) \land 0 \leq i < i_0]$
> **fi**

Two applications of the assignment rule, then lead to the following:

> **if** $odd(i) \to i, z := i - 1, z.b$
> [] $even(i) \to i, b := i/2, b.b$
> **fi**

As usual, this last step requires that one ensures that assignment rule proviso $pre \Rightarrow post[x \backslash E]$ should hold. The details are left to as an exercise.

However, note that there is a key insight here regarding what should happen when i is odd. Given that we wish to reduce i by one in order to arrive at the efficient even number scenario, the question reduces to: what must happen if we reduce i by one in order to preserve the invariant ($z.b^i = a^n$). Clearly, we then have to multiply z by b (and not by a as in our earlier abortive attempt).

Note also how the final iteration of the loop (if the loop is executed at all) will always be with i as the odd number, 1. Therefore, z will always be updated in the last iteration, even if it is never updated in any prior iteration.

The net result is the following delightful (and non-obvious) little algorithm:

> $i, b, z := n - 1, a, a;$
> **do** $i \neq 0 \to$
>   **if** $odd(i) \to i, z := i - 1, z.b$
>   [] $even(i) \to i, b := i/2, b.b$
>   **fi**
> **od**

In empirical tests, this algorithm, implemented in Java, was found to be considerably faster than a call to the pow() function in Java's Math package. It is naturally also considerably faster than an algorithm that merely multiplies a together n times. Notice that the algorithm is $\mathcal{O}(\log n)$, which is typically the case when one halves intervals. This means that to raise something to the power 1000, say, the algorithm does about 10 iterations, whereas the straightforward approach would take 1000 iterations. As for Java's pow() function, it would seem that it relies on series expansions to compute a^n, where n need not be integer.

One may well ask: is efficiency an issue? Of course, that depends on the application. In the case of this particular algorithm one could well imagine some "hard" real-time system (e.g. on board a missile, computing the flight path!) in which a small processor needs to compute the value of a^n over and over again, as rapidly as possible. An algorithm that is more efficient than others, such as the one above, could be critically important.

Finally, the reader should consider how to extend this code to handle the more general cases: if $n = 0$, or if $n < 0$.

3.5.4 Discussion

The above text could easily have been tidied up to show a direct path to the required answer. However, it is a little difficult to argue *ab initio* that a loop invariant should be $z.b^i = a^n$ instead of $z.a^i = a^n$. Indeed, it is not even obvious why one should choose the latter as an invariant until it is realised that it is nothing other than an assertion that $z = a^{n-i}$ should hold. Some text books propose the loop invariant "out of the air"—as if one could have thought it out in the first place. However, the deliberate decision to expose the reader to a "false path" was intended to demonstrate several matters. Here is a quick summary of some of the lessons learnt from the derivation above.

1. Finding loop invariants generally requires a lot of creative thinking—it is not necessarily a trivial matter at all.
2. Sometimes, you can build on or learn from your mistakes.
3. A good loop invariant often leads to a highly efficient algorithm.
4. Following the rules rigorously, while perhaps tedious, can expose one's errors and help one to develop correct code. If we did not bother about rigorously ensuring that the assignment rule's proviso, $pre \Rightarrow post[x \backslash E]$, actually held, we might not have picked up on the error. We might have felt quite comfortable with a solution that simply squared z when i is even. Taking the trouble to carefully check the assignment rule's proviso led to the mistake being picked up.
5. Following the rules rigorously and careful logical reasoning also helped us to identify appropriate initialization values. Some versions of this algorithm in fact start more obviously: with the assignment $i, b, z := n, a, 1$. This works, but requires one iteration more than necessary.
6. The use of "odd" and "even" tests can be very useful on occasions. It is left as an exercise to show how to derive a more naïve algorithm that does not differentiate between the odd- and even-ness of i. Relying on our initial invariant, one can dispense with the need for a select statement, but instead have the following assignment in the loop body: $i, z := i - 1, z.a$. This would preserve the invariant and lead to the "inefficient" version of the algorithm.

3.6   Integer Logarithm Approximation

3.6.1   Problem Statement and Invariant

We end this chapter of simple algorithms, by deriving an algorithm that finds the best possible integer approximation of the logarithm to the base 2 of a given integer. To see what is meant by this, consider the identity relationship that holds in real-valued arithmetic:

$$\ell = log_2(N) \Longleftrightarrow 2^\ell = N$$

Suppose we are given N and we need to find an integer ℓ that approximates $log_2(N)$. We can deduce from the real arithmetic identity relationship that an ℓ such that $N \in [2^\ell, 2^{\ell+1})$ is just such an approximation.[5] This is what we shall use as our postcondition. The specification to be refined is therefore:

$$\ell : [N > 0, N \in [2^\ell, 2^{\ell+1})]$$

Note that N is a constant. It is our task to change ℓ, and thus also the interval $[2^\ell, 2^{\ell+1})$, so that the interval "finds" N, as it were. Given our experience to date of the value of invariants, perhaps it would be useful to define an interval in terms of some parameter, n, that has the property of invariantly containing N. For example, suppose we tried to derive an algorithm where it was invariantly the case that $N \in [n.2^\ell, n.2^{\ell+1})$. The postcondition is then attained when $n = 1$. Letting inv' be defined as

$$inv' \triangleq N \in [n.2^\ell, n.2^{\ell+1})$$

and introducing n as a frame variable, the specification can now be stated as:

$$\ell, n : [N > 0, inv' \wedge (n = 1)]$$

Our initial approach to this problem was based on the invariant above, but the resulting algorithm turned out to be rather complicated. An alternative invariant could be:

$$inv \triangleq N \in [n.2^\ell, (n + 1).2^\ell)$$

Note that

$$inv \wedge (n = 1) \equiv inv' \wedge (n = 1) \equiv N \in [2^\ell, 2^{\ell+1}),$$

the latter being the problem's postcondition.

---

[5]As suggested later, if N is closer to $2^{\ell+1}$ than it is to 2^ℓ, then $(\ell + 1)$ would be a better approximation of $log_2(N)$ than ℓ would be. However, this can only be established by explicitly computing 2^ℓ and $2^{\ell+1}$—something which we wish to avoid in the algorithm to be derived.

3.6.2 Refinement Steps

Refinement using this invariant proceeds as follows:

$$\ell : [N > 0, N \in [2^\ell, 2^{\ell+1})]$$

$\sqsubseteq$ {Strengthen postcondition}

$$\ell : [N > 0, inv \wedge (n = 1)]$$

$\sqsubseteq$ {sequence rule}

$$\ell, n : [N > 0, inv];$$

$$\ell, n : [inv, inv \wedge (n = 1)]$$

$\sqsubseteq$ {assignment rule, since $N \in [N.2^0, 2^0(N + 1))$}

$$n, \ell := N, 0;$$

$$\ell, n : [inv, inv \wedge (n = 1)]$$

$\sqsubseteq$ {repetition rule, variant is $n - 1$}

$$n, \ell := N, 0;$$

do $n \neq 1 \rightarrow$

$$\ell, n : [(n \neq 1) \wedge inv, inv \wedge 0 \leq n - 1 < n_0 - 1]$$

od

$\sqsubseteq$ {assignment rule (justified below)}

$$n, \ell := N, 0;$$

do $n \neq 1 \rightarrow$

$$n, \ell := \lfloor \tfrac{n}{2} \rfloor, \ell + 1$$

od

Note that $n-1$ instead of n was used as the variant. This is because, by convention, the variant is bound from below by 0, while n would be bound from below by 1. However, it is not necessary to abide by the convention—everything still works if you do not.

3.6.3 Justifying the Assignment

The details of the justification for the assignment in the loop are not as straightforward as one might initially believe. (We leave aside a discussion of the variant part, since that is straightforward.) Since integer division is involved, we have to assume that rounding down always takes place. We have to therefore prove that $(n \neq 1) \wedge inv \Rightarrow inv[n, \ell \backslash \lfloor \tfrac{n}{2} \rfloor, \ell + 1]$. We proceed as follows, where we assume that $\tfrac{n}{2}$ is a real value:

$$inv[n, \ell\backslash\lfloor\tfrac{n}{2}\rfloor, \ell+1]$$

$\equiv$ {Expand inv}

$$(N \in [n.2^{\ell}, (n+1).2^{\ell})[n, \ell \backslash \lfloor\tfrac{n}{2}\rfloor, \ell+1]$$

$\equiv$ {Substitute}

$$N \in [\lfloor\tfrac{n}{2}\rfloor.2^{\ell+1}, (\lfloor\tfrac{n}{2}\rfloor+1).2^{\ell+1})$$

$\equiv$ {Focus on the lower bound: re-arrange terms}

$$N \in [(\lfloor\tfrac{n}{2}\rfloor).2.2^{\ell}, (\lfloor\tfrac{n}{2}\rfloor+1).2^{\ell+1})$$

$\Leftarrow$ {Since $\lfloor\tfrac{n}{2}\rfloor.2 \leq n$—see Sect. 3.6.4}

$$N \in [n.2^{\ell}, (\lfloor\tfrac{n}{2}\rfloor+1).2^{\ell+1})$$

$\equiv$ {Focus on the upper bound: re-arrange terms}

$$N \in [n.2^{\ell}, (\lfloor\tfrac{n}{2}\rfloor+1)2.2^{\ell})$$

$\equiv$ {Letting $\lfloor\tfrac{n}{2}\rfloor = \tfrac{n}{2} - \delta$, where $\delta = 0 \vee \delta = \tfrac{1}{2}$) }

$$N \in [n.2^{\ell}, (\tfrac{n}{2} - \delta + 1)2.2^{\ell})$$

$\equiv$ {Algebra}

$$N \in [n.2^{\ell}, (n + 2(1 - \delta)).2^{\ell})$$

$\Leftarrow$ {Since $(n + 2(1 - \delta)) \geq (n+1)$—see Sect. 3.6.4}

$$N \in [n.2^{\ell}, (n+1).2^{\ell})$$

$\equiv$ {Definition of inv}

inv

3.6.4   Strengthening Predicates by Decreasing Ranges

In two places in the above derivation, we used the notation $X \Leftarrow Y$ to indicate that a predicate X is weaker than another predicate Y. The predicate X had the form $N \in [bot, top)$ and Y had the form $N \in [bot', top')$. Clearly if the range in Y is smaller than the range in X, then X is indeed weaker than Y, i.e. $X \Leftarrow Y$. It is also clear that the range in Y is indeed smaller than that in X if $bot \leq bot'$, and/or if $top \geq top'$. We show that this indeed holds in each of the relevant instances in the derivation.

In the first of these two instances, we had

$$N \in [(\lfloor\tfrac{n}{2}\rfloor).2.2^{\ell}, (\lfloor\tfrac{n}{2}\rfloor+1).2^{\ell+1}) \Leftarrow N \in [n.2^{\ell}, (\lfloor\tfrac{n}{2}\rfloor+1).2^{\ell+1})$$

Since it is easy to see that $(\lfloor\tfrac{n}{2}\rfloor).2 \leq n$, and therefore that $(\lfloor\tfrac{n}{2}\rfloor).2.2^{\ell} \leq n.2^{\ell}$, the bottom limit of the range has increased (or stayed the same), and thus the $\Leftarrow$ is justified.

In the second instance, we had

$$N \in [n.2^\ell, (n + 2(1 - \delta)).2^\ell) \Leftarrow N \in [n.2^\ell, (n + 1).2^\ell)$$

Since $2(1 - \delta)$ either evaluates to 1 (when $\delta = \frac{1}{2}$) or to 2 (when $\delta = 0$), it follows that $n + 2(1 - \delta) \geq n + 1$, and therefore that $(n + 2(1 - \delta)).2^\ell \geq (n + 1).2^\ell$. Thus, in the second case, the top limit of the range has decreased (or stayed the same), and hence the $\Leftarrow$ is justified.

In summary, then, the derivation shows that

$$inv \Rightarrow inv[n, \ell \backslash \lfloor \frac{n}{2} \rfloor, \ell + 1]$$

thus justifying the refinement of the loop's body to the assignment $n, \ell := \lfloor \frac{n}{2} \rfloor, \ell + 1$

3.6.5 Discussion

A lot of effort seems to have gone into deriving the following apparently rather simple algorithm:

$$\{N > 0\}$$
$$n, \ell := N, 0$$
$$; \mathbf{do} \ i \neq 1 \rightarrow$$
$$\qquad n, \ell := \lfloor \frac{n}{2} \rfloor, \ell + 1$$
$$\mathbf{od}$$
$$\{N \in [2^\ell, 2^{\ell+1})\}$$

Of course, things always seem easier in hindsight. Without our formal approach, you would no doubt have been able to work out the basic principle of successively halving the original value of N. However, getting the initialisation values and termination condition of the loop right, tends to be rather error-prone. Moreover, our very formal reasoning has at least left us with an assurance that the algorithm is correct in terms of its pre- and postconditions.

It is less certain that the algorithm in fact delivers the *best* integer approximation of $log_2(N)$. The claim is only true if our notion of *best* co-incides with the postcondition, $N \in [2^\ell, 2^{\ell+1})$, which effectively results in an ℓ such that $N - 2^\ell \geq 0$.

For example, if $N = 1,023$, our algorithm would determine ℓ to be 9, so that $1,023 \in [2^9, 2^{10})$ and $1,023 - 2^9 = 1,023 - 512 = 511 \geq 0$. However, most people would regard 10 as being a better integer approximation of $log_2(1,023)$

Thus, it could be argued that in such cases it would be better to increase the algorithm's final value of ℓ by 1, even if that meant that $N - 2^\ell < 0$. Specifically, we would want to increase ℓ by 1 if N was closer to $2^{\ell+1}$ than to 2^ℓ, i.e. if ℓ were such that

$$(N - 2^\ell) > (2^{\ell+1} - N)$$

With some algebraic manipulation, it will be seen that this is equivalent to

$$N > 3.2^{\ell-1}$$

Thus, some might wish to augment the derived algorithm as follows:

$$\{N > 0\}$$
$$n, \ell := N, 0$$
$$\text{;do } i \neq 1 \rightarrow$$
$$\qquad n, \ell := \lfloor \tfrac{n}{2} \rfloor, \ell + 1$$
$$\textbf{od}$$
$$\{N \in [2^\ell, 2^{\ell+1})\}$$
$$\text{;if } ([N > 3.2^{\ell-1}) \rightarrow \ell := \ell + 1$$
$$\text{\rlap{[}}\quad ([N \leq 3.2^{\ell-1}) \rightarrow \textbf{skip}$$
$$\textbf{fi}$$

Unfortunately, such a select command would significantly undermine the algorithm's efficiency. You might have noticed that the loop's body can be implemented extremely efficiently in machine code: it requires the execution of a right shift instruction, and an increment instruction (generally executed in 1 clock cycle each). Indeed, the derived algorithm amounts to counting the number of times an integer word needs to be right-shifted in order to move its left-most 1 bit into the right-most position of the word. The select command introduces the complexity of computing 3.2^{l-1}. It is left to the reader as an exercise to derive an alternative algorithm which relies on an additional variable and computes $2^{\ell-1}$ in that variable as part of the existing loop.

As a final comment, we remark that the entire derivation can be generalised to an algorithm to approximate the logarithm to the base b instead of 2. In that case, the loop's condition should no longer be $n \neq 1$ but $n \geq b$. Additionally, the argument justifying the assignment in the body has to be generalised. It is very similar to that given above. However, $\delta = 0 \vee \delta = \tfrac{1}{b} \vee \ldots \delta = \tfrac{(b-1)}{b}$. Details are left as an exercise.

3.7 Revision Exercise

1. Derive a linear search algorithm that does not assume certainty of a successful search. Thus, the specification can be taken as: $i : [\text{true}, ((i \geq 0) \Rightarrow (A_i = x))]$.

It will be seen that the algorithm has the same initializing assignment statement as the linear search algorithm derived in this chapter, the same loop body, and its derivation relies on the same invariant and variant. However, its loop condition is different from the loop condition in the derived algorithm.

2. In answering the questions below, use X^r to indicate the reverse of array X and $X^r_{[i,j)}$ to denote the reverse of the subarray $X_{[i,j)}$.

   a. Propose an invariant, a variant, and a postcondition for the following loop.

   $\{A.len = B.len\}$
   $i := 0;$
   do $(i \neq A.len) \rightarrow$
       $B_{B.len-(i+1)}, i := A_i, i+1$
   od

   b. Refine $\{A.len = B.len\}\ B : S\ \{Post\}$ to code, where

   $$Post \triangleq \forall j : [0, A.len) \cdot \begin{cases} B_j = A_j & \text{if } A_{A.len-j+1} > 0, \\ B_j = 0 & \text{otherwise.} \end{cases}$$

3. A student produces the following version of insertion sort:

   ```
   pre  {A.len > 0}
   i, j := 0, 0
   ;do (i < A.len) →
          j := i − 1
          ;do (j ≥ 0) →
                 if (A_j > A_i) → A_{j+1} := A_j  fi
                 ; j := j − 1
          od
          A_{j+1}, i := A_i, i + 1
   od
   post  {sorted(A)}
   ```

   where the predicate $sorted(A)$ is defined as

   $$sorted(A) \triangleq \forall x, y : [x, y) \cdot (A_x \leq A_{x+1}) \wedge (x < y)$$

   Assume that the program's precondition is correct.

   a. In what way the definition of $sorted(A)$ deficient? Give an alternative. What, if anything, is being assumed when the given definition for $sorted(A)$ (and probably your improved version as well) is used as a postcondition to the sorting program?

b. Indicate which statement in the program could cause it to fail, and justify your claim.

c. Redefine the body of the outer loop. Do this by deciding what the inner loop's postcondition should be. Rely on this postcondition to propose a suitable loop invariant for the inner loop as well as a suitable inner loop condition. Then, in the normal way, derive code to initialize and construct the inner loop.

4. Consider a program consisting of an "infinite" loop which reads in, as its first statement, some integer value into variable v. Thereafter, a select statement updates two arrays A and B of unspecified length, the updating happening as described below. Code in the remainder of the loop is not relevant to this question, since it does not change any of the variables that are mentioned. You may assume the following:

- Before the execution of the select statement $A_{[0,n)}$ contains, in sorted order, the largest $X\%$ of the values read into variable v to date.
- Also before the execution of the statement array $B_{[0,m)}$ contains the remaining values that have been read into v.
- A routine $insert(X, y)$ is available that inserts a value y into an array X in its correctly sorted position relative to other values already placed in the array X.
- A routine $remove(X, i)$ is available that removes the ith element from the array X, copying $A_{(i+1)}$ into A_i, $A_{(i+2)}$ into $A_{(i+1)}$, etc.
- No two values that are read into variable v are the same.

Propose a select statement to update the arrays A and B so that they retain their properties with respect to the most recently read in value for v—i.e. $A_{[0,n)}$ still contains, in sorted order, the largest $X\%$ of the values read into variable v to date, while array $B_{[0,m)}$ still contains the remaining values that have been read into v. You should invoke the $insert$ and $remove$ routines as appropriate in your select statement. However, also include code to appropriately update the variables that indicate the number of elements that have been placed into arrays A and B respectively to date, namely n and m. Thus, do not assume that n and m are updated by $insert$ and/or $remove$. Do not use nested select statements in the select statement that you propose.

5. Indicate what each of the following programs achieves. Do this by (a) suggesting a loop invariant and (b) a variant for each of the programs. Then say what holds after the loop terminates.

a.
```
{A.len > 0}
i, j := 0, 1;
do (j ≠ A.len) →
    if  A_j > A_i → i, j := j, j + 1
    ▯  A_j ≤ A_i → j := j + 1
    fi
od
```

b.

$\{sorted(A) \wedge (A.len > 0)\}$
$i, p := 1, 1;$
do $(i \neq A.len) \rightarrow$
    if $A_i \neq A_{(i-p)} \rightarrow i := i + 1$
    $[\!]$ $A_i = A_{(i-p)} \rightarrow i, p := i + 1, p + 1$
    fi
od

c.

$\{A.len > 0\}$
$\ell, h, r, i := 0, A.len, 0, 1;$
do $(i \neq A.len) \rightarrow$
    if $(A_r = A_i) \rightarrow i := i + 1$
    $[\!]$ $(A_r \neq A_i) \rightarrow$
        if $(h - \ell) \leq (i - r) \rightarrow r, i := i, i + 1$
        $[\!]$ $(h - \ell) > (i - r) \rightarrow \ell, h, r, i := r, i, i, i + 1$
        fi
    fi
od

d.

$\{sorted(A) \wedge sorted(B) \wedge sorted(C)\}$
$i, j, k, r := 0, 0, 0, 0$
$;$**do** $((i \neq A.len) \wedge (j \neq B.len) \wedge (k \neq C.len)) \rightarrow$
    if $(A_i > B_j) \rightarrow j := j + 1$
    $[\!]$ $(B_j > C_k) \rightarrow k := k + 1$
    $[\!]$ $(C_k > A_i) \rightarrow i := i + 1$
    $[\!]$ $((A_i = B_j) \wedge (B_j = C_k)) \rightarrow i, j, k, r, D_r := i + 1, j + 1, k + 1, r + 1, A_i$
    fi
od

e.

$\{$ **Pre:** $(r \in [0, A.len)) \wedge (A.len > 0) \wedge mni(A, k) \wedge (sum(A) = S) \wedge (r = R)$ $\}$
do $(r \neq 0) \rightarrow$
    if $(k \neq A.len - 1) \rightarrow A_k, k := A_k + 1, k + 1$
    $[\!]$ $(k = A.len - 1) \rightarrow A_k, k := A_k + 1, 0$
    fi
    $; r := r - 1$
od

where following definitions hold

$$sum(A) \triangleq \sum_{i=0}^{A.len-1} A_i$$

$$eq(A_{[l,h)}) \triangleq \forall i, j : [l, h) \cdot A_i = A_j$$

$$mni(A, k) \triangleq k \in [0, A.len) \land eq(A_{[0,k)}) \land eq(A_{[k,A.len)})$$

$$\land (k \in [1, A.len) \Rightarrow (A_{k-1} = A_k - 1))$$

6. Consider a non-empty sorted array of integers, A. Develop an $O(A.len)$ algorithm that searches for two indices, i and j, in A such that $A_i + A_j = 0$. Assume that $i \leq j$ and call your invariant $Inv(A, i, j)$.

   To cater for the possibility that no two such indices can be found, the following code should be assumed immediately after the loop:

```
{Inv(A, i, j) ∧ ¬G}
if (i ≤ j) → print(Indices are "i" and "j")
‖ (i > j) → print("Indices not found")
fi
{post: (A_i + A_j = 0) ∨ (∀ p, q : [0, A.len) · ((A_p + A_q) ≠ 0))}
```

7. Derive an algorithm for a printer to print a document in so-called *booklet* format, using the guidelines given below.

   - The document to be printed has n pages, where $4 \leq n \leq P.len$, n is a multiple of four, and P is an array to be used by the printing algorithm. (The assumption that n is a multiple of four is intended to simplify this problem. In cases where a document does not comply with this requirement, for the purposes of this exercise it is assumed that the tail end of the document is "padded" with enough blank pages to ensure that the multiple of four assumption holds.)
   - The printer stores in P pointers that reference pages of the document to be printed. Thus, for $i = 0, 1, \ldots (n - 1)$, P_i refers to the $i + 1^{st}$ page.
   - *getSheet*() draws a blank sheet of paper into the printer for printing, and *ejectSheet*() returns a sheet of paper which is in the printer to the out-tray.
   - *printFront*(P_i, P_j) prints pages $i + 1$ and $j + 1$ on the front of the sheet of paper (in landscape and in the given order: first page $i + 1$ then page $j + 1$).
   - Similarly, *printBack*(P_i, P_j) prints pages $i + 1$ and $j + 1$, but the back of the sheet of paper.
   - *Booklet* format means that four document pages are printed on each sheet of paper. The pages are therefore printed in the following order:

     - Pages 1 and n are printed onto the "front" of the first sheet of paper;
     - Pages 2 and $(n - 1)$ are printed onto the "back" of this sheet of paper.
     - Pages 3 and $(n - 2)$ are printed onto the "front" of the next sheet of paper.
     - Pages 4 and $(n - 3)$ are printed onto the "back" of the next sheet of paper.
     - etc.

- *printed*($P_{[i,j)}$) is a predicate asserting that pages $i + 1$ to j (i.e. pages referenced by the pointers in $P_{[i,j)}$) have been printed onto one or more sheets of paper in booklet format.
- Your code should have a loop whose variant is $(j - i)$ and whose invariant is *printed*($P_{[0,i)}$) $\wedge$ *printed*($P_{[j+1,n)}$)

8. Assume that A is a non-empty array of integers. The subarray, $A_{[\ell,h)}$, is to be regarded as *monotonically non-decreasing* if and only if:

$$\begin{cases} h = \ell + 1 \text{ or} \\ h \in [\ell + 2, A.len) \wedge \forall j : [\ell, h - 1) \cdot A_j \leq A_{j+1} \end{cases}$$

i.e. a subarray is monotonically non-decreasing if and only if it either consists of only one element, or it consists of two or more elements (perhaps extending to the end of the array) where these elements are in non-descending order.

A developer has derived the algorithm below to find i such that the subarray $A_{[0,i)}$ is the longest monotonically non-decreasing subarray in A that starts at A_0.

```
i := 1
;do ((i ≠ A.len) cand (A_{i-1} ≤ A_i)) →
    i := i + 1
od
```

NB: In GCL, **cand** and **cor** denote "conditional and" and "conditional or" respectively. In C++/Java, these correspond to the well-known short-circuit operators && and || respectively. In the context above, **cand** will ensure that no attempt is ever made to evaluate the non-existent entry $A_{A.len}$.

Derive the above algorithm. Pay particular attention to the following:

- Formulation of pre- and postcondition
- Loop's postcondition as an invariant and negated guard
- Loop initialisation
- Formulation of the variant
- Proof of loop body

Chapter 4
Intermediary Examples

This chapter provides further examples of the software correctness by construction method. The examples are fairly diverse. They range from sorting in a specialised context (the Dutch National Flag problem), discovering segmental properties of an array (the longest segment and the longest palindrome problems), raster drawing algorithms, the majority voting problem and an example from computational geometry. It will be clear that conventional "hack into correctness" approaches to software development would be hard-pressed to come up with correct versions of these algorithms.

4.1 Dutch National Flag

Given an array, A, that contains an arbitrary number of objects marked as r, w and b[1] in some arbitrary order, sort the entries so that all the r's come first, followed by the w's, followed by the b's.

This is one of the many sorting algorithms, but it involves a rather specialised case—namely there are only three possible entries (at most) to be sorted. It is a well-known result in computation theory that the general sorting problem can at best be carried out in $\mathcal{O}(n \log n)$ time. However, in this special case, it is possible to sort in $\mathcal{O}(n)$ time.

An easy and obvious way of doing this is to run through the array and count up the number of r, w and b entries. Then one can simply over-write all the entries, filling in as many r's then as many w's, and finally as many b's as were determined in the initial run. Although this occurs in $\mathcal{O}(n)$ time, it in fact iterates through the

---

[1] These stand for red, white and blue—the colours of the Dutch National Flag, hence the title of the subsection. However, they are also the colours of the French flag, the Tricolour, and some francophone authors characterise the problem accordingly. This text should not be construed as a display of bias towards any particularly country.

D.G. Kourie and B.W. Watson, *The Correctness-by-Construction Approach to Programming*, DOI 10.1007/978-3-642-27919-5_4,
© Springer-Verlag Berlin Heidelberg 2012

array twice. The classical algorithm to be developed below improves on this by 50%—i.e., the sorting can be done with a single iteration through the array. In any case, this counting and overwriting approach would not work if the entries were complex objects with multiple attributes other than the r, w and b attributes that form the search basis.

Strictly speaking, in all sorting problems we should specify as part of our requirements, that the entries in the sorted array must match the entries that were originally in the array. Without this constraint, an array could be "sorted" by writing arbitrary values into the array in sorted order! One way of specifying this would be to have the following as part of the problem's pre- and postcondition:

$$count(A,r) = N_r \wedge count(A,w) = N_w \wedge count(A,b) = N_b, \qquad (4.1)$$

where $count(A,x) = N_x$ means that the number of x-entries in the array A is some value, N_x. For the purposes of this present exercise, we will simply assume that this always holds, both as part of the precondition and as part of the postcondition—without specifying it explicitly.[2]

4.1.1   Formulating the Problem

In order to specify the problem more concisely, let us define two predicates. The first (called c for "colour") asserts that all the entries in the subarray $A_{[l,h)}$ are the colour x:

Definition 4.1.1. $c(A,l,h,x) \triangleq \forall i : [l,h) \cdot (A_i = x)$.

Recall that if the range referenced in the colour predicate is empty, then the predicate is true. The colour predicate in Definition 4.1.1 is merely required to assist in formally defining a second predicate, given in Definition 4.1.2. This second predicate asserts that a certain interim state of sortedness of the array prevails. (The predicate is called s for "sorted".) It is formally defined as follows:

Definition 4.1.2.

$$s(A,l,h,wb,wt,bb) \triangleq c(A,l,wb,r) \wedge c(A,wb,wt,w) \wedge c(A,bb,h,b)$$

$$\wedge 0 \leq l \leq wb \leq wt \leq bb \leq h \leq A.len.$$

---

[2]The interested reader may refer to Morgan's book (p. 94) that provides a more sophisticated approach to specifying the same thing, but in the general case where the values in the array are not known a priori. He lays down in formal terms a requirement that says: if the array's contents are collectively regarded as a bag of items, then the sorted array must still represent the same bag.

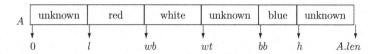

Fig. 4.1 The most general state for predicate $s(A, l, h, wb, wt, bb)$

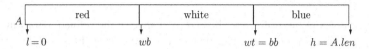

Fig. 4.2 A is sorted: $s(A, 0, A.len, wb, wt, bb) \land (wt = bb)$

The sorted predicate expresses the general scenario in Fig. 4.1, showing regions of array A already sorted into red, white and blue, respectively, and regions where no information is assumed about the colour. Here, wb stands for white/bottom, wt stands for white/top and bb stands for blue/bottom.

The indices wb, wt and bb have been constrained to specific upper and lower bounds in such a way as to allow for the possibility that—in the range of the sorted items $[l, h)$—there are

1. no reds in sorted position (i.e., $wb = l$); and/or
2. no whites in sorted position (i.e., $wb = wt$); and/or
3. no blues in sorted position (i.e., $bb = h$).

Clearly, if all these three conditions apply, and if l and h are 0 and $A.len$ respectively, then s is an assertion that the array is unsorted. It could also be the case that $A.len = 0$, but even in this case, the array is to be construed initially as unsorted.[3] This is precisely what we require to specify our precondition.

On the other hand, if l and h correspond to 0 and $A.len$ respectively, and $wt = bb$, then we have arrived at the scenario depicted in Fig. 4.2 below—precisely our required postcondition. (Note that by requiring $wt = bb$ in the postcondition, we are stating that it is impossible for the three conditions enumerated above to apply simultaneously, unless the array is empty ($A.len = 0$). However, it is possible that at most two of the three conditions may apply—i.e., that the array contains only one colour.)

The problem can thus be specified as follows:

$$A, wb, wt, bb : [s(A, 0, A.len, 0, 0, A.len), s(A, 0, A.len, wb, wt, bb) \land (wt = bb)].$$

---

[3]The claim that A is unsorted should be understood as an abbreviated way of saying that the extent to which A may be sorted, has not yet been tested. It may be the case that, once the sortedness of A is checked, it is found that it was fully sorted from the start. Even in the case of an empty array, we initially construe it as unsorted. Once it is verified as being an empty array, then it is regarded as sorted.

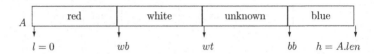

Fig. 4.3 Predicate $s(A, 0, A.len, wb, wt, bb)$ to serve as invariant

All variables in the frame are allowed to change in the refined algorithm. This includes the array, A, in that we can change its contents (e.g., by swapping contents of various cells around).

4.1.2 Choosing the Invariant

The next step, of course, is to identify a loop invariant. If one thinks about the problem, the invariant that suggests itself is one that expresses an interim situation where some regions of the array are not sorted, but others are. One could, theoretically, regard the scenario depicted in Fig. 4.1 as a generalised interim solution. As another example, instead of assuming that the red and white regions are contiguous as in that figure, we could allow for an additional unsorted region between the red and white entries. However, there is no apparent advantage in having more than one unsorted reason at any interim stage.

In the interest of keeping things simple, then, we limit ourselves to having one unsorted region. The question then becomes: where should the unsorted region start and end?

Let us suppose that the unsorted region is $A[bu, tu)$. Since the bottom boundary for the reds and the top boundary for the blues are always fixed (at indices 0 and $A.len$ respectively) there does not seem to be any sense in choosing bu as 0 or tu as $A.len$. Rather, it makes more sense to regard the unsorted region as one that falls somewhere between the top region of the already sorted whites, and the bottom region of the already sorted blues. We therefore choose as our unsorted region $A[wt, bb)$.

The invariant condition is depicted in Fig. 4.3 and the invariant can then be expressed as:

Definition 4.1.3. $inv \triangleq s(A, 0, A.len, wb, wt, bb)$.

At this point, it begins to look as if our Definition 4.1.2 was unnecessarily general: it is never necessary to use an l in that definition other than 0, or an h other than $A.len$. In the interests of simplicity, therefore, let us revise that definition to the following:

Definition 4.1.4.

$$s(A, wb, wt, bb) \triangleq c(A, 0, wb, r) \wedge c(A, wb, wt, w) \wedge c(A, bb, A.len, b)$$

$$\wedge 0 \leq wb \leq wt \leq bb \leq A.len.$$

The problem specification is also revised accordingly to:

$$A, wb, wt, bb : [s(A, 0, 0, A.len), s(A, wb, wt, bb) \wedge (wt = bb)]$$

and the invariant becomes:

Definition 4.1.5. $inv \triangleq s(A, wb, wt, bb)$.

4.1.3 Refining the Specification

At this stage, we can carry out the refinement to code in the sequence of steps given below.

$\qquad A, wb, wt, bb : [s(A, 0, 0, A.len), inv \wedge (wt = bb)]$

$\sqsubseteq \quad$ {sequence rule}

$\qquad A, wb, wt, bb : [s(A, 0, 0, A.len), inv];$

$\qquad A, wb, wt, bb : [inv, inv \wedge (wt = bb)]$

$\sqsubseteq \quad$ {assignment rule: $pre \Rightarrow inv[wb, wt, bb \backslash 0, 0, A.len]$ }

$\qquad wb, wt, bb := 0, 0, A.len;$

$\qquad A, wb, wt, bb : [inv, inv \wedge (wt = bb)]$

$\sqsubseteq \quad$ {repetition rule: variant: $bb - wt$}

$\qquad wb, wt, bb := 0, 0, A.len;$

$\qquad$ **do** $(wt \neq bb) \rightarrow$

$\qquad\qquad A, wb, wt, bb : [inv \wedge (wt \neq bb), inv \wedge (0 \leq (bb - wt) < bb_0 - wt_0]$

$\qquad$ **od**

Since A_{wt} can only be either red or white or blue, we can refine the specification for the loop's body to get the following:

$\qquad A, wb, wt, bb : [inv \wedge (wt \neq bb), inv \wedge (0 \leq (bb - wt) < bb_0 - wt_0]$

$\sqsubseteq \quad$ {selection rule; leave out frame variables to reduce clutter}

$\qquad$ **if** $(A_{wt} = r) \rightarrow [inv \wedge (wt \neq bb) \wedge (A_{wt} = r), inv \wedge (0 \leq (bb - wt) < bb_0 - wt_0]$

$\qquad \| \ (A_{wt} = w) \rightarrow [inv \wedge (wt \neq bb) \wedge (A_{wt} = w), inv \wedge (0 \leq (bb - wt) < bb_0 - wt_0]$

$\qquad \| \ (A_{wt} = b) \rightarrow [inv \wedge (wt \neq bb) \wedge (A_{wt} = b), inv \wedge (0 \leq (bb - wt) < bb_0 - wt_0]$

$\qquad$ **fi**

$\sqsubseteq \quad$ {assignment rule—to be justified later}

$\qquad$ **if** $(A_{wt} = r) \rightarrow A_{wt}, A_{wb}, wt, wb := A_{wb}, A_{wt}, wt + 1, wb + 1$

$\qquad \| \ (A_{wt} = w) \rightarrow wt := wt + 1$

$\qquad \| \ (A_{wt} = b) \rightarrow A_{wt}, A_{bb-1}, bb := A_{bb-1}, A_{wt}, bb - 1$

$\qquad$ **fi**

4.1.3.1   Remarks About the Last Step

1. In the next subsection, for illustrative purposes, it will formally and rigourously be shown that the third of the assignment statements in the three guarded commands, is a legitimate refinement of the specification from which it was derived. Here we offer an informal and intuitive sense of what the three assignment statements achieve by considering Fig. 4.3.

   - If $A_{wt} = r$, then swap it out with A_{wb} and increment both wb and wt. The first guarded command assignment does this.
   - If $A_{wt} = w$, then simply increment wt. The second guarded command assignment does this.
   - If $A_{wt} = b$, then swap it out with A_{bb-1} and decrement bb. The third guarded command assignment does this.

2. The multiple assignments in the first and third guarded command could have been expressed in at least two alternative ways. For example, in the first guard:

   - Assume a swap statement and then have:

     $$swap(A_{wb}, A_{wt}); wb, wt := wb + 1, wt + 1.$$

   - Alternatively, overwrite elements in the array A, but retain the constraint in (4.1) above:

     $$A_{wb}, A_{wt}, wb, wt := r, b, wb + 1, wt + 1.$$

4.1.4   Proving the Third Guard Command

It is appropriate to work through the full justification of at least one of the assignments above. Let us consider the third guard, since it is arguably the most complex. Working through the justifications for the other two guarded commands is left as an exercise to the reader. The refinement step at issue is:

$$[inv \wedge (wt \neq bb) \wedge (A_{wt} = b), inv \wedge (0 \leq (bb - wt) < bb_0 - wt_0]$$

$\sqsubseteq$ {assignment rule—to be justified later}

$$A_{wt}, A_{bb-1}, bb := A_{bb-1}, A_{wt}, bb - 1$$

To be convinced that the refinement is legitimate, we have to prove the proviso of the assignment law, i.e., we have to show that:

$$inv \wedge (wt \neq bb) \wedge (A_{wt} = b) \Rightarrow$$

$$(inv \wedge (0 \leq (bb - wt) < bb_0 - wt_0)[A_{wt}, A_{bb-1}, bb \backslash A_{bb-1}, A_{wt}, bb - 1]. \quad (4.2)$$

Make the substitution relevant to the variant part, and consider the result in relation to the conjuncts in the proviso that have a bearing on the variant. We have:

$$\cdots (wt \neq bb) \cdots \Rightarrow (0 \leq (bb - 1 - wt) < bb_0 - wt_0).$$

It easily follows from this that the variant part of the consequent behaves as expected. (Keep in mind that wt starts off as, and then remains, less than or equal to bb.)

Recall that Definition 4.1.5 of the invariant is given in terms of Definition 4.1.4 of the predicate s, which is, in turn, defined in terms of Definition 4.1.1. Let us expand inv in terms of these definitions, before making the substitutions required in (4.2) above.

inv

$\equiv$ {Definition 4.1.3}

$\quad s(A, wb, wt, bb)$

$\equiv$ {Definition 4.1.2}

$\quad c(A, 0, wb, r) \wedge c(A, wb, wt, w) \wedge c(A, bb, A.len, b) \wedge$
$\quad 0 \leq wb \leq wt \leq bb \leq A.len$

$\equiv$ {Definition 4.1.1}

$\quad \forall i : [0, wb) \cdot (A_i = r) \wedge$
$\quad \forall i : [wb, wt) \cdot (A_i = w) \wedge$
$\quad \forall i : [bb, A.len) \cdot (A_i = b) \wedge$
$\quad 0 \leq wb \leq wt \leq bb \leq A.len$

$\equiv$ {adding in two conjuncts that are tautologies}

$\quad \forall i : [0, wb) \cdot (A_i = r) \wedge$
$\quad \forall i : [wb, wt) \cdot (A_i = w) \wedge$
$\quad \forall i : [bb, A.len) \cdot (A_i = b) \wedge$
$\quad 0 \leq wb \leq wt \leq bb \leq A.len \wedge$
$\quad A_{wt} = A_{wt_0} \wedge A_{bb-1} = A_{(bb-1)_0}$

We now need to make the required substitutions, and to do so "simultaneously". That means, for example, that after substituting A_{wt} with A_{bb-1}, we *may not* try to apply the $[bb \backslash bb - 1]$ substitution to the index of A_{bb-1}. Notice that only the third universal quantifier conjunct is affected by the substitution. We get:

$$inv[A_{wt}, A_{bb-1}, bb \backslash A_{bb-1}, A_{wt}, bb - 1]$$

$\equiv$ {substitution is simultaneous}

$$(\forall i : [0, wb) \cdot (A_i = r)) \wedge$$

$$(\forall i : [wb, wt) \cdot (A_i = w)) \wedge$$

$$(\forall i : [bb - 1, A.len) \cdot (A_i = b)) \wedge$$

$$(0 \leq wb \leq wt \leq bb - 1 \leq A.len) \wedge$$

$$A_{bb-1} = A_{wt_0} \wedge A_{wt} = A_{(bb-1)_0}$$

$\equiv$ {replacing back in terms of the original definitions}

$$s(A, wb, wt, bb - 1) \wedge A_{bb-1} = A_{wt_0} \wedge A_{wt} = A_{(bb-1)_0}$$

This means that we have to show that:

$$s(A, wb, wt, bb) \wedge (wt \neq bb) \wedge (A_{wt} = b) \Rightarrow$$

$$s(A, wb, wt, bb - 1) \wedge A_{bb-1} = A_{wt_0} \wedge A_{wt} = A_{(bb-1)_0}$$

The antecedent and consequent parts of the $\Rightarrow$ relationship make the same claims about the sortedness of the subarray regions that are sorted into red and white. In addition, the antecedent asserts that $A_{[bb,A.len)}$ contains blue elements and that A_{wt} is also a blue element; while the consequent asserts that $A_{[bb-1,A.len)}$ contains blue elements and that A_{bb-1} contains the content previously held by A_{wt}. Taken together, this means that the $\Rightarrow$ relationship is valid. Thus, the multiple assignment was justified.

4.1.5 Putting it All Together

```
wb, wt, bb := 0, 0, A.len;
do (wt ≠ bb) →
    if (A_wt = r) → A_wt, A_wb, wt, wb := A_wb, A_wt, wt + 1, wb + 1
    ‖ (A_wt = w) → wt := wt + 1
    ‖ (A_wt = b) → A_wt, A_bb−1, bb := A_bb−1, A_wt, bb − 1
    fi
od
```

4.1.6 Discussion

The reader could be forgiven for believing that this derivation took a few long routes to achieve something that turned out to be quite simple. In a sense, this is indeed the case. However, we have deliberately decided not to polish up and shrink-wrap the derivation too much. We have done this to emphasise that the process of constructing an algorithm is, in practice, an iterative one, even though textbooks may give the impression that one is supposed to write everything down in a neat shrink-wrapped fashion from the start. Here are some of the matters that could be considered as superfluous.

Since l and h do not appear in either the precondition, postcondition or invariant, it was only in retrospect that the predicate s, originally defined to include these bounds, was revised. To have started off with the revised form would have been to anticipate the shape of the pre- and postcondition and of the invariant predicates. In particular, it would have anticipated that the subarrays $[0, l)$ and $[h, A.len)$ should be empty in the invariant, and this is not an obvious insight when one considers the problem for the first time. In not simplifying s, we intend to convey the sense that new algorithms can truly be *derived* (even if one sometimes goes down overspecified paths in trying to get to a solution), without somehow "first knowing the answer" and then reverse-engineering a refinement calculus argument to pretend that the algorithm was derived.

As an alternative to the invariant, we could have chosen the unsorted region to lie between the top of the already sorted reds and the bottom of the already sorted whites. Such an invariant will lead to an alternative solution to the one that was derived. It would require that the definition of s should change slightly, using an rt index to designate the top of the sorted reds, instead of a wt index to designated the top of the sorted whites. The reader may find this alternative solution as an exercise.

It might also be felt that the proof given to justify the assignment used in the third guard is unnecessary—that by merely looking at the various figures, one can see that the multiple assignment is valid. Such claims are normally made with the wisdom of hindsight. In this case, where the invariant was defined in terms of one predicate, which was defined in terms of another, the informal reasoning might have left one with an uncomfortable sense that something might have been missed—buried within those definitions within definitions. By exposing the underlying definitions in our formal argument, hopefully that sense of discomfort has been assuaged.

Finally, the reader is encouraged to walk through the algorithm for some boundary conditions: for example $A.len = 0$ or $A.len = 1$. There is much scope here for getting boundary conditions wrong, and this was an important consideration in defining s. We made sure that we defined and dealt with semi-open intervals in a clear and consistent manner throughout.

4.2 Longest Segment

There are a large variety of problems related to finding one or more segments in an array that have some particular characteristic. Pattern matching problems are one such group of problems. Even (linear/binary) search problems could be seen as finding a segment of length one that has some sought-after value. Another group of such problems are the so-called longest segment problems. Essentially the task is to identify the longest segment (i.e., subarray) in an array that has a given property.

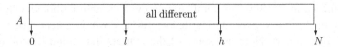

Fig. 4.4 Longest segment general idea

Unsurprisingly, there is also a class of shortest segment problems. Here we consider the following longest segment problem.

Given an array, A, find the longest segment $A_{[l,h)}$ such that no two elements in the segment are the same. For ease of reference, let $A.len = N$. We also assume that the array is not empty, i.e., $N > 0$.

We present a solution to this problem as it was developed at our first attempt— i.e., without any notion of reengineering the refinement "backwards" from a known answer. Of course, to derive the algorithm does not forbid one from using intuition, gut-feel, and from anticipating the general shape of the algorithm that you guess will emerge. The derivation should be used to affirm that gut feel, and to determine precisely the appropriate guards, loop conditions, instructions, etc. When necessary, we might need to backtrack from our initial intuition and reconsider another line of development.

4.2.1   Formulating the Problem

In the present case, what we hope to identify is the maximum length segment, $A_{[l,h)}$ whose elements are all different, as represented in Fig. 4.4.

We may anticipate a loop based on an index i, that runs through the array starting at 0 and ending at N. At the end of every iteration of the loop, we expect a picture similar to the one above, in that $A_{[l,h)}$ is guaranteed to be the required maximum length segment up to that point of processing. (We might intuitively anticipate that some or other decision has to be made during each iteration in order to check whether the maximum length segment should change; we might begin to build up an intuition of how the change should be made, etc. However, at this stage, one should "separate concerns" and leave those matters for later, when we need to develop the body of our loop. If necessary, we can always retrace our steps.)

At this point, it would be useful to define some notation to help us express our needs. In particular, it would be helpful to have predicates that express the following notions:

1. All the elements of some subarray are different;
2. A subarray whose elements are all different is the maximum length such subarray within a larger subarray.

To this end, define the following predicates:

Definition 4.2.1. $d(A, l, h) \triangleq \forall i, j : [l, h) \wedge (i \neq j) \cdot (A_i \neq A_j)$.

Note that if $A_{[l,h)}$ is a segment with one or zero elements, then the range of the $\forall$ quantifier is $\varnothing$ and thus $d(A, l, h)$ is true.

Definition 4.2.2.

$$maxd(A, l, h, p, q) \triangleq (l \in [p, q)) \wedge (h \in [p, q)) \wedge d(A, l, h) \wedge$$
$$\forall i, j : [p, q) \cdot (d(A, i, j) \implies (j - i \leq h - l)).$$

Of course, $maxd(A, l, h, p, q)$ is intended as a predicate that asserts that $A_{[l,h)}$ is a largest subarray of different elements in the subarray $A_{[p,q)}$. Once again, it should be noted that when the range of $\forall$ quantifiers reduces to $\varnothing$, then the predicate evaluates to true, i.e.:

$$\forall (l \in [0, N)) \cdot maxd(A, l, l, l, l) = maxd(A, l, l + 1, l, l + 1) = \text{true}.$$

Note, however that $maxd(a, l, l, l, l + 1) = \text{false}$ because an empty subarray is not the largest subarray in a subarray of length 1. Also note, in passing, that $maxd$ at these boundaries (e.g., $maxd(A, l, l, l, l)$) would not be defined if the assumption $A.len = N > 0$ did not hold, i.e., if $N = 0$.

4.2.2 A First Attempt at Refinement

Clearly, we would like to end up with values for l and h such that $maxd(A, l, h, 0, N)$ is true—this is precisely the postcondition to the problem. Let us then start with the problem specification and refine it in the now familiar way, as follows, where $maxd(A, l, h, 0, i)$ is used as the invariant:

$l, h : [N > 0, maxd(A, l, h, 0, N)]$

⊑   {rewriting bounds and introducing new frame variable}

$l, h, i : [N > 0, maxd(A, l, h, 0, i) \wedge i = N]$

⊑   {sequence rule with $mid = maxd(A, l, h, 0, i)$}

$l, h, i : [N > 0, maxd(A, l, h, 0, i)]; l, h, i : [maxd(A, l, h, 0, i), maxd(A, l, h, 0, i) \wedge i = N]$

⊑   {assignment rule: $(N > 0) \Rightarrow max(A, 0, 1, 0, 1) \equiv \text{true}$}

$l, h, i := 0, 1, 1 ; l, h, i : [maxd(A, l, h, 0, i), maxd(A, l, h, 0, i) \wedge i = N]$

⊑   {repetition rule, variant is $N - i$}

$l, h, i := 0, 1, 1 ;$

do $(i \neq N) \rightarrow$

$l, h, i : [maxd(A, l, h, 0, i) \wedge (i \neq N), maxd(A, l, h, 0, i) \wedge (i_0 < i \leq N)]$

od

Fig. 4.5 Longest segment interim status

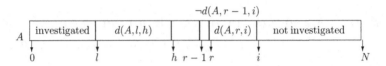

Fig. 4.6 The revised invariant scenario

By this time the reader should be thoroughly familiar with this sequence of refinement steps. Nevertheless, each step should still be carefully checked, ensuring that proviso's are valid in the case of assignments, etc. Hubris and high-handed self-confidence lie at the heart of most bugs!

Note that correctness arguments would be considerably complicated if we had to allow for the possibility of an empty array. In such a case, the specification's postcondition would be required to indicate appropriate values to assign for l and h if $N = 0$. Since $N > 0$ is a precondition of our specification, the matter does not arise—there will always be longest segment of different values—$[0, 1)$ in the case where $N = 1$.

The challenge now is to refine the specification that forms the loop's body. The general picture one might have in mind is probably something like the one in Fig. 4.5.

Clearly, to progress, we need to check whether the invariant will be violated if we increment i. If the invariant will be violated, then we need to do something as part of the loop body to restore it. We reason as follows:

Our invariant assures us that even though there may be one or more subsegments in the range $[0, i)$ in which the elements are all different, the length of no single such subsegment will exceed $(h - l)$.

Of the set of such subsegments, the length of only one of them can possibly be extended as a result of inspecting the value of A_i, namely the longest subsegment that starts at some value less than i, say r, and extends to i (excluded)—i.e., a segment for which $(d(A, r, i) \wedge \neg d(A, r - 1, i))$ holds.[4]

Thus, our picture can be augmented as in Fig. 4.6. This figure should not mislead the reader. It depicts a *general* scenario—one in which certain boundary situations are obscured. Specifically, the figure obscures the following special situations:

---

[4] The two terms in the conjunct are necessary. The first says that all elements in the subsegment are different. The second asserts that the length of the subsegment of different elements cannot be enlarged by starting that subsegment one position earlier.

- The figure does not indicate whether or not it is possible that $r \in [l, h)$. In general, there is no reason to suppose that this may not be the case. Indeed, in starting off the algorithm, it is hard to see how r can be anything other than the initial value of l and i be the same as h. In general, therefore, we shall allow these boundaries to be in the ranges:

  $(0 \le l \le r) \wedge (l < h \le i \le N) \wedge (r < i)$.

- The characterisation of interval $[r, i)$ we gave earlier, namely, $(d(A, r, i) \wedge \neg d(A, r - 1, i))$ is only reasonable when $r > 0$. A more precise description of this interval is: $(d(A, r, i) \wedge (r > 0 \implies \neg d(A, r - 1, i)))$.

Subject to these two special situations we note that if $d(A, r, i)$ is true and A_i is different from all elements in $A_{[r,i)}$, then $d(A, r, i + 1)$ holds. In such an event, it may be necessary to update the values of l and h to r and i respectively, depending on how $(i + 1 - r)$ and $(h - l)$ compare. On the other hand, if $d(A, r, i)$ is true and A_i is the same as some element in $A_{[r,i)}$, then $d(A, r, i + 1)$ will be false. We can then update r to a new value for which $d(A, r, i + 1)$ will hold. Note that there will always be such an r, since, in the limiting case, $d(A, r, i + 1)$ is true when $r = i$.

Having reflected on these matters, the reader may reach the same conclusion that we did, namely, that our previous invariant and refinement process should perhaps account for the value of r as well—i.e., it would seem appropriate that a variable, r is in the invariant whose value determines $d(A, r, i)$ as in the above figure.

Without going into detail, we note in passing that a naïve developer may decide that it is not absolutely necessary to keep such an updated value of r, since one could determine r afresh as part of the body of the loop that we have not yet refined. However, if one thinks about this carefully, it becomes clear that a double loop would then be needed to determine r—a double loop which would be part of the as yet unrefined body of the loop already derived. This would clearly be an unnecessarily inefficient, if not complicated, solution. We will not pursue the matter further here, but move on to a revised attempt to develop the algorithm, this time bringing r into the picture along the lines outlined above.

4.2.3   A Revised Attempt at Refinement

In our second attempt, we need to initialize r outside the outer loop and appropriately update it in the loop's body. Let us see where this idea takes us.

Begin by redefining the predicate, *maxd*, which was used as the basis for an invariant, giving it the additional parameter, r. We thus define the predicate *maxd'* with a fifth parameter in terms of the previous predicate, *maxd*, that has four parameters, as follows:

Definition 4.2.3.
$maxd'(A, l, h, p, q, r) \triangleq maxd(A, l, h, p, q) \wedge d(A, r, q) \wedge (r > 0 \implies \neg d(A, r - 1, q))$.

The intention is to use this new predicate as the basis for our new invariant.

The revised problem is now easily specified and refined in exactly the same way as before, except that we also include r as a frame variable, and initialize it to 0. Apart from now taking $maxd'(A,l,h,0,i,r)$ as the invariant, instead of $maxd(A,l,h,0,i)$, nothing else changes in the refinement process, so we end up with the following loop body to be refined:

$l,h,r,i := 0,1,0,1$;

{Invariant: $maxd'(A,l,h,0,i,r)$}

$\mathbf{do}\ (i \neq N) \rightarrow$

$l,h,r,i : [maxd'(A,l,h,0,i,r) \wedge (i \neq N), maxd]'(A,l,h,0,i,r) \wedge (i_0 < i \leq N)$

$\mathbf{od}$

{Invariant: $maxd'(A,l,h,0,i,r) \wedge (i = N)$}

The previous discussion suggests that we should drive towards developing an inner loop, based on an index, say j, that decrements from i down to r, with $d(A,j,i+1)$ as an invariant. The loop should terminate when $j = r$, or when $j = 0$ or when $A_i = A_{j-1}$ is discovered, whichever occurs first.

Note, however, that r has been initialised to 0 and can only increase. Also, if one of the loop's termination conditions is the conjunct $j = r$, then if j ever reaches 0, it can safely be assumed that $r = 0$ as well. In other words, the postcondition, Q_{inner}, of this inner loop could be stated as the following:

$$Q_{inner} \triangleq d(A,j,i+1) \wedge ((j = r)\ \mathbf{cor}\ (A_i = A_{j-1})).$$

The conditional or, $\mathbf{cor}$, is equivalent to short-circuit evaluation, and is intended to prevent an illicit attempt to reference A_{j-1} when $j = 0$.

Decrementing j in a loop that preserves this invariant leads to one of the following situations:

- If—before j is decremented down to r—it is found that $A_i = A_{j-1}$ while $d(A,j,i+1)$ is held invariant, then $d(A,r,i+1)$ will be false. In this case r has to be updated to the new value, j, so that $d(A,r,i+1)$ holds.
- If j has been decremented down to a point where $j = r$, then this would mean that we have established that A_i is different from all elements in $A_{[r,i)}$, and therefore that $d(A,r,i+1)$ holds. There is no need to change the value of r.

Once establishing that $d(A,r,i+1)$ holds, we need to check whether it is necessary to update the values of l and h to r and $i + 1$ respectively, depending on how $(i + 1 - r)$ and $(h - l)$ compare. We would also have to increment the value of i to make sure that the variant decreases.

With that fairly broad description of the task at hand as background, we now outline the sequence of steps to be followed in refining the loop's body:

$l,h,r,i : [maxd'(A,l,h,0,i,r) \wedge (i \neq N), maxd'(A,l,h,0,i,r) \wedge (i_0 < i \leq N)].$

The following layout shows, in Hoare triple notation, the refinement after successive applications of the sequence rule, where S, representing the outer loop's body, is expanded to the sequence of commands denoted by $S1; S2; S3$. Actually, the sequence rule has been applied twice, first expanding S to $S1; S'$ and then expanding S' to $S2; S3$.

$$\{maxd'(A, l, h, 0, i, r) \wedge (i \neq N)\}\, l, h, r, i : S\, \{maxd'(A, l, h, 0, i, r) \wedge (i_0 < i \leq N)\}$$

$\sqsubseteq$ {Successive sequence rule applications}

$$\{(maxd'(A, l, h, 0, i, r) \wedge (i \neq N)\}$$

$\qquad j : S1$

$$\{(maxd'(A, l, h, 0, i, r) \wedge (i \neq N) \wedge \underbrace{d(A, j, i + 1) \wedge ((j = r) \textbf{ cor } (A_i = A_{j-1}))}_{Q_{inner}}\}$$

$\qquad ; r : S2$

$$\{(maxd(A, l, h, 0, i) \wedge (i \neq N) \wedge d(A, r, i + 1) \wedge (r > 0 \implies \neg d(A, r - 1, i + 1))\}$$

$\qquad ; l, h, i : S3$

$$\{(maxd'(A, l, h, 0, i, r) \wedge (i_0 < i \leq N)\}$$

The pre- and postcondition Hoare triples involving $S1$, $S2$ and $S3$ are now discussed separately. Note that in each case, frame variables have been very specifically identified to indicate which variables are to change at each refinement step.

- The frame of $S1$ has been assigned the new frame variable, j. It is the task of $S1$ to determine j such that $Q_{inner} \triangleq d(A, j, i + 1) \wedge ((j = r) \textbf{ cor } (A_i = A_{j-1}))$ is attained, while preserving all other conjuncts in the precondition, namely $maxd'(A, l, h, 0, i, r) \wedge (i \neq N)$.
- $S2$ is concerned to set r to the value of j, since the precondition affirms that $d(A, j, i + 1)$. However, in so doing, we no longer have the certainty that the loop's invariant, $maxd'(A, l, h, 0, i, r)$, remains intact. Instead, we have to revert to the somewhat weaker postcondition, namely that $maxd(A, l, h, 0, i)$.
- $S3$ is used to reestablish the invariant $maxd'(A, l, h, 0, i, r)$ and also to ensure that the variant is decremented so that $(i_0 < i \leq N)$ holds. (Actually, this latter objective could have been achieved in a separate step, or by invoking the "following assignment" rule.

In elaborating $S1$, we will only change the value of j, and therefore, for simplicity will only write down predicates that relate to j. $S1$ can therefore be refined as follows:

$$\{\textsf{true}\}\, j : S1\, \{Q_{inner}\}$$

$\sqsubseteq$ {Sequence rule}

$$\{\textsf{true}\}$$

$\qquad j : S11$

$$\{d(A, j, i + 1)\}$$

$\qquad ; j : S12$

$$\{Q_{inner} \equiv d(A, j, i + 1) \wedge ((j = r) \textbf{ cor } (A_i = A_{j-1}))\}$$

$\sqsubseteq$ {Assignment rule: true $\Rightarrow d(A, j, i + 1)[j \backslash i]$}

{true}

   $j := i$

{$d(A, j, i + 1)$}

   $j : S12$

{$Q_{inner} \equiv d(A, j, i + 1) \wedge ((j = r) \textbf{ cor } (A_i = A_{j-1}))$}

$\sqsubseteq$ {Repetition rule. Invariant: {$d(A, j, i + 1)$}. Variant: $j - r$}

{true}

   $j := i$

   ; **do** $((j \neq r) \textbf{ cand } (A_i \neq A_{j-1})) \rightarrow j := j - 1$ **od**

{$Q_{inner} \equiv d(A, j, i + 1) \wedge ((j = r) \textbf{ cor } (A_i = A_{j-1}))$}

In the last refinement step shown, we have skipped several details. Clearly, $S12$ is envisaged as a loop with invariant $d(A, j, i + 1)$ that had been established by $S11$. The specification of this loop's body, according to the refinement rules would be:

$$j : [d(A, j, i + 1) \wedge ((j \neq r) \textbf{ cand } (A_i \neq A_{j-1})), d(A, j, i + 1) \wedge 0 \leq (j_0 - r) < (j - r)].$$

We leave it to the reader to verify that the proviso holds for applying the assignment $j := j - 1$ as a refinement to this specification.

Elaborating $S2$ merely involves setting r to the value of j, i.e., the assignment statement $r := j$. (We ignore the possibility that r already has the value j—using a select statement to only carry out the assignment if $r \neq j$ gains nothing in accuracy, and merely introduces an element of inefficiency.) To argue that this assignment is legitimate, we note that the postcondition of $S2$ where the substitution $[r \backslash j]$ is made, is given by

$$\{(maxd\,(A, l, h, 0, i) \wedge (i \neq N) \wedge d(A, j, i+1) \wedge (j > 0 \implies \neg d(A, j-1, i+1))\}.$$

Now the second and third conjuncts of this predicate identically match the second and third conjuncts in $S2$'s precondition. Moreover, the precondition's first conjunct, $maxd'(A, l, h, 0, i, r)$, is certainly stronger than postcondition's first conjunct, $maxd\,(A, l, h, 0, i)$. Thus, the proviso guaranteeing the legitimacy of this assignment will be established if we can argue that:

$$maxd'(A, l, h, 0, i, r) \wedge d(A, j, i + 1) \wedge ((j = r) \textbf{ cor } (A_i = A_{j-1}))$$

$$\Rightarrow (j > 0 \implies \neg d(A, j - 1, i + 1)).$$

To verify that this "implies everywhere" relationship holds, we need to consider two cases: $j = r$ and $j \neq r$ (actually $j > r$). In the first case, note that the predicate $maxd'$ contains a conjunct $(r > 0 \implies \neg d(A, r - 1, i))$. Thus

$$maxd'(A, l, h, 0, i, r) \land (j = r) \Rightarrow (j > 0 \implies \neg d(A, j - 1, i + 1)).$$

In the second case (which, by virtue of the **cor** operator, we only need to consider when $j > 0$), it easily follows that $(A_i = A_{j-1}) \Rightarrow \neg d(A, j - 1, i + 1)$.

Finally, a select statement is required for $S3$ to reestablish the invariant, so that $A_{[l,h)}$ remains the longest segment of different values in the range $A_{[0,i)}$. Using P and Q to represent the pre- and postconditions, respectively, the following refinement is that appropriate:

$\{(maxd(A, l, h, 0, i) \land (i \neq N) \land d(A, r, i + 1) \land (r > 0; \implies; \neg d(A, r - 1, i + 1))\}$
    $l, h, i : S3$
$\{(maxd'(A, l, h, 0, i, r) \land (i_0 < i \leq N)\}$
$\sqsubseteq$ {The select rule}
if $((h - l) \geq (i + 1 - r)) \rightarrow \{((h - l) \geq (i + 1 - r)) \land P\} l, h, i : S31 \{Q\}$
‖ $((h - l) < (i + 1 - r)) \rightarrow \{((h - l) < (i + 1 - r)) \land P\} l, h, i : S32 \{Q\}$
fi
$\sqsubseteq$ {Assignment rule applied twice}
if $((h - l) \geq (i + 1 - r)) \rightarrow i := i + 1$
‖ $((h - l) < (i + 1 - r)) \rightarrow i, l, h := i + 1, r, i + 1$
fi

The proviso of the select rule clearly holds, since the disjunction of the guards evaluates to true. Formal verification of the assignments in the guard statements is left as an exercise.

4.2.4 Putting it All Together

The result of the entire derivation is the following algorithm:

    $l, h, r, i := 0, 1, 0, 1$
    ;do $(i \neq N) \rightarrow$
        $; j := i$
        ;do $(j \neq r$ **cand** $A_{j-1} \neq A_i) \rightarrow j := j - 1$ **od**
        $; r := j$
        ;if $((h - l) < (i + 1 - r)) \rightarrow i, l, h := i + 1, r, i + 1$
        ‖ $((h - l) \geq (i + 1 - r)) \rightarrow i := i + 1$
        fi
    od

This can be slightly refactored by incrementing i only once before testing whether new values for l and h are required:

$l, h, r, i := 0, 1, 0, 1$
;**do** $(i \neq N) \rightarrow$
    ; $j := i$
    ;**do** $(j \neq r$ **cand** $A_{j-1} \neq A_i) \rightarrow j := j - 1$ **od**
    ; $r, i := j, i + 1$
    ; **as** $((h - l) < (i - r)) \rightarrow l, h := r, i$ **sa**
od

4.2.5 Discussion

This problem's solution is somewhere on the borderline between demanding a correctness-by-construction approach, and being amenable to a hacking-into-correctness approach. It would be interesting to know how long it would take the normal programmer to derive this algorithm in "hacking mode": sitting at a terminal and trying various experiments, deriving some sort of solution, checking it with a few test cases of boundary data, and iterating ahead until it was considered that the answer is correct. In saying this, we are not suggesting that the above refinement process was worked out very quickly. In fact, it took several hours. But we suspect that the algorithm could have been semi-formally derived by refinement (without all the didactic prose given above) somewhat more quickly than in hacking mode. What is more, one invariably has far greater confidence in the algorithm's correctness after (semi-)formally deriving it than if a solution had been hacked out in edit–compile–test cycles.

In practice one ought to be pragmatic about the degree of rigour deployed in refining down to code: employ enough formality to ensure that you derive a correct solution, without needing to justify every proviso of every assignment, for example, down to the fullest level of detail.

Nevertheless, we believe that for novices to this kind of material, it is a good idea to devote a lot of time to carrying out formal proofs rigorously, despite the amount of writing that needs to be done. Why? Because we believe that by experiencing the "pain" of deriving as much as possible with the fullest rigour possible, one comes to a deeper appreciation and insight of the kinds of mistakes that are possible, and the range of alternative paths that might have been taken.

4.3 Palindromes

Here is another instance of the longest segment problems: Given arrays A and M, both of length $N > 0$, for $i : [0, N)$ store j in M_i where $A_{[i,i+j)}$ is the longest palindrome in array A that starts at position i.

4.3.1   The Outer Loop

For any $k : [0, N)$, let $lpal(A, k)$ denote the length of the longest palindrome in A that starts at k. Let us take the liberty of writing down the outer loop immediately, giving an invariant in terms of $lpal$, as well as the variant for this loop. We also provide a number of relevant embedded assertions that should hold in the code. These assertions can also be seen as pre- and postconditions in Hoare triple specifications for different parts of the code.

$$i := 0;$$
$$\{inv(i) \triangleq \forall k : [0, i) \cdot M_k = lpal(A, k)\}$$
$$\{variant \triangleq N - i\}$$
$$\textbf{do } i \neq N \to$$
$$\qquad \{inv(i) \wedge i \neq N\}$$
$$\qquad j : S ;$$
$$\qquad \{j = lpal(A, i)\}$$
$$\qquad i, M_i := i + 1, j$$
$$\qquad \{inv(i)\}$$
$$\textbf{od}$$
$$\{inv(i) \wedge i = N\}$$

4.3.2   Formulating the Problem

Our task is to make explicit the code represented in this algorithm by the symbol S, where j is a frame variable. In doing so, we shall express S as a specification in Morgan's notation. Note that the precondition of S is the conjunction of the outer loop's invariant and the outer loop's guard. In the interest of economizing on the notation, we shall keep this in mind without writing these predicates out explicitly, using true as the precondition instead. The problem can therefore be specified as follows:

$$j : [\text{true}, j = lpal(A, i)].$$

To further refine the specification, it is useful to aid intuition by drawing pictures to represent the scenario we are developing. Start with that which is required in the problem, and try to generalize it to reflect an interim phase of the code's evolution. This has been done several times before in this text, and often aids in the formulation of sensible invariants for loops.

Before drawing these pictures, let us first define a few predicates that will be useful for annotating the pictures. To this end, let $pal(A, i, j)$ be the assertion that $A_{[i,i+j)}$ is a palindrome—i.e., that there is a palindrome of length j starting at A_i and ending at A_{i+j-1}.

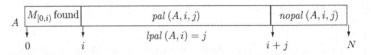

Fig. 4.7 $A_{[i,i+j)}$ is largest palindrome from i

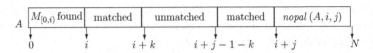

Fig. 4.8 $A_{[i,i+j)}$ not yet established as largest palindrome from i

Let $nopal(A, i, j)$ be the assertion that every subrange of A starting at index i and having length $(j + 1)$ or more is *not* a palindrome, i.e.,

- the subrange $A_{[i,i+j+1)}$, whose of length is $(j + 1)$, is not a palindrome, and

- the subrange $A_{[i,i+j+2)}$, whose of length is $(j + 2)$, is not a palindrome and

... and

- the subrange $A_{[i,N)}$, whose of length is $(N - i)$, is not a palindrome.

Formally, these assertions may be defined as follows:

$$pal(A, i, j) \triangleq \forall k : [0, j) \cdot A_{i+k} = A_{i+j-1-k}$$

$$nopal(A, i, j) \triangleq \forall k : [j + 1, N - i) \cdot \neg pal(A, i, k).$$

The final state of the problem we are considering is represented in Fig. 4.7. The figure shows that it has been established that $A_{[i,i+j)}$ is a palindrome, but that nothing larger than that, starting at i constitutes a palindrome. This means that $lpal(A, i) = j$. An interim scenario en route to this final scenario is represented in Fig. 4.8.

In this figure, it has already been established that there is no palindrome starting at i that is larger than j. In trying to determine whether $A_{[i,i+j)}$ is a palindrome, the first k elements have been tested, and found to match "in palindrome fashion" with the last k elements of the subarray. Here, we have let $matched(A, i, j, k)$ be the assertion that $A_{[i,i+k)}$ matches "in palindrome fashion" with $A_{[i+j-k,i+j)}$. By this, we mean that the following k equalities have been established: $A_i = A_{i+j-1}$ and $A_{i+1} = A_{i+j-1-1}$ and $\cdots A_{i+k-1} = A_{i+j-k}$ and Formally, we may write:

$$matched(A, i, j, k) \triangleq \forall \ell : [0, k) \cdot A_{i+\ell} = A_{i+j-1-\ell}.$$

Clearly, every time a match is found, the value of k should be incremented, thus decreasing the distance between the index on the left, $i + k$, and the index on the right, $i + j - 1 - k$, by two units. This matching should continue until a point is reached where the index from the left meets or crosses over with the index from the right, i.e., until:

$$(i + k \geq i + j - 1 - k) \equiv (2k + 1 \geq j). \tag{4.3}$$

There is quite a subtle point to note here about the equality case. The left and right indices point to elements which are next to be tested for equality. When equality holds in (4.3), then we have a state where an element is still to be tested for equality with itself. Clearly, this will hold and no formal test for equality is necessary. Thus, if $2k + 1 = j$, then we will have established that the subarray $A[i, i + j)$ is indeed a palindrome, without needing to carry out a final check to see whether $A_{i+k} = A_{i+j-1-k}$.

4.3.3 Refining the Specification

Figure 4.8 suggests the appropriate invariant to use in the refinement. Based on these figures, we can rewrite our specification and then refine it as follows:

$\qquad j : [\text{true}, j = lpal(A, i)]$

$\equiv \qquad$ {Rewriting the postcondition in a more explicit form}

$\qquad j : [\text{true}, pal(A, i, j) \wedge nopal(A, i, j)]$

$\sqsubseteq \qquad$ {Strengthening the postcondition and introducing k into frame }

$\qquad j, k : [\text{true}, matched(A, i, j, k) \wedge (2k + 1 \geq j) \wedge nopal(A, i, j)]$

$\equiv \qquad$ {$inv \triangleq matched(A, i, j, k) \wedge nopal(A, i, j)$}

$\qquad j, k : [\text{true}, inv \wedge (2k + 1 \geq j)]$

$\sqsubseteq \qquad$ {Sequence}

$\qquad j, k : [\text{true}, inv];$

$\qquad j, k : [inv, inv \wedge (2k + 1 \geq j)]$

$\sqsubseteq \qquad$ {Assignment}

$\qquad j, k := N - i, 0;$

$\qquad j, k : [inv, inv \wedge (2k + 1 \geq j)]$

$\sqsubseteq \qquad$ {Repetition. Variant: $V \triangleq jN + (j - 2k - 1)$}

$\qquad j, k := N, 0;$

$\qquad \textbf{do } (2k + 1 < j) \rightarrow$

$\qquad\qquad j, k : [inv \wedge (2k + 1 < j), inv \wedge 0 \leq V(j, k) < V(j_0, k_0)]$

$\qquad \textbf{od}$

The choice of the variant requires some explanation. In reference to Fig. 4.8, it is clear that k will be incremented for as long as matches are found between relevant items in A. Every such increment should let the variant decline. Since $j - 2k - 1$ will decline when k is incremented, the variant does indeed decline—provided j is held constant.

However, the figure also suggests that if a match is *not* found, then k will have to be reset to 0, thus *incrementing* the variant. This increment is maximally half of the size of the array, $N/2$. On the other hand when k is reset to 0, it is also necessary to decrement j by 1. To ensure that the variant declines, such a decrement by 1 of j should cause the variant to decline by at least $N/2$—i.e., to make up for the variant's increase as a result of k being set to 0. In the variant chosen above, a term jN has been inserted. This term causes the variant to decline by N when j declines 1. Thus, if j decrements by 1 and k is reset to 0, the variant will still decline.

Turning now to the refinement of the loop's body, we get the following:

$$j, k : [inv \land (2k + 1 < j), inv \land 0 \leq V(j, k) < V(j_0, k_0)]$$

$\sqsubseteq$ {Selection}

if $A_{i+k} = A_{i+j-1-k} \rightarrow k := k + 1$

$\|$ $A_{i+k} \neq A_{i+j-1-k} \rightarrow j, k := j - 1, 0$

fi

Again, we leave it as an exercise to fully prove that the provisos hold in the case of each assignment.

4.3.4   Putting it All Together

Our final algorithm is thus as follows:

$i := 0$;
$\{inv(i) \triangleq \forall k : [0, i) \cdot M_k = lpal(A, k)\}$
$\{variant \triangleq N - i\}$
do $i \neq N \rightarrow$
        $j, k := N - i, 0$;
        do $(2k + 1 < j) \rightarrow$
                if $A_{i+k} = A_{i+j-1-k} \rightarrow k := k + 1$
                $\|$ $A_{i+k} \neq A_{i+j-1-k} \rightarrow j, k := j - 1, 0$
                fi
        od
        $\{j = lpal(A, i)\}$
        $i, M_i := i + 1, j$
        $\{inv(i)\}$
od
$\{inv(i) \land i = N\}$

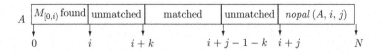

Fig. 4.9 $A_{[i,i+j)}$ not yet established as largest palindrome from i

4.3.5 Discussion

There is another approach to solving this problem, and it is suggested in Fig. 4.9. The implication here is that we begin by finding a k such that $i + k$ represents the "middle" of the interval $[i, j)$. We then decrement k down to 0 or until a match is no longer found.

This approach might seem to be advantageous in that it produces, as a byproduct, the lower bound for M_{i+k} for the various values of k, since the region marked "matched" in the figure will have been established as being a palindrome. However, upon reflection, to do this book-keeping on M not only mixes concerns, but it ends up without winning as much as it seemed to have promised. The reason is that, even if the lower bound of say M_{i+k} is known, once the loop has advanced i to investigate the largest palindrome at the current index $i + k$, it will still be necessary to investigate the possibility of all palindromes larger than this lower bound. Nothing is therefore gained by knowing a lower bound explicitly.

Furthermore, trying to identify the "middle" of the interval $[i, i + j)$ can be error-prone and confusing. One has to account for whether there are an odd or even number of elements in the interval and ensure that in all circumstances A_{i+k} and $A_{i+j-1-k}$ are the correct entries to be matched. Further investigation of these matters is left as an exercise.

4.4 Raster Lines

We now turn attention to a problem in the domain of computer graphics: draw the best approximation of a straight line between integer co-ordinates (x_ℓ, y_ℓ) and (x_h, y_h) using the function $draw(x, y)$ which colours a pixel at x and y where x and y are integers. (In the jargon of computer graphics: draw a raster line between (x_ℓ, y_ℓ) and (x_h, y_h).) For simplicity, the problem is restricted to a line whose slope is in the interval $(0°, 45°)$. It is easy to generalize the results for any other slope.

In [23] Gutknecht derived the solution to this problem in a correctness by construction fashion to illustrate the educational benefits of this development approach. The result is the famous Breshenham algorithm, normally presented in Graphics courses.

At first sight, the solution to the problem seems clear. It is easy to use simple secondary school geometry to determine the equation of a straight line between the

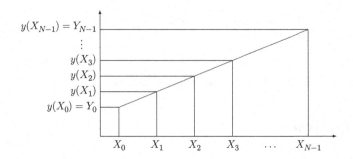

Fig. 4.10 Raster line problem

two given points. It is also easy to determine from this equation, for any real-valued
x-co-ordinate, the corresponding real-value of the y-co-ordinate. It would seem that
all we need is a loop in which the integer values $x_\ell, x_\ell + 1, x_\ell + 2, \ldots, x_h$ are caste
into real values, plug them into the equation to find the corresponding real-values of
y in each case, find the best integer approximation of y and invoke the $draw(x, y)$
method. However, real-valued arithmetic is inefficient in hardware and in graphics
applications, efficiency is at a high premium. The algorithm we derive executes in
integer-valued arithmetic only!

4.4.1   Formulating the Problem

It will be convenient to recast this problem slightly. The co-ordinates (x_ℓ, y_ℓ) and
(x_h, y_h) given in the initial formulation are will be seen as co-ordinates (X_0, Y_0)
and (X_{N-1}, Y_{N-1}) respectively, where X and Y are two arrays such that $X.len = Y.len = N \geq 2$. Instead of invoking a function $draw(x, y)$ to colour pixels, we
shall simply store in $(X_i, Y_i), i = 1, \ldots, N - 2$ the co-ordinates of the pixels that
need to be coloured. At the end, we will show that the resulting algorithm can easily
be transformed into one which invokes $draw(x, y)$ instead. The reason for relying
on array notation is to stay aligned with the derivations to date in this text.

If we are to colour in integer-valued pixels, it is clear that the X values are
separated by 1 unit from each other, i.e., that $\forall j : [1, N) \cdot (X_j = X_{(j-1)} + 1)$,
or alternatively:

$$\forall j : [0, N) \cdot (X_j = X_0 + j).$$

The problem is to step through these X values and determine the corresponding
integer Y value.

The scenario shown in Fig. 4.10 should be interpreted as showing integer X_i
values on the horizontal axis that determine the *real-valued* $y(X_i)$'s, shown on the
vertical axis. These y values have to be approximated by appropriate integer values.

Let $dx \triangleq X_{N-1} - X_0$ and $dy \triangleq Y_{N-1} - Y_0$, respectively. From elementary geometry, we know that the slope of the line is given by $\frac{dy}{dx}$ (which is a legitimate expression because we have assumed throughout that $dx > 0$). The equation of the line is therefore:

$$y(x) = Y_0 + (x - X_0)\frac{dy}{dx}. \tag{4.4}$$

Relying on Morgan's general notation, the problem can be roughly specified as follows:

$$X, Y : \left[(dx > 0) \wedge (dy > 0) \wedge \frac{dy}{dx} < 1, post \right],$$

where *post* can be informally stated as the following predicate:

$\forall j : [0, N) \cdot (j > 0 \implies X_j = X_{(j-1)} + 1) \wedge (Y_j = $ "the best integer approximation of $y(X_j)$ as determined from (4.4))".

Notice the following about this specification:

- *Per definition*, Y_0 is regarded as the best integer approximation of $y(X_0)$ and Y_{N-1}, as the best integer approximation of $y(X_{N-1})$. This can be seen by plugging X_0 and X_{N-1} respectively into (4.4): the result will be that $y(X_0) = Y_0$ and $y(X_{N-1}) = Y_{N-1}$ respectively.
- The precondition is, in fact, implicitly also an invariant over all the code, since it does not use any frame variables. In such circumstances, it is legitimate to use the precondition in reasoning at any point about the code that has been developed at that stage. This has been the case in several previous examples. For example, a precondition for binary search was the sortedness of an array, which is invariantly sorted. That fact was then used in reasoning about the code to be developed.
- In particular, at any point we may use the fact that $\frac{dy}{dx} < 1$ (i.e., the slope is less than 45°) when reasoning about code. We shall see later that this is in fact an important piece of information to use when refining to code.
- The postcondition requires each X value to be one unit larger than its predecessor.

Let us now try to capture more precisely the meaning of "best integer-approximated point".

For any $j : [0, N)$, a reasonable way to round off real-valued $y(X_j)$ to an integer-value, Y_j, is to choose Y_j in such a way that:

$$|y(X_j) - Y_j| \leq \tfrac{1}{2}$$
$$\equiv \quad \{\text{definition of } |z|\}$$
$$-\tfrac{1}{2} \leq (y(X_j) - Y_j) \leq \tfrac{1}{2}$$
$$\equiv \quad \{\text{adding } Y_j \text{ to the inequalities}\}$$
$$Y_j - \tfrac{1}{2} \leq y(X_j) \leq Y_j + \tfrac{1}{2}$$

$\equiv$ {using (4.4)}

$$Y_j - \tfrac{1}{2} \le Y_0 + (X_j - X_0)\tfrac{dy}{dx} \le Y_j + \tfrac{1}{2}$$

$\equiv$ {multiplying by $2dx$ to get rid of divisors}

$$2Y_j \cdot dx - dx \le 2Y_0 \cdot dx + 2(X_j - X_0)dy \le 2Y_j \cdot dx + dx$$

$\equiv$ {subtracting $2Y_j \cdot dx$ and rearranging terms}

$$-dx \le 2(X_j - X_0)dy - 2(Y_j - Y_0)dx \le dx$$

$\equiv$ {introducing a new variable d_j as a new conjunct}

$$(-dx \le d_j \le dx) \wedge (d_j = 2(X_j - X_0)dy - 2(Y_j - Y_0)dx)$$

Thus, every (X_j, Y_j) co-ordinate to be determined must conform to this predicate—a predicate that consists of three conjuncts, namely:

$$(-dx \le d_j) \wedge (d_j \le dx) \wedge (d_j = 2(X_j - X_0)dy - 2(Y_j - Y_0)dx).$$

Implicitly, d has been introduced as an auxiliary *array* variable. Its jth value, d_j, has a specific value for each (X_j, Y_j) pair. (Later it will be seen that there is no need for such array storage and we will simply overwrite d_j when its previous value is no longer necessary.)

To avoid non-determinism, let us decide to always choose Y_j and d_j so that the lower bound for d_j that is given above is always a strict inequality. Effectively, therefore, we strengthen the above predicate to:

$$(-dx < d_j) \wedge (d_j \le dx) \wedge (d_j = 2(X_j - X_0)dy - 2(Y_j - Y_0)dx).$$

Our previous postcondition can now be stated more formally, and more accurately, as:

$$post \triangleq \forall j : [0, N) \cdot ((j > 0 \implies X_j = X_{(j-1)} + 1) \wedge$$
$$(-dx < d_j \le dx) \wedge (d_j = 2(X_j - X_0)dy - 2(Y_j - Y_0)dx)).$$

As an aside, note that it is not obvious—merely by inspecting *post*—to conclude that for a given integer X_j there will be unique integer values for Y_j and d_j that will satisfy *post*. At this stage, we remain open to the possibility that there may be more than one pair of integer values for Y_j and d_j (or perhaps no pair of integer values at all), and let the mathematics sort the matter out as we go along.

Also note that since X_0 and Y_0 are given, and since it is also given that $dx > 0$, choosing $d_0 = 0$ ensures that this predicate holds for (X_0, Y_0).

4.4.2 Deriving the Loop

It is now easy to see how we can use generalize *post* into an invariant, namely:

$$inv(i) \triangleq \forall j : [0, i)((j > 0 \implies X_j = X_{(j-1)} + 1) \wedge$$
$$(-dx < d_j \leq dx) \wedge (d_j = 2(X_j - X_0)dy - 2(Y_j - Y_0)dx)). \quad (4.5)$$

Recalling that $pre = (dx > 0) \wedge (dy > 0) \wedge \frac{dy}{dx} < 1$, and noting that the array d should be included as a frame variable in our specification (since it will be necessary to set and change d if we are to attain the invariant), we refine the original specification in the now familiar fashion as follows:

$\quad X, Y, d : [pre, post]$

$\sqsubseteq \quad$ {Rewriting *post* and including i as a frame variable}

$\quad X, Y, i, d : [pre, inv(i) \wedge (i = N)]$

$\sqsubseteq \quad$ {Sequence rule to attain $inv(i)$}

$\quad X, Y, i, d : [pre, inv(i)];$

$\quad X, Y, i, d : [inv(i), inv(i) \wedge (i = N)]$

$\sqsubseteq \quad$ {Justified below }

$\quad i, d_0 := 1, 0$

$\quad ; X, Y, i, d : [inv(i), inv(i) \wedge (i = N)]$

$\sqsubseteq \quad$ {Repeat rule with variant: $N - i$}

$\quad i, d_0 := 1, 0;$

$\quad \textbf{do } (i \neq N) \rightarrow$

$\quad\quad X, Y, i, d : [inv(i) \wedge i \neq N, inv(i) \wedge 0 \leq N - i < N - i_0]$

$\quad \textbf{od}$

To justify the initialisation step, we have to show that $pre \implies inv(i)[i, d_0 \backslash 1, 0]$. This is easily done as follows:

$inv(i)[i, d_0 \backslash 1, 0]$

$\equiv \quad$ {Substituting the definition of $inv(i)$}

$(\forall j : [0, i)((j > 0 \implies X_j = X_{(j-1)} + 1) \wedge$
$(-dx < d_j \leq dx) \wedge (d_0 = 2(X_j - X_0)dy - 2(Y_j - Y_0)dx))[i, d_0 \backslash 1, 0]$

$\equiv \quad$ {Replacing i with 1, the interval of interest reduces to $[0, 1)$, only $j = 0$ is relevant}

$(-dx < d_0 \leq dx) \wedge (d_0 = 2(X_0 - X_0)dy - 2(Y_0 - Y_0)dx))[d_0 \backslash 0]$

$\equiv \quad$ {Replacing d_0 with 0}

$(-dx < 0 \leq dx) \wedge (0 = 0)$

$\equiv \quad$ { since $dx > 0$ is given}

true

Thus $pre \implies inv(i)[i, d_0 \backslash 1, 0]$ and the initialisation assignment is justified.

4.4.3   Developing the Loop's Body

At this stage, we need to refine the loop's body from the specification, and we proceed as follows. Since we know a priori that we will have to increment i in the loop, we might as well apply the "following assignment" rule as a first step to achieve this, and simultaneously remove from further consideration the variant predicate, since it is fairly obvious that it will be fulfilled.

$$X, Y, i, d : [inv(i) \wedge (i \neq N), inv(i) \wedge 0 \leq N - 1 - i < N - 1 - i_0]$$

$\sqsubseteq$ {Following assignment rule}

$$X, Y, d : [inv(i) \wedge (i \neq N), inv(i)[i \backslash i + 1]; i := i + 1$$

$\sqsubseteq$ {Substitution}

$$X, Y, d : [inv(i) \wedge (i \neq N), inv(i + 1)]; i := i + 1$$

In considering how to refine

$$X, Y, d : [inv(i) \wedge (i \neq N), inv(i + 1)]$$

it seems reasonable to change only the frame variables X_i, Y_i and d_i. All other variables in the arrays, X, Y and d remain unchanged. The way in which X_i should change is quite clear: set X_i to $X_{i-1} + 1$.

In considering how Y_i might change, the following is a key insight:

Because $\frac{dy}{dx} < 1$, when incrementing X_i by one unit, Y_i either stays the same as Y_{i-1}, or Y_i is one unit more than Y_{i-1}.

There are no circumstances under which Y_i should be increased by more than 1 (for then the slope of the line would be greater than 45°); neither should Y_i ever be decreased (for then the slope would be negative).

This key insight suggests that a select statement is needed in which there are at least two guards, say $G1$ and $G2$. Each guard should handle one of the different cases for updating Y_i. In both guard bodies, X_i should increment by 1 unit, as indicated above.[5]

However, at this point of our reasoning, it is not clear what $G1$ or $G2$ should be, and neither do we have any idea of how d_i should be updated in the respective cases. Let us suppose that d_i should be updated by two values are E_1 and E_2 respectively in the two respective cases. We therefore surmise that the following refinement will be possible:

---

[5]This fact suggests that the updating of X_i might have been handled by the earlier applied "following assignment" refinement step. However, nothing is lost by not doing so.

$X, Y, d : [inv(i) \wedge (i \neq N), inv(i + 1)]$

$\sqsubseteq$ {Assuming that $inv(i) \wedge (i \neq N) \Rightarrow G1 \vee G2$}

    if $G1 \rightarrow X, Y, d : [G1 \wedge inv(i) \wedge (i \neq N), inv(i + 1)]$

    $\|$ $G2 \rightarrow X, Y, d : [G2 \wedge inv(i) \wedge (i \neq N), inv(i + 1)]$

    fi

$\sqsubseteq$ {Assuming that the provisos for the respective assignments can be proved}

    if $G1 \rightarrow X_i, Y_i, d := X_{i-1} + 1, Y_{i-1}, E_1$

    $\|$ $G2 \rightarrow X_i, Y_i, d := X_{i-1} + 1, Y_{i-1} + 1, E_2$

    fi

To economise a little on notation, define the predicate:

$$dval(j) \triangleq (-dx < d_j \leq dx) \wedge (d_j = 2(X_j - X_0)dy - 2(Y_j - Y_0)dx)$$

and note that

$$inv(i + 1) \equiv inv(i) \wedge (X_i = X_{(i-1)} + 1) \wedge dval(i). \tag{4.6}$$

Begin by considering the first guard's postcondition, after substitution required because of the assignment, i.e.:

    $inv(i + 1)[X_i, Y_i, d_i \backslash X_{i-1} + 1, Y_{i-1}, E_1]$

$\equiv$ {Using equivalence (4.6)}

    $(inv(i) \wedge (X_i = X_{(i-1)} + 1) \wedge dval(i))[X_i, Y_i, d_i \backslash X_{i-1} + 1, Y_{i-1}, E_1]$

$\equiv$ {Since substituting in $(X_i = X_{(i-1)} + 1)$ yields true }

    $(inv(i) \wedge dval(i))[X_i, Y_i, d_i \backslash X_{i-1} + 1, Y_{i-1}, E_1]$

$\equiv$ {Since X_i, Y_i, d_i do not appear in $inv(i)$ }

    $inv(i) \wedge dval(i)[X_i, Y_i, d_i \backslash X_{i-1} + 1, Y_{i-1}, E_1]$

Recall that our intended assignment is only allowed if the precondition of the original specification (in guard 1) everywhere implies the above expression—i.e., we require that:

$$G1 \wedge inv(i) \wedge (i \neq N) \Rightarrow inv(i) \wedge dval(i) [X_i, Y_i, d_i \backslash X_{i-1} + 1, Y_{i-1}, E_1].$$

Now since that precondition contains the conjunct $inv(i)$, all we need to show to make the assignment legitimate is that:

$$G1 \wedge inv(i) \wedge (i \neq N) \Rightarrow dval(i) [X_i, Y_i, i, d_i \backslash X_{i-1} + 1, Y_{i-1}, i + 1, E_1].$$

Recall that $dval(i)$ consists of the conjuncts $-dx < d_i \leq dx$ and the equality $d_i = 2dy(X_i - X_0) - 2dx(Y_i - Y_0)$. Let us first consider the substitution in the latter conjunct, i.e., in the equality. We then have:

$$E_1 = 2dy(X_{i-1} + 1 - X_0) - 2dx(Y_{i-1} - Y_0)$$

$\equiv$ {Rearranging terms}

$$E_1 = 2dy(X_{i-1} - X_0) - 2dx(Y_{i-1} - Y_0) + 2dy$$

$\equiv$ {Since $d_{i-1} = 2dy(X_{i-1} - X_0) - 2dx(Y_{i-1} - Y_0)$}

$$E_1 = d_{i-1} + 2dy$$

If we now decide to assign to d_i the value $d_{i-1} + 2dy$, and make this substitution instead of E_1 in $dval(i)$, the first conjunct in $dval(i)$ becomes:

$$-dx < d_{i-1} + 2dy \leq dx$$

and the second conjunct becomes true. This means that the assignment in the body of the first guarded command is legitimate, only if the following can be shown:

$$G1 \wedge inv(i) \wedge (i \neq N) \Rightarrow -dx < d_{i-1} + 2dy \wedge d_{i-1} + 2dy \leq dx.$$

Now recall that $inv(i)$ contains a conjunct of the form $-dx < d_{i-1}$. Since it is given that $dy > 0$, this certainly means that if $dx < d_{i-1}$ holds, then $-dx < d_{i-1} + 2dy$ also holds.

On the other hand, we can be sure that $d_{i-1} + 2dy \leq dx$ if we choose to define $G1$ as:

$$G1 \triangleq d_{i-1} + 2dy \leq dx.$$

If we defined $G1$ any weaker, then the "implies everywhere" relationship will no longer be guaranteed. On the other hand, there does not seem to be any cogent reason for defining $G1$ stronger than it is.

What we have therefore shown is that the postcondition of the first guarded command will be guaranteed if the guarded command is formulated as:

$$(d_{i-1} + 2dy \leq dx) \rightarrow X_i, Y_i, d_i := X_{i-1} + 1, Y_{i-1}, d_{i-1} + 2dy.$$

Arguing along exactly the same lines for the second guard (we will not repeat all the details) leads to a derived value for d_i in the case where Y_i is assigned the value $Y_{i-1} + 1$. We proceed as follows:

$$E_2 = 2dy(X_{i-1} + 1 - X_0) - 2dx(Y_{i-1} + 1 - Y_0)$$

$\equiv$ {Rearranging terms}

$$E_2 = 2dy(X_{i-1} - X_0) - 2dx(Y_{i-1} - Y_0) + 2dy - 2dx$$

$\equiv$ {Since $d_{i-1} = 2dy(X_{i-1} - X_0) - 2dx(Y_{i-1} - Y_0)$}

$$E_2 = d_{i-1} + 2dy - 2dx$$

Again, deciding to assign to d_i the value $d_{i-1} + 2dy - 2dx$, and making this substitution instead of E_2 in $dval(i)$, means that the first conjunct of $dval(i)$

becomes: $-dx < d_{i-1} + 2dy - 2dy \leq dx$ and the second becomes true. Similarly to before, the following has to be shown:

$$G2 \wedge inv(i) \wedge (i \neq N) \Rightarrow (-dx < d_{i-1} + 2dy - 2dx) \wedge (d_{i-1} + 2dy - 2dx \leq dx).$$

This time around, we can argue as follows. From $\frac{dy}{dx} < 1$, it is clear that $dy < dx$ and therefore that $dy - dx < 0$. It follows that

$$2dy - 2dx = 2(dy - dx) < 0.$$

Since $d_{i-1} \leq dx$ (which is a conjunct of $inv(i)$) holds, it follows that $(d_{i-1} + 2dy - 2dx \leq dx)$ also holds. As a result, $G2$ can be taken as $(-dx < d_{i-1} + 2dy - 2dx)$. This simplifies to $(dx < d_{i-1} + 2dy)$.

Note that it indeed turns out that $G_2 = \neg G_1$, just as we had hoped for. This means that $inv(i) \wedge (i \neq N) \Rightarrow G1 \vee G2$, which justifies our original refinement to a select command.

4.4.4 Putting it All Together

We can therefore substitute for G_1 and G_2 in the above to get the final algorithm as follows:

```
i, d₀ := 1, 0
;do (i ≠ N) →
    if ((d_{i-1} + 2 · dy) ≤ dx) → X_i, Y_i, d_i := X_{(i-1)} + 1.Y_{(i-1)}, d_{(i-1)} + 2dy
    ▯ (dx < d_{i-1} + 2dy) → X_i, Y_i, d_i := X_{(i-1)} + 1, Y_{(i-1)} + 1, d_{(i-1)} + 2dy - 2dx
    fi
    ;i := i + 1
od
```

This can be refactored to eliminate all arrays, and to insert a $draw(x, y)$ command at appropriate points in the algorithm, thus arriving at a version commonly given as the Breshenham algorithm in Graphics text books. The arrays X, Y and d are really unnecessary from an operational standpoint: we do not need to preserve and explicitly record all pixel pairs that are drawn. Once a pair of pixel values has been computed and drawn, the same variables in which the information was stored may be overwritten with the new information. Furthermore, the i variable was only needed to track the next array index to be used, and may therefore also be eliminated. Finally, since $d + 2dy$ is computed along all computational paths (and also used in the guards) it may be precomputed at the start of each loop iteration and used wherever needed. The result is the following:

$$x, y, d := x_l, y_l, 0$$
$$; draw(x, y)$$
$$; \mathbf{do} \ (x \neq x_h) \rightarrow$$
$$\qquad d := d + 2dy$$
$$\qquad ; \mathbf{if} \ (d \leq dx) \rightarrow \mathbf{skip}$$
$$\qquad \| \quad (d > dx) \rightarrow y, d := y + 1, d - 2dx$$
$$\qquad \mathbf{fi}$$
$$\qquad ; x := x + 1$$
$$\qquad draw(x, y)$$
$$\mathbf{od}$$

4.4.5   Discussion

It was decided to use arrays in this example to retain a fairly familiar context for the reader. If arrays are not used, then the reasoning process becomes a little less familiar, though no less accurate. For example, in an invariant or postcondition, we would not be able to say things like: $\forall j \ : \ [0, i) X_j \cdots$ because we would have used a single variable x that is constantly overwritten in each iteration of the loop. If we wished to remain formal, we would need to extend our notational conventions. We would need some way of not only referring to the value of x before it was last changed, (currently we use x_0, which is admittedly a little ambiguous in that x could be construed as an array), but also to the value of x two iterations back, three iterations back, etc. Alternatively, we could have expressed the invariant, the postcondition, etc., semi-formally, using English narrative where formal mathematical symbols failed. This is not such a bad idea, and is arguably better than not explicitly formulating any invariant or postcondition at all.

In many ways, this example is rather different from previous ones. Previously, when a select statement was anticipated, we had a fair idea of what the guards should be, and then proceeded to determine the body of each guard. This example has thrown up the first occasion where the body of the guard, i.e., the assignments to be made, was predictable from the context. However, the conditions under which the assignments should be made (i.e., the guards themselves) were unknown. We used our theory, specifically the requirements of the proviso of the assignment rule, to reason out what the guards should be in each case.

The final result is indeed rather interesting. We have successfully avoided any real arithmetic. Notice that very few integer operations are needed. They are mostly add/subtract operations. Furthermore, the two multiplication operations involve 2 as an operand. Such a multiplication can be implemented very efficiently by a shift operation.

It should be noted that, because computer screens are not necessarily equally scaled in the X and Y directions, it is possible that the algorithm would produce slightly distorted results on different hardware platforms. Scaling has to take place to correct for such distortions.

4.5 Raster Circle

Following reasoning very similar to the previous section, a raster graphics algorithm for drawing a circle is developed below. The algorithm turns out to be slightly different from the one developed by Bresenham [7] and also from modifications of Bresenham's circle algorithm given in standard texts such as Foley et al. [14]. The resulting algorithm is as efficient as its rivals, and can be transformed into them. The development process focuses parallels that of the raster line drawing algorithm but contains a few more complexities.

4.5.1 Problem Statement

The problem to be addressed is the following:

Draw $\frac{1}{8}$th of the circumference of a circle which has a positive integer, r, as radius and which is centered at $(0,0)$. It is to be drawn on a rastered plain, implying that all co-ordinates (x, y) are integer-valued. The first point is to be drawn at $(0, r)$ and the algorithm should end just before $x > y$. This guarantees that no more than $\frac{1}{8}$th of the circle's circumference is drawn.

Assume that $draw(x, y)$ colours the pixel (x, y). If a complete circle was required, $draw(x, y)$ could be designed to colour 7 additional points on the circle's circumference. These points are easily determined from the point (x, y) using symmetry arguments. The reader can easily determine that if (x, y) lies on the circumference of a circle, then so do the points $(-x, y)$; $(x, -y)$; $(-x, -y)$; (y, x); $(-y, x)$; $(y, -x)$ and $(-y, -x)$. However, if it is important in the context of the problem that no point may be coloured more than once, then special consideration should be given to boundary situations such as $x = 0$, $y = 0$ and $x = y$.

As in the case of a raster line, we regard X and Y as arrays, and we consider that the task is to determine integer values for $(X_0, Y_0), (X_1, Y_1), \ldots$. The first point starts with $X_0 = 0$ and $Y_0 = r$. Once again, we step ahead in X with increments of 1, and this time, our decision is whether to retain the current value of Y with each X increment, or whether to *decrement* Y by 1. This decision is based on the appropriate integer approximation of the real value for Y for a given X, denoted by $y(X)$ and determined from the equation for a circle, namely:

$$y(X) = \sqrt{r^2 - X^2}. \tag{4.7}$$

We thus require that $\forall j \in [0, N) \cdot X_j = X_{j-1} + 1$. In this case, the point at which to stop drawing is not known a priori. Rather, it is determined by the requirement that we only draw $\frac{1}{8}$th of a circle. Thus, we stop drawing as soon as we reach a value j such that $X_j > Y_j$. We therefore assume that N, the length of arrays X and Y, has been chosen to be large enough for the problem at hand. (As in the case of the raster line, in practice it is not necessary to use arrays at all. We do so for explanatory purposes only.)

Once again, the problem can be specified as follows:

$$X_{[0,N)}, Y_{[0,N)} : [r > 0, post],$$

where *post* can be informally described in the following terms:

Some integer, i has been reached such that for $j = 0, 1, \ldots, i$ all the (X_j, Y_j) pairs have been determined in such a way that Y_j is the best integer approximation of $y(X_j)$ defined in (4.7), and $X_j = X_{j-1} + 1$. (However, in the case of $j = 0$, X_0 is given as 0 and is thus not computed from its predecessor. Y_0 is also given as r, but this would also be evident from (4.7).) Moreover, $X_j \leq Y_j$ for all but the last pair, i.e., for $X_j \leq Y_j$ for $j = 0, 1, \ldots, i-1$, but $X_i > Y_i$.

The challenge is to state this more formally, in a way that will aid our development. As before, for any arbitrary j, given X_j, the best integer approximation of $y(X_j)$ can be determined by reasoning as follows:

$$Y_j - 1/2 \leq \sqrt{r^2 - X_j^2} < Y_j + 1/2$$
$$\equiv \quad \{\text{squaring}\}$$
$$Y_j^2 - Y_j + 1/4 \leq r^2 - X_j^2 < Y_j^2 + Y_j + 1/4$$
$$\equiv \quad \{\text{subtracting } Y_j^2 + 1/4\}$$
$$-Y_j \leq r^2 - X_j^2 - Y_j^2 - 1/4 < Y_j$$
$$\equiv \quad \{\text{multiplying by 4 to remove real numbers}\}$$
$$-4Y_j \leq 4\left(r^2 - X_j^2 - Y_j^2\right) - 1 < 4Y_j$$
$$\equiv \quad \{\text{introducing a new variable, } d_j\}$$
$$(-4Y_j \leq d_j < 4Y_j) \wedge d_j = 4\left(r^2 - X_j^2 - Y_j^2\right) - 1$$

This suggests the following update of our informally defined postcondition:

$$post \triangleq \exists i : \mathbb{N} \cdot (X_i > Y_i) \wedge$$
$$\forall j : [0, i) \cdot (X_j \leq Y_j) \wedge$$
$$\forall j : [1, i+1) \cdot (X_j = X_{j-1} + 1) \wedge$$
$$\forall j : [0, i+1) \cdot \left((-4Y_j \leq d_j < 4Y_j) \wedge \left(d_j = 4\left(r^2 - X_j^2 - Y_j^2\right) - 1\right)\right).$$

Note that the various ranges have been chosen very specifically to co-incide with the meaning expressed in the informal description of the postcondition.

4.5.2   From Invariant to Loop

It is now a fairly simple matter to infer an invariant from the postcondition. Simply leave out the requirement that $X_i > Y_i$, but include all the other conjuncts of the postcondition into the invariant.

$$inv(i) \triangleq \forall j : [0,i) \cdot (X_j \leq Y_j) \wedge \tag{4.8}$$

$$\forall j : [1, i+1) \cdot (X_j = X_{j-1} + 1) \wedge \tag{4.9}$$

$$\forall j : [0, i+1) \cdot \left((-4Y_j \leq d_j < 4Y_j) \wedge \left(d_j = 4 \left(r^2 - X_j^2 - Y_j^2 \right) - 1 \right) \right) \tag{4.10}$$

It is thus clearly the case that $inv(i) \wedge (X_i > Y_i) \equiv post$, i.e., if we attain the invariant in a loop in which i is incremented, until the point where $X_i > Y_i$, then the purpose of the algorithm will have been attained. It will be convenient to view the invariant as consisting of three main conjuncts, shown in each line above—i.e., $inv(i) \equiv inv1(i) \wedge inv2(i) \wedge inv3(i)$.

The specification is therefore refined as follows:

$X, Y : [r > 0, post]$

⊑   {Strengthening postcondition and including variables i and d into the frame}

$X, Y, i, d : [r > 0, inv(i) \wedge X_i > Y_i]$

⊑   {Sequence rule to attain $inv(i)$}

$X, Y, i, d : [r > 0, inv(i)];$

$X, Y, i, d : [inv(i), inv(i) \wedge X_i > Y_i]$

⊑   {Assignment rule: $r > 0 \Rightarrow inv(i)[X_0, Y_0, i, d_0 \backslash 0, r, 0, -1] \equiv \textsf{true}$}

$X_0, Y_0, i, d_0 := 0, r, 0, -1;$

$X, Y, i, d : [inv(i), inv(i) \wedge X_i > Y_i]$

⊑   {Repeat rule with variant: $Y_i - X_i$}

$X_0, Y_0, i, d_0 := 0, r, 0, -1;$

$\textbf{do } (X_i \leq Y_i) \rightarrow$

   $X, Y, i, d : [inv(i) \wedge X_i \leq Y_i, inv(i) \wedge (0 \leq Y_i - X_i < Y_{i_0} - X_{i_0})]$

$\textbf{od}$

The assignments for initialization are easily verified.

4.5.3   Refining the Loop's Body

The general requirements of the loop are clear: we need to increment i and then update X_i to be one more than its predecessor. Then we need to set Y_i and d_i to the values required by the invariant. We will allow ourselves the luxury of not being further concerned with the variant part of the postcondition, since all manipulations to X values involve an increase, and all manipulation to Y values involve a decrease. In both these instances, the variant will decrease towards its bottom limit. We note that in incrementing i we will attain $inv1(i)$. In updating X_i we will attain $inv2(i)$. The challenge in updating Y_i and d_i is to attain $inv3(i)$. We proceed as follows:

$$X, Y, i, d : [inv(i) \wedge X_i \leq Y_i, inv1(i) \wedge inv2(i) \wedge inv3(i)]$$

$\sqsubseteq$ {Sequence rule}

$$i : [inv(i) \wedge X_i \leq Y_i, inv1(i) \wedge inv2(i-1) \wedge inv3(i-1)]$$
$$; X : [inv1(i) \wedge inv2(i-1) \wedge inv3(i-1), inv1(i) \wedge inv2(i) \wedge inv3(i-1)]$$
$$; Y, d : [inv1(i) \wedge inv2(i) \wedge inv3(i-1), inv1(i) \wedge inv2(i) \wedge inv3(i)]$$

$\sqsubseteq$ {Assignment rule: See justification below}

$$i := i + 1$$
$$; X : [inv1(i) \wedge inv2(i-1) \wedge inv3(i-1), inv1(i) \wedge inv2(i) \wedge inv3(i-1)]$$
$$; Y, d : [inv1(i) \wedge inv2(i) \wedge inv3(i-1), inv1(i) \wedge inv2(i) \wedge inv3(i)]$$

$\sqsubseteq$ {Assignment rule: See justification below.}

$$i := i + 1; X_i := X_{i-1} + 1$$
$$; Y, d : [inv1(i) \wedge inv2(i) \wedge inv3(i-1), inv1(i) \wedge inv2(i) \wedge inv3(i)]$$

The first assignment, $i := i + 1$, is justified on the grounds that

$$(inv1(i) \wedge inv2(i-1) \wedge inv3(i-1))[i \backslash i + 1] \equiv (inv1(i+1) \wedge inv2(i) \wedge inv3(i)).$$

Since $inv1(i+1) \equiv inv(i) \wedge X_i \leq Y_i$, and since the relevant specification's precondition and postcondition after substitution are identical, the assignment's proviso is fulfilled.

The second assignment, $X_i := X_{i-1} + 1$, is justified on the grounds that the postcondition after substitution transforms as follows:

$$(inv1(i) \wedge inv2(i) \wedge inv3(i-1))[X_i \backslash X_{i-1} + 1] \equiv (inv1(i) \wedge inv2(i-1) \wedge inv3(i-1))$$
$$(4.11)$$

and since this is equivalent to the relevant precondition, the assignment's proviso is again satisfied.

To be convinced of the equivalence claimed in equivalence (4.11) note, firstly, that $inv1(i)$ and $inv3(i-1)$ do not contain any references to X_i. These predicates are therefore unaffected by the substitution on the left hand side, and thus appear unchanged on the right hand side. In $inv2(i)$ the only conjunct that is affected by the substitution asserts that $X_i = X_{i-1} + 1$. However, the substitution changes this to the tautology: $X_{i-1} + 1 = X_{i-1} + 1$. As a result,

$$inv2(i)[X_i \backslash X_{i-1} + 1] \equiv inv2(i-1)$$

and thus equivalence (4.11) holds.

Having updated X_i and i, the task of the last specification in our partially refined loop body, namely,

$$Y, d : [inv1(i) \wedge inv2(i) \wedge inv3(i-1), inv1(i) \wedge inv2(i) \wedge inv3(i)]$$

is to determine values of Y_i and d_i that correspond with the updated X_i value. To do this, we have to do something that renders $inv3(i)$ true, given that $inv3(i-1)$ is the starting position.

Analogously to the previous line-drawing example, we turn to domain-specific information for clues about how this may be done—i.e., we know that in drawing this particular $\frac{1}{8}$th of a circle, for each increment in the X co-ordinate, the Y co-ordinate will either stay the same in each iteration, or will be one *less* than its predecessor. Thus, we again anticipate a select command with two guards, the first retaining Y_i at its previous value, and the second, decrementing Y_i by 1. As before, we need to work out the conditions under which these values are assigned to Y_i, as well as the values to be assigned to d_i in each case.

The refinement step thus has the following form:

$$X, Y, i, d : [inv1(i) \wedge inv2(i) \wedge inv3(i-1), inv1(i) \wedge inv2(i) \wedge inv3(i)]$$
$$\sqsubseteq \{\text{Select role, anticipating that the precondition} \Rightarrow G_1 \vee G_2\}$$

if $G_1 \rightarrow$
$\quad \{\ inv1(i) \wedge inv2(i) \wedge inv3(i-1) \wedge G_1\ \}$
$\quad Y_i, d_i := Y_{i-1}, E_1$
$\quad \{\ inv(i) \equiv inv1(i) \wedge inv2(i) \wedge inv3(i)\ \}$
$\parallel\ G_2 \rightarrow$
$\quad \{\ inv1(i) \wedge inv2(i) \wedge inv3(i-1) \wedge G_2\ \}$
$\quad Y_i, d_i := Y_{i-1} - 1, E_2$
$\quad \{\ inv(i) \equiv inv1(i) \wedge inv2(i) \wedge inv3(i)\ \}$
fi

Once more, note that for each guarded command, we need to choose a guard, G, and assignments to Y_i and d_i so that, loosely speaking the following holds: $inv3(i-1) \wedge G \Rightarrow inv3(i)[\text{substitution}]$. And since $inv3(i) \equiv inv3(i-1) \wedge (-4Y_i \leq d_i < 4Y_i) \wedge (d_i = 4(r^2 - X_i^2 - Y_i^2) - 1)$, the essence of our task for each guard, is to find G, Y_i and d_i such that:

$$G \Rightarrow (-4Y_i \leq d_i < 4Y_i) \wedge \left(d_i = 4\left(r^2 - X_i^2 - Y_i^2\right) - 1\right) \text{[substitution]}.$$

Again, we use the predicate $\left(d_i = 4\left(r^2 - X_i^2 - Y_i^2\right) - 1\right)$ to fix a value to be assigned to d_i for a given Y_i (i.e., depending on whether Y_i stays the same as Y_{i-1} or decrements by 1). To find such a d_i means to render this predicate true when the associated values for Y_i and d_i are plugged into it.

Having found such values for Y_i and d_i, we then have to select a value for the guard such that

$$G \Rightarrow (-4Y_i \leq d_i < 4Y_i) \text{[substitution]} \wedge \text{true}.$$

With the forgoing as a general outline of our refinement strategy, we now determine values to be assigned to d_i in each guarded command.

4.5.4   Determining the Guards

As just pointed out, the values to be assigned to d_i can be determined by considering $d_i = 4\left(r^2 - X_i^2 - Y_i^2\right) - 1$ in the $inv3(i)$ part of the postcondition, when making the substitutions prescribed by the assignment rule's proviso. Note that in simplifying the expressions that we get after substitution, we are allowed to rely on equality relationships that otherwise form part of the postcondition context under consideration. In particular, since $inv2(i)$ contains a conjunct stating that $X_i = X_{i-1} + 1$, we will be justified in replacing X_i by X_{i-1} if it suites out purpose.

Considering the first guard, we get:

$$\left(d_i = 4\left(r^2 - X_i^2 - Y_i^2\right) - 1\right)[Y_i, d_i \backslash Y_{i-1}, E_1]$$

$\equiv$ {Substitution and since $X_i = X_{i-1} + 1$ by $inv2(i)$}

$$E_1 = 4\left(r^2 - (X_{i-1} + 1)^2 - Y_{i-1}^2\right) - 1$$

$\equiv$ {Squaring}

$$E_1 = 4\left(r^2 - \left(X_{i-1}^2 + 2X_{i-1} + 1\right) - Y_{i-1}^2\right) - 1$$

$\equiv$ {Arithmetic}

$$E_1 = 4\left(r^2 - X_{i-1}^2 - (2X_{i-1} + 1) - Y_{i-1}^2\right) - 1$$

$\equiv$ {Arithmetic}

$$E_1 = 4\left(r^2 - X_{i-1}^2 - Y_{i-1}^2\right) - 1 - 4(2X_{i-1} + 1)$$

$\equiv$ $\{d_{i-1} = 4(r^2 - X_{i-1}^2 - Y_{i-1}^2) - 1\}$

$$E_1 = d_{i-1} - 8X_{i-1} - 4$$

In the second case we get:

$$\left(d_i = 4\left(r^2 - X_i^2 - Y_i^2\right) - 1\right)[Y_i, d_i \backslash Y_{i-1} - 1, E_2]$$

$\equiv$ {Substitutions and since $X_i = X_{i-1} + 1$ by $inv2(i)$}

$$E_2 = 4(r^2 - (X_{i-1} + 1)^2 - (Y_{i-1} - 1)^2) - 1$$

$\equiv$ {Expanding $(X_{i-1} + 1)^2$}

$$E_2 = 4(r^2 - X_{i-1}^2 - (2X_{i-1} + 1) - (Y_{i-1} - 1)^2) - 1$$

$\equiv$ {Expanding with $-(Y_{i-1} - 1)^2$}

$$E_2 = 4\left(r^2 - X_{i-1}^2 - (2X_{i-1} + 1) - Y_{i-1}^2 + (2Y_{i-1} - 1)\right) - 1$$

$\equiv$ {Arithmetic}

$$E_2 = 4\left(r^2 - X_{i-1}^2 - (2X_{i-1} + 1) - Y_{i-1}^2 + (2Y_{i-1} - 1)\right) - 1$$
$$-4(2X_{i-1} + 1 - 2Y_{i-1} + 1)$$

$$\equiv \quad \{d_{i-1} = 4\left(r^2 - X_{i-1}^2 - Y_{i-1}^2\right) - 1\}$$
$$E_2 = d_{i-1} - 4(2X_{i-1} + 1 - 2Y_{i-1} + 1)$$
$$\equiv \quad \{\text{Simplification}\}$$
$$E_2 = d_{i-1} + 8(Y_{i-1} - X_{i-1} - 1)$$

The specification to be refined is therefore the following:

> **if** $G_1 \rightarrow \{inv1(i) \wedge inv2(i) \wedge inv3(i - 1) \wedge X_{i-1} \leq Y_{i-1} \wedge G_1\}$
> $Y_i, d_i := Y_{i-1}, d_{i-1} - 4(2X_{i-1} + 1)$
> $\{inv(i)\}$
> **|** $G_2 \rightarrow \{inv1(i) \wedge inv2(i) \wedge inv3(i - 1) \wedge X_{i-1} \leq Y_{i-1} \wedge G_2\}$
> $Y_i, d_i := Y_{i-1} - 1, d_{i-1} + 8(Y_{i-1} - X_{i-1} - 1)$
> $\{inv(i)\}$
> **fi**

However, by the assignment rule, this refinement will only be valid if the precondition in each case everywhere implies the postcondition in which all occurrences of Y_i and d_i are replaced by their new values.

4.5.5 Deriving the Guards

For the first guard, it is required to show the following "implies everywhere" relationship:

$$inv1(i) \wedge inv2(i) \wedge inv3(i - 1) \wedge X_{i-1} \leq Y_{i-1} \wedge G_1$$
$$\Rightarrow inv(i)[Y_i, d_i \backslash Y_{i-1}, d_{i-1} - 4(2X_{i-1} + 1)]. \tag{4.12}$$

In order to do that, consider the following steps to transform the consequent.

$inv(i)[Y_i, d_i \backslash Y_{i-1}, d_{i-1} - 4(2X_{i-1} + 1)]$
$\equiv \quad$ {Since $inv1(i)$ and $inv2(i)$ do not contain terms to be substituted}
$inv1(i) \wedge inv2(i) \wedge inv3(i)[Y_i, d_i \backslash Y_{i-1}, d_{i-1} - 4(2X_{i-1} + 1)]$
$\equiv \quad$ {Since $inv3(i - 1)$ does not contain terms to be submitted}
$inv1(i) \wedge inv2(i) \wedge inv3(i - 1) \wedge$
$((-4Y_i \leq d_i < 4Y_i) \wedge (d_i = 4\left(r^2 - X_i^2 - Y_i^2\right) - 1)) [Y_i, d_i \backslash Y_{i-1}, d_{i-1} - 4(2X_{i-1}+1)]$
$\equiv \quad$ {Second conjunct evaluates to true after substitution}
$inv1(i) \wedge inv2(i) \wedge inv3(i - 1) \wedge$
$(-4Y_{i-1} \leq d_{i-1} - 4(2X_{i-1} + 1) < 4Y_{i-1}) \wedge \text{true}$
$\equiv \quad$ {Making implied conjuncts explicit}
$inv1(i) \wedge inv2(i) \wedge inv3(i - 1) \wedge$
$(-4Y_{i-1} \leq d_{i-1} - 4(2X_{i-1} + 1)) \wedge (d_{i-1} - 4(2X_{i-1} + 1) < 4Y_{i-1})$

$\equiv$ {Since $d_{i-1} < 4Y_{i-1}$ is a conjunct in $inv3(i-1)$ and $-4(2X_{i-1}+1) < 0$}
  $inv1(i) \wedge inv2(i) \wedge inv3(i-1) \wedge (-4Y_{i-1} \le d_{i-1} - 4(2X_{i-1}+1))$

Noting the correspondence between the antecedent this form of the consequence in (4.12), it is clear that a sufficient condition for the "implies everywhere" relationship to hold, is when

$$G_1 \equiv -4Y_{i-1} \le d_{i-1} - 8X_{i-1} - 4$$

or, equivalently

$$G_1 \equiv d_{i-1} \ge 4(2X_{i-1} - Y_{i-1} + 1)$$

Arguing along similar lines, it will be found that

$$G_2 \equiv d_{i-1} < 4(2X_{i-1} - Y_{i-1} + 1)$$

The details are left as an exercise.

4.5.6   Putting it All Together

From all of the above, the following circle-drawing algorithm has been derived:

```
X₀, Y₀, i, d₀ := 0, r, 0, −1;
{ invariant: inv(i) }
do  Xᵢ ≤ Yᵢ →
      i := i + 1; Xᵢ := Xᵢ₋₁ + 1;
      if  dᵢ₋₁ ≥ 4(2Xᵢ₋₁ − Yᵢ₋₁ + 1) → Yᵢ, dᵢ := Yᵢ₋₁, dᵢ₋₁ − 4(2Xᵢ₋₁ + 1)
      ▯  dᵢ₋₁ < 4(2Xᵢ₋₁ − Yᵢ₋₁ + 1) → Yᵢ, dᵢ := Yᵢ₋₁ − 1, dᵢ₋₁−8(Xᵢ₋₁ − Yᵢ₋₁+1)
      fi
od
```

If we rewrite this algorithm without the use of arrays, we can, as before, eliminate variable i, and overwrite x, y and d values to get the following. Before overwriting a previously computed (x, y) co-ordinate we call the $draw(x, y)$ function to display the co-ordinate as a pixel on the screen.

However, there are a number of points that need careful consideration.

• It is not entirely clear where to invoke $draw(x, y)$. Notice that x and y are first updated (in the loop's body) and then checked (in the loop's condition) to see whether they are still in the range of the first $\frac{1}{8}$th of the circumference of the circle. Therefore, if we simply insert a $draw(x, y)$ invocation as the last command in the loop's body, we run the risk of possibly drawing a pixel that is outside of those bounds in the final iteration of the loop. Should this be an important consideration in the context of some problem, then we would need a select statement that checks whether the x and y values computed are still within range, only invoking $draw(x, y)$ if they are. Furthermore, if we took this approach, then we would also have to invoke $draw(x, y)$ before the loop, otherwise the first pixel will not be drawn.

An alternative solution would invoke $draw(x, y)$ at the beginning of the loop, without invoking it before the loop starts. There is no need for concern that the command will not be invoked if the loop is never entered, since our initialisation of x and y to 0 and r respectively guarantees that the loop always completes at least one iteration.

- We should also give consideration to the fact that the assignments in the guarded command above rely on X_{i-1} whose value is actually $X_i - 1$. Now if, below, we update x by overwriting it, then later references to X_{i-1} in the above algorithm should be replaced with $x - 1$ instead of by x.

Accounting for these two points, the revised algorithm becomes:

$$x, y, d := 0, r, -1;$$
$$\{ \text{ invariant: } inv(i) \ \}$$
$$\textbf{do } x \le y \rightarrow$$
$$\quad draw(x, y);$$
$$\quad x := x + 1;$$
$$\quad \textbf{if } d \ge 4(2x - y - 1) \rightarrow d := d - 4(2x - 1)$$
$$\quad \textbf{|} \ \ d < 4(2x - y - 1) \rightarrow y, d := y - 1, d - 8(x - y)$$
$$\quad \textbf{fi}$$
$$\textbf{od}$$

Although this software correctness-by-construction approach has derived an algorithm that is fully correct, it differs from the so-called mid-point circle drawing algorithm that appears in many graphics text books. This algorithm is given below:

$$x, y, d, p, t := 0, r, 3, (1 - r), (-2 * r + 5);$$
$$\textbf{do } x \le y \rightarrow$$
$$\quad draw(x, y);$$
$$\quad \textbf{if } p < 0 \rightarrow d, p, t := d + 2, p + d, t + 2$$
$$\quad \textbf{|} \ \ p \ge 0 \rightarrow y, d, p, t := y - 1, d + 2, p + t, t + 4$$
$$\quad \textbf{fi};$$
$$\quad x := x + 1;$$
$$\textbf{od}$$

Our derived algorithm is less efficient than the mid-point circle drawing algorithm in that the former involves relatively complicated guards to be tested, as well as several more operations per guard body than required by the latter. On the other hand, our derived algorithm only needs 3 variables, whereas the conventional one needs 5, so we have a slight gain in space efficiency.

Furthermore, quite a lot of refactoring can be carried out on our derived algorithm to make it more efficient. For example, noting that $4(2x - 1)$ is computed several times and noting that it increases in every iteration by 4 (since x increases by 1), the value could be stored in a variable, say z, initialized to -4 (i.e., since

$4(2.0 - 1) = -4)$ and then incremented by 4 in every iteration. This yields the somewhat simpler algorithm that has an additional variable, namely:

$$x, y, z, d := 0, r, -4, -1;$$
$$\{ \text{ invariant: } inv(i) \ \}$$
$$\textbf{do } x \le y \rightarrow$$
$$\quad draw(x, y);$$
$$\quad x, z := x + 1, z + 4;$$
$$\quad \textbf{if } d \ge z - 4y \rightarrow d := d - z$$
$$\quad \textbf{|} \ d < z - 4y \rightarrow y, d := y - 1, d + 8(x - y)$$
$$\quad \textbf{fi}$$
$$\textbf{od}$$

There are yet further possibilities for transformation, and it can be shown that after several such transformations, the mid-point circle algorithm is derived. However, details are beyond the scope of this present text.

4.6   Majority Voting

The problem solved in this section is also briefly discussed in the previously mentioned guest editorial by Gutknecht [23]. The problem is a rather strange one, and is very cryptically explained in that editorial. It can be stated as follows.

> Each element in a sequence, b, of length $M > 0$, is a vote for some arbitrary individual. Write a program that eliminates all but one individual, x, in such a way that no individual who is eliminated has a majority of votes.

You should note the requirements of the problem very carefully: the claim is not that x has the majority of votes. Rather, it is that if the algorithm selects x as its outcome, then no individual other than x may have the majority of votes. In other words, the problem statement requires that x has to be the winning candidate if x has *strictly more than* 50% of the votes. If no-one has more than 50% of the votes, then x may be *any arbitrary individual*. This latter statement holds, even if some individual other than x has exactly 50% of the votes.

Furthermore, the problem statement is entirely silent about how many different candidates there may be. The algorithm is intended to function properly, irrespective of the number of candidates, and it is not required that this number is known beforehand!

To take a few concrete examples, consider the five different ballot count scenarios for candidates A, B and C given in the table below. (Ignore the last two columns for the moment.) The table is intended to illustrate that each of the five scenarios could be a legitimate outcome of the majority voting algorithm.

In each scenario, A and B are assumed to have been eliminated as majority candidates by the algorithm, and C is left as x—the *possible* majority candidate.

	A	B	C (x)	Total (M)	s range wrt (4.14) and (4.15)	s range wrt C and Total
Scenario 1	5	5	90	100	5–50	5–10
Scenario 2	20	10	70	100	20–50	20–30
Scenario 3	40	5	55	100	40–50	40–45
Scenario 4	30	30	40	100	30–50	30–60
Scenario 5	40	40	20	100	40–50	40–80

In scenarios 1, 2 and 3, C is *in fact* the majority candidate. In scenario 4, neither C nor any other candidate is the majority candidate, but C, still designated the *possible* majority candidate, happens to have the most number of votes (although not more than 50%). In scenario 5, C does not even have the most votes, but A and B have been explicitly excluded from being majority candidates and the algorithm has still designated C as the *possible* majority candidate.

The algorithm *has to* deliver $x = C$ as outcome in the first three scenarios. It may (but need not) deliver $x = C$ as outcome in the fourth and fifth scenario.

4.6.1 Formulating the Problem

To formalize the required postcondition, we rely on the notation relating to sequences which was introduced in Sect. 2.6.2. If you have forgotten it, it would probably be a good idea to briefly review that section at this stage.

We claim that for any candidate, y, who appears on the ballot, if $y \neq x$ then it must be the case that $b.y \leq M/2$—the number of votes for y in sequence b is less than or equal to the total number of votes. If this were not so, then it would be incorrect to designate x as the possibly winning candidate.

However, as will be demonstrated below, sometimes this upper bound of $M/2$ on $b.y$ can be much too liberal. Let us take s to be an alternative upper bound of all such $b.y$'s, where we assume that $s \leq M/2$. We thus have:

$$\forall y : (y \neq x) \cdot b.y \leq M/2, \tag{4.13}$$

$$\forall y : (y \neq x) \cdot b.y \leq s \tag{4.14}$$

$$\text{and } 2s \leq M. \tag{4.15}$$

In fact, it is clear that if we rely on (4.14) and (4.15) alone, then (4.13) can be treated as redundant. The problem can thus be specified as:

$$x, s : [\text{true}, \forall y : (y \neq x) \cdot b.y \leq s \wedge 2s \leq M].$$

Now consider the *penultimate* column in the above table. It shows the ranges over which s may be chosen, while still complying with (4.14) and (4.15). In each case, the lower bound is the maximum of A and B's votes (shown in the first two columns), while the upper bound is $50 = M/2$.

The question arises: can we not constrain s more tightly? Clearly, one cannot constrain the lower bound any more—the bound is fully determined by the votes for A and B to date. However, the upper bound in the second last column seems overly generous in some scenarios. For example, in scenario 1, any value of s more than 10 (which is the number of votes not allotted to C) represents an overly generous upper limit.

In the last column of the table above, an alternative upper limit on s is used, namely $(M - b.x)$—i.e., the number of votes left after allocating votes given to x. It is clear that in some cases, this bound overrides the bounds implied by (4.14) and (4.15), while in other cases, this does not happen. This suggests that an alternative bound could be placed on s, namely:

$$s \leq M - b.x. \tag{4.16}$$

We can therefore refine the above specification, by strengthening the postcondition with the bound in (4.16), as follows:

$$x, s : [\text{true}, \forall y : (y \neq x) \cdot b.y \leq s \wedge 2s \leq M \wedge s \leq M - b.x].$$

Note in passing, that this last bound, (4.16), is not strictly necessary in the postcondition, in the sense that if (4.14) and (4.15) hold, then the result will already comply strictly with the statement of the majority voting problem.

4.6.2   Arriving at an Invariant and Developing the Loop

An invariant predicate can now be defined; one that asserts that after the first m ballots have been counted, (4.14), (4.15) and (4.16) will hold. Such an invariant clearly specialises to the required postcondition when m is M.

$$inv(x, s, m) \triangleq \forall y : (y \neq x) \cdot b \uparrow m.y \leq s \wedge 2s \leq m \wedge s \leq m - b \uparrow m.x.$$

We can easily ensure that the invariant holds initially (vacuously) by the initialization actions given below. Refinement now proceeds as follows:

$x, s, m : [\text{true}, inv(x, s, m) \wedge m = M]$

$\sqsubseteq$ {sequence}

$x, s, m : [\text{true}, inv(x, s, m)] \; ; x, s, m : [inv(x, s, m), inv(x, s, m) \wedge m = M]$

$\sqsubseteq$ {assignment}

$x, s, m := b_0, 0, 1;$

$x, s, m : [inv(x, s, m), inv(x, s, m) \wedge m = M]$

$\sqsubseteq$ {repetition, variant $M - m$}

$x, s, m := b_0, 0, 1;$

do $(m \neq M) \rightarrow$

   $x, s, m : [inv(x, s, m) \wedge (m \neq M), inv(x, s, m) \wedge 0 \leq M - m < M - m_0]$

od

We already have a broad notion of how the loop's body will emerge after refinement. Obviously m will have to be incremented (thus decreasing the variant). Each such step will point to a fresh vote in the sequence b, and we will need to decide on how to change the x and/or s (if at all) in each iteration, based on the newly encountered vote. Clearly the loop's body will require a select statement. At this point, let us make a design decision to have the body as a single select statement, with an unknown number of guarded commands, and let us anticipate that the increment in m will take place in each guarded command. Refactoring afterwards can always take place if we find it necessary or desirable.

4.6.3   Developing the Guards

Since we will be refining using selection, we will be dealing with guarded commands of the form:

$G \rightarrow x, s, m : [G \wedge inv(x, s, m) \wedge (m \neq M), inv(x, s, m) \wedge 0 \leq M - m < M - m_0].$

In each case, we shall also want to change the specification into an assignment of the form $x, s, m := E_1(x), E_2(s), E_3(m)$ and to do this we will have to use the assignment rule to argue that the following $\Rightarrow$ holds:

$$G \wedge (m \neq M) \wedge inv(x, s, m) \Rightarrow (inv(x, s, m) \wedge 0 \leq M - m < M - m_0)$$

$$[x, s, m \backslash E_1(x), E_2(s), E_3(m)]. \qquad (4.17)$$

For the present purposes, we will make these arguments rather informally.

The first question we face is: what guards shall we construct? Two possibilities immediately come to mind: guards that determine what to do when $b_m = x$ and those that say what to do when $b_m \neq x$. In the former case, the value of s (upper bound of all $b.y$'s that exclude $b.x$) need not change. Neither should the current "winner" x change. We need merely increment m in order to decrease the variant. The first guarded command can therefore be taken as:

$$b_m = x \rightarrow m := m + 1.$$

We note that the guarded command fulfills the formal requirements: it indeed preserves the invariant, and it ensures that the variant strictly decreases. (The reader may formally check these claims, via the arguments implied by (4.17) above.)

In considering the case of $b_m \neq x$, the situation is a little more complicated. We have to distinguish between two cases: when $2s < m$ and when $2s = m$. (Note that one would have to think the matter through quite deliberately before reaching this conclusion. The fact that we have simply stated this to be the case should not be construed to imply that it should be entirely obvious, even at first sight.)

In the case of $(b_m \neq x) \wedge (2s < m)$, the question arises: do we have reason to change the "winner" from the current value of x? Seemingly not, since there is no candidate $y \neq x$ such that $b \uparrow (m+1).y$ becomes a majority count. When probing b_m, such a y would only become a majority candidate if, just prior to probing b_m, $(b \uparrow m.y = s) \wedge (2s = m)$ is true.

However, in order to guarantee the invariant, the upper bound on the count of y, namely s, should be increased by one, just in case some y is already at its upper bound. We can do this without violating the $(2s \leq m)$ conjunct of the invariant, provided that m is also incremented—something that we need to do in any case in order to decrease the variant. Since both s and m are incremented by 1, and since $b \uparrow m.x$ is unchanged, the third conjunct of the invariant is also preserved. As a result of the foregoing, the second guarded command can be specified as:

$$(b_m \neq x) \wedge (2s < m) \rightarrow s, m := s + 1, m + 1.$$

Once again, we note that the guarded command fulfills the formal requirements: it indeed preserves the invariant, and ensures that the variant strictly decreases. Again, this can be formally checked as an exercise via the arguments implied by (4.17) above.

The case that now remains is where $(b_m \neq x) \wedge (2s = m)$. Here we cannot simply increment both s and m by 1, since that would result in a violation of the invariant conjunct: $(2s \leq m)$. But we must increment m in order to decrease the variant. It seems that we now have no alternative but to change the value of x. To what should we change it? The most likely option seems to be to change it to whatever the value of b_m is at that stage. Furthermore, there is nothing to suggest that s has to be changed in any way. As a result of the foregoing, the third guarded command thus appears to be:

$$(b_m \neq x) \wedge (2s = m) \rightarrow x, m := b_m, m + 1.$$

Our argumentation to arrive at this command might have seemed rather arbitrary. Let us therefore argue the case more convincingly by formally showing that the "implies everywhere" relation in (4.17) holds for this particular guarded command. This means that the following has to be shown:

$$(b_m \neq x) \wedge (2s = m) \wedge (m \neq M) \wedge inv(x, s, m) \Rightarrow$$

$$(inv(x, s, m) \wedge 0 \leq M - m < M - m_0)[x, m \backslash b_m, m + 1].$$

As before, the variant strictly decreases, because m is incremented. The conjuncts referring to the variant are thus true and need not be further considered in our argumentation.

But is the invariant preserved after the assignment? To answer this question, let us substitute $inv(x, s, m)$ by its definition in both the antecedent and consequent, and also carry out the substitution $[x, m \backslash b_m, m + 1]$ required in the consequent. We then get the following:

$$(b_m \neq x) \wedge (2s = m) \wedge (m \neq M) \wedge \tag{4.18}$$

$$\forall y : (y \neq x) \cdot b \uparrow m.y \leq s \wedge \tag{4.19}$$

$$2s \leq m \wedge s \leq m - b \uparrow m.x \tag{4.20}$$

$$\Rightarrow$$

$$\forall y : (y \neq b_m) \cdot b \uparrow (m + 1).y \leq s \wedge \tag{4.21}$$

$$2s \leq m + 1 \wedge \tag{4.22}$$

$$s \leq m + 1 - b \uparrow (m + 1).b_m \tag{4.23}$$

We argue that the antecedent (LHS) everywhere implies the consequent (RHS) by showing that each one of the three conjuncts on the RHS will necessarily also hold, if some combination of conjuncts on the LHS holds. If this can be shown, it will mean that if all of the conjuncts in the LHS hold, then all of the conjuncts on the RHS will also be true.

First conjunct (4.21): Since this conjunct is a universally quantified predicate, it can also be seen as the *set* of conjuncts over each instance of the quantification. The corresponding antecedent set of conjuncts, (4.19), matches those in the consequent in all cases except two candidates: the consequent includes candidate x but excludes candidate b_m; while the antecedent excludes the x candidate, but includes the b_m candidate. Here, our only concern is to argue that if the antecedent holds, then the consequent's conjunct that claims $b \uparrow (m + 1).x \leq s$, will also hold. This can be established by considering the following three antecedent conjuncts, two of which appear in (4.18) and the other in (4.20):

$$(b_m \neq x) \wedge (2s = m) \wedge (s \leq m - b \uparrow m.x)$$

$\Rightarrow$ {Substituting m by $2s$ in last conjunct}

$$(b_m \neq x) \wedge (s \leq 2s - b \uparrow m.x)$$

$\equiv$ {simplifying and rearranging}

$$(b_m \neq x) \wedge (b \uparrow m.x \leq s)$$

$\Rightarrow$ {$b_m \neq x$, means that $b \uparrow m.x = b \uparrow (m + 1).x$ }

$$b \uparrow (m + 1).x \leq s$$

Thus, (4.21) will always hold if the antecedent holds.

Second conjunct (4.22): The relationship $(2s = m)$ holds in (4.18) of the antecedent. This implies everywhere that $(2s \leq m + 1)$ holds. Thus, (4.22) will always hold if the antecedent holds.

Third conjunct (4.23): This conjunct can be seen to be implied everywhere by the antecedent, by considering several of the antecedent's conjuncts collectively, namely the first two conjuncts in (4.18) and the universally quantified conjunct in (4.19):

$$(b_m \neq x) \wedge (2s = m) \wedge \forall y : (y \neq x) \cdot b \uparrow m.y \leq s$$

$\Rightarrow$ {Since $(b_m \neq x)$, consider only $y = b_m$ in $\forall y : (y \neq x) \cdot b \uparrow m.y \leq s$}

$$(2s = m) \wedge b \uparrow m.b_m \leq s$$

$\Rightarrow$ {Since $(2s = m) \equiv (s = m-s)$, replace s by $(m - s)$ in second conjunct}

$$b \uparrow m.b_m \leq m - s$$

$\equiv$ {rearranging terms}

$$s \leq m - b \uparrow m.b_m$$

$\equiv$ {Since $b \uparrow m.b_m = b \uparrow (m + 1).b_m - 1$}

$$s \leq (m + 1) - b \uparrow (m + 1).b_m$$

Again we see that (4.23) will always hold if the antecedent holds.

These arguments, taken together, formally justify our proposed guard and assignments for the third guarded command. As a result of all the above argumentation, we arrive at the following final refinement:

$$
\begin{aligned}
&x, s, m := b_0, 0, 1; \\
&\textbf{do } (m \neq M) \rightarrow \\
&\quad \textbf{if } (b_m = x) \rightarrow m := m + 1 \\
&\quad \|\ (b_m \neq x) \wedge (2s < m) \rightarrow s, m := s + 1, m + 1 \\
&\quad \|\ (b_m \neq x) \wedge (2s = m) \rightarrow x, m := b_m, m + 1 \\
&\quad \textbf{fi} \\
&\textbf{od}
\end{aligned}
$$

4.6.4 Discussion

This is a rather strange, almost magical, algorithm. Neither its derivation, nor its final form, nor the interpretation of its output is obvious.

In regard to its derivation, presumably the conventional informal approach to solving this problem would be to keep a total in memory of the number of votes for each candidate as one iterated through the sequence of ballots. The maximum total would then be determined at the end of the iteration. This would normally require that we knew, a priori, how many candidates there are, or else that we dynamically determined this number as we iterated through the ballot sequence. The present algorithm is totally oblivious of the number of candidates. It merely chugs through the ballot sequence and comes up with an answer, which is admittedly a little obscure as discussed below, but nevertheless correct in terms of the stated postcondition.

In following a less conventional but more formal approach to achieve the postcondition, we needed to derive a loop invariant. The determination of the invariant required quite a lot of thought. To some extent, it could be argued that (4.15) and (4.13) above are be fairly obvious. However, the need for the strengthening brought about by (4.16) is not at all obvious. We only became fully convinced of its necessity (Gutknecht's exposition implies that it is a sort of "nice-to-have") when trying to argue the case for the third guard of the alternation statement. The reader is encouraged to check that it was specifically required in the argumentation at that stage of the above discussion. Without taking note of this invariant relationship, one cannot prove the proviso.

The final form of the algorithm could certainly not be written down by the average programmer without some sort of formal derivation. One of the questions that might be asked about this final form is: should one not also cater for the possibility that $(b_m \neq x) \wedge (2s > m)$? Clearly this would be redundant, since the entire argument in deriving the algorithm is that the invariant must hold before each loop iteration, and it is preserved after each loop iteration. If at any stage $(2s > m)$ became true, then the invariant would be violated. Recall that the semantics of the selection statement is that it fails if none of its guards are satisfied. In the current context, failure in the event of the invariant being violated would be entirely appropriate. It would signal that an error had occurred in our logical reasoning— hopefully something that has not occurred in the foregoing reasoning process.

At the end of the algorithm, s and x have specific values and, of course, M is also given. There does not seem to be any obvious way of using these results to say whether x is definitely the majority candidate or not. At best, one can conclude that if $2s = M$ then x is not a majority candidate. (Why?) But if this happens, one is not entitled to conclude that x is the candidate with the maximum (non-majority) number of votes. Furthermore, it is not legitimate to conclude that if $2s < M$ then x is indeed the majority candidate. This may be the case, but is not necessarily so. The algorithm seems to be based on the notion that: "This is a democracy. Unless the citizens elect a clear winner, then anyone on the ballot list may be chosen as the winner."

Another application of the algorithm (appropriately adapted in terms of the loop's stopping condition) could be where voting takes place on a continuous basis, with the current "winner" being fed back to the voters. One might expect the voters to alter their votes away from worst-choice candidates towards more popular candidates as the voting progresses. Eventually, one might expect a convergence towards the winning candidate as the voting progresses. This kind of scenario is not so far-fetched: it could well be used as a strategy in fault-tolerant computing where several processors are sometimes required to compute the same result and the majority-voted result is used as the correct answer, but only after a period of convergence over time with the same machines somehow moderating their computation according to the current winning outcome, x. Similar scenarios could be considered in optimization algorithms (e.g., particle swarms needing to decide a search direction) where different processes have to "vote" for the next appropriate direction of search.

4.7 Computational Geometry

There are numerous interesting algorithms in a domain of study called computational geometry. We present here, a very simple example taken from work on so-called axial line placement in collections of convex polygons.

4.7.1 Background and Notation

Figure 4.11 depicts a "chain" of convex polygons. The polygons are marked as $A, \ldots, J$. These convex polygons are said to form a chain because they have the following characteristics:

- Polygons A and J each share exactly one side with a neighbouring polygon (namely with B and I respectively).
- All the other polygons each share two sides: one with each of two neighbours.

These shared sides are called adjacencies. The figure also indicates four axial lines crossing adjacencies between polygons. The first runs from polygon A to polygon C; the second from C to E; the third from E to G; and the fourth from H to J. An axial line is therefore characterised by the adjacencies that it intersects. The axial lines that will be of interest must be maximal. A maximal axial line has the property that it cannot be extended in any direction without crossing a side of a polygon that is not an adjacency. All axial lines in Fig. 4.11 are maximal—they cannot be extended in either direction in such a way that they

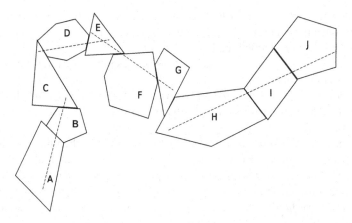

Fig. 4.11 Chain of convex polygons

cross an additional adjacency, even if their orientation (gradient) is changed, or if they are shifted upwards, downwards, left or right.

Our general task is to develop an algorithm to perform maximal axial line placement on a chain of convex polygons. In particular, we want to construct a smallest set of maximal axial lines that ensures that every adjacency is crossed at least once. Note that the axial lines in Fig. 4.11, though maximal, do not conform to the problem's requirements: they leave the adjacency between G and H uncrossed. At least another maximal axial line from F to H is required.[6]

As an aside, one should also note that the minimal set of maximal lines crossing all adjacencies may not necessarily be unique. However, we shall be content with any single solution.

In order to construct the smallest set of maximal axial lines that ensures that every adjacency is crossed at least once, assume that the following is given[7]:

- C is a chain of n convex polygons, $C = c_1, c_2, \ldots c_n$.
- There is an adjacency between polygon c_j and c_{j+1}, denoted by $c_j | c_{j+1}$, for $j = 1, \ldots, n-1$. (Note, therefore, that the first adjacency is $c_1 | c_2$ and the last adjacency is $c_{n-1} | c_n$.)
- $vis(j, i)$ is a predicate method that returns **true** if adjacency $c_j | c_{j+1}$ is partially visible to $c_{i-1} | c_i$. This means that:

---

[6]The figure is obviously just an example and our above conclusion is based on simple visual observation. If the precise co-ordinates of the various vertices in the convex polygons were known, it might turn that an axial line could be drawn from E to H. However, such precision is not of concern in this discussion.

[7]The notation used here is taken from the original formulation of the problem, and therefore deviates from our convention to date of enumerating entities from 0.

- When the predicate is **true**, then an axial line can be drawn that crosses through adjacencies $c_j|c_{j+1}, c_{j+1}|c_{j+2}, \ldots, c_{i-1}|c_i$.
- The predicate is defined for $1 \le j \le i \le n$
- Note that $vis(j, j)$ is construed as **true** because the set of adjacencies to be crossed is empty.
- For all $1 < j < i < n$, if $vis(j, i) \wedge \neg vis(j-1, i) \wedge \neg vis(j, i+1)$ holds, then the axial line that crosses through adjacencies $c_j|c_{j+1}, c_{j+1}|c_{j+2}, \ldots, c_{i-1}|c_i$ is maximal.
- For all $1 \le i < n$, if $vis(1, i) \wedge \neg vis(1, i+1)$ holds, then the axial line that crosses through adjacencies $c_1|c_2, c_2|c_3, \ldots, c_{i-1}|c_i$ is maximal.
- For all $1 < j \le n$, if $vis(j, n) \wedge \neg vis(j-1, n)$ holds, then the axial line that crosses through adjacencies $c_j|c_{j+1}, c_{j+1}|c_{j+2}, \ldots, c_{n-1}|c_n$ is maximal.
- If $vis(1, n)$ holds, then the axial line that crosses through adjacencies $c_1|c_2, c_2|c_3, \ldots, c_{n-1}|c_n$ is maximal.

- *axline*(j, i) is a method that returns an axial line which crosses all adjacencies from $c_j|c_{j+1}$ to $c_{i-1}|c_i$.

  - The precondition of the *axline*(j, i) method is $vis(j, i) \wedge 1 \le j < i \le n$.

- F is a set that contains maximal axial lines in the chain of polygons, C.

4.7.2   The Approach to Solving the Problem

Our task is to construct set F so that it contains the minimal number of maximal axial lines needed to ensure that all adjacencies are crossed at least once. Since F will grow incrementally as part of the algorithm, and therefore have a different content as the algorithm progresses, we will refer to its final state as F^f.

The essential idea is encapsulated in the following, which we shall refer to as the left-to-right approach and abbreviate to the *LRA*:

> Start in the first polygon and extend an axial line from it that crosses as many adjacencies as possible. This is a maximal axial line and it is inserted into the minimal set. The polygon in which this maximal axial line ends is then used as a starting point for a new maximal axial line which is *first* extended as far to the right as possible; and *then* as far to the left as possible. This maximal axial line, too, is inserted into the minimal set, F. This is repeated from each rightmost termination point (i.e., polygon) of a maximal axial line in F, until all adjacencies have been intersected.

Of course, care should be taken in the LRA not to attempt to extend a maximal axial line to the right of the rightmost polygon, or to the left of the leftmost polygon. Furthermore, it is essential that one first extends as far right as possible, and only thereafter, as far left as possible.

It can be shown that the LRA leads to a minimal set of maximal axial lines crossing all adjacencies. Even though this claim might seem obvious, it is nevertheless requires proof. Such a proof is given in the original work from which this material is taken, but will not discussed here. Rather, we wish to develop an algorithm that executes the LRA, based on the correctness-by-construction approach.

Start by defining $F(j)$ as a predicate to serve as part of a loop invariant. The predicate asserts that when the LRA has investigated polygon c_j in polygon chain C, then F will contain all and only the maximal axial lines in F^f that end in a polygon of the subchain $c_1, \ldots, c_j$. Thus $F(j)$ is defined, informally, as follows:

$$F(j) \triangleq (c_i|c_{i+1} \ldots c_{h-1}|c_h) \in F \iff (h \leq j) \wedge (c_i|c_{i+1} \ldots c_{h-1}|c_h) \in F^f.$$

The following should be noted about this predicate, $F(j)$:

- The truth value of $F(j)$ depends on the current contents of the set F. For $F(j)$ to be true, every axial line in F^f that ends in or before c_j has to be in the F; and every axial line in F has to correspond with an axial line in F^f that ends in or before c_j.
- However, $F(j)$ may be true, even if there are no axial lines in F ending in c_j. If there is no such axial line in the final set, F^f, then $F(j)$ will only be true if there is no such axial line in F. Likewise, if there is indeed such axial line in the final set, F^f, then $F(j)$ will only be true if there is also such axial line in F.
- The definition of $F(j)$ implies that $F(1)$ is true, if and only if $F = \varnothing$.
- The definition of $F(j)$ also implies that $F(n)$ is true, if and only if $F = F^f$.

4.7.3 Deriving the Solution Constructively

What is needed is an algorithm, S such that $\{n \geq 2\}$ $F{:}S$ $\{F(n)\}$.

In thinking about the steps needed in the algorithm, suppose that we already have determined $F(j)$; a maximal axial line running through polygon c_j is to be determined as the next axial line to insert into F. In order to determined this next axial line, we need to probe adjacencies as far to the right as possible, starting with adjacency of $c_j|cj + 1$. We then need to probe adjacencies as far to the left as possible, stating with $c_j|cj + 1$. We use index h to demarcate the rightmost polygon probed to date, and index ℓ to demarcate the leftmost index to date. We therefore define an invariant in terms of j, ℓ and h as follows:

$$inv(\ell, j, h) \triangleq F(j) \wedge vis(\ell, h) \wedge 1 \leq \ell \leq j \leq h \leq n.$$

Since

$$inv(\ell, n, h) \equiv F(n) \wedge vis(\ell, h) \wedge 1 \leq \ell \leq n = h$$

it follows that $inv(\ell, j, h) \wedge (j = n) \Rightarrow F(n)$ and therefore that $inv(\ell, j, h) \wedge (j = n)$ can be used to refine by strengthening the postcondition.

However, in doing so, there could be some uncertainty about the values that ℓ and h will assume at the end of the loop. In the case of h, the matter is quite clear: as seen above, it is explicitly part of the invariant that when $j = n$, then h will have the value n.

The final status of ℓ in a loop whose postcondition is $inv(\ell, j, h) \wedge (j = n)$ is less clear. The invariant contains the conjunct $vis(\ell, h)$ (which would actually be $vis(\ell, n)$ at the end of the loop) but does not explicitly require that $\neg vis(\ell - 1, h)$ holds (assuming $\ell > 1$). From the point of view of correctness argumentation, it is irrelevant whether or not $\neg vis(\ell - 1, h)$ holds or not. All that is required is that $F(n)$ holds, since that assures us that the will be in F a maximal axial line that ends in polygon c_n. Provided this holds, it does not matter whether or not $\neg vis(\ell - 1, h)$ holds or not. It just so happens that in the loop we construct below, it does indeed hold, subject to the requirement that $\ell > 1$

With these remarks in mind, we now refine the problem specification given above as follows (this time, remaining with Hoare triple notation):

$\{n \geq 2\}\ F{:}S\ \{F(n)\}$

$\sqsubseteq$ {Strengthening postcondition}

$\{n \geq 2\}\ F : S\ \{inv(\ell, j, h) \wedge (j = n)\}$

$\sqsubseteq$ {Introducing frame variables}

$\{n \geq 2\}\ F, \ell, j, h : S\ \{inv(\ell, j, h) \wedge (j = n)\}$

$\sqsubseteq$ {Sequence rule}

$\{n \geq 2\}\ F, \ell, j, h : S1\ \{inv(\ell, j, h)\}$;
$\{inv(\ell, j, h)\ F, \ell, j, h : S2\ \{inv(\ell, j, h) \wedge (j = n)\}$

$\sqsubseteq$ {Assignment rule}

$F, \ell, j, h := \phi, 1, 1, 2;$
$\{inv(\ell, j, h)\}\ F, \ell, j, h : S2\ \{inv(\ell, j, h) \wedge (j = n))\}$

$\sqsubseteq$ {Iteration rule}

$F, \ell, j, h := \phi, 1, 1, 2;$
$\{inv(j, \ell, h)\}$
do $(j \neq n) \rightarrow$
        $\{inv(j, \ell, h) \wedge (j \neq n)\}\ F, \ell, j, h : S2\ \{inv(\ell, j, h) \wedge 0 \leq V < V_0\}$
od
$\{inv(\ell, j, h) \wedge (j = n)\}$

The justifications for each refinement step above are fairly straightforward and are left as an exercise. The complete algorithm with a refined loop body is given below without further proof.

pre $\{n \geq 2\}$
$F, j, l, h := \phi, 1, 1, 2$
$\{inv(\ell, j, h) \triangleq F(j) \wedge vis(\ell, h) \wedge 1 \leq \ell \leq j \leq h \leq n\}$
$\{V \triangleq (n+1)(n - |F|) + (n - (h - \ell))\}$
;**do** $(j \neq n) \rightarrow$
$\quad$ **if** $h < n$ **cand** $vis(\ell, h + 1) \rightarrow h := h + 1$
$\quad$ | $(h = n$ **cor** $\neg vis(\ell, h + 1)) \wedge (l > 1$ **cand** $vis(\ell - 1, h)) \rightarrow \ell := \ell - 1$
$\quad$ | $(h = n$ **cor** $\neg vis(\ell, h + 1)) \wedge (l = 1$ **cor** $\neg vis(\ell - 1, h)) \rightarrow$
$\quad\quad F, j, \ell, h := F \cup \{axline(\ell, h)\}, h, h, h + 1$
$\quad$ **fi**
od
$\{inv(\ell, j, h) \wedge j = n\}$
post $\{F(n)\}$

Although the guards in the select statement may seem rather complex, a little thought will convince you of their accuracy and comprehensiveness. However, the variant, V, which is specified in the comments, and which was used to refine the loop is non-trivial and requires an explanation. This variant is given as:

$$V \triangleq (n+1)(n - |F|) + (n - (h - \ell)).$$

V accounts for the fact that in each iteration, either:

- $h - \ell$, the current length of an axial line being considered at this point in the algorithm, comes closer to n (which happens either because h is increased or because ℓ is decreased); or
- the number of adjacencies in F increases by 1, so that $|F|$ comes closer to its upper bound, namely n. Put differently, $n - |F|$ comes closer to its lower bound of 0.

However, when the latter happens, then $h - \ell$ is also reset to 0, meaning that $n - (h - \ell)$ might actually *increase*. Thankfully, it can never increase by more than n!

To offset this potential increase, therefore, and to ensure that the variant decreases by at least 1 in each iteration, any possible unit increase in $|F|$, which is also a decrease in $n - |F|$, is magnified by a factor of $(n + 1)$. This accounts for the term $(n + 1)(n - |F|)$ in the variant. As a result, if the term $(n - (h - \ell))$ in the variant increases by at most n, then the term $(n + 1)(n - |F|)$ decreases by $n + 1$, thus ensuring that the variant decreases by at least 1.

As seen in the first guard, the final algorithm increases h as much as possible. Then (only if h can no longer be increased) it decreases ℓ by as much as possible, as seen in the second guard. If neither of these two actions are possible, (as seen in the third guard) then the axial line from ℓ to h is maximal. This line is therefore added into F, and j is increased to h. Furthermore, ℓ and h are reset to h and $h + 1$ respectively. Note that the guards are mutually exclusive.

Recall that **cand** and **cor** are used to indicate the "conditional and" and "conditional or" operations (also known as short circuit operations). x **cand** y only evaluates expression y if expression x evaluates to true; otherwise it returns false. Similarly, x **cor** y only evaluates expression y if expression x evaluates to false; otherwise it returns true.

4.7.4   Discussion

The algorithm for this problem that was proposed in its original publication looks rather different from the one we have derived. For comparative purposes, it is given below, restated in GCL notation. Variable names have been changed to coincide with those used in the derived algorithm, and "conditional or" expressions, not in the original, have been used where appropriate.

> Input: a chain of convex polygons C and $n = |C|$
> Output: a minimal set of maximal axial lines F
> $j := 1$ {Source of current axial line in the loop}
> $F := \phi$ {Will contain final set of axial lines}
> **for** $h = 2$ to n
>   **as** $((h = n)$ **cor** $\neg vis(j, h + 1)) \rightarrow$
> $\ell := j - 1$
> $;\textbf{do } \ell \neq 0 \textbf{ cor } vis(\ell, h) \rightarrow$
> $\ell := \ell - 1$
>   **od**
> $; F := F \cup axline(\ell + 1, h)$
> $; j := h$
>   **sa**
> **rof**

It is left to the reader to understand the algorithm in this form, and to become convinced of its correctness.

Here are some matters of concern about this form of the algorithm—concern, not in the sense that the algorithm is incorrect, but rather in the sense that an added intellectual burden is imposed on the reader in trying to verify the algorithm's correctness:

- The fact that ℓ is not initialized, means that the reader has to be convinced that it will acquire a correct value eventually.
- It is left to the reader to infer the condition under which the loop does nothing more than start the next iteration. Use of the classical GCL select statement would explicitly have a guarded command: $((h \neq n)$ **cand** $vis(j, h + 1)) \rightarrow skip$.

- This means that the condition under which the search for the right-most end of the axial line is advanced—i.e., the condition under which h is incremented—is not made explicit.
- The notation obscures the fact that there is an underlying symmetry involved in either incrementing h by as much as possible, then decrementing ℓ by as much as possible, and then generating the axial line.
- It is disconcerting that ℓ has to be decremented one past its required value, and then incremented in generating the axial line.
- The assignment of h to j makes more sense when a loop invariant statement drives the motivation to do this.
- Some effort is required to verify that the algorithm is correct at boundary values (e.g., when $j = 1$ or when $h = n$) and, in the absence of a structure or checklist, one is often left with a feeling of uncertainty about whether every boundary condition has been checked.

No doubt, criticisms could also be made of the first variation of the algorithm. For example, it might have been better to have constructed separate loops within the main loop that increment h and decrement ℓ respectively. However, we contend that, in general, by constructively deriving code from specifications, the overall structure and purpose of the code tends to be more transparent and elegant than if unguided intellectual effort is brought to bear on the problem.

4.8 Revision Exercises

1. Study the so-called "stable marriage problem" and its solution, as outlined in Wikipedia (http://en.wikipedia.org/wiki/Stable_marriage_problem). Suggest a suitable variant and invariant for the problem. Attempt to write these down in natural language. Only once you have this should you attempt to formally state the invariant and variant.
2. Study the "Convex Hull Problem" and the "Graham Scan Algorithm" It is given at http://softsurfer.com/Archive/algorithm_0109/algorithm_0109.htm# Convex%20Hulls

    Suggest an appropriate variant and invariant for the loop in this problem. Do not be too concerned about specifying the invariant as a predicate—just give an English narrative description of it.

    Note that the pseudocode given at the above website is actually rather flakey. It is reproduced below. You will notice that i is not properly initialised, and is also not properly incremented in the loop.

```
Input: a set of points S = {P = (P.x,P.y)}
    Select the rightmost lowest point P0 in S.
    Sort S angularly about P0 as a center.
        For ties, discard the closer points.
    Let P[N] be the sorted array of points.
```

```
Push P[0]=P0 and P[1] onto a stack W.
while i < N
{
    Let PT1 = the top point on W
    Let PT2 = the second top point on W
    if (P[i] is strictly left of the line PT2 to PT1) {
        Push P[i] onto W
        i++      // increment i
    }
    else
            Pop the top point PT1 off the stack
}
Output: W = the convex hull of S.
```

A more accurate rendition of the loop, given in GCL, follows below. A few stack operations have been assumed, using a Java-like style for calling stack methods.

$i := 2$

{ **Variant:** ... }

{ **Invariant:** ... }

do $(i \neq P.len) \rightarrow$

$\qquad PT1, PT2 := W.top(1), W.top(2)$

$\qquad ;\textbf{if } (P_i.isLeft(PT2, PT1)) \rightarrow W.push(P_i)$

$\qquad \textbf{|} \quad \neg(P_i.isLeft(PT2, PT1)) \rightarrow W.pop()$

$\qquad \textbf{fi}$

$\qquad ;i := i + 1$

od

{ **Invariant:** $\wedge \ (i = P.Len)$ }

3. *Square root approximation* We are given a natural number s, and we must set the natural number r to the greatest integer not exceeding $\sqrt{s}$, where $\sqrt{}$ takes the non-negative square root of its argument. Thus starting from $s = 9$, for example, we would expect to finish with $s = 29 \wedge r = 5$.

4. Derive an algorithm to find indices ℓ and h such that $A_{[\ell,h)}$ is a shortest maximal run in the array A. Assume that $A.len > 0$. Rely on the following definitions:

   A run in an array is a subarray whose values are all the same.
   A left run in an array is a run in the array that cannot be extended further to the left
   A maximal run in an array is a left run in the array that cannot be extended further to the right.

   Suggestions:

   • The following figure (Fig. 4.12) might aid in determining an invariant and variant
   • Of course, the shortest possible maximal run is necessarily of length 1. You may therefore be tempted to build tests into your algorithm that enforce termination when a run of length 1 is found. Ignore this matter in

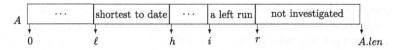

Fig. 4.12 Invariant and variant

deriving your code. It will complicate reasoning about more fundamental questions. The derived code can always be refactored to account for maximal runs of length 1 at a later stage.

- Map the algorithm derived above to a program in your favourite programming language, and test your code against arrays such as the following:

  [1111000011000]

  [1]

  [000011]

  [00001]

  [1110000]

  [0011]

  [101010] etc.

5. The code below was provided as a hacked solution to the shortest maximal run problem described in the previous exercise. Is it correct? If you have difficulty reaching a conclusion, it would be wise to draw a life-lesson from your experience about the consequences of hacking code into correctness.

$\ell, h, i, r := 0, A.len, 0, 1$

;**do** $(r \neq A.len) \rightarrow$

   do $((r \neq A.len) \wedge (A_i = A_r)) \rightarrow r := r + 1$ **od**

   ;**if** $((h - l) \leq (r - i)) \rightarrow i := r$

   ∥ $((h - l) > (r - i)) \rightarrow l, h := i, r$

   fi

od

6. You are given an array, A, $(A.len > 0)$ that is described by the following diagram.

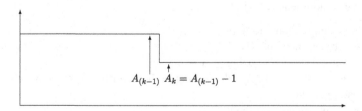

Thus, all elements of the subarray $A_{[0,k)}$ are the same; all elements of subarray $A_{[k,A.len)}$ are the same; and $A_k = A_{(k-1)} - 1$. However, we also allow for the possibility that $k = 0$, in which case, all elements in the array are the same. We can express this by saying that array A is monotonically non-increasing,[8] and its elements never differ by more than 1 unit.

Derive an algorithm to add r units (where $r \in [0, A.len)$) to elements of A in such a way that A retains this property of being monotonically non-increasing with elements never differing by more than 1 unit. You may assume that k is known at the start of the algorithm.

Use these guidelines:

- Regard A, r and k as frame variables.
- Define a predicate, $mni(A, k)$ that asserts that A is monotonically non-increasing, with a difference occurring at between elements $A_{(k-1)}$ and A_k, provided $k > 0$; and all elements are the same if $k = 0$. Use in your definition, the predicate $eq(A_{[\ell,h)})$ that asserts that all elements in the interval $[\ell, h)$ are the same.
- Specify the precondition, but include in it the predicate that $sum(A) = S$, where $sum(A)$ denotes the sum of the elements in the array. Also include in the precondition an assertion that the $r = R$. Thus S and R denote the initial values of $sum(A)$ and r, respectively.
- Specify the postcondition, including in it conjunct(s) that clarify the relationship between the updated values of $sum(A)$ and r on the one hand, and their respective initial values R and S.
- The problem statement strongly suggests a loop invariant. Give this invariant.
- Use the invariant to solve the problem in a single loop.
- Make clear what you are using for a *variant*.

Aside:

This is the simplest in a whole family of possible load-balancing algorithms. In such problems, the objective is to balance out the load between different processors/workers/units, the load here being represented by the value stored in different array elements.

One could imagine variations such as:

- A has more than one step;
- k is not known initially;
- r is not restricted to being $\leq A.len$;
- A is monotonically non-decreasing without further restrictions about only one step; and
- no restriction on the shape of A.

---

[8] A formal definition of a monotonically non-decreasing subarray was given in Exercise 8, Sect. 3.7.

The latter is probably the most complex case. It is not immediately obvious whether there is a "best" way to balance the load. There could be several strategies to try to obtain a smooth shape for A, but it is not obvious whether there is a uniquely best way.

7. Derive an algorithm to find the intersection of three integer sets. Assume that each set is implemented as a sorted integer array (possibly empty). The three sets are therefore stored in arrays A, B and C respectively, and their intersection should be stored as a sorted array in array D. Assume that $D.len$ is large enough to store the intersection, i.e., $D.len \geq \max(A.len, B.len, C.len)$

To simplify notation, it will be handy to use set notation on arrays, or subarrays. Thus, the problem statement can be specified as follows, where i, j, k and r are indices into arrays A, B, C and D respectively:

$$i, j, k, r, D : [sorted(A) \wedge sorted(B) \wedge sorted(C), sorted(D) \wedge D = A \cap B \cap C]$$

or, more simply, if we assume throughout that the sortedness of arrays is implied, then:

$$i, j, k, r, D : [\text{true}, D = A \cap B \cap C].$$

Note that there are some subtle issues around the question of when the loop should terminate. One solution would be to arrange for each index in each array to reach the end of the array. Another (more efficient approach) would be to terminate the loop when any index reaches the end of an array.

8. *A Small Case-Study*[9]

Andile received an email from her friend Adam containing the following extract—

"... what prompted me to write this email, was that we had to write a simple algorithm: a function which reads chunks of predetermined size from a file, sending each chunk in turn without reading the entire file into memory. The trick is that the algorithm should start from a specified starting position, and the file should be read only up to (and including) a particular end position. And, the end position may not be specified, in which case you should read up to the end of the file. Similarly, the starting position may also not be specified, in which case you should start reading from the start of the file. ... "

The email included the Python solution in Fig. 4.13 that had been developed. Adam asked whether "formal methods" would provide a cleaner solution to their problem.

Never having used Python, Andile studied the algorithm and decided the following:

---

[9]This case study describes an interaction between a very smart former postgraduate student and one of the authors. In order to preserve anonymity, names have been changed in the narrative

```
1    def app_iter_range(self, start=None, end=None):
2        current = 0
3        if start:
4            current = start
5
6        with open(self.full_path, 'rb') as fileobj:
7            fileobj.seek(current)
8            done = False
9            while not done:
10               # Invariant: chunk and (not end or current < end+1)
11               chunk = fileobj.read(self.chunk_size)
12               if not chunk:
13                   done = True
14               else:
15                   current += len(chunk)
16                   if end and current > end+1:
17                       overshot = end-current+1
18                       chunk = chunk[:overshot]
19                       done = True
20               if chunk:
21                   yield chunk
```

Fig. 4.13 Supplied Python version

- As in C, variables in Python can be interpreted as Booleans, as is the case in lines 3, 12, 16 and 20.
  In line 3, evidently the variable start used as a Boolean, evaluates to true if it is given explicitly in the method call.
  Similarly, in line 12, evidently chunk used as a Boolean, evaluates to false if and only if the reading action on the file has reached the end of the file.
  Line 16 uses end in a similar fashion to start in line 3, but also uses end as an ordinary integer type.
  Finally, in line 20, chunk is used as a Boolean and evaluated similarly to line 12.
- The essence of the given Python algorithm could be rewritten in GCL-like pseudocode as in Fig. 4.14. The following is assumed:
  The data is read from array A instead of from some file. To mimic the Python code in line 11, the pseudocode uses a *read* method to move information from a subarray to chunk.
  In the GCL pseudocode, it is assumed that if $s = -1$ then the intention of the method caller was to read from the beginning of the file; and similarly if $e = -1$ then read to the end of the file.
  A method called *yield* is used to do something with the chunk at the end of the loop, corresponding to line 21 of the Python program.
- Finally, Andile articulated the pre- and postcondition require of this code as shown in Fig. 4.14.

She then wrote down a much cleaner GCL algorithm for the problem, following the kind of development strategy advocated in this book, without

```
proc range(s, e)
    pre {s, e ∈ [−1, A.len) ∧ (s ≤ e)}
    c := 0;
    ; as (s < 0) → c := s sa
    ; done := FALSE
    ; do (¬done) →
        ; chunk := read(A[c,chunk.len))
        if (¬chunk) → done := TRUE
        ▯ (chunk) → c := c + chunk.len
            ; as ((e < 0) ∧ (c > e + 1)) →
                over := e − c + 1
                ; chunk := chunk[: over]
                ; done := TRUE
            sa
        fi
        as (chunk) → yield(chunk) sa
    od
    post {A[s,e+1) has been processed}
corp
```

Fig. 4.14 GCL version of supplied Python algorithm

fully elaborating each refinement step on paper. The entire exercise took her about 30 min, and it probably took about 10 min to write down her proposed algorithm. She sent back her solution with the following comments:

I found the range.py example interesting. . . . my thoughts about your solution were that your loop seemed to try to mix several concerns that should be separated.

- What are the bounds over which the task is to take place
- What is the normal flow of logic to be handled by a loop
- What is the exceptional case, i.e., to deal with the last chunk that may be smaller than previous chunks.

It seems to me that by trying to deal with all these concerns in the same loop, you ended up with a load of logic and flags that were unnecessarily complicated. . . . my solution tried to deal with each concern separately. The essence of my approach is

that I sought a loop invariant that was simple—everything "processed" in the range [start,exclude). Next, I asked: What must be true at the end of the loop? Answer: Invariant AND predicate that says "can't go further in the loop"—i.e., if I read another chunk, then I would pass "end". The negation of that predicate became the loop's condition.

After that, everything is pretty simple: Need a loop body to read a chunk, do the processing, and step ahead one increment. Need a bit of code after the loop to handle the tail end processing, need something before the loop to set it up, etc.

Adam translated the GCL-like solution back into Python, thoroughly tested it, found no errors, and confessed to feeling embarrassed at his original version. The main concern in his version was to avoid reading the length of the file at the beginning (in Andile's GCL example, she simply assume it to be available

proc *range*(s, e)
  pre $\{s, e \in [-1, A.len) \wedge (s \leq e)\}$
  S_1
  $\{$**Invariant**$??\}$
  $\{$**Variant** $??\}$
  ;**do** $(G) \rightarrow$
        S_2
  od
  $\{$**Invariant** $\wedge (\neg G)\}$
  ; S_3
  post $\{A_{[s,e+1)}$ has been processed$\}$
corp

Fig. 4.15 Solution outline

as *A.len*) because he felt that this would involve an inefficient system call. His subsequent remarks in this regard are worth hearing:

> "I do believe that you should let performance influence your design if and only if after profiling you discover that you indeed have a performance problem. And, XP has this principle called "YAGNI" (You ain't gonna need it.) So, maybe I've violated that principle and built in a performance improvement of questionable value (because it has not been profiled) which I may not need (because I have not experienced the problem)."

Your Task:

Reconstruct Andile's version of the algorithm. Use the solution outline in Fig. 4.15. Of course, you have to articulate the invariant, variant, loop condition, etc.

9. (a) Derive a GCL program to solve the following problem:

$$L : \left[N > 0 \wedge b > 1, N \in \left[b^L, b^{L+1} \right) \right],$$

i.e., derive an integer approximation, L, of $log_b(N)$. This is of course a generalisation of the problem that was discussed in Sect. 3.6, namely:

$$L : \left[N > 0, N \in \left[2^L, 2^{L+1} \right) \right].$$

(b) Note that the above will may not give the "best" approximation. For example, if $N = 723$ and $b = 10$, it will deliver $L = 2$ because $N \in \left[10^2, 10^3 \right)$. Constructively develop code to find the *best* integer approximation, L, of $log_b(N)$.

    Start by formulating a formal postcondition that depends on the various parameters and that expresses what is required, so that the problem becomes:

$$L : [N > 0 \wedge b > 1, post(b, N, L)].$$

You are likely to find that refining $post(b, N, L)$ is the most challenging part of this question. Thereafter it is simply a matter of "reusing" your solution in the first part of the exercise, and taking a fairly obvious step thereafter.

10. *Longest prefix matching* Given arrays S and p of characters, find the index i of the leftmost occurrence of the longest prefix of p in S. For example, when $S = WatkinsWatson$, $p = Walsh$ we would obtain $i = 0$ since no prefix longer than Wat matches, and it matches leftmost at the beginning of S. On the other hand, for $p = Watsonville$ we would have $i = 7$.

11. *Longest strictly descending subsequence* Given an array Q of numbers, find the rightmost indices i and j such that the $j - i$ is maximal and for all $k : i < k \le j$

$$Q_{k-1} > Q_k.$$

For example, if $Q = [-1000, 2, 1.5, -1, 6, 5, 4]$ the answer is $i = 4, j = 6$. Q is guaranteed to be non-empty.

12. *Longest alternating subsequence* Given an array Q of numbers, find the leftmost indices i and j such that the $j - i$ is maximal and for all integers $Q_i, \ldots, Q_j$, the sequence is alternating (strictly) increasing–decreasing. It may start decreasing or increasing and end on either. For example, if $Q = [-5000, -1000, 2, 2.1, -1, -0.5, 6, 7]$ the answer is $i = 1, j = 6$ because from $Q_1 = -1000$ to $Q_6 = 6$ the sequence starts increasing and then alternates. Q is guaranteed to be non-empty.

Chapter 5
Procedures and Recursion

5.1 Introduction

Procedures[1] offer a well-known way of reusing code. A procedure may be viewed as a named block of code, characterised by its pre- and postconditions. It may be called (or invoked) from other parts of a program. A correctness-by-construction approach can be used to derive the body of the procedure, thus ensuring that it conforms to its stated pre- and postconditions. However, to date we have not explicitly shown how *calling* a procedure can be incorporated into our refinement rules. Section 5.2 provides the relevant refinement rules, while Sect. 5.3 provides a broad strategy for deriving procedures.

The rest of the chapter the focusses on recursion. This is a well-known and powerful algorithmic device in terms of which procedures *call themselves* during execution—hence the unsettling aphorism:

> To understand recursion, you have to understand recursion!

Although it takes a little time to become familiar with the idea of recursion, once the ice has been broken, recursive algorithms turn out to have a kind of magically succinct quality about them.

Recursion is useful in solving problems through a *Divide and Conquer* strategy: a problem is broken down into smaller pieces that can be easily solved, and then all the smaller solutions are merged together. Recursive procedures are also often used to traverse recursive data structures, such as lists, graphs, trees and lattices.

Many problems are amenable to both recursive and iterative algorithmic solutions. For example, Kaldewaij [25] uses correctness-by-construction techniques to derive iterative solutions for both Quicksort and Mergesort—classically presented

---

[1]Synonyms are *subprocedure, subprogram, routine, subroutine, function* and *method*. In this text, we will keep to the terms *procedure* and *function* as they were classically used in languages such as Pascal.

D.G. Kourie and B.W. Watson, *The Correctness-by-Construction Approach to Programming*, DOI 10.1007/978-3-642-27919-5_5,
© Springer-Verlag Berlin Heidelberg 2012

as recursive algorithms. Recursive algorithmic solutions often have advantages over their equivalent iterative versions. Many are more elegantly expressed in their recursive forms, making such algorithms easier for programmers to understand, remember and implement. In the case of template meta-programming in C++, variables cannot be used to support iteration, so recursion for performing repetition [2] is obligatory. On the downside, recursion is more space- and time-expensive when implemented on a real machine.

Nevertheless, on grounds of elegance alone, it is worth investigating how to incorporate recursion into the correctness-by-construction approach. In Sect. 5.4, refinement rules for deriving recursive procedures will be presented, as well as a discussion of total correctness. Section 5.5 shows how variants can be used to ensure termination of recursive programs. The section offers a strategy for constructing such procedures, somewhat analogous to the loop construction strategy of Chap. 2. Section 5.6 then provides a number of examples to demonstrate how the material in Sects. 5.2–5.5 can be used to derive recursive algorithms in practice.

5.2   Procedures

This section draws on the refinement rules provided by Morgan's refinement calculus. A procedure is a named block of code, characterised by a pre- and postcondition, and possibly by so-called "formal" parameter variables. It can be invoked by giving its name and so-called "actual" parameters to be passed on to and/or retrieved from the procedure. The scope of the parameters can be set in different ways. However, for simplicity, in this discussion we will assume that all variables to be considered *other than actual and formal parameters* have global scope—i.e. they are visible from both the calling environment, and within the procedure.

5.2.1   Parameterless Procedures

The simplest of procedure refinement rule deals with procedures with no parameters. Let $R()$ denote a call to a procedure defined as **proc** $R()$ S **corp**—i.e. the procedure has name R and body S. The following refinement applies.

Rule 10. $Spec(P, S, Q) \sqsubseteq Spec(P, R(), Q)$

In other words, if we wish to derive code that terminates in $State_Q$ if commenced in $State_P$, and we already know that the body, S, of the parameterless procedure, $R()$ complies with this requirement, then we might as well just call $R()$! We don't even need to know the details of what S does—if, given the precondition, $R()$ terminates and produces the specified postcondition, then it is good enough.

Consider, for example, the following simple procedure which sets a global variable, x, to 1.

$$\textbf{proc } \textit{SetToOne}() \; x := 1 \textbf{ corp}$$

The body of this procedure just happens to comply with the following specification.[2]

$$Spec(x < 20, x : S, x > 0)$$

It is easy enough to prove that the body of $\textit{SetToOne}()$ indeed complies with this specification (a simple exercise left to the reader). But whether we know that $Spec(x < 20, x : S, x > 0)$ holds as a matter of proof, or as a matter of externally supplied information, Rule 10 asserts that invoking $\textit{SetToOne}()$ from $State_{x<20}$ will result in a new state in $State_{x>0}$.

Clearly, $x : [x < 20, x > 0]$ is not the most specific characterisation of what the body of $\textit{SetToOne}()$ accomplishes. Such a specification would require maximal weakening of the precondition and strengthening of the postcondition, namely $x :$ [true, $x = 1$]. Rule 10 would also apply in this case, so that we could assert that:

$$[\text{true}, x = 1] \sqsubseteq \textit{SetToOne}()$$

Parameterless procedures such as $\textit{SetToOne}()$ are, however, very limited in their usefulness. For example, $\textit{SetToOne}()$ is restricted to both the global variable x and the constant value 1. The procedure would be far more useful if it could accept, as a parameter, a variable other than x on which to perform its assignment, and/or a value other than 1 to be used in the assignment.

There are three classically-known types of parameters: "pass-by-value", "pass-by-result" and "pass-by-value-result."[3] Refinement rule are defined to handle each of these types of parameters in procedures.

In the rule explanations that will follow below, a *formal parameter* is the variable declared in the procedure definition whose scope is limited to the procedure. An *actual parameter* refers to the variable or value sent through at the procedure call. In the following code snippet, z is the formal parameter and a is the actual parameter.

$$\textbf{proc } \textit{Proc}(z) \ldots \textbf{ corp}$$

$$\vdots$$

$$a := p * q + r;$$
$$Proc(a)$$

---

[2]Recall the three equivalent notational options introduced in Chap. 2. There we introduced $Spec(x < 20, x : S, x > 0)$ as just another form of the Hoare triple notation $\{x < 20\} \; x : S \; \{x > 0\}$. Morgan's notation of $x : [x < 20, x > 0]$ suppresses explicit reference to abstract code, S, whereas concrete code is explicitly given and any inference about such code's pre- and postconditions has to rely on previous refinement steps. We freely alternate between notations in order to highlight various aspects of a specification.

[3]Some contexts speak of "in", "out" and "in out" parameters, respectively. The terms "call-by-value" and "call-by-reference" are also encountered, the latter being more or less equivalent to "pass-by-value-result".

This example takes some notational liberties, in that *Proc* does not specify the type of its formal parameter as pass-by-value, pass-by-result or pass-by-value-result. As will be seen below, this is normally required.

We will now indicate the refinement rules that can be used in the presence of each of these three types of parameters. Throughout we will refer to a procedure $R(z)$, that has the formal parameter z, and which is invoked as $R(a)$, where a is the actual parameter. We will mention in passing various constraints that apply to the contents of the pre- and postconditions when these rules are applied. However, for the sake of simplicity, we will not fully elaborate on them, nor methodically check for compliance with those constraints in subsequent examples, since—in the main—they forbid rather extreme situations which are seldom relevant.

5.2.2　Pass by Value

A pass-by-value parameter initialises the formal parameter's value to that of the actual parameter's value, but changes made to the value of the formal parameter during execution of the procedure do not affect the value of the actual parameter, a. Essentially the parameter is used to pass a *value* to the procedure, and therefore the parameter a is best thought of as an expression (which is evaluated before control is passed to the procedure body) rather than as a variable.[4]

Suppose we are given the procedure specified as **proc** $R(\textbf{value } z)$ $w, z : R_{body}$ **corp**. This specification emphasises that the frame variables (or perhaps variable lists) w and z may change when R_{body} is executed. The pass-by-value rule to be given below indicates the circumstances under which $R(a)$ may be invoked.

The rule will rely on the notation a_0 to denote the actual parameter, a, after all occurrences of w in a have been substituted by w_0, i.e. $a_0 \equiv a[w \backslash w_0]$. Now to see why this makes sense, one has to understand that the expression a may include the variable w. For example, a could be the expression $w + 4x$ (x being some other arbitrary variable). Since frame variable w may change during the execution of R, we have an interest in noting its initial value w_0, as well as the initial value of a, namely $a_0 \equiv w_0 + 4x$. Note that there is no need to be concerned about how x will change during a call to R: we may assume that it does not change at all, since it does not appear as a frame variable in relation to R_{body}.

Using this notation, the pass-by-value refinement rule is as follows.

---

[4]An expression is a programming construct that returns a *value*. A variable to which a value has been assigned is thus one special form of an expression. Other kinds of expressions are constants, expressions with operators, etc. A function call is also conventionally regarded as an expression.

Rule 11. *Pass by value rule*[5]
Given: **proc** $R(\textbf{value}\, z)\, \{P\}\, w, z : R_{body}\, \{Q\}$ **corp**
Rule: $\{P[z\backslash a]\}\, w : S\, \{Q[z_0\backslash a_0]\} \sqsubseteq \{P[z\backslash a]\}\, R(a)\, \{Q[z_0\backslash a_0]\}$

Suppose we have a library containing the utility procedure R. To be useful, we would obviously expect that its documentation contains information about the pre- and postconditions, P and Q, under which it operates—i.e. under which $\{P\}\, w, z : R_{body}\, \{Q\}$ is true. Of course, the details of R_{body} is assumed to be unknown. However, we do know that R_{body} may only change values of the pass-by-value formal parameter z and the globally known variable w. (Throughout, we assume z and w to be single variables. The discussion trivially generalises to the case where they represent lists of variables instead.) Note that P and/or Q are allowed to refer to variables w and z.

The rule indicates that the a call to $R(z)$, i.e. the concrete code $R(a)$, then conforms to the specification
$\{P[z\backslash a]\}\, R(a)\, \{Q[z_0\backslash a_0]\}$.

Moreover, the rule indicates that this specification is a refinement of any abstract specification that has the same pre- and postconditions and allows for the changes in w—i.e. it is a refinement of $\{P[z\backslash a]\}\, w : S\, \{Q[z_0\backslash a_0]\}$.

Note that it would not make any sense to specify in the postcondition, Q, any kind of expectations on the range of *final* values of the formal value parameter, z. Why not? Well, because the scope of z is limited to within R_{body}, and any such information would be of no use to a caller of R. However, it is well within expectation that the designer of R_{body} might need to specify, in postcondition Q, something about how the initially passed value of z, namely z_0, features in relation to other variables that have been manipulated during the execution of R. For example, the purpose of R_{body} may have been to ensure that $w > z_0$.

Now suppose that you need to change the value of w at a point where you know that predicate P' will hold, and you believe that by using the actual parameter a in the call $R(a)$, your purpose would be achieved—i.e. say Q' will hold. How can you know whether or not the call $R(a)$ complies with your requirements in a given context? Rule 11 will assist you in answering your question.

The information you have at hand is that $\{P\}\, w, z : R_{body}\, \{Q\}$ holds. The rule tells you that by calling $R(a)$, you may be confident that $\{P[z\backslash a]\}\, R(a)\, \{Q[z_0\backslash a_0]\}$ will hold.

If P' and Q' do not coincide exactly with $P[z\backslash a]$ and $Q[z_0\backslash a_0]$ respectively, you would still not know whether or not the call to $R(a)$ achieves your purpose. To be affirmed of that, you would need to show is that

$$\{P'\}\, w, z : S\, \{Q'\} \sqsubseteq \{P[z\backslash a]\}\, R(a)\, \{Q[z_0\backslash a_0]\}$$

---

[5]The rule is given in Hoare triple notation, because the pre- and postconditions that apply when the call is issued are explicitly shown. For this reason Hoare notation will also be used in subsequent rules. However, the essential equivalence of the two notations should constantly be borne in mind. In Morgan's notation this particular rule is: $w : [P[z\backslash a], Q[z_0\backslash a_0]) \sqsubseteq R(a)$.

You would have to rely on other refinement rules to show this—typically using rules relating to strengthening postconditions, weakening preconditions, etc. You might even have to rely on the sequence rule where $P[z \backslash a]$ and $Q[z_0 \backslash a_0]$ feature as *mid* predicates en route to attaining Q' from P'.

As an example of the rule in action, consider the following procedure, which merely sets the global variable, w, to its pass-by-value parameter incremented by 1.

$$\textbf{proc } R(\textbf{value } z) \ w := z + 1 \ \textbf{corp}$$

Now suppose that the designer of this procedure had placed it in a library and, for reasons related to the context of its intended use, advertises that $R(\textbf{value } z)$ conforms to the specification:

$$w, z : [w \geq 0 \wedge z < 100, w > z_0]$$

It is a simple matter to show that the procedure's body indeed conforms to the specification. (Of course, it also conforms to various other specifications, and in practice, it might have been more sensible for the designer to specify a precondition that is as weak as possible, and a postcondition that is as strong as possible, for example $w, z : [\textsf{true}, w = w_0 + 1 \wedge x = z_0 + 1]$. However, the given specification is used for illustrative reasons.)

Note that, as required for the application of the rule, the postcondition is independent of the formal parameter, z. It indeed reference its initial value z_0, but this was tolerated by the rule's constraints. As a result we may apply Rule 11, using $(w \geq 0 \wedge z < 100)$ and $(w > z_0)$ as P and Q, respectively.

Let us consider applying the rule under two circumstances. In the first case, suppose we want to use an actual parameter of 5, i.e. we wish to call $R(5)$. To apply the rule we need to determine the precondition under the substitution $[z \backslash 5]$, which becomes

$$w \geq 0 \wedge 5 < 100 \equiv w \geq 0 \wedge \textsf{true} \equiv w \geq 0.$$

Also needed is the postcondition under the substitution $[z_0 \backslash a_0]$, where

$$a_0 \equiv a[w \backslash w_0] \equiv 5[w \backslash w_0] \equiv 5$$

The postcondition under the substitution $[z_0 \backslash 5]$ then becomes

$$(w > w_0 z_0)[z_0 \backslash 5] \equiv (w > 5)$$

Rule 11 then assures us that:

$$\{(w \geq 0)\} \ w : S \ \{(w > 5)\}$$
$$\sqsubseteq \{(w \geq 0)\} \ R(5) \ \{(w > 5)\}$$

Thus, Rule 11 assures us that if $w > 0$ and the call $R(5)$ is made, then the call will terminate and $w > 5$ when it does so.

To illustrate the use of the rule when the actual parameter is slightly more complicated, suppose we wished to make the call $R(3w + 1)$. In this case, we need to make the substitution $[z \backslash 3w + 1]$ in the precondition to get: $(w \geq 0) \wedge (3w_0 + 1 < 100)$

Since $a_0 = (3w + 1)[w \backslash w_0] = 3w_0 + 1$, we need the substitution $[z_0 \backslash 3w_0 + 1]$ in the postcondition. This gives $(w > 3w_0 + 1)$. The result would be the following application of Rule 11:

$$\{(w \geq 0) \wedge (3w_0 + 1 < 100)\} \, w : S \, \{(w > 3w_0 + 1)\}$$
$$\sqsubseteq \{(w \geq 0) \wedge (3w_0 + 1 < 100)\} \, R(3w_0 + 1) \, \{(w > 3w_0 + 1)\}$$

It does no harm at this stage to eliminate the explicit reference to initial values in P, so that, because of Rule 11 we could have confidence in the following specification:

$$\{(0 \leq 3w + 1 < 100)\} \, R(3w + 1) \, \{(w > 3w + 1)\}$$

Of course, the developer who wished to ensure that the postcondition holds after the call to $R(3w + 1)$ would have to ensure that the precondition holds before the call. That seems like a lot more trouble than it is worth in the case of this rather contrived example.

In summary, we have seen that if we know something about behaviour of a procedure's body in terms of pre- and postconditions that comply with the rule's restrictions, and if we invoke the procedure with appropriate actual parameters, then Rule 11 informs us of a pre-post specification to which that invocation will conform.

5.2.3 Pass by Result

A "pass-by-result" actual parameter *has to be* a variable—it may not be any other kind of expression. It is assigned the value of its corresponding formal parameter when the procedure terminates. Such parameters pass values "out" of the procedure whereas pass-by-value parameters pass values "into" the procedure.

The pass-by-result rule is given below, where it is now assumed that a in the call $R(a)$ is a variable.

Rule 12. *Pass by result rule*
Given: **proc** $R(\textbf{result } z) \, \{P\} \, w, z : R_{body} \, \{Q\}$ **corp**
Rule: $\{P\} \, w, a : S \, \{Q[z \backslash a]\} \sqsubseteq \{P\} \, R(a) \, \{Q[z \backslash a]\}$

The rule is contingent on certain constraints in the way P and Q are constituted: z_0 may not appear in Q and z may not appear in P. These constraints are entirely sensible.

z is used to return a result from R_{body}; when the call is made it is assumed to be unassigned (to have no value). Thus, its initial value, z_0, is irrelevant to the final outcome of R_{body} and therefore ought not to appear in the postcondition, Q.

Similarly, it would not make sense to refer to z in the precondition, P. Since z's value is not communicated to R_{body}, its initial value cannot play any meaningful role in the procedure's outcome and therefore has no place in the procedure's precondition, P.

A simple example illustrates the rule in action. Consider the following procedure.

$$\textbf{proc } R(\textbf{result } z) \ z, w := x + 1, w + 1 \ \textbf{corp}$$

Here, x may be viewed as a global variable, or perhaps as a local constant. Whatever the case, the procedure's designer would have to advertise that the procedure conforms to a specification that assumes knowledge that the user knows something about the value of x. For example, the following specification may be advertised:

$$z, w : [P, Q] \text{ where } P \equiv \textbf{true} \text{ and } Q \equiv (w > w_0 \wedge z > x)$$

(That the body actually adheres to this claim can readily be verified.)

Suppose that we, as users of the procedure, require that the call $R(a)$ should result in $Q' \equiv (w > w_0 \wedge a > x)$. From the designer's specifications it is evident that $Q' \equiv Q[z\backslash a]$. The rule allows us to conclude that

$$\{\textbf{true}\} \ w, a : S \ \{(w > w_0 \wedge a > x)\}$$
$$\sqsubseteq \{\textbf{true}\} \ R(a) \ \{(w > w_0 \wedge a > x)\}$$

which is just another way of saying that the call $R(a)$ is a refinement of a specification that seeks to attain the postcondition from an arbitrary (true) starting scenario, and that, in turn, is a longwinded way of saying that the $R(a)$ will achieve our desired postcondition, irrespective of the starting state.

5.2.4 Pass by Value Result

A "pass-by-value-result" parameter is a combination of the previous two parameter types. The actual parameter, which is again constrained to be a variable, both initialises the value of the formal parameter at the start of the procedure and the value of the formal parameter is passed back to the actual parameter at the termination of the procedure. The rule indicates the circumstances under which $R(a)$ may be invoked when we are given the procedure **proc** $R(\textbf{value result } z) \ R_{body}$ **corp**. The rule appears as a combination of Rule 11 and Rule 12.

Rule 13. *Pass by value-result rule*
Given: **proc** $R(\textbf{value result } z) \ \{P\} \ w, z : R_{body} \ \{Q\}$ **corp**
Rule: $\{P[z\backslash a]\} \ w, a : S \ \{Q[z_0, z\backslash a_0, a]\} \sqsubseteq \{P[z\backslash a]\} \ R(a) \ \{Q[z_0, z\backslash a_0, a]\}$

In contrast to the pass-by-result rule, the rule does not require that z may not be appear in P. Similarly, in contrast to the pass-by-value rule, the rule does not require that z may not appear in Q.

Consider the simple example that differs from the previous one only in that z is now passed by value-result, and z replaces the role of x in the previous example.

$$\textbf{proc } R(\textbf{value result } z) \; z, w := z + 1, w + 1 \; \textbf{corp}$$

It is easy to verify that the procedure's body complies with the specification:

$$\{\textsf{true}\} \; z, w := x + 1, w + 1 \; \{(w > w_0 \wedge z > z_0)\}$$

Taking P in the rule as $\textsf{true}$, Q as $(w > w_0 \wedge z > z_0)$ and applying the rule's substitutions, we get:

$$\{\textsf{true}\} \; w, a : S \; \{(w > w_0 \wedge a > a_0)$$

$$\sqsubseteq \{\textsf{true}\} \; R(a) \; \{(w > w_0 \wedge a > a_0)\}$$

Thus, invoking $R(a)$ from any start state guarantees that both w and a will be larger than their respective values before the invocation.

5.2.5 Functions

Functions are easily refined as they are special cases of procedures. A function returns values, and thus any function can be expressed as a procedure with an additional pass-by-result parameter for each of its return values. For example, the following snippet

$$\textbf{proc } Example(\textbf{result } x, \textbf{result } y, \textbf{value } x) \ldots x, y := 0, 1 \; \textbf{corp}$$

$$\ldots$$

$$Example(p, q, r)$$

is equivalent to

$$\textbf{func } Example(\textbf{value } z) : \langle x, y \rangle \ldots a, b := 0, 1 \; \textbf{ncuf}$$

$$\ldots$$

$$p, q := Example(r)$$

To refine a specification into a function call, simply show that the refinement is valid for the procedure version of the procedure and then rewrite the procedure in its function form.

5.3 Procedure Refinement Strategy

The procedure refinement rules can be used as the basis of the following steps to develop a procedure.

1. Choose a name for the procedure that describes its functionality. Suppose we choose *Compute* for illustrative purposes. We also use *Parms* as a temporary placeholder for the unspecified parameters. The procedure then has form:

$$\textbf{proc } Compute(Parms) \; Body \; \textbf{corp}$$

2. Decide what the procedure should do in terms of the pre- and postconditions of *Body*. This will put the procedure in the form:

$$\textbf{proc } Compute(Parms) \; \{P\} \; Body \; \{Q\} \; \textbf{corp}$$

3. Decide on what inputs the procedure should take and what outputs it should produce. Then add parameters to reflect these. The pre- and postconditions should provide a clue as to the mode of each parameter. Variables in the precondition only are probably pass-by-value parameters; variables in the postcondition only are probably pass-by-result parameters; and variables in both the pre- and postcondition are probably pass-by-value-result parameters. This will put the procedure in the following form:

$$\textbf{proc } Compute(\textbf{value } in; \; \textbf{result } out; \textbf{value result } inout)$$

$$\{P\} \; in, out, inout : S \; \{Q\}$$

corp

where *in*, *out* and *inout* may represent lists of parameters of those respective modes. Note that at this stage S represents an abstraction of the code that is yet to be instantiated.

4. Refine the body of the procedure into code using refinement laws such as the assignment and selection laws. This will put the procedure in the form:

$$\textbf{proc } Compute(\textbf{value } in; \; \textbf{result } out; \textbf{value result } inout)$$

$$\{P\} \dots \text{code} \dots \{Q\}$$

corp

5. Decide on the actual parameters to be used when calling the procedure from the main program. Let *ina*, *outa* and *inouta* represent the actual pass-by-value, pass-by-result and pass-by-value-result parameters, respectively. The refinement rules indicate that a call to the procedure with these actual parameters will result in the following correct specification:

$\{P[in, inout \backslash ina, inouta]\}$
    $Compute(ina, out, inouta)$
$\{Q[in_0, in, `out, inout_0, inout \backslash ina_0, ina, outa, inouta_0, inouta]\}$

6. If the procedure has pass-by-result parameters, it may be refactored into a function, making the necessary adjustments to the call in the main program. This step is entirely optional, but may make the final program easier to read and understand.

5.4 Recursive Procedures

Now that the refinement laws for procedures have been presented, we should be able to refine recursive procedures. Let us begin with a classic recursive example, the factorial function.

The factorial of some positive integer n, written $n!$, is defined as the number $1 \times 2 \times \cdots \times n$, or, in product of a sequence notation:

$$n! = \prod_{k=1}^{n} k$$

$0!$ is considered to be a special case and is defined as having the value 1.

Following the strategy in Sect. 5.3, we choose a name for the procedure giving

proc *Factorial(Parms) Body* **corp**

The procedure should take a non-negative integer, say n, as input and produce as output its factorial value, say f. We replace *Body* with this specification:

$$\{n \geq 0\}\, n, f : Body\, \{f = n_0!\}$$

Note that we use n_0 in the postcondition instead of n. This clarifies that even if the value of n changes within the procedure, f must eventually be the factorial of the initial value of n. If, instead, the specification had simply been $\{n \geq 0\}\, Body\, \{f = n!\}$, then $n, f := 0, 1$ would be a valid refinement of the specification, but contrary to what we intended to specify.

Since n appears in the precondition but not in the postcondition (n_0 appears in the postcondition instead), n may be a pass-by-value parameter (or even a pass-by-value-result parameter, but not a pass-by-result parameter).

On the other hand, f does not appear in the precondition, but does appear in the postcondition. Hence it may be a pass-by-result parameter (but not a pass-by-value parameter and not a pass-by-value-result parameter). The procedure now looks like this:

proc *Factorial*(**value** n, **result** f) $\{n \geq 0\}\, n, f : Body\, \{f = n_0!\}$ **corp**

The next step is to refine the body of the specification into code. Since this is a recursive procedure, we know that as part of the code refinement, *Factorial* should call itself. Since the formal and actual parameters of a recursive function will have the same names, we distinguish the formal parameter corresponding to some actual parameter x by x'.

Using this notation, and leaving aside termination issues for the moment, suppose that we wanted to argue that the following refinement is allowed by the procedure refinement rules:

$$\{n' \geq 0\}\, n, f : Body\, \{f' = n_0'!\}$$

$\sqsubseteq$ Using Rule 11 for n and Rule 12 for f

$$\{n' \geq 0\}\, Factorial(n', f')\, \{f' = n_0'!\} \tag{5.1}$$

This code is supposed to set f' to $n'!$ when it terminates, and since $f = f'$ and $n = n'$ in the first recursive call, the final outcome should indeed then be that $f = n$.

The problem here, though, is that the refinement is premised on the assumption that

proc *Factorial*(**value** n, **result** f) $\{n \geq 0\}\, n, f : Body\, \{f = n_0!\}$ **corp**

is given (check the rules to see this), and in particular, that

$$\{n \geq 0\}\, n, f : Body\, \{f = n_0!\} \tag{5.2}$$

is given—i.e. known to be a true predicate. However, we do not know yet that the predicate is true. To prove it true, we would have to show that if the precondition holds, and *Body* executes, *then Body will terminate* and the postcondition will hold. This cannot be done directly, since the contents of *Body* has not yet been determined.

We could, in principle, make an assumption about the content of *Body*. We could say: suppose predicate 5.2 is true, and on this assumption, we apply a procedure refinement rule. Do we then end up with something contradictory or not? If so, then the assumption would have been invalid; otherwise it can be accepted.

In the present case, if we made that assumption and applied the procedure rule as just discussed above, then *Body* would contain a recursive call to itself, and the call would have the actual parameters that correspond exactly to the formal parameters. The procedure would clearly end up recursing infinitely! In fact, therefore, predicate 5.2 would have been shown, ex post facto, to be false.

In deriving recursive procedures, we therefore face the two common problems hinted at above: finding a way of recursively calling the procedure that guarantees termination; and applying the refinement rules on the assumption that their application is valid, and only being able to verify that application thereafter. This latter verification can usually be done by using induction as a proof technique. In the material below we shall not carry out these proofs, since this will deflect from our main purpose. However, they are not difficult, and can easily be developed by the interested reader.

The following section, then, proposes a strategy for developing terminating recursive procedures. Even though the strategy does not pretend to be a universal recipe for developing recursive algorithms, it will be useful for many problems.

5.5 Terminating Recursive Programs

Chapter 2 presented a strategy for guaranteeing loop termination. Using this strategy for iteration as a guide, we will formulate a strategy to develop recursive procedures that are guaranteed to terminate once called. This strategy is offered, not as a panacea, but as an approach that will work for most recursive algorithms.

The second step of Chap. 2's iteration strategy mentions a predicate, G, which serves as the loop's condition. While G is true the loop continues to execute, and when G becomes false the loop terminates. It turns out that a similar predicate will be useful in recursive procedures as well.

For any recursive procedure we need to find one or more *base cases*. A base case refers to a condition under which the result to be returned is directly known or can easily be computed—i.e. a recursive call is not to be made. Suppose that there are $i > 0$ different base cases and that they occur respectively under the conditions B_1, $B_2, \ldots, B_i$. Let $G = (B_1 \vee B_2 \vee \cdots \vee B_i)$. The general idea is therefore to execute one of the base cases whenever conditions warrant it, and to make a recursive call whenever $\neg G$ holds.

However, merely to include code to handle base cases is not enough. Even though the recursion is guaranteed to terminate if G holds, there is no guarantee that conditions will eventually be reached to ensure that G does in fact hold.

Again we look to the iteration strategy for inspiration. This strategy, as part of its third step, introduced a variant, V, which must satisfy the conjuncts $(0 \leq V) \wedge (V < V_0)$ at the end of each iteration of the loop (as part of the loop body's postcondition).

For recursion, we also introduce a variant V, but with a few special properties.

- V is formulated in terms of variables and/or formal parameters. This has several implications. For discussion purposes below, we denote the variant as

$V(in, inout, x)$, where in is a **value** parameter, $inout$ is a **value result** parameter and x is a variable (or possibly a list of variables).

- Since V is used for logical reasoning only, the scope of x is not critical. It may be global or local. Local implies that, in the current recursive execution, the variable's value from a previous recursive execution will be unknown at the *code level*. However, reasoning at an *abstract/logical level* about its value in previous recursions and how its value may affect V, remains a perfectly legitimate exercise.
- In reasoning about the value of the variant at any particular stage of the computation, the formal parameters in and $inout$ obviously need to be replaced by the value of the actual variables (say ina and $inouta$) at each stage.
- In the context of recursion , a variant will not be formulated in terms of **result** parameters.

• The variant expression should consistently decline with each recursive invocation of the procedure, i.e. the predicate $(0 \leq V) \wedge (V < V_0)$ should hold. But this raises two related questions. At which point should the predicate hold? And what should V_0 designate at that point?

- In answer to the first question, we require that $(0 \leq V)$ and $(V < V_0)$ should hold just before executing the first command in the body of the called recursive procedure—i.e. $(0 \leq V)$ and $(V < V_0)$ should be conjuncts of the recursive procedure's precondition.
- In answer to the second question, we need to consider two scenarios. In the first scenario, we assume that a recursive call had been issued by a previous execution of the procedure. In that case, $V_0 = V_0(in, inout, x))$ is taken as the variant's value at a particular point in the previous recursive execution; namely, the point just before determining which guarded command of the select statement should be executed. At that point, V_0's value is such that the $\neg G$ guarded command will be selected. Subsequent to selecting that command but prior to issuing the recursive call, V_0's value might be changed.

The second scenario needing consideration is when a procedure is called for the first time—i.e. it is called from a main program. In this case, for convenience we shall assume that the value of $V_0 = Max$, where Max is the maximum value that can be represented in the system—i.e we assume that $V < V_0$ always holds at the first call.

These two additional considerations (base cases and variants) suggest a strategy for developing recursive procedures that are guaranteed to terminate. The recursive refinement strategy is as follows:

1. Follow steps 1 through 3 of the general strategy for defining a procedure presented in Sect. 5.3—i.e. choose a name for the procedure, determine the pre- and postconditions of the procedure and determine the parameters for the procedure.

2. Identify base case guards, B_1, B_2, ..., B_i. Also identify the values R_1, $R_2, \ldots, R_i$ that should be returned in each of these cases respectively. Introduce a select command with guards B_1, B_2, ..., B_i and $\neg G$.[6] Following the convention used in the general strategy for defining a procedure, the procedure should now be in the form:

$$
\begin{aligned}
&\textbf{proc } \textit{Compute}(\textbf{value } \textit{in}; \ \textbf{result } \textit{out}; \ \textbf{value result } \textit{inout}) \\
&\quad \{pre\} \\
&\quad \textbf{if } B_1 \rightarrow \{pre \wedge B_1\} \ out := R_1 \ \{post\} \\
&\quad \vdots \\
&\quad \| \ \ B_i \rightarrow \{pre \wedge B_i\} \ out := R_i \ \{post\} \\
&\quad \| \ \ \neg G \rightarrow \{pre \wedge \neg G\} \ S \ \{post\} \\
&\quad \textbf{fi} \\
&\quad \{post\} \\
&\textbf{corp}
\end{aligned}
$$

3. Define a variant, V, for the recursion . As shown in the procedure outline below, revise the precondition by adding $(0 \leq V) \wedge (V < V_0)$ as additional conjucts. The revised precondition is denoted as pre'.

$$
\begin{aligned}
&\textbf{proc } \textit{Compute}(\textbf{value } i\,n; \ \textbf{result } \textit{out}; \ \textbf{value result } \textit{inout}) \\
&\quad \{pre' \equiv (pre \wedge (0 \leq V) \wedge (V < V_0))\} \\
&\quad \textbf{if } B_1 \rightarrow \{pre' \wedge B_1\} \ out := R_1 \ \{post\} \\
&\quad \vdots \\
&\quad \| \ \ B_i \rightarrow \{pre' \wedge B_i\} \ out := R_i \ \{post\} \\
&\quad \| \ \ \neg G \rightarrow \{pre' \wedge \neg G\} \ S \ \{post\} \\
&\quad \textbf{fi} \\
&\quad \{post\} \\
&\textbf{corp}
\end{aligned}
$$

4. Refine $\{pre \wedge \neg G\} \ S \ \{post\}$. Notionally, one might typically use the sequence rule to arrive at the form

$$\{pre \wedge \neg G\} \ S0; \ \{mid0\} \ S1; \ \{mid1\} \ S2 \ \{post\}$$

---

[6]It is not necessary to prove the proviso for the select rule here since the disjunction of the guards is $(G \vee \neg G)$ which is always true. Since all preconditions everywhere imply true, this select command as part of the recursive refinement strategy will always be valid.

where $S0$ involves a phase of preparation for a recursive call in $S1$. This preparation might typically include a decrementing of V. Indeed, very often no explicit preparation is necessary so that $S0$ is simply empty, and may be ignored.

The choice of the $mid1$ predicate should articulate one or more subproblems implicit in $post$ that can be solved by one or more recursive calls to this procedure. $S1$ should then be refined to attain $mid1$. The actual parameters of all recursive calls (and global variable values before the calls) should be such that they comply with the preconditions of the recursively called procedure, specifically in regard to the variant.

In each recursive call revisions to the pass-by-value parameters, in, and/or pass-by-value-result parameters $inout$ will typically drive down the variant in the recursively called procedure. For descriptive purposes below, we notionally describe this by assuming functions F and F' which transform in and $inout$ to their values required in the call. These functions may be evaluated as part of $S0$ indicated above, and/or they might represent direct substitutions of formal parameters by appropriate expressions (in the case of in variables). Thus, we assume that $S1$ may be represented by the recursive call $Compute(F(in), out, F'(inout))$. Of course, in practice this might be very simplistic, since additional computation might be required before and after the recursive call, and indeed, more than one recursive calls may be required.

5. Derive code, here generically denoted by a function H, such that

$$\{mid\}\ out := H(out)\ \{post\}$$

is satisfied. After refinement, this puts the procedure in the form:

$$\{pre \wedge 0 \le V < V_0\}$$
$$\textbf{if}\ \ B_1 \rightarrow out := R_1$$
$$\vdots$$
$$\|\ \ \ B_i \rightarrow out := R_i$$
$$\|\ \ \ \neg G \rightarrow \{\text{Possible preparation code for recursive call}\}$$
$$Compute(F(in), out, F'(inout));$$
$$out := H(out)$$
$$\textbf{fi}$$
$$\{post\}$$

6. Finally, follow steps 5 and 6 of the general strategy for defining a procedure presented in Sect. 5.2. That is, refactor the procedure into a function if desired, and call the procedure from the main program. In the case where the variant V includes global variant variables, the main program call may involve initialising these variables to appropriate values to satisfy $0 \le V < V_0$. Recall, however, that we will always assume that this predicate is satisfied at the first invocation of the recursive procedure.

5.6 Recursive Examples

In this section, we will use the recursive refinement strategy to develop several recursive algorithms from specification.

5.6.1 Factorial

First, we will use the recursive refinement strategy to develop a terminating refinement of *Factorial* developed in Sect. 5.4. To recap, after steps 1 through 3 of the general procedure refinement strategy, we have a *Factorial* procedure of the form

$$\textbf{proc } Factorial\,(\textbf{value } n, \textbf{result } f)\ \{n \geq 0\}\, n, f : S\ \{f = n_0!\}\ \textbf{corp}$$

so step 1 of the recursive refinement strategy is complete. Step 2 requires the identification of base cases. To complete this step, consider the definition

$$n! = \begin{cases} \prod_{k=1}^{n} k & \text{if } n > 0 \\ 1 & \text{if } n = 0 \end{cases} \tag{5.3}$$

which shows that 0! is a base case since its value is known and trivially returnable.

Many implementations of recursive factorial use only this base case and work properly, but from a semantic point of view, 0! is considered a special case of the factorial function rather than a trivially simple case (since $\prod_{k=1}^{0} k$ is not defined). Keeping this in mind, 1! is trivially simple and also a good semantic fit since it represents the simplest defined case of $\prod_{k=1}^{n} k$. For this reason, we declare $B_1 \overset{\Delta}{=} (n = 0)$ and $B_2 \overset{\Delta}{=} (n = 1)$. Since the precondition specifies that $(n \geq 0)$ we may take $\neg G$ to be

$$\neg G \equiv (n \neq 0 \wedge n \neq 1) \wedge (n \geq 0) \equiv (n \geq 2)$$

The refinement is therefore:

$$\begin{aligned}
&\textbf{proc } Factorial(\textbf{value } n, \textbf{ result } f) \\
&\quad \{n \geq 0\} \\
&\quad \textbf{if } (n = 0) \rightarrow f := 1 \\
&\quad \textbf{|} \ (n = 1) \rightarrow f := 1 \\
&\quad \textbf{|} \ (n \geq 2) \rightarrow \{n \geq 2\}\ S\ \{f = n_0!\} \\
&\quad \textbf{fi} \\
&\quad \{f = n_0!\} \\
&\textbf{corp}
\end{aligned}$$

For step 3, it is necessary to define a variant V which will satisfy $0 \leq V < V_0$ as part of the precondition of each recursive call. Intuitively, n makes a good choice for V, since n is bounded from below by zero. (We know that when n is 0 or 1 there is no recursive call.)

We now have $V \equiv n$, and we add $0 \leq n < n_0$ to the precondition. The precondition to the procedure is therefore modified to

$$(n \geq 0) \wedge (0 \leq n < n_0) \equiv (n \geq 0) \wedge (n < n_0)$$

The resulting procedure outline is therefore:

> **proc** *Factorial*(**value** n, **result** f)
> $\qquad \{(n \geq 0) \wedge (n < n_0)\}$
> $\qquad$**if** $(n = 0) \rightarrow f := 1$
> $\qquad$∥ $(n = 1) \rightarrow f := 1$
> $\qquad$∥ $(n \geq 2) \rightarrow \{n \geq 2\} \ S \ \{f = n_0!\}$
> $\qquad$**fi**
> $\qquad \{f = n_0!\}$
> **corp**

Recall that we assume that when the initial call from the main program is made, then the variant part of the precondition is initially met by default.

Step 4 now advises us to use the composition rule, as part of step 4, to refine the specification of the last guard into

$$\{n \geq 2\} \, n, f : S1 \, \{mid\}; \, n, f : S2 \, \{f = n_0!\}$$

The challenge is to determine *mid* in such a way that: (1) $S1$ can be refined to a recursive call that attains *mid*; and (2) as part of $S2$, something can be done to f so that $f = n_0!$ is satisfied.

Equation (5.3) shows that the factorial's definition can be restated recursively as

$$n! = n \times (n - 1)! \qquad\qquad (5.4)$$

provided that $n > 0$. This broadly suggests the way ahead:

- Define *mid* as $\{f = (n_0 - 1)!\}$ and satisfy *mid* by regarding $S1$ as the recursive call *Factorial*$((n - 1), f)$.
- Then refine $S2$ to $f := f \times n$ to attain the postcondition $\{f = n_0!\}$. (Thus, in terms of the earlier discussion, the function $H(f)$ is defined as $f \times n$.)

Let us therefore show that the following is true.

$$\{n \geq 2\} \, Factorial \, ((n - 1), f) \, \{f = (n_0 - 1)!\}; \, f := f \times n \, \{f = n_0!\} \quad (5.5)$$

We begin by addressing the first part of (5.5). Assume the that the specification of the *Factorial* program is correct, i.e. that $\{(n \geq 0) \wedge (n < n_0)\}$ R_{body} $\{f = n_0!\}$ is true, where R_{body} designates the body of the program that is still being evolved. (As suggested earlier, this can later be verified by an inductive argument.) Noting that $(n - 1)$ is to be used as an actual parameter for the formal parameter n we apply Rule 11 to get:

$$\{(n \geq 0) \wedge (n < n_0)[n \backslash (n - 1)]\}\, n, f : S1\, \{f = n![n \backslash (n - 1)]\}$$

$$\sqsubseteq \{\text{Rule } 11\}$$

$$\{(n - 1 \geq 0) \wedge (n - 1 < n_0)\}\, Factorial((n - 1), f)\, \{f = (n - 1)!\}$$

$$\equiv \{\text{Since } (n - 1 \geq 0) \equiv (n \geq 1) \text{ and since } (n - 1 < n_0) \equiv \text{true} \}$$

$$\{(n \geq 1)\}\, Factorial((n - 1), f)\, \{f = (n - 1)!\} \tag{5.6}$$

This refinement sequence assures us that starting from $n \geq 1$ and calling *Factorial*$((n - 1), f)$ will guarantee that $f = (n - 1)!$ will subsequently hold. The postcondition of (5.6) happily co-incides with the first postcondition encountered in the specification (5.5). However, specification (5.5) has a stronger precondition than (5.6), namely $(n \geq 2)$ instead of $(n \geq 1)$. Clearly, then,

$$\{n \geq 2\}\, Factorial((n - 1), f)\, \{f = (n - 1)!\} \tag{5.7}$$

is guaranteed to hold, if (5.6) holds.[7]

Seen in terms of the function F mentioned in the narrative of step 4, this function has implicitly been defined as $F(x) = x - 1$, so that the recursive call *Factorial*$(n - 1, f)$ and *Factorial*$(F(n), f)$ are equivalent.

To verify the assignment in the second part of (5.5) we need to prove that $f = (n_0 - 1)! \Rightarrow f = n_0![f \backslash f \times n]$. This follows directly done.

Sticking all the pieces of code together gives the final refinement of the factorial procedure:

```
proc Factorial(value n, result f)
    {n ≥ 0}
    if (n = 0) → f := 1
    ▌ (n = 1) → f := 1
    ▌ (n ≥ 2) → Factorial(n − 1, f); f := n × f
    fi
    {f = n!}
corp
```

---

[7]Note carefully that we are not arguing here that (5.7) refines (5.6). It patently does not, since it involves a strengthening of the precondition, not a weakening thereof. Indeed, the reverse is true, by virtue of the "weaken precondition" refinement rule, i.e. (5.7) $\sqsubseteq$ (5.6). Rather, we are claiming that if a specification is known to be true for a weak precondition, it is guaranteed to remain true for a stronger precondition.

While this refinement is already complete, in the interests of completing all the steps in the strategy, the procedure can be easily refactored into a function by making f into a return value and compacting the recursive call and assignment of f into a single statement as follows:

> **func** *Factorial*(**value n**) : $\langle f \rangle$
> $\qquad \{n \geq 0\}$
> $\qquad$ **if** $(n = 0) \rightarrow f := 1$
> $\qquad$ | $(n = 1) \rightarrow f := 1$
> $\qquad$ | $(n \geq 2) \rightarrow \{n \geq 0\}\ f := n \times Factorial(n - 1)\ \{f = n!\}$
> $\qquad$ **fi**
> $\qquad \{f = n!\}$
> **cnuf**

Finally, suppose that a main program has been specified by

$$\{x = 7\}\ y : S\ \{y = x_0!\}$$

Intuitively, we would want to replace S by a recursive call to the derived function, and return its value in y, i.e. we would simply say that this specification is adhered to by $y := Factorial(x)$. Let us verify this intuition by meticulous adherence to the refinement rules. Since we rely on our convention that this first call always complies with the variant used to derive the recursive procedure, we will not include the variant as part of the procedure's precondition.

$\qquad \{x = 7\}\ y : S\ \{y = x_0!\}$

$\sqsubseteq \qquad$ {Weaken precondition}

$\qquad \{x > 0\}\ y : S\ \{y = x_0!\}$

$\equiv \qquad$ {Reversed substitution}

$\qquad \{n > 0[n\backslash x]\}\ y : S\ \{f = n_0![n_0, f\backslash x_0, y]\}$

$\sqsubseteq \qquad$ {Rule 11 (pass-by-value) and Rule 12 (pass-by-result)}

$\qquad \{n > 0[n\backslash x]\}\ y := Factorial(x)\ \{f = n_0![n_0, f\backslash x_0, y]\}$

$\equiv \qquad$ {Forward substitution}

$\qquad \{x > 0\}\ y := Factorial(x)\ \{y = x_0!\}$

This final form gives code that is a refinement of the specification stated for the main program. It guarantees that if the actual variable x is initialised to *any* positive value, the code will terminate and deliver in y a value that is the factorial of x. In particular, if x is initialised to 7 to conform with the main program's precondition, the code will compute 7!. Henceforth, we will take the liberty of following our intuition, instead of giving this complete justification for making the recursive call from the main program.

5.6.2   Searching a List

In Chap. 3, an iterative linear search algorithm was developed that searches through elements of an array. Here we develop a recursive linear search algorithm that searches through elements of a list.

Consider a list $\mathcal{L}$ of elements E_0, E_1, ..., E_{n-1} where n is the length of $\mathcal{L}$ and each element contains some arbitrary integer value. The following concepts and operations are defined:

- $Val(E)$ denotes the value of the element E.
- $H(\mathcal{L})$ denotes the first element (index zero) of the list $\mathcal{L}$.
- $T(\mathcal{L})$ denotes a sublist of $\mathcal{L}$ that contains all the elements of $\mathcal{L}$ in order, except for $H(\mathcal{L})$.[8]
- A special "terminating element" T is defined as having the property that $Val(T)$ returns the special value NULL.
- The predicate $NT(\mathcal{L})$ returns true if and only if the last element of list $\mathcal{L}$ and only the last element is a terminating element. We say that such a list is null-terminating.
- The length of a null-terminating list, $\mathcal{L}.len$, does not include the terminating element, so for an empty null-terminating list $\mathcal{L}$, we have $\mathcal{L}.len = 0$.[9]

Let x denote some integer value and $\mathcal{L}$ denote a non-terminating list as defined above. We are going to consider a problem whose precondition is:

$$pre \triangleq NT(\mathcal{L})$$

We will develop a recursive linear search algorithm to search $\mathcal{L}$ for the value of x. If the value of x appears in an element within $\mathcal{L}$, then variable i must represent the index of that element (starting from index zero), otherwise i must have the value -1.

We rely on a similar predicate to the one used for developing the iterative array linear search algorithm developed in Chap. 3, namely

$$appears(\mathcal{L}, V) \triangleq \exists j : [0, \mathcal{L}.len) \cdot (V = Val(\mathcal{L}_j))$$

which is true if an element with the value of V appears in $\mathcal{L}$ and false otherwise.

As discussed above, x may or may not match an element in $\mathcal{L}$ and the postcondition must take both of these possibilities into account. Thus, the postcondition can be expressed as

$$post(\mathcal{L}, x, i) \triangleq (appears(\mathcal{L}, x) \wedge Val(E_i) = x) \vee (\neg appears(\mathcal{L}, x) \wedge (i = -1))$$

---

[8]*Head* and *Tail* are analogous to the CAR and CDR pointers in LISP.

[9]This terminating list design is based on the Typelist struct developed by Alexandrescu for the Loki library [2].

The specification of the problem can be stated formally as

$$i : [NT(\mathcal{L}), post(\mathcal{L}, x, i)]$$

Commencing at step 1 of the suggested strategy for developing recursive procedures, note that the procedure that we will develop finds an index of an element. Hence we select *IndexOf* as its name. The formal specification statement of *IndexOf* is almost the same as that just given for the problem, namely $i :$ $[NT(L), post(L, z, i)]$. The only difference is that the specification of *IndexOf* relies on formal parameters L and z, whereas the previous specification referenced the specific values $\mathcal{L}$ and x which will later serve as actual parameters for *IndexOf*.

Since L appears in both the pre- and postcondition we could pass it as a value-result parameter. However, since the procedure should not change the list itself, it is safer to pass L by value. z appears in the postcondition but once again, z should not be changed as part of the algorithm, so we also pass it by value. i is the output of the procedure and is passed by result. This gives us an initial form of

proc *IndexOf*(**value** L, **value** z, **result** i)
$\qquad \{NT(L)\}$
$\qquad i : S$
$\qquad \{post(L, z, i)\}$
corp

With step 1 complete, step 2 requires that base cases be identified and handled. One obvious base case is where the list is empty (except, of course, for its terminating element whose presence is enforced by the precondition $NT(L)$). In such a case, the list cannot contain z, so i should be assigned to -1 to satisfy the postcondition.

A second base case exists when the first element of a list is an element with the value of z. Formally stated, when $Val(H(L)) = z$ we can return the index 0.

As suggested by step 2, we introduce a selection statement to handle these base cases. To reduce notational clutter, we leave out from the precondition to S explicit reference to the conjunct corresponding to $\neg G$ as well as to $V = V_0$. These conjuncts should always be regarded as implicitly present in subsequent reasoning. The result is:

proc *IndexOf*(**value** L, **value** z, **result** i)
$\qquad \{NT(L)\}$
$\qquad$ **if** $(Val(H(L))) = NULL) \rightarrow i := -1$
$\qquad \| \quad (Val(H(L))) = z) \rightarrow i := 0$
$\qquad \| \quad ((Val(H(L)) \neq NULL) \vee (Val(H(L))) \neq z))) \rightarrow$
$\qquad\qquad\qquad \{NT(L) \wedge ((Val(H(L)) \neq NULL) \vee (Val(H(L))) \neq z))\}$
$\qquad\qquad\qquad S$
$\qquad\qquad\qquad \{post(L, z, i)\}$
$\qquad$ **fi**
$\qquad \{post(L, z, i)\}$
corp

Now we must define a variant in such a way that we can guarantee the recursive calls terminate. By passing an empty null-terminating list to the procedure it will not recurse, so by passing ever smaller sublists recursively, we can guarantee termination. Keeping this in mind, a good choice for V appears to be $V = L.len$. Step 3 is now complete.

Step 4 requires the use of composition to split the specification of the recursive case. We need to choose mid such that it is satisfied by a recursive call. Consider information that is inherent in the guard of this recursive case. It consists of two disjuncts. One of the disjuncts affirms that the $H(L) \neq z$; the other, $H(L) \neq NULL$, affirms that there is at least one more non-terminating element remaining in the tail of the list. This information indicates that a reasonable aim for mid would be to assert that i indicates where—if at all—z is to be found in the tail of the list. This is precisely what is asserted by $post(T(L), z, i)$, which we therefore select as our version of mid in this case.

From this point, to cut back on notational clutter, we will not refer to the guard conjuncts $H(L) \neq z$ and $H(L) \neq NULL$ in our subsequent reasoning. Neither will we refer to the variant, except to note that it will indeed decline from one recursive call to the next.

We want to refine as follows:

$$\{NT(L)\}\ S\ \{post(L, z, i)\}$$

$\sqsubseteq$ {Sequence rule}

$$\{NT(L)\}\ S1\ \{post(T(L), z, i)\}\ ;\ S2\ \{post(L, z, i)\} \tag{5.8}$$

$\sqsubseteq$ {By some suitable justification}

$$\{NT(L)\}\ IndexOf(T(L), z, i);\ \{post(T(L), z, i)\} \tag{5.9}$$

$$S2$$

$$\{post(L, z, i)\}$$

How do we justify the second refinement step—i.e. the step that leads from (5.8) to (5.9)? Clearly we have to appeal to Rule 11.

Rule 11 assumes the correctness of the body of *IndexOf* with respect to its stated pre- and postconditions. For our purposes, this correctness is assumed but it can be separately verified using induction subsequent to its derivation.

The rule then requires us to make the substitution $[L \backslash T(L)]$ in the precondition $\{NT(L)\}$ of the body of *IndexOf*. The rule also requires us to make the substitution $[L_0 \backslash T(L_0)]$ in the postcondition $\{post(L, z, i)\}$ of the body of *IndexOf*. Here, the L in postcondition $\{post(L, z, i)\}$ references the incoming list, L. It may therefore be treated as L_0 and replaced by its initial tail, denoted by $T(L)$. Applying the rule then explains the first step of following refinement sequence.

$$\{NT(T(L))\}\ S1\ \{post(T(L), z, i)\} \tag{5.10}$$

$\sqsubseteq$ {Using Rule 11}

$$\{NT(T(L))\}\ IndexOf(T(L), z, i)\ \{post(T(L), z, i)\}$$

$\sqsubseteq$ {Since $NT(L) \iff NT(T(L))$}

$$\{NT(L)\}\ IndexOf(T(L), z, i)\ \{post(T(L), z, i)\} \tag{5.11}$$

But notice carefully the following: we wanted to show (5.8) $\sqsubseteq$ (5.9), and we have shown that (5.10) $\sqsubseteq$ (5.11) holds instead. Fortunately, (5.9) and (5.11) match. However, the preconditions in (5.8) and (5.10) do not match. Nevertheless, as pointed out above, the precondition in (5.8) is equivalent to the precondition in (5.10)—i.e. $NT(L) \iff NT(T(L))$. We may therefore confidently assert that (5.8) $\sqsubseteq$ (5.9).

The function F mentioned in step 4 of the refinement strategy corresponds in this present instance to $T(x)$. At the conclusion of this step we have:

> **proc** *IndexOf*(**value** L, **value** z, **result** i)
> $\qquad \{NT(L) \land 0 \le L.len < L_0.len\}$
> $\qquad$ **if** $(Val(H(L))) = NULL) \to i := -1$
> $\qquad \|\ (Val(H(L))) = z) \to i := 0$
> $\qquad \|\ ((Val(H(L))) \neq NULL) \lor (Val(H(L))) \neq z))) \to$
> $\qquad\qquad\qquad \{NT(L)\}$
> $\qquad\qquad\qquad\qquad IndexOf(T(L), z, i);$
> $\qquad\qquad\qquad \{post(T(L), z, i)\}$
> $\qquad\qquad\qquad\qquad S2$
> $\qquad\qquad\qquad \{post(L, z, i)\}$
> $\qquad$ **fi**
> $\qquad \{post(L, z, i)\}$
> **corp**

To execute step 5, we note that if the index of element x in a list is denoted by i, then the index of x in a superlist created by appending an element to the beginning of the list must be $i+1$. Thus, if the sought-after entry is found at index i in the tail of L, then it must be at $i + 1$ in L itself. This suggests that we can define the H function as $H(x) = x + 1$.

Note, however, that we must also consider the possibility that the element does not occur in the sublist, $(i = -1)$, and in such a case, i retains the value $i = -1$ with respect to the full list. This leads to the full definition of

$$H(x) = \begin{cases} x + 1 & x \ge 0 \\ x & x = -1. \end{cases}$$

Using an "as" command to represent this conditional change in the value of x, we have the complete code for the recursive function *IndexOf*:

```
proc IndexOf(value L, value z, result i)
    {NT(L) ∧ 0 ≤ L.len < L₀.len}
    if (Val(H(L))) = NULL) → i := −1
    ▯ (Val(H(L))) = z) → i := 0
    ▯ ((Val(H(L))) ≠ NULL) ∨ (Val(H(L))) ≠ z))) →
                    {NT(L) ∧ 0 ≤ L.len < L₀.len}
                    IndexOf(T(L, z), i);
                        as (i ≥ 0) → i := i + 1 sa
                    {post(L, z, i)}
    fi
    {post(L, z, i)}
corp
```

If desired, the procedure can now be refactored into a function. Either way, the procedure is ready to be called from a main program.

5.6.3 Evaluating an Expression Tree

Expression trees are often used in compilers to represent expressions as part of syntax analysis [1]. In this section a recursive algorithm will be developed to evaluate the expression represented in a binary expression tree (BET).

The primary use of recursion in this algorithm will be to traverse a recursive structure in order to carry out a specific computation. As such, it will be prudent to define exactly what is expected of this recursive structure.

The structure to be used is a BET. The predicate $BET(T)$ evaluates to true if and only if T abides by the following rules:

- $G(T, A)$ is a connected acyclic graph with set of nodes T and set of arcs A. Because A is not further referenced in this discussion, we shall simply refer to the graph as T.
- $T = N_0, N_1, \ldots, N_{k-1}$, where $|T| = k < \infty$ denotes the number of nodes in T.
- Each node in T has exactly one parent, which is another node in T, except for the single "root" node. The $Root(T)$ function returns the root node of T.
- Each node in T has either zero children or two children. The predicate $Term(N)$ is true if and only if the node N has zero children.
- If a node N has two children, one is referred to as the left child and the other is the right child and these are returned for node N by $L(N)$ and $R(N)$ respectively. The parent of both $L(N)$ and $R(N)$ is of course N.
- If $Term(N)$ is false for some N, then N holds a reference to an operator. For simplicity we will deal only with two binary operators. $Op(N)$ returns either the special value '+' for addition or the special value '×' for multiplication.

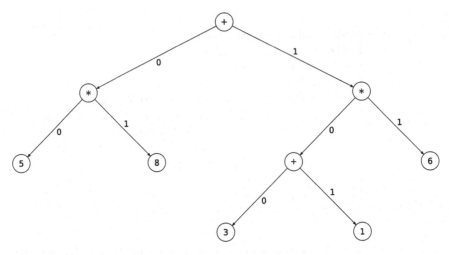

Fig. 5.1 A binary expression tree that evaluates to 64

- If *Term*(*N*) is **true** for some *N*, then *N* holds a reference to an integer value. This value is denoted by *Val*(*N*)
- The function *T*(*R*) returns the tree *T* formed with the node *R* as its root.

The above rules imply that all the nodes *N* in a BET *T* share a single common ancestor: the root node of the tree.

A BET is evaluated by evaluating each node, starting from leaf nodes and working upwards. A leaf node, *N* has the value *Val*(*N*). The value of a non-leaf node, *N*, whose two children are leaf nodes *L* and *R* respectively is *Val*(*L*) *Op*(*N*) *Val*(*R*). This value is recursively used to evaluate non-leaf nodes higher up in the tree. The value of the BET (i.e. the value of the binary expression which the tree represents) is given is the value of the tree's root.

The value of the BET *T* will be denoted by *Eval*(*T*). Note carefully that *Eval*(*T*) as used here is a mathematical function, not the name of a procedure or function in a computer program.

Consider, for example, the BET in (Fig. 5.1). The evaluation of the binary tree T is $(5 \times 8) + ((3 + 1) \times 6) = 64$, i.e. *Eval*(*T*) = 64.

We develop here a recursive procedure to evaluate an arbitrary BET that conforms to the description given above.

Step 1 requires that we pick a name, specification and choose parameters for the procedure to be defined. Since we are evaluating a tree, *Evaluate* will be the name for the procedure. Note throughout that this procedure name should be sharply distinguished from the mathematical function previously mentioned, *Eval*, which returns an integer value.

The procedure's precondition asserts that the tree structure, *T*, to be traversed is a BET as defined above, since we will be using these rules to refine the specification, so

$$pre \triangleq BET(T)$$

The postcondition asserts that some integer variable, say r, has the value of the evaluated tree, so

$$post \triangleq r = Eval(T)$$

T and r appear in the pre- and postconditions, so they make good candidates for *Evaluate*'s parameters. However, we know that later we will probably want to pass subtrees recursively to *Evaluate*, so a reference to a single root node, N, may be more useful than a reference to a tree T. Whenever we wish to refer to the full tree T, we can easily represent it as $T(N)$. Moreover, we can represent the two subtrees of node N as $T(L(N))$ and $T(R(N))$. Rewriting the pre- and postcondition in this form, the resulting specification becomes:

$$r : [BET(T(N)), r = Eval(T(N))]$$

This particular recursive algorithm does not change the tree structure or values in the nodes, so we pass N by value.[10] The output variable r only appears in the postcondition and should be passed by result. We now have a procedure skeleton:

$$\textbf{proc } Evaluate(\textbf{result } r, \textbf{value } N)$$
$$\{BET(T(N))\}$$
$$r : S$$
$$\{r = Eval(T(N))\}$$
$$\textbf{corp}$$

The specification needs to be refined with respect to S, the body of the recursive procedure to be developed.

It is necessary to determine base conditions where no recursive call is required. From the BET rules, it is known that when a node is terminal (it has no children) it holds a reference to an integer value that represents its evaluation. Under such circumstances, $Val(N)$ can simply be returned through an assignment of r. A select statement can be used to deal with this single base case. This leads to the procedure outline:

---

[10]However, a node will generally by represented by an object in an object-oriented programming languages, and most of these languages pass object parameters by a reference to the object. Semantically, a pass by reference is the same as a pass by value result, so in this example N could have been passed by value result. This would help to develop an algorithm that will be correct when implemented in an object oriented language such as Java, where objects can only be passed by reference.

```
proc Evaluate(result r, value N)
    {BET(T(N))}
    if Term(N) → r := PVal(N)
    ‖  ¬Term(N) → r : [BET(T(N)), r = Eval(T(N))]
    fi
    {r = Eval(T(N))}
corp
```

Ideally, each node in the tree should be visited exactly once for a complete traversal. As it turns out, this can be achieved by calling *Evaluate* on the left and right children of each non-terminal node N as long as we start at the root of the full tree: since the BET rules assert that the tree is connected and each non-root node has a parent, then clearly each node will be traversed (at least) at some point as the child of its parent beginning with the children of the root.

The rules also state that there are no loops or cycles among nodes, so each node will be traversed at most once. Since each node must be visited at least once and at most once, each node must be visited exactly once. This fact makes it easy to find a variant V.

We assume a global variable, L, is a set of nodes that is initialized to $\varnothing$ before *Evaluate* is called. Assume that the call to *Evaluate* passes on the BET B as actual parameter.

Each time a node is visited *Evaluate* must insert the visited node into L, thus increasing its size. This way, as B is traversed, L will become larger until it is equal in size to B (at which point all the nodes of B will have been visited and no more recursive calls should be allowed.) This gives a variant that depends on the actual parameter used during the call, namely $V = |B| - |L|$. The code thus far is

```
proc Evaluate(result r, value N)
    {BET(T(N)) ∧ (0 ≤ |B| − |L| < |B| − |L₀|}
    L := L ∪ {N};
    if Term(N) → r := Val(N)
    ‖  ¬Term(N) → r : [BET(T(N)), r = Eval(T(N))]
    fi
    {r = Eval(T(N))}
corp
```

Note that we have inserted at the beginning of the code an assignment statement to update L, since every entry into the procedure represents a visit to a node. This means that for every subsequent recursive call, the variant relative to its value at the beginning of this current recursive execution will have declined by one.

The recursive refinement strategy now suggests the use of composition to split the specification of the $\neg G$ guard into two. A *mid* must be found such that it is satisfied by a recursive call to *Evaluate*.

The evaluation of any tree is found be performing the operation of its root on operands derived from evaluating its left and right subtrees respectively. This suggests that *mid* should be satisfied by not one, but two recursive calls to *Evaluate*. As this is the case, it does not seem possible to store the result of the recursive calls in r as the second call will overwrite the first. Instead, it makes sense to introduce two temporary variables t_1 and t_2 to store the values of the evaluation of the left and right subtrees respectively. Later we will find a formula to derive the value of r from t_1 and t_2. By using the composition rule a second time we are left with the sequence of specifications

$$r : [BET(T(N)), r = Eval(T(N))]$$
$\sqsubseteq$ {Composition rule applied twice}
$$L, r, t_1, t_2 : [BET(T(N)), t_1 = Eval(T(L(N)))];$$
$$L, r, t_1, t_2 : [t_1 = Eval(T(L(N))),$$
$$t_1 = Eval(T(L(N))) \wedge t_2 = Eval(T(R(N)))];$$
$$L, r, t_1, t_2 : [t_1 = Eval(T(L(N))) \wedge t_2 = Eval(T(R(N)))$$
$$r = Eval(T(N))]$$

Noting that the predicate $BET(T(N))$ is invariant, it is carried over into each *mid* predicate as an extra conjunct, and we get

$\sqsubseteq$ {Rules 11 and 12 }
$$\{BET(T(N))\}$$
$$Evaluate(t_1, T(L(N)));$$
$$\{BET(T(N)) \wedge t_1 = Eval(T(L(N)))\}$$
$$Evaluate(t_2, T(R(N)));$$
$$BET(T(N)) \wedge t_1 = Eval(T(L(N))) \wedge t_2 = Eval(T(R(N)))\};$$
$$L, r, t_1, t_2 : S$$
$$r = Eval(T(N))\}$$

We will not justify the refinement step in detail. It relies on Rules 11 and 12 and requires substituting formal parameters with actual parameters, as specified by those rules. It also requires of us to ensure that only BETs are passed as actual parameters. That the left- and right subtrees passed as actual parameters in the recursive calls are indeed BETs follows directly from the fact that $BET(N)$ holds prior to the relevant call. This is the reason for writing $BET(N)$ explicitly as a conjunct in the various preconditions above.

The foregoing refinement can now be inserted into the code derived thus far. Refinement of the last part of the above specification can then proceed in terms of step 5 of our general strategy, the purpose being to derive appropriate code for S.

What is needed is a function H that will assign to r a value, in terms of t_1 and t_2 such that $r = Eval(T(N))$ is true. As previously pointed out, the value of a tree is equal to the root's binary operator applied to the evaluation of its left subtree (which we happen to have stored in t_1) and the evaluation of its right subtree (which we happen to have stored in t_2.) Since N is non-terminal ($Term(N)$ returned false during the guard evaluation of the selection statement) the BET rules tell us that the function $Op(N)$ will return the operator of N, which will be either "+" or "×". Using this knowledge, H can be written as

$$H(N, x, u, v) = \begin{cases} x := u + v & \text{if } Op(N) = \text{``+''} \\ x := u \times v & \text{if } Op(N) = \text{``}\times\text{''} \end{cases}$$

and this refines the procedure to its final form. The main program can now be refined to a call to *Evaluate*, sending through the root of B as a parameter:

```
proc  Evaluate(result r, value N)
        {BET(T(N))}
        L := L ∪ {Address(N)};
        if  Term(N) → r := Val(N)
        ‖  ¬Term(N) →
              Evaluate(t₁, T(L(N)));
              Evaluate(t₂, T(R(N)));
              if  (Op(N) = "+") → r := t₁ + t₂
              ‖  (Op(N) = "×") → r := t₁ × t₂
              fi
        fi
        {r = Eval(T(N))}
corp
```

We draw attention to the following general matters regarding $Evaluate()$.

Firstly, note that the global variant variable, L, need not have been global at all. Instead, L could easily have been passed by value-result to the procedure. However, passing these extra parameters to a procedure can make it cluttered and difficult to understand. In fact, L can be refactored out of the program altogether—its only purpose was to make explicit a variant in support of reasoning about termination. This would make the procedure slightly more portable, in the sense that the user (caller) would not need to initialise L or be otherwise concerned with it.

As a second closing observation, note that although the final algorithm defined for $Evaluate()$ is relatively short and simple, this only because the algorithm relies heavily on the fact that it is traversing a well defined BET structure with many helpful restrictions and rules. When writing an algorithm to traverse over a recursive structure like a tree, graph or lattice, it pays off to spend time identifying and defining what is expected from the structure. Doing so will make the algorithm simpler to write, as there is more information with which to work.

5.6.4 MergeSort

The final example details the derivation of the well-known von Neumann Merge-Sort algorithm. The algorithm is based on the idea that two sorted arrays can be easily merged into a single sorted array. A single array is broken down into many arrays of size one and zero, then these mini arrays are all merged together again to form a sorted array.

The function to merge two lists together is iterative, and thus will not be refined here. Instead, we will simply assume that it is already implemented with the signature

func $Merge(\textbf{value } Y, \textbf{value } Z) : \langle X \rangle$

and satisfies the specification: $X : [sorted(Y) \wedge sorted(Z), (X = Y \cup Z) \wedge sorted(X)]$

The first step, as always, is to choose a name, parameters and specification for the procedure. *MergeSort* is as good a name as any, and it should take an array as input. Its output should be the sorted array. To keep these two concerns separate, we pass the input array A by value and the output sorted array S by result. Let $perm(A, S)$ denote that S is a permutation of A. This gives us:

$$S : [\text{true}, perm(A, S) \wedge sorted(S)]$$

The obvious base cases are that either A is empty or A contains only one element. In either case, A is already sorted and $S := A$ satisfies the specification. This gives:

proc $MergeSort(\textbf{value } A, \textbf{result } S)$
  if $(A.len = 0) \rightarrow S := A$
  $\|$ $(A.len = 1) \rightarrow S := A$
  $\|$ $(A.len > 1) \rightarrow S : [\text{true}, perm(A, S) \wedge sorted(S)]$
  fi
corp

The variant is where things get tricky. Consider the diagrams in Fig. 5.2a, b. Clearly there are two different "stages" in performing a merge-sort: The array is split, then merged. However, these actions are interleaved: calls to merge will happen in between calls to split, and thus a variant must be found to take into account both of these types of calls. Each of these two stages needs to be considered when constructing the variant, so *splitPart* + *mergePart* seems like a good place to start.

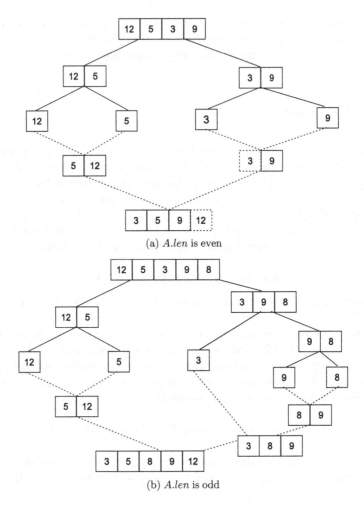

Fig. 5.2 *MergeSort* where *A.len* is even and where *A.len* is odd. (**a**) *A.len* is even (**b**) *A.len* is odd

We begin by considering the *splitPart*. The diagrams show that splitting the array forms a kind of tree (shown as black edges) with a particular depth. We begin by defining the maximum size, *maxSize*, of this tree to be the depth of the tree multiplied by the size of the array. This way we can also define a global variant variable, say *splitCount*, that stores combined sizes of the subarrays that have been split. As the arrays are split, their sizes are added to the variant variable, so that (*maxSize - splitCount*) approaches zero.

The depth of the tree has a logarithmic relation to the size of the array. Since the array is split in two, the depth of the tree is $log_2(A.len)$ rounded up to the closest integer, in addition to the depth (1) of the original array. This makes *maxSize* = $(log_2(A.len) + 1) \times size)$ and thus *splitPart* = $(((log_2(A.len) + 1) \times size) - splitCount)$. Now to consider the *mergePart*. The diagrams show that the merge part also forms a kind of tree (shown as grey edges) and has depth equal to one less than the spilt tree: $log_2(A.len)$. After each merge, we add the size of the newly formed subarray to a global variable, say *mergeCount*. This way, as the subarrays are merged together $((log_2(A.len) \times A.len) - mergeCount)$ approaches zero.

Combining all of this together we are left with

$$V = (log_2(A.len) \times (A.len) - splitCount) + (log_2(A.len)$$

$$\times (A.len) - mergeCount)$$

The recursive refinement strategy now suggests the use of the composition rule. In a similar way to the *Evaluate* problem from the previous section, an array can be thought of as the concatenation of its left subarray and its right subarray. We should use the composition rule twice so that the specification is divided into three parts: The first part should be satisfied by a recursive call on the left subarray and the second part should be satisfied by a recursive call on the right subarray. To store the sorted versions of these arrays we will use two temporary variables T_1 and T_2. We define

$mid1 \triangleq (perm(A_{[0,A.len/2)}, T_1) \wedge sorted(T_1))$ and

$mid2 \triangleq (perm(A_{[A.len/2,A.len)}, T_2) \wedge sorted(T_2))$

which leads to the specification of the body of the $\neg G$ guard as

$S : [\text{true}, mid1]; S : [mid1, mid1 \wedge mid2]; S : [mid1 \wedge mid2, perm(A, S) \wedge sorted(S)]$

Before refining specifications to recursive calls we need to make sure the variant is satisfied. This can be done by making sure that *splitCount* increases in size before either left or right is called and that *mergeCount* increases after merge is called. The easiest way to achieve this is to carry out the assignment of *splitCount* before the select statement and the assignment of *mergeCount* after the call to *Merge*(). We can now refine to recursive calls, leaving the program in the form:

```
proc MergeSort(value A, result S)
    if (A.len = 0) → S := A
    ▌ (A.len = 1) → S := A
    ▌ (A.len > 1) →
        MergeSort(A[0,A.len]/2), T₁); MergeSort(A[A.len/2,A.len), T₂)
        S : [mid1 ∧ mid2, perm(A, S) ∧ sorted(S)]
    fi
corp
```

Now all that is required is to find a H which assigns the value of S in terms of T_1 and T_2. It turns out that a call to $Merge(T_1, T_2)$ produces the required value of S, so

$$S : [mid1 \wedge mid2, perm(A, S) \wedge sorted(S)] \sqsubseteq S := Merge(T1, T2)$$

We must also remember to add *mergeCount* := *mergeCount* + *S*.*len* to satisfy the variant. This leaves the procedure in its final form:

> **proc** *MergeSort*(**value** *A*, **result** *S*)
>   *splitCount* = *splitCount* + *A*.*len*;
>   **if** (*A*.*len* = 0) → *S* := *A*
>   ▌ (*A*.*len* = 1) → *S* := *A*
>   ▌ (*A*.*len* > 1) →
>   *MergeSort*(*A*$_{[0,A.len/2)}$, *T*$_1$)
>   ; *MergeSort*(*A*$_{[A.len/2,A.len)}$, *T*$_2$)
>   ; *S* := *Merge*(*T*1, *T*2)
>   ; *mergeCount* := *mergeCount* + *S*.*len*
>   **fi**
> **corp**

Now the procedure can be called from a main program that sets the initial values of the global variant variables, *mergeCount* and *sortCount* to zero. As in the previous example, however, these counters are not an essential part of the algorithm, but were introduced in order to support reasoning about termination.

5.7   Conclusion

This chapter has illustrated how recursive algorithms can be derived in a formal correctness-by-construction fashion. A general strategy for deriving recursive algorithms has been outlined and illustrated by way of a number of examples. The strategy relies on refinement rules that indicate how a procedure invocation can be a refinement of a specification. The specification, in turn, corresponds to the pre- and postcondition of the called procedure, but where formal parameters are substituted by actual parameters. The way in which the substitution is to take place depends on the mode of the parameter: pass by value, result, or value-result.

Two important issues arise in the applying these rules. In the first place, the rules assume that the called procedure is correct in that it has a body that conforms to a specified pre- and postcondition. However, in the case of recursion , there is no way of knowing whether or not the called recursive program is indeed correct, because it is still under construction. It can only be formally shown to be correct once the algorithm has been developed. Induction would be the most suitable mathematical strategy for providing such proofs. However, no such proofs have been given in this chapter. Although we recognise the value and validity of mathematical rigour in providing such proofs, we nevertheless regard such proofs as outside the scope of this text. Instead, this chapter serves as a starting point for those who would wish to pursue more rigourously the theme of refinement calculus in the context of procedure invocation and recursive procedure construction.

A second issue worth mentioning at this point is the introduction of a variant as part of the general solution strategy. Although the formal definition of a variant indeed gives confidence that the recursion will not be infinite, in most situations it might be something of an overkill. This became evident in the last two examples, where we saw that variables keeping track of the variant could be refactored out of the final solution—they serve no other role in the program except to indicate that progress is being made towards arriving at the base cases. From a pragmatic point of view, one could dispense with a variant if you have sufficient assurance that your successive recursive calls will always be on ever-smaller problems and therefore that the base case scenarios will eventually be reached. This is specifically the case when the recursive calls deal with data structures such as graphs, trees, lists, sets, etc which are partitioned into smaller data structures at each call.

The algorithm to be derived in the next chapter will depend significantly on recursion. However, we will neither prove the final algorithm correct by use of induction, nor will we formally define a variant to describe its progress towards termination, since this will be self-evident.

Chapter 6
Case Study: Lattice Cover Graph Construction

In this chapter, the correctness by construction approach is applied to an algorithmic problem that lies well off the beaten track of classical text book examples. The algorithm has been in the public domain since about 2000, but was only clearly explained and its correctness shown in 2010 [26]. The algorithm has also been shown to be considerably more efficient than its rivals.

The principle reason why we choose to devote an entire chapter to the derivation of this algorithm is to impress upon the reader that correctness by construction as an approach to developing software is not merely a classroom exercise. Instead, it can be used to discover new and important algorithms. When adopted as a general approach to working out new algorithms, the results tend to be both elegant and fruitful.

6.1 Introduction

The problem to be addressed is to construct the so-called cover graph of a special type of set called a lattice. Now this task is crucial in an emerging field in computer science called formal concept analysis (FCA). FCA relies on lattices to study sets of objects and their associated discrete attributes. In fact, organising such information in a lattice structure provides the richest, most detailed possible view of the data. It allows for the deployment of inferencing mechanisms, so that these structures can be used in fields such as machine learning, linguistics, ontology building, knowledge representation, data mining, etc.

Formal concept analysis has been around for about three decades. Various algorithms, many rather inefficient, have been proposed to construct the cover graphs required by the theory. In fact, one of the alleged shortcomings of the FCA approach is that these cover graphs can, in worst case scenarios, grow exponentially. The graph construction algorithm developed here evolved from the efforts of a postgraduate project at Pretoria University in which a cover graph construction algorithm, known in the literature as *AddIntent*, was proposed. The algorithm turned

D.G. Kourie and B.W. Watson, *The Correctness-by-Construction Approach to Programming*, DOI 10.1007/978-3-642-27919-5_6,
© Springer-Verlag Berlin Heidelberg 2012

out to be significantly faster than others under almost all scenarios, particularly when applied to live data. However, the algorithm's workings were rather opaque, and consequently it was difficult to be convinced of its correctness. This chapter shows how a variant of that algorithm can be derived in a way that is transparent, comprehensible and correct. Refactoring to the original algorithm is quite easily done. The material covered is derived from a published version in [26].

The next section will introduce the required basic theory about lattices in general, and the notion of a special kind of lattice to be used in the chapter, called a set intersection-closed lattice (SICL). An algorithm is then developed in a correctness by construction fashion that inserts an element into an existing SICL, and that expands its existing cover graph accordingly. The refactorings needed to derive the original *AddIntent* algorithm are then provided, and the reader is also given a brief introduction to the FCA study domain, so that the practical applicability of the algorithm may more fully be appreciated.

6.2 Preliminaries

6.2.1 Lattices

First, we recall basic definitions from lattice theory [4, 11]. We will be concerned with a finite set, L. We do not really care what type of elements are in the set. However, we insist that some (but perhaps not all) elements of the set can be compared to one another, and we denote the comparator by the symbol $\leq$. The fact that this symbol corresponds to the well known "less or equal to" symbol used to indicate the ordering of numbers (either real or integer) is co-incidental. For example, L could represent a set of people, and $a \leq b$ could be used to represent the fact either that the symbols a and b represent the same person, or that person a is a descendent of person b. Alternatively, L could represent a set of sets, and $a \leq b$ could be used to represent the fact that set a is a subset of set b (i.e., $a \subseteq b$). A set whose elements can be compared by some such comparator is called a partially ordered set under the following circumstances.

Definition 6.2.1. Set L is *partially ordered* by $\leq$ if and only if:

- $\leq$ is reflexive, i.e., $\forall a : L \cdot (a \leq a)$
- $\leq$ is antisymmetric, i.e., $\forall a, b : L \cdot ((a \leq b) \wedge (b \leq a)) \implies (a = b)$
- $\leq$ is transitive, i.e., $\forall a, b, c : L \cdot ((a \leq b) \wedge (b \leq c)) \implies (a \leq c)$

A partially ordered set (abbreviated to a poset) will be denoted by $(L, \leq)$ if we wish to emphasise that $\leq$ is the ordering relationship. The following are examples of posets:

$$(L_{sets}, \subseteq) \text{ where } L_{sets} = \{\{a, b, c, d\}, \{a, b, c\}, \{a, b, d\}, \{b, c\}\}$$

$$\left(L_{fam}, \leq\right) \text{ where } L_{fam} = \{\texttt{pete}, \texttt{mary}, \texttt{bob}, \texttt{bill}\}$$

In the second example, we are assuming that Pete and Mary are siblings, and that they have grandfathers Bob and Bill. We are using $\leq$ to indicate descendant relationships, but also assume that $\leq$ is reflexive—i.e., that, for example, pete $\leq$ pete holds.

In such posets it is not necessary that *all* pairs of elements are comparable by the ordering. Thus, it is neither the case that pete $\leq$ mary, nor that mary $\leq$ pete. Similarly, bob and bill bear no descendant relationship to one another—at least no relationship that is evident in set L_{fam}. Similarly, in poset L_{sets}, there is no subset relation between $\{a, b, c\}$ and $\{a, b, d\}$.

Moreover, depending on how L is chosen, it may or may not be the case that given an arbitrary set of elements $T \subseteq L$, a u can be found such that $\forall x : T(x \leq u)$. If it is the case, then u is called an *upper bound* of the set T.

Definition 6.2.2 (Upper bound). Let $(L, \leq)$ be a poset, and $T \subseteq L$. Then u is an upper bound of T if and only if $(\forall x : T \cdot (x \leq u))$.

Thus, $\{a, b, c\}$ is an upper bound of the set $T_{sets} = \{\{a, b, c\}, \{b, c\}\}$. Also bob is an upper bound of the set $T_{fam} = \{\text{pete}, \text{mary}\}$. Notice that since $\{a, b, c\} \in T_{set}$ but bob $\notin T_{fam}$, the upper bound of set T may or may not be an element of T.

Also notice that a set T may have many upper bounds. For example T_{fam} has the set of upper bounds $T_{ufam} = \{\text{bob}, \text{bill}\}$. Similarly, T_{set} has the following set of upper bounds $T_{uset} = \{\{a, b, c\}, \{a, b, c, d\}\}$. Now T_{uset} possesses a property that T_{ufam} does not have, namely, there is an element of T_{uset} that is "smaller" than all other elements of T_{uset}. This is the set $\{a, b, c\}$. This element is the least upper bound (LUB) of T_{set}. We define separately this key notion about posets.

Definition 6.2.3 (Supremum or LUB). Let $(L, \leq)$ be a poset, and $T \subseteq L$. Then u is the supremum (or least upper bound or LUB, or join) of T if and only if T has a non-empty set of upper bounds, call it T_{up}, and $\forall x \in T_{up} \cdot (u \leq x)$.

We provide the following observations about the notion of a supremum:

- The terms supremum, LUB and join are synonyms.
- If a set T has no upper bounds, then it does not have a supremum.
- The fact that a set has upper bounds is not a guarantee that the set has a supremum. For example, the set T_{fam} mentioned above does not have a supremum.
- It is not difficult to prove that the supremum, if it exists, is unique.
- A set that has only one upper bound will obviously have that upper bound as its supremum.
- The supremum of set T may or may not be an element of T. For example, consider the poset $(\mathbb{R}, \leq)$, where $\mathbb{R}$ represents the real numbers. The subset of $\mathbb{R}$ represented by the interval $[0, 1)$ has as its supremum 1, but $1 \notin [0, 1)$. As another example, the supremum of $T = \{\{b, c\}, \{a, b, d\}\}$ in the poset $(L_{sets}, \subseteq)$ mentioned above, is $\{a, b, c, d\} \notin T$.
- The term "join" is more commonly encountered in literature about lattices (see below) and the symbol $\vee$ is often used as an infix operator to denote a join. Thus,

if u is the join of $T = \{a, b\}$ then we could write $u = a \vee b$. Less commonly one might encounter the notation $u = \bigvee T$ to denote the supremum or join of set T.

Dual concepts apply in regard to lower bounds in a poset: T could have a lower bound in poset $(L, \leq)$. The set of lower bounds may or may not have a greatest lower bound (GLB). The reader may, as an exercise, formulate the precise meaning of these concepts. The GLB of $T \subseteq L$ is also called the *infimum* or *meet* of T. The meet of a and b is sometimes denoted by $a \wedge b$.

We are now finally in a position to give the definition of a lattice:

Definition 6.2.4 (Lattice).   A *lattice* is a poset $(L, \leq)$ in which every pair of elements has a supremum and an infimum.

Where the ordering relation $\leq$ is clear from the context, the lattice is simply indicated by L. Because every set of elements of a non-empty lattice L has a supremum and infimum, it can easily be shown that L has a maximum element (denoted by $\top_L$) and a minimum element (denoted by $\bot_L$).

Definition 6.2.5 (Child, parent and cover relationships).   If $c, p \in L$ then we say that c is a *child* of p (p is a *parent* of c) if and only if

$$(c \leq p) \wedge (\forall r : (L \setminus \{c, p\}) \cdot (\neg(c \leq r \leq p))).$$

We also say that p *covers* c.

Notation 6.2.6 ($\prec_L$).   *We denote such a child–parent relationship between the elements of a lattice by $c \prec p$ or by $c \prec_L p$ where required by the context. Note that $\prec_L$ is called the* cover relation *of L. It is a binary relation on the set L, i.e., it is the set of pairs from the elements of L that are in a child–parent or cover relation to one another. Specifically:*

$$\prec_L \triangleq \{(c, p) \mid c \prec_L p\}.$$

This cover relation on a lattice can be represented visually by a graph called a line (or Hasse) diagram. Figure 6.1 is an example of such a line diagram. Its contents will be discussed in more detail below. For the moment, note that in this line diagram, lattice elements are nodes; parent nodes are drawn above their child nodes; and an arc is drawn between every two nodes c and p for which $c \prec p$ holds. Following the normal convention of denoting a graph by a pair of sets, the first being the set of nodes, and the second being the set of arcs, the line diagram of L can be denoted by the graph $(L, \prec)$. Unsurprisingly, we also refer to this graph as the *cover graph* of L.

This rest of this chapter is about using the correctness-by-construction approach to develop an algorithm that constructs the cover graph of a particular kind of lattice. The next subsection introduces this particular kind of lattice, as well as other concepts that will be used in developing the algorithm.

6.2.2 Set Intersection-Closed Lattices

The notion of a set of subsets from an alphabet, A, is quite well-known. The maximal set of subsets of A, the powerset, denoted $\mathbb{P}(A)$, consists of all possible subsets of A, including $\emptyset$ and A itself. Clearly the intersection of any two elements chosen from $\mathbb{P}(A)$ will also be an element of $\mathbb{P}(A)$. We say that $\mathbb{P}(A)$ is closed with respect to set intersection and we call $\mathbb{P}(A)$ a *closure system*. We are interested in closure systems, of which $\mathbb{P}(A)$ is but one example. The general definition of a closure system is the following.

Definition 6.2.7 (Closure system). A *closure system* C on some alphabet A is a collection of subsets of A that contains A and that is closed under set intersection—i.e.:

$$C \text{ is a closure system on } A \iff (A \in C) \wedge \left(\forall \mathcal{X} \subseteq C : \left(\bigcap \mathcal{X} \in C\right)\right).$$

In this definition, C is a set of subsets formed from the alphabet A, and $\mathcal{X}$ is to be interpreted as a subset of the set elements of C—i.e., $\mathcal{X}$ is a set of subsets of C. The intersection of all the sets in $\mathcal{X}$, denoted above by $\bigcap \mathcal{X}$, will obviously be another set, possibly the set $\emptyset$. For C to be closed under set intersection, it is required that this resulting set is also an element of C.

There are very many possible ways of ordering two arbitrary elements, X and Y, of a closure system, C, depending on the given context. For example, we could order the decide to order a closure system whose elements are all of different sizes, in terms of the respective sizes of the elements, i.e., $X \leq Y$ if and only if $|X| \leq |Y|$. Alternatively, we may flip a coin to decide whether two randomly selected elements of a closure system, say X and Y, are to be regarded as $X \leq Y$.

In general, we cannot claim that an arbitrary ordering of a closure system is a lattice, because the ordering may not comply with the rules of a partial order, and/or because it might not be the case that every pair of elements has a supremum and infimum.

In this text, we are interest in one very specific way of ordering the elements of a closure system, namely by set inclusion—i.e., $X \leq Y$ if and only if $X \subseteq Y$. It turns out that such a closure system (i.e., closure system ordered by set inclusion, $\subseteq$) is indeed a lattice—it is a partially ordered set in which every non-empty set of elements has a unique LUB (supremum) and a unique GLB (infimum). We will not prove this result from lattice theory, but merely accept it.

Definition 6.2.8 (SICL). If C is a closure system on A, then we call the lattice $(C, \subseteq)$ a *SICL*.

Figure 6.1 shows a line diagram of a SICL with alphabet $\{a, b, c, d\}$. In this figure, as well as in forthcoming examples, a set $\{a, b, c, d\}$ is abbreviated to abcd, $\{a, b, c\}$ to abc, etc. The SICL is the set of nodes in the diagram, $\{abcd, abd, ad, bd, bc, d, b, \emptyset\}$. The line diagram represents the cover graph of

Fig. 6.1 Example line diagram/cover graph of lattice L

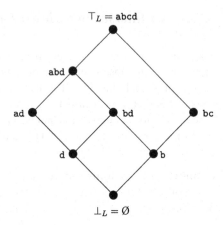

this SICL, where a node p is connected by a downward arc to a node c if $c \prec p$. (For example, the fact that abd $\prec$ abcd means that, in the diagram, abcd should be connected by the downward arc to abd, etc.).

The top element of the lattice in the figure is abcd, the bottom element is $\emptyset$ and there are various other elements in between. Notice that set intersection closure indeed holds: the intersection of every pair of nodes in the figure (actually of every set of nodes in the figure) is also a node in the figure. Some examples are:

$$ad \cap bd = d,$$

$$abd \cap bd = bd,$$

$$abd \cap bc = b,$$

$$ad \cap bc = \emptyset,$$

$$abd \cap ad \cap bc = \emptyset,$$

$$etc.$$

Notice also that the meet operation ($\wedge$) on sets in a SICL coincides with the intersection operation. For example, ad $\cap$ bd $=$ d $=$ ad $\wedge$ bd. One can easily find the meet of a set of nodes in the diagram by traversing down paths from each node in the set to where these paths "meet" in a common node. Notice, too, that there will always be one and only one such meet. We can formulate this as the following general property.

Property 6.2.9. *In a SICL, the meet of a set of nodes is the same as the intersection of the set of nodes.*

In a similar way, one can easily find the join of a set of nodes in the diagram by traversing *up* paths from each node in the set to where these paths "join" in a common node. Nevertheless, one should not infer that there is a symmetry in a SICL between the meet and the join ($\vee$) operation. It is sometimes but not *always* the case that if x and y are two arbitrary nodes in a SICL then $x \vee y = x \cup y$. There is a danger of being confused by this. For example, in Fig. 6.1, it is indeed the case that $\text{ad} \cup \text{bd} = \text{ad} \vee \text{bd} = \text{abd}$. However the figure also exhibits the following counter-example: $\text{bcd} = \text{bd} \cup \text{bc} \neq \text{bd} \vee \text{bc} = \text{abcd}$. Perhaps it would be wise to state this fact as well as a property.

Property 6.2.10. *In a SICL, the join of a set of nodes is sometimes, but not always the same as the union of the set of nodes.*

Furthermore, not every node in the figure is produced by intersecting some other two nodes. For example, nodes abcd, abd, ad, bd and bc are not produced by the intersection of any other nodes. Notice that these nodes only have a single parent in the cover relation (or no parent in the case of the top node, abcd). We state this fact as a formal SICL property.

Property 6.2.11. *In a SICL, any node with two or more parents is the intersection of those parents. A node with less than two parents is not the result of intersection.*

We shall require following SICL property (actually of any lattice) and the associated notation in developing the algorithm below.

Property 6.2.12. *If C is an arbitrary element of a SICL $\mathcal{L}$, then the set $\{R \in \mathcal{L} \mid R \subseteq C\}$ (denoted by $\downarrow C$ and called a principal ideal) is also a SICL whose top element is C. The cover relationship (arcs in the cover graph) of SICL $\downarrow C$ will be denoted by $\prec_{\downarrow C}$.*

Thus, for example, in Fig. 6.1, the principal ideal of abd is a SICL, we denote it by $\downarrow \text{abd}$ and it consists of the following elements: $\{\text{abd}, \text{ad}, \text{bd}, \text{b}, \text{d}, \emptyset\}$. The arcs in the cover graph of $\downarrow \text{abd}$ are thus given by $\prec_{\downarrow \text{abd}} = \{(\text{abd}, \text{ad}), (\text{abd}, \text{bd}), (\text{bd}, \text{b}),$ $(\text{bd}, \text{d}), (\text{ad}, \text{d}), (\text{d}, \emptyset), (\text{b}, \emptyset)\}$. Similarly, $\downarrow \text{bc}$ is a SICL consisting of $\{\text{bc}, \text{b}, \emptyset\}$ and the arcs in its cover graph are given by $\prec_{\downarrow \text{bc}} = \{(\text{bc}, \text{b}), (\text{b}, \emptyset)\}$.

It will also be important in developing the algorithm to be aware of the following property of SICLs (actually of any lattice).

Property 6.2.13. *Some nodes in $\downarrow C$ might be children of some nodes in $\mathcal{L} \setminus \downarrow C$. However, no node in $\downarrow C$ can be a parent of a node in $\mathcal{L} \setminus \downarrow C$.*

This is evident in Fig. 6.1. For example, none of the nodes in $\downarrow \text{abd}$ is a parent to any node outside of $\downarrow \text{abd}$. However, some nodes in $\downarrow \text{abd}$ are children of nodes in the original SICL—for example abd is a child of $\top_L$ and b is a child of bc.

Property 6.2.13 is crucial to the algorithm we shall develop since it has the following important consequence. Suppose we add a node to a principal ideal of a node in SICL $\mathcal{L}$, say to $\downarrow C$, without changing anything else in $\mathcal{L} \setminus \downarrow C$. However, we do it in such a way as to preserve the SICL nature of $\downarrow C$—i.e., we add all additional nodes needed in $\downarrow C$ to ensure that it is set intersection-closed. Then, Property 6.2.13 assures us that none of the new nodes will have children in $\mathcal{L} \setminus \downarrow C$.

As a concrete example of this, suppose we wished to add ab into SICL $\downarrow$abd in Fig. 6.1, and we specifically wanted to retain the new structure as a SICL. Then we would also have to add a to the revised $\downarrow$abd since a = ab ∩ ad. In addition, we would have to add arcs (abd, ab), (ab, b), (ab, a), (ad, a) and (a, Ø) to the arcs of the original $\prec_{\downarrow abd}$. Nodes abcd and bc are still parents of nodes in both the original and revised $\downarrow$, but nodes in neither the original nor revised SICL are parents to nodes in $\mathcal{L} \backslash \downarrow$ abd.

In order to formulate the problem to be addressed, let us define the following predicates:

$$SICL(\mathcal{L}, \top_{\mathcal{L}}) \triangleq \mathcal{L} \text{ is a SICL defined on the alphabet } A = \top_{\mathcal{L}}$$

$$CG(\mathcal{L}, \prec_{\mathcal{L}}) \triangleq \text{The cover graph of SICL } \mathcal{L} \text{ consists of nodes } \mathcal{L} \text{ and arcs } \prec_{\mathcal{L}}$$

$$pre \triangleq SICL(\mathcal{L}, \top_{\mathcal{L}}) \wedge CG(\mathcal{L}, \prec_{\mathcal{L}}) \wedge X \subset \top_{\mathcal{L}}$$

$$post' \triangleq SICL(\mathcal{L}, \top_{\mathcal{L}}) \wedge CG(\mathcal{L}, \prec_{\mathcal{L}}) \wedge X \in \mathcal{L}$$

The problem to be addressed is then almost (but not quite): $(\mathcal{L}, \prec_{\mathcal{L}}) : [pre, post']$. Formulated in this way, the problem stated in natural language is more or less:

> Given a SICL $\mathcal{L}$ and its cover graph with arcs $\prec_{\mathcal{L}}$, as well as a new set X which is a subset of the SICL's top element, update the SICL and its arcs so that it incorporates the new set X.

Clearly, in order to do this update, not only the new set X must be added into the SICL, but all additional sets that are needed to ensure set intersection-closedness. Our formulation indeed embodies this requirement, since it requires as part of *post'* not only that $X \in \mathcal{L}$ but also that the updated $\mathcal{L}$ must be a SICL. What is wrong with the above formulation is that it does not insist that the new SICL must differ *minimally* from the original one. It is not enough to preserve the SICL property— we must do so without adding additional sets into the SICL that are not specifically required because of the addition of X.

We therefore require a way of saying unambiguously that $\mathcal{L}$ must be enlarged to include only X and pairwise intersections of X with all elements of $\mathcal{L}$. This is the purpose of Definition 6.2.14 that introduces the notion of an X-extension of a set.

Definition 6.2.14. Let $\mathcal{L}_0$ and $\mathcal{L}$ each be a set of sets from the alphabet A such that $\mathcal{L}_0 \subseteq \mathcal{L}$. Let $X \subseteq A$ and suppose $X \in \mathcal{L}$. Then $\mathcal{L}$ is said to be an X-*extension* of $\mathcal{L}_0$, denoted by $\mathcal{L}_0 \sqsubseteq_X \mathcal{L}$, if

$$\forall Y \in \mathcal{L} \setminus \mathcal{L}_0 : ((X = Y) \vee (\exists Z \in \mathcal{L}_0 : Y = (X \cap Z))).$$

Note that if $\mathcal{L}_0 = \mathcal{L}$, then the universal quantification in the above predicate is over an empty range and so the predicate is true, implying that a set of sets can be taken to be an X-extension of itself, where X is any element of that set.

This definition means that each element in $\mathcal{L}$ that is not in $\mathcal{L}_0$, aside from X itself, can be derived by intersecting some element in $\mathcal{L}_0$ with X.

As an example, suppose $\mathcal{L}$ is taken as all the elements in the lattice in Fig. 6.1, and $\mathcal{L}_0$ is taken as all excluding ad, d and $\varnothing$—i.e.:

$$\text{Suppose that } \mathcal{L} = \{\text{abcd}, \quad \text{abd}, \quad \text{ad}, \quad \text{bd}, \quad \text{bc}, \quad \text{d}, \quad \text{b}, \quad \varnothing\}$$

$$\text{and } \mathcal{L}_0 = \{\text{abcd}, \quad \text{abd}, \quad \text{bd}, \quad \text{bc}, \quad \text{b}\}$$

$$\text{so that } \mathcal{L} \setminus \mathcal{L}_0 = \{\text{ad}, \quad \text{d}, \quad \varnothing\}$$

Then $\mathcal{L}_0 \sqsubseteq_{\text{ad}} \mathcal{L}$.

To prove that this is indeed the case, we need to consider all elements in $\mathcal{L} \setminus \mathcal{L}_0$ other than ad itself. These are d and $\varnothing$. We need to show that each of these elements is the result of intersecting ad with an element in $\mathcal{L}_0$.

This is indeed the case, since both bd and b are in $\mathcal{L}_0$ and:

$$\text{d} = \text{ad} \cap \text{bd},$$

$$\varnothing = \text{ad} \cap \text{b}.$$

On the other hand, if $\mathcal{L}_0$ consists of all elements of $\mathcal{L}$ apart from b and d, i.e.,

$$\mathcal{L} = \{\text{abcd}, \quad \text{abd}, \quad \text{ad}, \quad \text{bd}, \quad \text{bc}, \quad \text{d}, \quad \text{b}, \quad \varnothing\} \text{ and}$$

$$\mathcal{L}_0 = \{\text{abcd}, \quad \text{abd}, \quad \text{ad}, \quad \text{bd}, \quad \text{bc}, \quad \varnothing\}$$

then $\mathcal{L}_0 \not\sqsubseteq_{\text{b}} \mathcal{L}$. This is because d in $\mathcal{L} \setminus \mathcal{L}_0$ cannot be derived by intersecting b with any element in $\mathcal{L}_0$. Similarly, under this scenario, $\mathcal{L}_0 \not\sqsubseteq_{\text{d}} \mathcal{L}$.

The problem to be solved refines the earlier version by strengthening the postcondition, i.e.,

$$(\mathcal{L}, \prec_{\mathcal{L}}) : [pre, post'] \sqsubseteq (\mathcal{L}, \prec_{\mathcal{L}}) : [pre, post],$$

$$\text{where } pre \triangleq SICL(\mathcal{L}, \top_{\mathcal{L}}) \wedge CG(\mathcal{L}, \prec_{\mathcal{L}}) \wedge X \subset \top_{\mathcal{L}}$$

$$\text{and } post \triangleq SICL(\mathcal{L}, \top_{\mathcal{L}}) \wedge CG(\mathcal{L}, \prec_{\mathcal{L}}) \wedge X \in \mathcal{L} \wedge \mathcal{L}_0 \sqsubseteq_{\text{x}} \mathcal{L}$$

6.3 The Algorithm

We shall now derive a procedure, *insert*, whose pre- and postconditions are as described above. The input, $(\mathcal{L}, \prec_L)$, is the cover graph of a SICL $\mathcal{L}$, and the updated version of this cover graph is returned by the procedure. The updating is in terms of the input set X, which is a subset of $\top_{\mathcal{L}}$. The returned cover graph is of a new

SICL, $\mathcal{L}$, which is the X-extension of the original SICL $\mathcal{L}_0$.[1] The procedure outline is therefore:

> **proc** *insert* (**value result** $(\mathcal{L}, \prec_{\mathcal{L}})$, **value** X)
>   **pre** $\{SICL(\mathcal{L}, \top_{\mathcal{L}}) \wedge CG(\mathcal{L}, \prec_{\mathcal{L}}) \wedge X \subset \top_{\mathcal{L}}\}$
> $(\mathcal{L}, \prec_{\mathcal{L}}) : S$
>   **post** $\{SICL(\mathcal{L}, \top_{\mathcal{L}}) \wedge CG(\mathcal{L}, \prec_{\mathcal{L}}) \wedge X \in \mathcal{L} \wedge \mathcal{L}_0 \sqsubseteq_x \mathcal{L}\}$
> **corp**

As seen in the previous chapter, the formal parameter X is designated a **value** parameter because it passes on a value to the procedure without changing in the procedure, whereas the graph parameter $(\mathcal{L}, \prec_L)$ is designated **value result** because it not only provides an input value to the procedure, but also serves to return the result. In the interests of economising on notation, we shall take the liberty of dropping the **value result** and **value** descriptions of the formal parameters from this point on.

6.3.1   The Basic Structure

As a strategy to refine S, finding the position of X in $CG(\mathcal{L}, \prec_{\mathcal{L}})$ seems like a sensible thing to do. As a first step to do this, suppose we decide to test whether or not $\top_{\mathcal{L}}$ is the parent of X. Let $C_{\top_{\mathcal{L}}} = \{C \mid C \prec \top_{\mathcal{L}}\}$ be the of children of $\top_{\mathcal{L}}$ and suppose that $|C_{\top_{\mathcal{L}}}| = n$. In the algorithm below, we assume that these children are ordered, and they are indicated by $C_i, i = 0, \ldots, n-1$. It seems reasonable to iterate over all these children and test whether any of them give an indication of whether or not $X \prec \top_{\mathcal{L}}$ holds. What should be tested in order to gain such an indication?

Well, we know for sure that $X \prec \top_{\mathcal{L}}$ does *not* hold if, for some C_i, we find that $X \subset C_i$. In that case the parent of X in the new SICL will either be C_i itself, or some node below C_i in the line diagram (since all of those nodes will, per definition of a SICL be subsets of C_i). In the notation introduced in Property 6.2.12, the parent of X will be in $\downarrow C_i$.

Furthermore, if it turns out that $X = C_i$ for some i, then it is indeed the case that $X \prec \top_{\mathcal{L}}$, but because of the equality our job is already done. The procedure can return because the postcondition is already satisfied.

If neither of these circumstances arise—i.e., if $\forall C_i \cdot X \not\subseteq C_i$—then we can infer that X is indeed the child of $\top_{\mathcal{L}}$ and proceed further. We therefore consider the following refinement strategy for S:

---

[1] It is trivial to adapt the algorithm for cases where $\neg(X \subset \top_{\mathcal{L}})$. Two cases then need to be handled. If $X \supset \top_{\mathcal{L}}$ then X simply becomes the new top of the enlarged SICL. If $\neg(X \subset \top_{\mathcal{L}} \wedge X \supset \top_{\mathcal{L}})$ then insert $X \cap \top_{\mathcal{L}}$ into $\mathcal{L}$, create a supremum for X and $\top_{\mathcal{L}}$ and join X and $\top_{\mathcal{L}}$ to their supremum.

$i := 0$;
let $\{C_0, C_i, \ldots C_{n-1}\}$ *be the set of* $\top_{\mathcal{L}}$'s *children.*
do $((i \neq n) \wedge (X \not\subseteq C_i)) \rightarrow i := i + 1$ **od**
$\{ (i = n) \vee (X \subseteq C_i) \}$
if $(i = n) \rightarrow \{X \prec \top_{\mathcal{L}}\} \{S_1$ entails connecting X to $\top_{\mathcal{L}}$ and X to its children$\}$
   $\{post\}$
⫿ $((i < n) \wedge (X = C_i)) \rightarrow$ **return** $\{post\}$
⫿ $((i < n) \wedge (X \subset C_i)) \rightarrow \{$Insert X in$\downarrow C_i\}$ S_2 $\{post\}$
fi

6.3.2 Articulating and Attaining $inv1(i)$

This loop is rather naïve for several reasons, and we shall progressively upgrade
it, as well as articulate a loop invariant that emerges from the upgraded form. For
the moment, we limit attention to one particular shortcoming of the loop: we are
ignoring the possible children of X in the new SICL that might be discovered as we
examine each C_i.

For example, if we discover that $C_i \subset X$, then we can be sure that $C_i \prec X$ in the
new SICL. Let us enhance the loop by introducing a select statement to test whether
$C_i \subset X$ holds, and if so, to collect C_i as a possible child of X into the set $\mathcal{C}$. Of
course, this set should be initialised to $\varnothing$.

We may now well inquire what to do if $\neg(C_i \subset X)$ holds. In that case, attention
falls on $C_{iX} = C_i \cap X$: to preserve set intersection-closedness, clearly C_{iX} will have
to become part of the new SICL, if it is not already in there. (Note in passing that
this holds even if $C_{iX} = \varnothing$—it cannot be assumed that every SICL already has $\varnothing$
as its bottom element.) Moreover, in the new SICL, it is possible that $C_{iX} \prec X$ will
hold. The loop should ideally deal with both these possibilities: namely, take note
of C_{iX} as a possible child of X and insert C_{iX} into $\mathcal{L}$. For the moment, however,
we limit the loop to collecting all possible children of X into set $\mathcal{C}$. The matter of
installing any C_{iX} as part of the new SICL will be addressed later. Thus, the select
statement should be provided with a second guard $\neg(C_i \subset X)$ which adds C_{iX}
to $\mathcal{C}$.

After i iterations, this loop will have ensured that $\mathcal{C}$ contains all potential children
of X in the new SICL that are present in the first i principal ideals of the children
of $\top_{\mathcal{L}}$. The set of nodes represented by all the elements in these principal ideals is
visually depicted in Fig. 6.2 where $\mathcal{M}_i$ is defined as:

$$\mathcal{M}_i = \begin{cases} \bigcup_{k=0}^{i-1}(\downarrow C_k) & \text{if} \quad i > 0 \\ \varnothing & \text{if} \quad i = 0 \end{cases}.$$

Another way of saying that $\mathcal{C}$ contains all potential children of X in $\mathcal{M}_i$ is to say that
every element of $\mathcal{M}_i$ that is a subset of X must also be a subset of some element

Fig. 6.2 $\mathcal{M}_i = \bigcup_{k=0}^{i-1}(\downarrow C_k)$

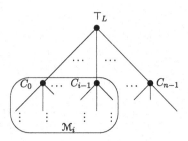

of $\mathcal{C}$. However, it is not enough to merely describe $\mathcal{C}$ in this way. We should also assert that it does not contain unnecessary elements—i.e., it only contains elements that are subsets of X. This description of $\mathcal{C}$ is formally captured in the following loop invariant:

$$inv1(i) \triangleq (\forall Y:((Y \in \mathcal{M}_i) \wedge (Y \subset X)) \cdot (\exists C \in \mathcal{C}: Y \subseteq C)) \wedge (\forall C \in \mathcal{C}: C \subset X).$$
$$(6.1)$$

As a consequence of the above, we can now enhance the procedure outline to date as shown below, where the added parts have been underlined.

> **let** $\{C_0, C_i, \ldots C_{n-1}\}$ *be the set of* $\top_{\mathcal{L}}$*'s children.*
> $i, \mathcal{C} := 0, \varnothing;$
> $\{inv1(i)\}$
> **do** $((i \neq n) \wedge (X \not\subseteq C_i)) \rightarrow$
>   **if** $(C_i \subset X) \rightarrow \mathcal{C} := \mathcal{C} \cup \{C_i\}$
> $\|$ $\neg(C_i \subset X) \rightarrow \mathcal{C} := \mathcal{C} \cup \{C_i \cap X\}$
>   **fi**
> $i := i + 1$
> **od**
> $\{ ((i = n) \vee (X \subseteq C_i)) \wedge inv1(i)\}$
> **if** $(i = n) \rightarrow \{X \prec \top_{\mathcal{L}}\} \overline{\{S_1 \text{ entails connecting } X \text{ to } \top_{\mathcal{L}} \text{ and } X \text{ to its children}\}} \{post\}$
> $\|$ $((i < n) \wedge (X = C_i)) \rightarrow$ **return** $\{post\}$
> $\|$ $((i < n) \wedge (X \subset C_i)) \rightarrow \{\text{Insert } X \text{ in} \downarrow C_i\} S_2 \{post\}$
> **fi**

6.3.3 Articulating and Attaining $inv2(i)$

Although we have not installed into the SICL the set $C_{iX} = C_i \cap X$ that is implicit in the second guard, this has to be done at some stage in order to retain the set intersection-closedness property in the final SICL. It would be convenient to do so as part of the second guard in the select statement of the loop. The alternative would be to store C_{iX} and handle its insertion into the SICL at a later stage. Though the latter seems possible (and thus a possible avenue to explore for future research), the former seems preferable. At first sight, it might not be entirely clear how one could do this.

However, given that we wish to add a node to a SICL, and that we are writing the procedure *insert* to do precisely that, the possibility of recursion naturally arises. Can we not make a recursive call to *insert* as part of the second guard, passing it $C_i \cap X$ instead of X? Careful consideration of the pre- and postconditions of *insert* will show that this can indeed be done: before such a call, the precondition of *insert* with formal parameters suitably replaced by actual parameters will be valid. After the call we will have a new SICL which is a $(C_i \cap X)$-extension of the starting one, and which now has $C_i \cap X$ as part of it. Thus we could change the second guarded command to the following:

$$\{\neg(C_i \subset X) \wedge SICL(\mathcal{L}, \top_{\mathcal{L}}) \wedge CG(\mathcal{L}, \prec_{\mathcal{L}}) \wedge (C_i \cap X) \subset \top_{\mathcal{L}}\}$$
$$\neg(C_i \subset X) \rightarrow \mathcal{C} := \mathcal{C} \cup \{C_i \cap X\};\ insert((\mathcal{L}, \prec_{\mathcal{L}}), (C_i \cap X))$$
$$\{SICL(\mathcal{L}, \top_{\mathcal{L}}) \wedge CG(\mathcal{L}, \prec_{\mathcal{L}}) \wedge (C_i \cap X) \in \mathcal{L} \wedge \mathcal{L}_0 \sqsubseteq_{C_i \cap X} \mathcal{L}\}$$

Although this would work correctly, we evidently have an inefficiency built into such a call. We are forcing a search for a position for $C_i \cap X$ in $\mathcal{L}$ starting with the children of $\top_{\mathcal{L}}$. These children will be examined from left to right, even though we know a priori that $C_i \cap X$ in $\mathcal{L}$ *has to be* installed somewhere below the node C_i. All iterations of the loop prior to that point would have been redundant. Let us endure this inefficiency for the time being, and refactor it later.

We now focus on the whether or not the *first guard* of the select statement conforms to the same pre- and postcondition specification as the second guard, i.e., does the following hold:

$$\{(C_i \subset X) \wedge SICL(\mathcal{L}, \top_{\mathcal{L}}) \wedge CG(\mathcal{L}, \prec_{\mathcal{L}}) \wedge (C_i \cap X) \subset \top_{\mathcal{L}}\}$$
$$(C_i \subset X) \rightarrow \mathcal{C} := \mathcal{C} \cup \{C_i\}$$
$$\{SICL(\mathcal{L}, \top_{\mathcal{L}}) \wedge CG(\mathcal{L}, \prec_{\mathcal{L}}) \wedge (C_i \cap X) \in \mathcal{L} \wedge \mathcal{L}_0 \sqsubseteq_{C_i \cap X} \mathcal{L}\}$$

This is trivially the case for the first two conjuncts of the postcondition, which remain unchanged by the command of the first guard. In verifying that the third conjunct remains true, note that since the guard is $C_i \subset X$, it must be the case that $C_i = (C_i \cap X)$. So the third conjunct amounts to the assertion that $\mathcal{L} \sqsubseteq_{C_i} \mathcal{L}_0$. Since $\mathcal{L} = \mathcal{L}_0$ and since $\mathcal{L}$ is an extension of itself with respect to any node that is in $\mathcal{L}$, including C_i, the third conjunct is true as well. Thus, the first guard preserves the postcondition. Since the second guard also preserves it (albeit potentially quite inefficiently) the following invariant is preserved by the loop as a whole:

$$inv2(i) \triangleq SICL(\mathcal{L}, \top_L) \wedge CG(\mathcal{L}, \prec_{\mathcal{L}}) \wedge (\forall k : [0, i) \cdot (\mathcal{L}_0 \sqsubseteq_{C_k \cap X} \mathcal{L})). \quad (6.2)$$

The invariant of the loop is now $inv1(i) \wedge inv(2)$, and the following structure has been evolved:

let $\{C_0, C_i, \ldots C_{n-1}\}$ *be the set of* $\top_{\mathcal{L}}$'s *children.*
$i, \mathcal{C} := 0, \varnothing;$
$\{inv1(i) \wedge inv2(i)\}$
do $((i \neq n) \wedge (X \nsubseteq C_i)) \rightarrow$
    if $(C_i \subset X) \rightarrow \mathcal{C} := \mathcal{C} \cup \{C_i\}$
    ▌ $\neg(C_i \subset X) \rightarrow \mathcal{C} := \mathcal{C} \cup \{C_i \cap X\};$ *insert*$((\mathcal{L}, \prec_{\mathcal{L}}), C_i \cap X)$
    fi
    $i := i + 1$
od
$\{ ((i = n) \vee (X \subseteq C_i)) \wedge inv1(i) \wedge inv2(i)\}$
if $(i = n) \rightarrow$ {Since $X \prec \top_{\mathcal{L}}$, connect X to $\top_{\mathcal{L}}$ and X to its children} S_1 {*post*}
▌ $((i < n) \wedge (X = C_i)) \rightarrow$ **return** {*post*}
▌ $((i < n) \wedge (X \subset C_i)) \rightarrow$ {Insert X in$\downarrow C_i$} S_2 {*post*}
fi

6.3.4   Filling in S_1

Suppose the loop terminates with $i = n$. Then $(\forall k : [0, i) \cdot (\mathcal{L}_0 \sqsubseteq_{C_k \cap X} \mathcal{L}))$, which is the third conjunct of $inv2(n)$, assures us that $\mathcal{L}$ already embodies all sets needed for X to be included into it—i.e., if we insert X into $\mathcal{L}$ it will still be set intersection-closed. Moreover, the fact that the second conjunct holds, namely $CG(\mathcal{L}, \prec_{\mathcal{L}})$, means that all sets that have been added into $\mathcal{L}$ are correctly connected in the cover graph. All that remains is to include node X in $\mathcal{L}$ (this is achieved by the assignment command $\mathcal{L} := \mathcal{L} \cup \{X\}$) and to correctly connect X to its parent and children.

Since $i = n$ we can be sure that X is not a subset of any child of the top element. Hence, the top element is the only parent of X. The arcs in the cover graph should therefore be updated by the assignment: $\prec_{\mathcal{L}} := \prec_{\mathcal{L}} \cup \{(\top_{\mathcal{L}}, X)\}$.

Children of X in the final lattice, $\mathcal{L}$, have to be the largest subsets of X that are in $\mathcal{L}$. Obviously, every such subset is the intersection of X and a child, C, of the top element in $\mathcal{L}_0$; of course, this intersection may be equal to C (in which case, C is a child of X). The set $\mathcal{C}$ consists of all such intersections obtained. It can easily be verified that not every element of $\mathcal{C}$ need necessarily be a *maximal* subset of X in $\mathcal{L}$: some may be proper subsets of others. Only the maximal subsets of X in $\mathcal{C}$ have to be identified and connected to X. Assume that $getMax(\mathcal{C})$ is a function that returns as a set the maximal sets in $\mathcal{C}$—i.e., sets in $\mathcal{C}$ that are not contained in any other sets in $\mathcal{C}$.

To finish the insertion of X into $(\mathcal{L}, \prec_{\mathcal{L}})$, we therefore have to connect X to all the maximal subsets of X in $\mathcal{C}$ so that they become children of X. If any child of X, say C is linked to $\top_{\mathcal{L}}$, then the corresponding arc must be removed. The assignment

$$\prec_{\mathcal{L}} := (\prec_{\mathcal{L}} \setminus \{(\top_{\mathcal{L}}, C)\}) \cup \{(X, C)\}$$

expresses this removal of arc $(\top_{\mathcal{L}}, C)$ (if it exists) from $\mathcal{L}$ and installation of (X, C) as a new parent–child arc in the cover graph of the SICL. The command S_1 in the guard of the select statement following the loop can thus be elaborated as follows.

$$
\begin{aligned}
&\textbf{if } (i = n) \rightarrow \\
&\qquad \mathcal{L} := \mathcal{L} \cup \{X\} \\
&\qquad ; \prec_{\mathcal{L}} := \prec_{\mathcal{L}} \cup \{(\top_{\mathcal{L}}, X)\} \\
&\qquad ; \textbf{for } C : getMax(\mathcal{C}) \rightarrow \\
&\qquad\qquad \prec_{\mathcal{L}} := (\prec_{\mathcal{L}} \setminus \{(\top_{\mathcal{L}}, C)\}) \cup \{(X, C)\} \\
&\qquad \textbf{rof} \\
&[\!]\ ((i < n) \wedge (X = C_i)) \rightarrow \textbf{return } \{post\} \\
&[\!]\ ((i < n) \wedge (X \subset C_i)) \rightarrow \{\text{Insert } X \text{ in} \downarrow C_i\}\ S_2\ \{post\} \\
&\textbf{fi}
\end{aligned}
$$

6.3.5   Completing the Select Command

The implications need to be considered if the loop does not iterate through all the children of $\top_{\mathcal{L}}$, but instead terminates because it is found—possibly after one or more recursive calls in the loop—that $(X \subseteq C_i)$ for some $i < n$. If this happens, then the foregoing derivation shows that the loop ends in the state $(i < n) \wedge (X \subseteq C_i) \wedge inv1(i) \wedge inv2(i)$. One of the last two guarded commands in the select command after the loop will then be executed. Formulated as Hoare triple specifications that need to be proven true, the bodies of these last two commands have the following forms respectively:

$$\{(i < n) \wedge (X = C_i) \wedge inv1(i) \wedge inv2(i)\} \textbf{ return } \{post\}, \tag{6.3}$$

$$\{(i < n) \wedge (X \subset C_i) \wedge inv1(i) \wedge inv2(i)\}\ S_2\ \{post\}, \tag{6.4}$$

where S_2 represents the code needed to ensure that we "Insert X in $\downarrow C_i$". The definitions of $inv2(i)$ and $post$ are copied below as a reminder of their formulation, and so that they can easily be compared against one another. However, in $inv2(i)$ we use the notation $\mathcal{L}_0$ to indicate the SICL before executing the **return** statement or S_2, and we indicate the originally input SICL as $\mathcal{L}_{00}$.

$$inv2(i) \stackrel{\triangle}{=} SICL(\mathcal{L}_0, \top_{L_0}) \wedge CG(\mathcal{L}_0, \prec_{\mathcal{L}_0}) \wedge (\forall k : [0, i) \cdot (\mathcal{L}_{00} \sqsubseteq_{C_k \cap X} \mathcal{L}_0)), \tag{6.5}$$

$$post \stackrel{\triangle}{=} SICL(\mathcal{L}, \top_{\mathcal{L}}) \wedge CG(\mathcal{L}, \prec_{\mathcal{L}}) \wedge (X \in \mathcal{L}) \wedge (\mathcal{L}_0 \sqsubseteq_X \mathcal{L}). \tag{6.6}$$

For correctness reasoning purposes, **return** can be viewed as similar to **skip**: the specification $\{P\}$ **return** $\{Q\}$ is true provided $P \Rightarrow Q$. Obviously variable values remain unchanged, so that $\mathcal{L} = \mathcal{L}_0$. Taking this into account, the definitions (6.5) and (6.6) clearly show that $(X = C_i) \wedge inv2(i) \Rightarrow post$ so that the **return** in specification (6.3) can be regarded as valid. Note that the last conjunct of $inv2(i)$ plays no role in the reasoning. Moreover, in considering the last conjunct of $post$, note that if $(X \in \mathcal{L}) \wedge (\mathcal{L}_0 = \mathcal{L})$, which is indeed the case here, then $(\mathcal{L}_0 \sqsubseteq_X \mathcal{L}) =$ true—as noted previously, any set is an extension of itself with respect to any one of its own elements.

All that remains, therefore, is to determine S_2. Once more, a recursive call to *insert* suggests itself, this time inserting X into $\downarrow C_i$, i.e., $insert((\downarrow C_i, \prec_{\downarrow C_i}), X)$. The precondition of the following Hoare triple would have to be true to permit such a recursive call, and the result would be the indicated postcondition. (Note that C_i has been used to indicate the top of this SICL, instead of the equivalent but more cumbersome notation $\top_{\downarrow C_i}$.)

$$\{SICL(\downarrow C_{0_i}, C_{0_i}) \wedge CG(\downarrow C_{0_i}, \prec_{\downarrow C_{0_i}}) \wedge (X \subset C_{0_i})\} \tag{6.7}$$

$$insert((\downarrow C_i, \prec_{\downarrow C_i}), X) \tag{6.8}$$

$$\{SICL(\downarrow C_i, C_i) \wedge CG(\downarrow C_i, \prec_{\downarrow C_i}) \wedge (X \in \downarrow C_i) \wedge (\downarrow C_{0_i} \sqsubseteq_X \downarrow C_i)\} \tag{6.9}$$

Using Property (6.2.12), it is easy to see that if the precondition of specification (6.4) holds, then (6.7) will also hold, i.e., $SICL(\downarrow C_{0_i}, C_{0_i}) \wedge CG(\downarrow C_{0_i}, \prec_{\downarrow C_{0_i}}) \wedge (X \subset C_{0_i})$ will also hold. The call to *insert* in (6.8) may thus be made and the indicated postcondition in (6.9) is then guaranteed to be attained.

The question, then, is whether this resulting postcondition (6.9) $\Rightarrow$ *post* in (6.6). In other words, if we update the SICL $\downarrow C_i$ which is within the SICL $\mathcal{L}$ by minimally inserting X into it (minimally in the sense that $\downarrow C_{i_0} \sqsubseteq_X \downarrow C_i$ holds) so that its cover graph is now described by $CG(\downarrow C_i, \prec_{\downarrow C_i})$, can we then reasonably claim each of the conjuncts of *post* will hold? Let us argue the case by showing that (6.9) everywhere implies each of *post*'s conjuncts in turn.

- Showing that (6.9) $\Rightarrow$ $SICL(\mathcal{L}, \top_{\mathcal{L}})$:
  Property 6.2.12 states that $SICL(\mathcal{L}, \top_{\mathcal{L}}) \Rightarrow SICL(\downarrow C_i, \top_{\downarrow C_i})$. It cannot simply be asserted that the reverse holds, namely $SICL(\downarrow C_i, \top_{\downarrow C_i}) \Rightarrow SICL(\mathcal{L}, \top_{\mathcal{L}})$. In the absence of other contextual information about $\mathcal{L}$ and $\downarrow C_i$ this claim cannot be affirmed or denied. However, consider the situation when we add two conjuncts to the left hand side that are true.

  The first, $SICL(\mathcal{L}_0, \top_{\mathcal{L}_0})$, is a conjunct of *inv2* in (6.5), and is thus true ahead of the *insert*. Furthermore it is unaffected by the call.

  The second, $\downarrow C_{i_0} \sqsubseteq_X \downarrow C_i$, is true because it is a conjunct of the call's postcondition, as see in (6.9).

  We thus consider the following assertion, which we claim indeed holds:

$$SICL(\mathcal{L}_0, \top_{\mathcal{L}_0}) \wedge \downarrow C_{i_0} \sqsubseteq_X \downarrow C_i \wedge SICL(\downarrow C_i, \top_{\downarrow C_i}) \Rightarrow SICL(\mathcal{L}, \top_{\mathcal{L}}). \tag{6.10}$$

Here we are claiming that if we take into account that $\mathcal{L}_0$ started off as a SICL, and that C_i, which is now an X-extension of its original form, is embedded into $\mathcal{L}$ without anything else in $\mathcal{L}$ changing, then the resulting $\mathcal{L}$ indeed constitutes a SICL.

This claim can only be falsified if the intersection of a node in $\mathcal{L} \setminus \downarrow C_i$, say p, with a new node in $\downarrow C_i$, say q, is absent from $\mathcal{L}$.

But we can see that this will never be the case if we consider the intersection (the meet) of p and C_i, say m. This set would necessarily be in both $\downarrow C_{i_0}$ (because of the set intersection-closedness property of $\mathcal{L}_0$) and in $\downarrow C_i$ (because *insert* does not remove any nodes). Because $\downarrow C_i$ is a SICL, it must also be the case that the meet of m and q, call it m', is in $\downarrow C_i$. It is easy to show that this set, m', corresponds with $p \cap q$. Formally:

$$p \cap q$$
$$\equiv \quad \{(q \in (\downarrow C_i)) \implies (q \subset C_i) \implies (q = C_i \cap q)\}$$
$$p \cap C_i \cap q$$
$$\equiv \quad \{\text{Set intersection is associative, and } m = p \cap C_i\}$$
$$m \cap q$$
$$\equiv \quad \{m' = m \cap q\}$$
$$m'$$

Thus, the intersection of an arbitrary node in $\mathcal{L} \setminus \downarrow C_i$ with any new node in $\downarrow C_i$ is always in $(\downarrow C_i) \subseteq \mathcal{L}$.

Hence, (6.10) is always true.

- Showing that $(6.9) \implies CG(\mathcal{L}, \prec_\mathcal{L})$:

In a similar manner, we would like to show that the following holds:

$$CG(\mathcal{L}_0, \prec_{\mathcal{L}_0}) \wedge \downarrow C_{i_0} \sqsubseteq_X \downarrow C_i \wedge CG(\downarrow C_i, \prec_{\downarrow C_i}) \implies CG(\mathcal{L}, \prec_\mathcal{L}).$$

To do this, we need to argue that it is sufficient to add the new arcs of $\prec_{\downarrow C_i}$ into $\prec_\mathcal{L}$ in order to obtain all the arcs of the cover graph of $\mathcal{L}$ (which we have just proven to be a SICL). Since the call's postcondition guarantees that the arcs in $\prec_{\downarrow C_i}$ accurately represent parent–child relationships in $\downarrow C_i$, and since the call to *insert* neither adds new arcs, nor deletes any existing arcs between nodes in $\downarrow C_i$ and nodes in $\mathcal{L} \setminus \downarrow C_i$, we are left with two possible concerns: should new arcs involving nodes in $\downarrow C_i$ and nodes $\mathcal{L} \setminus \downarrow C_i$ be added to $\prec_\mathcal{L}$; and/or should any existing arcs involving nodes in $\downarrow C_i$ and nodes $\mathcal{L} \setminus \downarrow C_i$ be removed from $\prec_\mathcal{L}$?

Property 6.2.13 eliminates any concerns in regard to arcs starting from nodes in $\downarrow C_i$ and ending at nodes in $\mathcal{L} \setminus \downarrow C_i$: none could have existed before the call, and none should be installed after the call. That leaves for consideration arcs where a parent is in $\mathcal{L} \setminus \downarrow C_i$ and a child is in $\downarrow C_i$.

An argument against the need to *remove* or *replace* any existing arc runs as follows. Suppose (p, q) is such an arc in the cover graph of the original SICL. That would mean that q is the meet (infimum) of p and any other node in $\downarrow C_i$ that is a superset of q, including the meet between p and C_i. That means that q is the largest set of common elements shared by p and C_i. The insertion of X into $\downarrow C_i$ does not add to this set of common elements. Therefore existing arcs should not be removed or replaced from the cover graph of the new SICL. Either removal or replacement would incorrectly imply that the largest set of common elements between p and C_i has changed.

There is a similar argument against the need to *insert* an arc (as opposed to replacing an existing one). Per definition of a lattice, C_i and every node in

$p \in \mathcal{L} \setminus \downarrow C_i$ has a meet in both the original and resulting SICL. If there was previously no arc from p to a node in $\downarrow C_i$ then inserting such a parent–child arc would change the meet of p and C_i. But since p and C_i have exactly the same elements in common before and after the placement of X in the SICL, it would be illegitimate to change this meet, which is precisely what the introduction of an arc would do.

- Showing that $(6.9) \Rightarrow (X \in \mathcal{L})$:
  Since $X \in \downarrow C_i \Rightarrow X \in \mathcal{L}$, the third conjunct of *post* is quite obviously everywhere implied by the postcondition of *insert*'s call.
- Showing that $(6.9) \Rightarrow (\mathcal{L}_0 \sqsubseteq_X \mathcal{L})$:
  Since the guard's condition prior to the *insert* call requires that $X \subset C_i$, it is quite clear that the intersection of any element in $\mathcal{L}$ with X will be in $\downarrow C_i$. As a result, it easily follows that $(\downarrow C_{i_0} \sqsubseteq_X \downarrow C_i) \Rightarrow (\mathcal{L}_0 \sqsubseteq_X \mathcal{L})$ holds.

6.3.6   The Completed Algorithm

Putting all the pieces together delivers the following algorithm for insert:

Algorithm 6.3.1.
proc *insert*(**value result** $(\mathcal{L}, \prec_{\mathcal{L}})$, **value** X)
pre $\{SICL(\mathcal{L}, \top_{\mathcal{L}}) \wedge CG(\mathcal{L}, \prec_{\mathcal{L}}) \wedge X \subset \top_{\mathcal{L}}\}$
let $\{C_0, C_i, \ldots C_{n-1}\}$ be the set of $\top_{\mathcal{L}}$'s children.
$i, \mathcal{C} := 0, \varnothing$
$; \{inv1(i) \wedge inv2(i)\}$
do $((i \neq n) \wedge (X \not\subseteq C_i)) \rightarrow$
    if $(C_i \subset X) \rightarrow \mathcal{C} := \mathcal{C} \cup \{C_i\}$
    $\|$ $\neg(C_i \subset X) \rightarrow \mathcal{C} := \mathcal{C} \cup \{C_i \cap X\}; \ insert((\mathcal{L}, \prec_{\mathcal{L}}), C_i \cap X)$
    fi
    $; i := i + 1$
od
$\{ ((i = n) \vee (X \subseteq C_i)) \wedge inv1(i) \wedge inv2(i)\}$
$;$ **if** $(i = n) \rightarrow$
    $\mathcal{L} := \mathcal{L} \cup \{X\}$
    $; \prec_{\mathcal{L}} := \prec_{\mathcal{L}} \cup \{(\top_{\mathcal{L}}, X)\}$
    $;$ **for** $C : getMax(\mathcal{C}) \rightarrow$
        $\prec_{\mathcal{L}} := (\prec_{\mathcal{L}} \setminus \{(\top_{\mathcal{L}}, C)\}) \cup \{(X, C)\}$
    rof
    $;$ **return**
$\|$ $((i < n) \wedge (X = C_i)) \rightarrow$ **return**
$\|$ $((i < n) \wedge (X \subset C_i)) \rightarrow insert((\downarrow C_i, \prec_{\downarrow C_i}), X)$
fi
post $\{SICL(\mathcal{L}, \top_{\mathcal{L}}) \wedge CG(\mathcal{L}, \prec_{\mathcal{L}}) \wedge X \in \mathcal{L} \wedge \mathcal{L}_0 \sqsubseteq_X \mathcal{L}\}$
corp

Table 6.1 Comparing X against C_f and then against sibling C_s: logical possibilities

	$X = C_s$	$X \subset C_s$	$C_s \subset X$	$C_{sX} = C_s \cap X$
$X = C_f$	$C_f = C_s$	$C_f \subset C_s$	$C_s \subset C_f$	$C_{sX} = C_{fs}$
	No/No	No/No	No/No	Yes/No
$X \subset C_f$	$C_s \subset C_f$	$X \subset C_f \wedge X \subset C_s$	$C_s \subset C_f$	$C_{sX} \subseteq C_{fs}$
	No/No	Yes/No	No/No	Yes/No
$C_f \subset X$	$C_f \subset C_s$	$C_f \subset C_s$	$C_f, C_s \in C$	$C_f, C_{sX} \in C$
	No/No	No/No	Yes/Yes	Yes/Yes
$C_{fX} = C_f \cap X$	$C_{fX} = C_{fs}$	$C_{fX} \subseteq C_{fs}$	$C_{fX}, C_s \in C$	$C_{fX}, C_{sX} \in C$
	Yes/Yes	Yes/Yes	Yes/Yes	Yes/Yes

There is much that could be said about this algorithm. On the one hand, there are several refactoring possibilities as well as previously published variants of the algorithm. One variant has been used in the context of FCA and been shown to be very efficient from a practical point of view. On the other hand, the "almost magical" impact of the recursion obscures a number of interesting operational details that are worth reviewing. In the next section we shall consider some of these operational details, and return to the refactored variations after that.

6.3.7 The Operational Implications

While the previous correctness by construction argumentation guarantees the algorithm's correctness, it has bypassed a number of details about possible execution traces that may be followed, depending on the data to be processed. A consideration of these will provide further insight into the algorithm. However, this section may be skipped at first reading.

Table 6.1 identifies logical possibilities of how children of a common parent in a SICL (in the present case $\top_C$) may be matched against X. In the algorithm's main loop, these children are compared sequentially against X, and it is of interest to discover matching combinations that might be both logically and operationally possible, those that might be logically possible but operationally impossible, and those that are not logically possible at all. By "operationally possible" we refer to the possible traces of events as the loop is executed.

Row headers in the table indicate possible outcomes when X is compared to child C_f and column headers, when X is compared to child C_s. The f and s subscripts are intended to signify the order of comparison: the C_f comparison first takes place and then (secondly) the C_s comparison. In each case, the outcome could be equality ($=$), or the child contains X ($C \subset X$), or X contains the child ($X \subset C$), or none of these, in which case the intersection of X and the child is denoted by C_{fX} and C_{sX}, respectively. We also use C_{fs} to refer to $C_f \cap C_s$. For ease of reference, we shall refer to the cell in the ith row and jth column as cell (i, j).

Each cell contains three entries: a predicate about C_f and/or C_s on a first row; and, on a second row, a pair consisting of the words "Yes" and/or "No". The first row entry of cell (i, j) indicates what we could logically infer if the outcome of the first X comparison (with C_f) was as indicated in row i, and the subsequent outcome of the X comparison (with C_s) was as indicated in column j. The first bottom entry in each cell indicates whether such an outcome is logically possible for children of the same parent in a SICL. The second bottom entry indicates whether the outcome is operationally possible in the algorithm when it is logically possible—i.e., whether the algorithm's loop will continue after comparing X against C_f to subsequently compare X against C_s.

Thus, cell $(1, 1)$ indicates that if C_f was found to be equal to X, and subsequently it was found that C_s was also equal to X, this would logically mean that $C_f = C_s$. Since a parent in a SICL cannot have two identical children, the word "No" appears twice in that cell to indicate that this is neither logically nor operationally possible. Similarly, the first row of cell $(1, 2)$ indicates if $X = C_f$ and $X \subset C_s$, then logically, $C_f \subset C_s$. However, in a SICL X cannot be equal to a child of the top node and then subsequently found to be contained by another child, since that would mean that C_f should be located somewhere in $\downarrow C_s$.

As a final example, consider cell $(2, 2)$. The "Yes" entry in the bottom row of this cell affirms that it is logically possible for X to be a proper subset of two children of the top node in a SICL, C_f and C_s. The "No" entry affirms that once the algorithm's loop establishes that $X \subset C_f$, it will terminate, and the loop will not discover that $X \subset C_s$.

Collectively, the scenarios reflected in the table's first two rows correspond to conditions under which the loop terminates— i.e., when $X \subseteq C_f$ the loop's condition no longer holds. All cell entries in these two rows are labelled as "No/No" because it is logically not possible to encounter the given scenario in a SICL, or as or "Yes/No" because the algorithm's design is such that X will not be tested against C_s even the indicated relationship between X and C_s is permitted by the definition of a SICL. It is therefore unnecessary to inquire further about the operational consequences in these contexts.

Row three shows that if $(C_f \subset X)$ then it is not possible that $(X \subseteq C_s)$. Column three shows that if $(C_s \subset X)$ then it is not possible that $(X \subseteq C_f)$. Taken together, this means that if X is a superset of any one of the children of SICL $\top_{\mathcal{L}}$, then this logically excludes the possibility that X is a subset or equal to some other child of $\top_{\mathcal{L}}$. Thus, if X is a superset of some child, then—even if this fact has not been established operationally—the loop will iterate through all the children of $\top_{\mathcal{L}}$, possibly finding that X is also a superset the other children (indicated as a possibility in cell $(3, 3)$) and/or finding that the second guard fires so that C_{sX} has to be inserted into the lattice, which is the case indicated in cell $(3, 4)$. In each of these cases, the loop collects the possible children of X into $\mathcal{C}$, as suggested by the entries cell $(3, 3)$ and cell $(3, 4)$.

Row four shows what happens if none of the conditions in the headers of first three rows are encountered when testing C_f (i.e., when it is neither the case that $C_f \not\subseteq X$ nor that $X \not\subseteq C_f$). In this case—both logically and

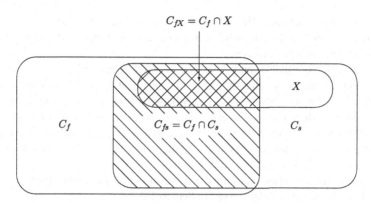

Fig. 6.3 The scenario in cell $(4, 2)$: $X \subset C_s \implies C_{fX} \subset C_{sf}$

operationally—"anything" can subsequently be anticipated with respect to C_s: i.e., subsequent iterations of the loop might discover that $(C_s = X)$, or that $(X \subset C_s)$, or that $(C_s \subset X)$ or, if none of these alternatives occur, that $C_{sX} = (C_s \cap X)$ has to be inserted into the lattice.

The information in cell $(4, 3)$ and cell $(4, 4)$ is consistent with the information just discussed in regard to the third row: the loop collects possible child information to preserve invariant (6.1) and traverses more children of $\top_{\mathcal{L}}$ without any problems. However, unlike the case of row three (i.e., $C_i \subset X$), which logically guaranteed that all n children would be tested, a row four occurrence does not give any assurance of whether or not this will be the case. It is possible that the loop may subsequently terminate because of equality (column one) or child containment of X (column 2).

These two cases, shown in cell $(4, 1)$ and cell $(4, 2)$ might, for some, raise troubling questions. Can we be sure that the recursive call inserting C_{fX} into the SICL was legitimate if we subsequently discover that $X = C_s$ or $X \subset C_s$? What effect does the recursive call have on the overall structure that is later handled by these cases?

In the case of $X = C_s$ (cell $(4, 1)$) there is evidently no problem. Since $\mathcal{L}$ is per definition set intersection-closed, it must be the case that $C_f \cap C_s = C_{fs}$ was already in $\mathcal{L}$. Thus inserting $C_{fX} = C_f \cap X = C_f \cap C_s = C_{sf}$ into $\mathcal{L}$ is not problematic. An attempt is made to insert an existing node into $\mathcal{L}$ and has no effect at all on $\mathcal{L}$. The loop will complete having done one, or perhaps more, "useless" but harmless recursive calls and then terminate when it is discovered that $X = C_s$. The select statement after the loop will simply return from *insert* with an unchanged $\mathcal{L}$.

If we insert $C_{fX} = C_f \cap X$ into $\mathcal{L}$ and then subsequently discover that $X \subset C_s$ holds (i.e., the cell $(4, 2)$ scenario), no problem exists either. We know this because $X \subset C_s$ means that C_{fX} must be a subset of or equal to $C_{fs} = C_f \cap C_s$ (symbolically $C_{fX} \subseteq C_{fs}$). The matter is illustrated in Fig. 6.3. The figure shows that the first recursive call will insert the set C_{fX} into $\mathcal{L}$ somewhere in $\downarrow C_s$. Because $\mathcal{L}$ is set intersection-closed, C_{fs} will already be in $\downarrow C_s$, and C_{fX} will be installed somewhere below this set. The subsequent call to install X in $\downarrow C_s$ will occur in an updated version of $\downarrow C_s$ in which some of the work which it would in any case need to do, has already been done.

Note that since equality may hold (i.e., it may be that $C_{fX} = C_{fs}$ or, even more generally that C_{fX} already exists in $\downarrow C_{fs}$), it is possible that $\mathcal{L}$ may be unchanged by the call. Either way (i.e., whether equality holds or updating takes place) makes no difference to the ultimate correctness argument. Operationally, the loop will eventually terminate by discovering that $X \subset C_s$. It will then execute the relevant guard of the subsequent select statement, making the recursive call to *insert* to install X in $\downarrow C_i$, where $i = s$ in this context.

It is these considerations that inform some of the refactorings suggested below, particularly the refactoring discussed in Sect. 6.4.2.

6.4 Refactorings

There are numerous ways in which Algorithm 6.3.1 can be refactored. Here we shall only consider two: one reasonably obvious measure to improve efficiency, and then a refactoring which will bring the algorithm more closely in line with other published versions.

6.4.1 Efficiently Inserting $C_i \cap X$

In elaborating the select command in the algorithm's main loop, we proposed in Sect. 6.3.3 that the second guard should use the recursive call $insert((\mathcal{L}, \prec_{\mathcal{L}}), C_i \cap X)$ to place $C_i \cap X$ into $\mathcal{L}$. It was pointed out that this implied that the children of $\top_{\mathcal{L}}$ would be examined against $C_i \cap X$ from left to right and that this was quite obviously inefficient, since we already know at that $C_i \cap X$ should be installed somewhere below C_i. Nevertheless, the call was issued in that form and, since the pre- and postconditions match the loop's invariant, there was no need for a lengthy justification about its correctness.

Subsequently, it was shown that if $X \subset C_i$, then a recursive call to $insert((\downarrow C_i, \prec_{\downarrow C_i}), X)$ could be made after the loop which would insert X into $\mathcal{L}$. This was justified in some detail in Sect. 6.3.4. It was shown that minimally updating the principal ideal, $\downarrow C_i$ does not undermine any of the SICL properties of $\mathcal{L}$, and therefore achieves the required postcondition.

In like manner, the first recursive call could just as well be started from C_i rather than $\top_{\mathcal{L}}$, thus avoiding the unnecessary examination of other children of $\top_{\mathcal{L}}$. Because arguments to legitimate such a call closely parallel those already given in Sect. 6.3.4, they need not be repeated here. This then is our first suggested refactoring: in Algorithm 6.3.1, replace the call $insert((\mathcal{L}, \prec_{\mathcal{L}}), C_i \cap X)$ in the main loop by $insert((\downarrow C_i, \prec_{\downarrow C_i}), C_i \cap X)$. It will be seen that this form is used in the Algorithm 6.4.3 to be presented below.

6.4.2 Finding the Parent of X

The original version of Algorithm 6.3.1 was published in [41, 42] and was called *AddIntent* for reasons that will be hinted at later. It was not derived using correctness by construction methods. As a matter of fact, most people found the algorithm very difficult to follow, and were quite uncertain of its correctness. Confidence in its correctness was largely dependent on test data.

Subsequently, a rather more elegant version of the algorithm was derived and has been discussed in [26]. This latter version checks for $X = C_i$ or $X \subset C_i$ as two additional guards in the select statement in the main loop. If one of these guards fire, a flag is set and, where necessary, the recursive call is made from the body of that additional guard in the loop to insert X somewhere in $\downarrow C_i$. The flag is then used to terminate the loop. This renders the loop's invariant slightly more complicated, because it has to account for the change in state that is possibly brought about if one of these guards fires. Algorithm 6.3.1 pleasingly avoids the need for such flags and has a simpler invariant.

A subsequent discussion and refactoring in [26] is based on the desirability of a simpler select statement in the loop, so that the resulting loop in [26] would contain only the two guards—as we already have in Algorithm 6.3.1. However, this is achieved is by a refactoring that leads to an algorithm that is similar in structure to the original in [41, 42]: prior to the loop, the parent P of X is sought, relying on a function called $getP$. The subsequent loop then has the same select statement as that Algorithm 6.3.1. The function for $getP$ is not derived, but merely described verbally.

It turns out that $getP$ is actually a stripped down version of Algorithm 6.3.1. All that is needed is to remove from Algorithm 6.3.1 all the commands associated with $inv1(i)$ and the installation of X into $\mathcal{L}$, and to appropriately adapt the select statement after the loop. Furthermore, since $\mathcal{L}$ remains unchanged, $inv2(i)$ is no longer relevant. Instead, the loop's invariant is a statement that the region searched to date does not contain the parent of X, i.e.:

$$inv3(i) \triangleq \nexists P : \mathcal{M}_i \cdot (X \prec_\mathcal{L} P). \tag{6.11}$$

The result is Algorithm 6.4.1 below, given in function format, rather than as a procedure.

Algorithm 6.4.1.
func $getP(\textbf{value } (\mathcal{L}, \prec_\mathcal{L}), \textbf{value } X) : \langle P \rangle$
pre $\{SICL(\mathcal{L}, \top_\mathcal{L}) \wedge CG(\mathcal{L}, \prec_\mathcal{L}) \wedge X \subset \top_\mathcal{L}\}$
let $\{C_0, C_i, \ldots, C_{n-1}\}$ be the set of $\top_\mathcal{L}$'s children.
$i, := 0$
$; \{inv3(i)\}$
do $((i \neq n) \wedge (X \not\subseteq C_i)) \rightarrow i := i + 1$ **od**
$\{((i = n) \vee (X \subseteq C_i)) \wedge inv3(i)\}$

$$; \textbf{if } (i = n) \rightarrow P := \top_{\mathcal{L}}$$
$$\parallel \quad ((i < n) \wedge (X = C_i)) \rightarrow P := X$$
$$\parallel \quad ((i < n) \wedge (X \subset C_i)) \rightarrow P := getP((\downarrow C_i, \prec_{\downarrow C_i}), X)$$
$$\textbf{fi}$$
post $\{(X = P) \vee (X \prec_{\mathcal{L}} P)\}$
$; \textbf{return}$
cnuf

Justifying the commands in the guard bodies of the select command following the loop is straight forward. Notice that the $getP$ returns X if it is established that it already exists in $\mathcal{L}$. This is reflected in its postcondition.

Algorithm 6.3.1 can now be refactored by first invoking $getP$ to return the parent of X. If it is found that X is already in $\mathcal{L}$, we of course return directly. Otherwise the main loop of Algorithm 6.3.1 may be used as before, but with the strengthened precondition that $X \prec_{\mathcal{L}} P$. As a result, the loop simply iterates over all children of P and assembles the possible children of X in set $\mathcal{C}$ as before. After the loop, X is installed into $\mathcal{L}$ in exactly the same way as before.

Putting all the pieces together delivers the following refactored algorithm for insert that relies on $getP$ and matches other published versions.

Algorithm 6.4.2.
proc $insert(\textbf{value result } (\mathcal{L}, \prec_{\mathcal{L}}), \textbf{value } X)$
pre $\{SICL(\mathcal{L}, \top_{\mathcal{L}}) \wedge CG(\mathcal{L}, \prec_{\mathcal{L}}) \wedge X \subset \top_{\mathcal{L}}\}$
let $\{C_0, C_i, \ldots, C_{n-1}\}$ be the set of $\top_{\mathcal{L}}$'s children.
$P := getP((\mathcal{L}, \prec_{\mathcal{L}}), X)$
$\{(P = X) \vee X \prec P)\}$
$; \textbf{if } P = X \rightarrow \textbf{return}$
$\parallel \quad P \neq X \rightarrow$
$\qquad \mathcal{C} := \varnothing$
$\qquad ; \{inv1(i) \wedge inv2(i) \wedge (X \prec_{\mathcal{L}} P)\}$
$\qquad \textbf{for all } (C_i \prec P) \rightarrow$
$\qquad\qquad \textbf{if } (C_i \subset X) \rightarrow \mathcal{C} := \mathcal{C} \cup \{C_i\}$
$\qquad\qquad \parallel \quad \neg(C_i \subset X) \rightarrow \mathcal{C} := \mathcal{C} \cup \{C_i \cap X\}; \ insert((\downarrow C_i, \prec_{\downarrow C_i}), (C_i \cap X))$
$\qquad\qquad \textbf{fi}$
$\qquad \textbf{rof}$
$\qquad \{ (i = n) \wedge inv1(i) \wedge inv2(i)\}$
$\qquad ; \mathcal{L} := \mathcal{L} \cup \{X\}$
$\qquad ; \prec_{\mathcal{L}} := \prec_{\mathcal{L}} \cup \{(P, X)\}$
$\qquad ; \textbf{for } C : getMax(\mathcal{C}) \rightarrow$
$\qquad\qquad \prec_{\mathcal{L}} := (\prec_{\mathcal{L}} \setminus \{(P, C)\}) \cup \{(X, C)\}$
$\qquad \textbf{rof}$
$\textbf{fi}$
$; \textbf{return}$
post $\{SICL(\mathcal{L}, \top_{\mathcal{L}}) \wedge CG(\mathcal{L}, \prec_{\mathcal{L}}) \wedge X \in \mathcal{L} \wedge \mathcal{L}_0 \sqsubseteq_x \mathcal{L}\}$
corp

6.4.3 Discussion

Algorithms 6.3.1 and 6.4.3 are *incremental* algorithms: they can be used to grow a given SICL $\mathcal{L}$ by set X and all other sets implied by the insertion of X into $\mathcal{L}$. Clearly, they can be used to construct a SICL ab initio that contains a prespecified set of sets.[2] For example, suppose we wanted to construct a SICL out of the set of sets $\mathcal{X}$. We would first need to compute the top element of the SICL, which is given by the union of all the sets in $\mathcal{X}$, i.e., $\top = \bigcup \mathcal{X}$, using $\{\top\}$ as the starting SICL, and then successively placing elements of into the incrementally growing SICL:

> **Algorithm 6.4.3.**
> **proc** $makeSICL(\textbf{result } (\mathcal{L}, \prec_{\mathcal{L}}), \textbf{value } \mathcal{X})$
> $(\mathcal{L}, \prec_{\mathcal{L}}) := (\bigcup \mathcal{X}, \varnothing)$
> ; **for all** $(X \in ToDo) \rightarrow$
> $insert((\mathcal{L}, \prec_{\mathcal{L}}), X)$
> **rof**
> **corp**

Assuming that $|\bigcup \mathcal{X}| = n$, the worst case order-of-magnitude performance of any general SICL construction algorithm to build a SICL out of $\mathcal{X}$ is $\mathcal{O}(2^n)$. Algorithms 6.3.1 and 6.4.3 are no exceptions. This is because the maximum number of subsets that can be built out of a set of n elements is 2^n. (Put differently, the so-called powerset of $\mathcal{X}$ consists of $2^{|\mathcal{X}|}$ subsets of $\mathcal{X}$.)

It is nevertheless interesting to reflect on circumstances under which one the two algorithm may be better than the other, for there appear to be trade-offs to be made between the two of them.

Algorithm 6.3.1 recognises the need to insert the node $C_i \cap X$ (as well as other new child nodes of this inserted node) at some stage, and does the work needed to install these nodes on the spot, as it were. This seems like an efficient action to take, provided that one does not have to search too frequently and too deeply for the parent of $C_i \cap X$ in subsequent recursive calls. In other words, if $|C_i \cap X|$ is fairly large—i.e., if we may reasonably anticipate that the parent of $C_i \cap X$ is high up in the cover graph—then Algorithm 6.3.1 may have some advantage over Algorithm 6.4.3. On the other hand, the latter algorithm avoids the accumulation of potential children of X in $\mathcal{C}$ that may turn out subsequently to have been unnecessary. It would require an empirical study over many different kinds of data sets to establish whether these theoretical considerations play a significant role in actual performance.

---

[2]Of course, we assume that $|\mathcal{X}| < \infty$. However, the algorithm specifications above are not inherently limited to dealing with finite sets. They could, in principle, be implemented on a computer that had some way of representing infinitely large sets and which could carry out the required set operations (intersection, membership, union) on those infinite sets.

From a theoretical perspective, one could perhaps argue that Algorithm 6.3.1 is more elegant in that it seamlessly wraps the search for a parent of X into the same overall structure of the algorithm, whereas Algorithm 6.4.3 requires a call to $getP$. Again, there is a counter-argument to this, namely that the latter separates the concerns of finding a parent of X and of inserting X into $\mathcal{L}$—a well-established and sound software engineering principle.

There are several additional refactorings that could marginally affect the overall performance of this algorithm. For example, one could improve on the efficiency of $getMax$ by noting that whenever $C_i \subset X$ holds, we have found a definite child of X. Only the sets $(C_i \cap X)$ that are placed in $\mathcal{C}$ in the second guard may turn out to be subsets of the actual children of X, instead of being actual children of X once all the information has been collected. Arrangements can be made to account for this by collecting definite children of X separately from potential children of X. The subsequent establishment of actual children could then, in some cases, be speeded up. Again, such a refactoring will not affect the algorithm's worst case performance.

6.5   A Gentle Introduction to Formal Concept Analysis

Under what circumstances, one might ask, would one want to construct a SICL? It turns out that SICL-construction lies at the heart of a field of study called FCA [19]. FCA relies on graphs that represent so-called concept lattices [8, 19, 48] (also referred to as Galois lattices or formal concept lattices) to provide a rich source of information about the inter-relationship between a set of objects under study that share certain discrete attributes. These concept lattices provide a framework for representing, discovering, inferring and managing knowledge in various domains, including linguistics [35], social network analysis [17, 36], ontology building [38] and information retrieval [9]. Concept lattices also play a role in some machine learning methods [29] and data mining techniques [40]. Another area of application is software construction and engineering. (See, for example, [3,12,21,24,30,37] and a survey in [39]). A comprehensive introduction to concept lattices and, especially, its applications in computer science is provided in [8]. Below we give a gentle introduction to the topic.

Essentially, a concept lattice is built from a set, M, of *attributes*, subsets of which characterize each element in a set, G, of *objects*. Each node in a concept lattice is characterized by two sets (A, B) where $A \subseteq G$ and $B \subseteq M$. The pair may only appear in the concept lattice if A consists of *all* objects that possess *all* the attributes in B. Additionally it has to be the case that B is maximal, meaning that there are not any additional attributes shared by A that are not included in B.

Such a pair (A, B) is then called a *concept*.

Note carefully that a concept has to have the largest sets possible for the given context. By this we mean the following. Suppose that you pick a set of objects, say A, and discover that these objects have attributes in B in common. This does not yet entitle you to conclude that (A, B) is concept. You first have to establish that, in the context under consideration, no other object also possess the attributes B. You also have to establish that the objects in A do not possess some other attributes in common that are not in B. Only if these conditions hold can you conclude that (A, B) is a concept.

As our running example, consider the cross-table at the top of Fig. 6.4. Such a table is called a context. The particular context displayed in the figure is one of the classical examples used in FCA, and is known as the Living Context. Its ten columns consist of "attributes" (chosen to be of interest for a particular purposes) of living things and its rows enumerate nine living "objects" that are to be studied. An "X" in a given cell indicates that the particular object possesses the associated attribute. Thus M = { Needs water, Lives in water, ..., Suckles young} and G = { Leech, Bream, ..., Maize}. Cells indicate attributes that characterise the various objects. An example of a concept is the set of all objects that need water, live on land, need chlorophyll and have 1-leaf germination, i.e., the concept ({Reed,Maize}, {Needs water, Lives on land, Needs chlorophyll, 1-leaf germination}). Note that the objects and attributes are tightly coupled: if you leave out one attribute, you inadequately describe what maize and reeds have in common, and if you add "Lives in water" as an attribute to describe the concept of a reed, then you are no longer describing the concept that includes maize. Likewise, if you leave out one of the objects, you no longer describe the objects that share those particular attributes. Neither may you add "bean" to the set of objects, because then you no longer limit the concept description to 1-lead germinating objects.

The concept (A, B) is said to have an *extent* of A and an *intent* of B. Now it turns out that if you determine all concepts in a given context, and then consider the extents of these concepts, they will form a closure system on G. This claim might not be self-evident, but can be strictly proven. Similarly, it can also be proven that the intents of all concepts constitute a closure system on M. Thus, if two subsets of G (or M), say A and A', are the extents (respectively, intents) of nodes in a concept lattice, then $A \cap A'$ will also be the extent (intent) of some node in the lattice.

From the information given above, we could imagine drawing two different cover graphs for the two different SICLs for these two closure systems—one for the set of set intersection-closed object sets, and one for the set intersection-closed attribute sets. Nodes in each set could be labelled by the associated concepts. Note that in each case, we will have all the concepts in the cover graph, ordered differently from top to bottom. In the one case, nodes with the largest extents will be at the top, and in the other case, nodes with the largest intents. However, it is a remarkable fact that if you flip one of the cover graphs over so that its smallest nodes are on top (e.g., the cover graph for the attributes), then the nodes in the two graphs will match one another on an exact pair-wise basis! Each such pair matching gives the extent and intent for a concept. In effect, we only need the one cover graph to get the other.

The set of concepts drawn up from a context can therefore be regarded as forming a lattice—a so-called concept lattice—which embodies two SICLs. To set up a concept lattice and its associated cover graph, we could use the algorithm discussed in this chapter (or any one of several others), making slight adaptations for keeping track of each node's extent (if a SICL based on intents is constructed), or of each

	Needs water	Lives in water	Lives on land	Needs chlorophyl	1 leaf germinate	2 leaf germinate	Is motile	Has limbs	Suckles young
Leech	X	X					X		
Bream	X	X					X	X	
Frog	X	X	X				X	X	
Dog	X		X				X	X	X
Spike-weed	X	X		X	X				
Reed	X	X	X	X	X				
Bean	X		X	X		X			
Maize	X		X	X	X				

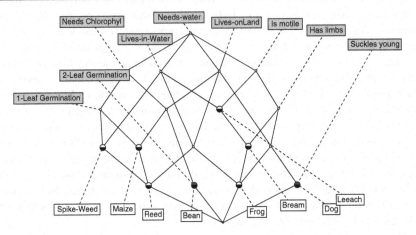

Fig. 6.4 Living context and cover graph

node's intent (if a SICL based on extents is constructed). The resulting cover graph would be the same. However, we would not know which way the arcs should point in such a cover graph, because we have not yet specified an ordering on concepts. When is one concept smaller than another?

By FCA convention, concepts are assumed to be ordered by set-containment of their *intents*—the smaller the extent, the smaller the concept. Thus, for concepts (A, B) and (C, D), we have $(A, B) \leq (C, D)$ iff $A \subseteq C$. (It can easily be shown that, alternatively, $(A, B) \leq (C, D)$ iff $D \subseteq B$.) The relation $\prec$ is defined as above.

Thus the largest concept is the one with the most attributes in its intent, and the least objects (possibly none) in its extent. The smallest concept is the one with the least attributes in its intent (possible none) and the most objects in its extent. Somewhat perversely, however, it has become an FCA convention to draw and depict concept lattices with the smallest node on the top, and the largest node at the bottom of the drawing—the exact opposite to the SICLE drawing in Fig. 6.1 previous given. The cover graph for the living context's concept lattice is drawn in Fig. 6.4 according to this counter-intuitive convention. This concept lattice was set up using the open source tool known as Concept Explorer.[3]

---

[3]*Note*: Concept Explorer's author has requested that users cite his Russian text, [49].

Certain nodes are tagged by attribute or object labels. To infer the concept represented by a given node, one can infer the extent by collecting together all the object labels that can be found by tracing paths radiating out from the node in a downward direction. Similarly, the intent can be found by collecting all the attribute labels encountered on paths moving from the node in an upward direction. Thus the top and bottom concepts of the lattice (counter-intuitively placed in the reverse direction in the diagram) are as follows:

$$\top = (\varnothing, \{\text{Needs water, Lives in water}, \ldots, \text{Suckles young}\})$$
$$\bot = (\{\text{Leech, Bream}, \ldots, \text{Maize}\}, \{\text{Needs water}\})$$

In all, there are nineteen concepts in the cover graph. The reader may find, as an exercise, the node representing the concept ({Frog, Reed}, {Needs water, Lives in water, Lives on land}).

To construct a concept lattice and cover graph from a given context using Algorithm 6.3.1 or 6.4.3, initialise the graph structure with a single node, M, which forms the top node of a singleton lattice, and remains the top node in all subsequently generated lattices. The construction then proceeds by successively calling the algorithm for every object from G, where the set to be inserted into the lattice corresponds to the set of attributes that characterize the particular object, and the lattice generated by each call is used as the starting lattice for the next call. Although our algorithms generate only concept intents, they can be easily adapted to generate extent–intent pairs, i.e., concepts.

For several decades, a variety of algorithms for constructing concept lattices have been proposed, e.g., [20, 34, 41]. See [28] for a review and comparison. To date, the algorithm reported in [34] appears to have the best *theoretical* worst-case complexity estimate, namely $O(|\mathcal{L}|(|G| + |M|)|G|)$, where $|\mathcal{L}|$ is the number of concepts in the resulting lattice. Note that this is the complexity of constructing the lattice from scratch rather than updating an existing lattice by inserting a new object. In [26] an upper bound worst case complexity of $O(|G|^3|M||\mathcal{L}|)$ is derived for Algorithm 6.4.3 in the general case. However, in the case of very dense lattices, a worst case upper bound estimate of $O(|G|^2|M||\mathcal{L}|)$ was derived.

In [42] empirical experiments were undertaken to compare the performance of several of the most efficient (according to [28]) and/or most popular lattice construction algorithms: *Norris* [33], *Ganter* (a.k.a. *NextClosure*) [18], a version of *Bordat* [6] from [28], *Godin* [20] and *Nourine* [34].[4]

It was found that an algorithm called *AddIntent* in [41] in the form very close to Algorithm 6.4.3) generally outperformed the others, except for two scenarios where it was ranked second. Most experiments were based on randomly generated data, or on constructing Boolean lattices of various sizes (i.e., maximally large lattices for various attribute set sizes). However, when four real-world data-sets taken from the UCI repository [5] were used, *AddIntent dramatically* outperformed

---

[4]Algorithms were implemented in C++ on the same codesbase. Tests were performed on a Pentium™ 4–2 GHz computer with 1 Gigabyte RAM running under Windows XP™.

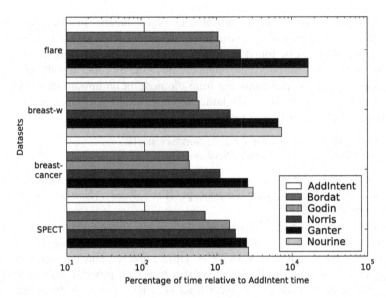

Fig. 6.5 Performance of *AddIntent* and other algorithms using empirical data (Based on data from [42])

the other algorithms as seen in Fig. 6.5. SPECT (Single Proton Emission Computed Tomography) is a real data set that contains 267 objects and 23 attributes, generating a lattice with 21,550 concepts. The remaining datasets (Breast Cancer Wisconsin Breast Cancer, and Solar Flare databases) are given in the form of many-valued tables and the QuDA program [22] was used to transform vector representations of objects in these data sets into attribute sets.

Chapter 7
Case Study 2: Classifying MADFA Construction Algorithms

The previous chapter illustrated the potency of software correctness by construction for developing a new and elegant algorithm. In this chapter we focus on classifying and taxonomising algorithmic problems by relying on correctness by construction thinking.

Systematic classification and taxonomisation is somewhat underdeveloped in computer science. One can see this, for example, in text books on data structures and algorithms. Quite sensibly, algorithms that address a common problem domain—for example, sorting—will be grouped in the same chapter. However, the presentation of the material seldom reflects, in any fundamental sense, the underlying common-alities and differences between the algorithms.

As will be illustrated, software correctness by construction methods can be a significant aid in articulating the commonalities and differences between algorithms. In our experience, the advantages are not merely pedagogic in nature. The taxonomising effort may well expose gaps in the taxonomic structure of related algorithms, thus suggesting avenues of potential research.

In this chapter, we illustrate how to classify a subset of algorithms that minimize acyclic deterministic finite automata. A comprehensive loop-invariant-based taxonomisation of such algorithms is given in [43]. That taxonomy resulted in the invention of a number of algorithms that were previously unknown. Clearly it is beyond the scope of the present text to attempt anything more than a brief illustration of the general idea. Nevertheless, in order to do that, we need to introduce relevant concepts related to finite automata.

7.1 Introduction

In the world of software, there is a vast number of applications to handle, recognize, search for and otherwise manipulate sequences of characters from some alphabet. Some that immediately come to mind are: compilation, word processing, text searching, natural language translation and many more.

D.G. Kourie and B.W. Watson, *The Correctness-by-Construction Approach*
to Programming, DOI 10.1007/978-3-642-27919-5_7,
© Springer-Verlag Berlin Heidelberg 2012

In each of these cases, elements of an alphabet—i.e. elements of some set of entities—are arranged in sequences (or strings). At the core of most of these problems is the notion that a "language" consists of a (possibly infinite) set of permissable strings. Here the term "language" is used in a technical and generic sense. In some contexts, it could mean a natural language such as English. In this case, the language is defined to be the set of strings that constitute legitimate English sentences. In another context, the language could designate some programming language, say Java. Again, in this case, the Java language is defined by the set of all strings that constitute syntactically correct Java programs. In yet other cases, the language could be taken to mean the set of all legitimate keywords in a programming language (which is different from the set of all syntactically correct programs in that language); or the set of words in a natural language (which is different from the set of all sentences in the language); or the set of possible strings of nucleotides (molecules that occur in DNA, normally designated by the letters A, C, G and T) in a genomic sequence that have some specific property, etc.

There are many challenges in processing strings in such languages, principally centered on identifying whether or not a string is an element of a given language. Since it is generally impractical explicitly to store all legitimate strings of the language, one of the problems is that of representing the language in some way. Language theorists have developed various formalisms for doing this, the most common being the use of so-called production rules. Chomsky classified languages into a four level hierarchy, based on the kinds of production rules that may be used to describe a language. Going from the most complex to the most simple, the classes of languages are called, respectively: recursively enumerable, context sensitive, context free and regular (or right linear). A natural language such as English is an example of a context sensitive language. Programming languages (Java, C^{++}, etc.) are context free. These matters are well documented, and the interested reader can refer to any number of text books for further information.

This chapter is all about a subset of regular languages—i.e., a subset of those languages that can be recognised by acyclic deterministic finite automata. The need for processing such regular languages arises in a large number of contexts: network intrusion detection systems, pattern matching, predictive text editing, spell checking, lexical analysis in compiling, DNA analysis, etc. In this chapter, we will not focus so much on how to recognise whether a given string is an element of a such regular language. Instead, we will focus on strategies for building minimal data structures for representing such regular languages.

7.2 From DFAs to MADFAs

7.2.1 Deterministic Finite Automata—DFAs

With each regular language is associated a formalism called a deterministic finite automaton (DFA). Such an automaton is an abstract computational device that is considered to be in some *state* at any given point in its computation. Formally, a DFA can be defined as follows:

Definition 7.2.1 (Deterministic Finite Automaton). A DFA is a five-tuple $(Q, \Sigma, \delta, F, s)$ where:

Q is a finite set of states;
Σ is a finite set of symbols called the alphabet;
$\delta : Q \times \Sigma \nrightarrow Q$ is a transition function that maps a state and an alphabet symbol to a state;
$F \subseteq Q$ is a set of so-called final states; and
$s \in Q$ is the start state.

The DFA is thus initially considered to be in state s. It "processes" symbols from the alphabet, by transiting to a new state when presented with a symbol. This new state is determined by the transition function, δ, which maps the current state and symbol to the next state.

Note that the $\nrightarrow$ used in the signature of the function δ in the above definition is conventionally used to indicate that δ is a *possibly partial* function. We therefore do *not* assume that the function δ is defined for every state / alphabet symbol pair.[1] If a state/symbol pair, (q, a), is undefined for δ, this will be denoted this by $\delta(q, a) = \perp$.

Every automata may be depicted as a transition graph. In such a graph, states are depicted as circles, start states have an in-edge from nowhere and final states are represented by two concentric circles. Transitions are depicted as labeled directed edges. Figure 7.1 gives an example of a transition graph.

The graph represents the DFA, M, in which

$$M = (Q, \Sigma, \delta, F, s)$$
$$Q = \{0, 1, 2, 3\},$$
$$\Sigma = \{a, b\},$$
$$\delta = \{\langle(0, a), 1\rangle, \langle(0, b), 2\rangle \langle(1, b), 3\rangle, \langle(2, a), 3\rangle\},$$
$$F = \{3\},$$
$$s = 0$$

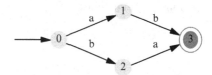

Fig. 7.1 Transition graph example

---

[1]In many texts, δ is assumed to be a total function. That means that instead of δ being undefined for certain state/alphabet pairs, the automaton is assumed to transit to a special "sink" state when encountering such state/alphabet pairs.

$$\mathcal{L}(M) = \{ab, ba\} \ (\mathcal{L}(M) \text{ denotes the language of } M\text{—see later})$$

$$|M| = 4 \ (|M| \text{ denotes the size of } M\text{—see later})$$

Here, we have followed the convention of representing the function δ as a set of pairs, the first element of each pair being from the domain, and the second element being from the range. Thus, for example, $\delta(0, a) = 1$ can be represented as $\langle (0, a), 1 \rangle$, etc. Because δ is a function, there can only be one out-transition of a node in a transition graph labelled by a given symbol. If, for example, Fig. 7.1 had a transition from state 0 to state 1 labelled a, and another from state 0 to state 2, also labelled a, this would mean that $\delta(0, a)$ maps to two states—which is not possible for a function.

As an example of where $\perp$ is used, note that since there is no out transition from state 2 on symbol b, this means that $\delta(2, b) = \perp$.

7.2.2 Acyclic Deterministic Finite Automata—ADFAs

In this text we are concerned a with very specific type of DFA: the subset of DFAs whose transition graphs do not have cycles. The transition graph in Fig. 7.1 is just such an example. DFAs associated with such transition graphs are called *acyclic* DFAs (abbreviated to ADFAs). Henceforth, all discussion should be assumed to be in reference to ADFAs. However, some of the properties also apply to DFAs in general. Readers interested in additional information about DFAs and related matters (such as non-deterministic finite automata) should refer to other standard sources.

ADFAs are of great practical importance because they can be used to represent languages whose elements (also referred to as words) are finite in length.

Given a transition graph of some ADFA, it is typically used to check whether a given string from the alphabet is in fact a word represented within the graph. To discuss this further, we introduce some notation that will be used in the rest of the chapter.

Let Σ^* be the Kleene closure of Σ—i.e., the set of all possible strings that can be formed from the alphabet Σ, including the empty string, normally designated by ϵ. In addition $\Sigma^+ = \Sigma^* \setminus \{\epsilon\}$.

Let $a \in \Sigma$ and $v \in \Sigma^*$. Then av denotes a string in Σ^+. We assume throughout the following functions:

$$head : \Sigma^+ \to \Sigma \text{ such that } head(av) = a,$$

$$tail : \Sigma^+ \to \Sigma^* \text{ such that } tail(av) = v.$$

Consider a finite string $x \in \Sigma^*$ and some ADFA, $M = (Q, \Sigma, \delta, F, s)$. Broadly speaking, to determine whether M accepts x we need to do the following:

Find the state, say q_1, that is returned by $\delta(head(x), s)$. Then find the state, say q_2, that is returned by $\delta(head(tail(x)), q_1)$. Continue in this way until the entire string has been processed. If the resulting state, say $q_n \in F$ then we say that M has accepted x; otherwise x has been rejected by M. Of course, if $x = \epsilon$ then it is accepted by M if and only if the start state, $s \in F$.

Algorithm 7.2.2 indicates how to determine algorithmically whether or not a string $x \in \Sigma^*$ is accepted or rejected by M.

> **Algorithm 7.2.2.**
> $\{ (x \in \Sigma^*) \wedge (|x| < \infty) \}$
> $t, q := x, s_0;$
> $\{ \text{ inv} \triangleq t \text{ is untested and the current state is } q \}$
> **do** $((t \neq \epsilon) \textbf{ cand } (\delta(head(t), q) \neq \bot)) \rightarrow$
> $q, t := \delta(head(t), q), tail(t)$
> **od**
> $\{inv \wedge ((t = \epsilon) \textbf{ cor } (\delta(head(t), q) = \bot))\}$
> **if** $((t = \epsilon) \wedge (q \in F)) \rightarrow$ *accept x*
> $[\!]\ ((t = \epsilon) \wedge (q \notin F)) \rightarrow$ *reject x*
> $[\!]\ (t \neq \epsilon) \rightarrow$ *reject x*
> **fi**

$\mathcal{L}(M)$ is used to denote the set of all words accepted by ADFA M. It is called the *language* of M. Algorithm 7.2.2 can be used to check—positively or negatively—whether an arbitrary word of finite length is in $\mathcal{L}(M)$. In this sense, the algorithm defines $\mathcal{L}(M)$.[2]

However, Algorithm 7.2.2 assumes that the relevant transition graph is available. In practice, one often starts off, not with a transition graph representing $\mathcal{L}(M)$, but just with $\mathcal{L}(M)$ itself—for example, with a list of words in a dictionary. The first challenge is efficiently (in space and time) to construct the transition graph that represents all these words.

7.2.3 Minimum Acyclic Deterministic Finite Automata—MADFAs

As shall be seen, there are many ways in which this can be done. Indeed, in general many ADFAs (and thus also many transition graphs) may have the same language. Such ADFAs will typically have differently defined δ's and/or Q's and/or F's. Each such automaton, M, can be assigned a size, denoted by $|M|$, that corresponds to its

---

[2]Note as an aside that this claim cannot be extended to DFAs in general (i.e., to DFAs that are not ADFAs) since the algorithm cannot affirm whether a word of infinite length (represented in a finite way) is part of a given DFA's language.

number of states, $|Q|$. (Other notions of size are possible, for example, involving the total number of transitions. We do not consider them here.)

Now it turns out that, associated with each regular language $\mathcal{L}$ whose elements consist of finite length words, there is a *unique* smallest ADFA.[3] If M is an ADFA, we shall use the predicate $MIN(M)$ to assert that it is the smallest ADFA recognising the language $\mathcal{L}(M)$.

Determining this minimum ADFA (henceforth abbreviated to MADFA)—or even an approximation of it—is a vital task in large-scale applications of automata theory. This is because construction of an ADFA from a set of words without giving attention on the ADFA's size tends to result in a state-space explosion. In practice, minimisation could reduce an ADFA's size by a factor of 10 or more, in some cases making the difference between determining whether or not an application will be feasible on a given hardware platform.[4]

Because of the practical importance of the task, the last couple of decades have seen a variety of algorithms being proposed for deriving a MADFA from a given set of finite words. Although authors of new algorithms typically cite and perhaps briefly explain existing algorithms, the presentation, style of explanation, notation differs considerably from one another. It therefore becomes increasingly difficult to gain an overall understanding of how the set of algorithmic solutions inter-relate, and to identify potential gaps that could be exploited by further research.

Experience with several problem domains has shown that a methodical correctness by construction derivation of each relevant algorithm can be a potent means of finding and articulating the intrinsic differences and similarities between a set of related algorithms. This was recently done in [43] with respect to the MADFA construction algorithms. Interested readers can read the source document for full details. Here we intend giving a brief overview of what the approach entails, but in order to do this, some additional MADFA-related concepts need to be explained.

7.2.4   Concepts for MADFA Construction Algorithms

The concepts presented in this subsection are needed to illustrate the elegant classification of MADFA construction algorithms that is provided in [43]. Because we will not be examining the details of each and every algorithm in this present text, we can conveniently skip over several of the additional definitions and concepts presented in [43]. However, the reader should be aware that the articulation of such concepts constitutes a significant part of the intellectual effort required to

---

[3]Up to isomorphism. *Note*: This claim is also true for regular languages and DFAs in general.

[4]At the 2009 annual FSMNLP workshop, a speaker from Google demonstrated the company's prototype voice recognition system that was based on DFA technology where a minimisation algorithm had been used to reduce the initially derived DFA of size about 10 million, down to about 3 million.

achieve a fundamental and elegant taxonomisation. Part of the effort may involve a restatement of widely known concepts. Another part may be to articulate predicates implicitly relied upon by other authors, but not explicitly stated. In general, the challenge should not be underestimated of providing a unified notation and vocabulary at an appropriate level of formality. The effort is well worth it, since the rewards will be seen in terms of elegance that facilitates pedagogic and research objectives.

For notational convenience, we will assume throughout that we are referencing an ADFA, $M = (Q, \Sigma, \delta, F, s)$. In terms of this assumption, we will take the liberty of not including M as a parameter of a predicate or function. We will assume that the various symbols associated with M are globally known and we will freely use them and reference them. In addition, if we refer to state p, for example, then we are assuming that $p \in Q$. Similar remarks apply to start state references, references to δ, etc. On the other hand, whenever relevant we will allow ourselves the freedom to include M as a parameter of a predicate or function. For example, we have already noted that $\mathcal{L}(M)$ represents the language of M, and that MIN(M) asserts that M is a MADFA. Henceforth we will generally simply write $\mathcal{L}$ to represent this language, and simply write MIN to assert that M is a MADFA.

Under this assumption, we start with following definitions, leading to the definition of a trie.

Definition 7.2.3 (Confluence state). A state p is a *confluence* state, written *Is_Confl*(p), iff it has more than one in-transition in the transition graph of M.

Definition 7.2.4 (Confluence-free set of states). A set of states X is confluence-free, written *Confl_free*(X), iff $\forall p : X \cdot (\neg Is\_Confl(p))$

Definition 7.2.5 (Trie). M is a *trie*, written *Is_Trie*, iff its transition graph is a tree rooted at start state s.

For our purposes we shall assume that the start state s of an ADFA is never a confluence state. A trie is therefore an ADFA without any confluence states whatsoever. Note that all leaves of a trie are final states. The ADFA associated with the transition graph in Fig. 7.1 is not a trie: the graph is not a tree, and *Is_Confl*(3) is true. On the other hand, the ADFA of the transition graph in Fig. 7.2 is indeed a trie—it is a tree whose leaves are final states, and there are no confluence states.

Notation 7.2.6. *For a state p, Σ_p denotes the subset of Σ on which p has out-transitions. That is, $\Sigma_p = \{a | a \in \Sigma \wedge \delta(p, a) \neq \perp\}$.*

Thus, in reference to Fig. 7.2, $\Sigma_0 = \{h\}$, $\Sigma_1 = \{a, e\}$, $\Sigma_2 = \{d, r\}$, $\Sigma_3 = \varnothing$, etc.

Definition 7.2.7 (Extending δ). We extend δ to the function $\delta^* : Q \times \Sigma^* \nrightarrow Q$ where

$$\delta^*(p, w) = \begin{cases} p & \text{if } w = \epsilon \\ \delta^*(\delta(p, a), v) & \text{if } (w = av) \wedge (v \in \Sigma^*) \wedge (a \in \Sigma_p) \\ \perp & \text{otherwise} \end{cases}.$$

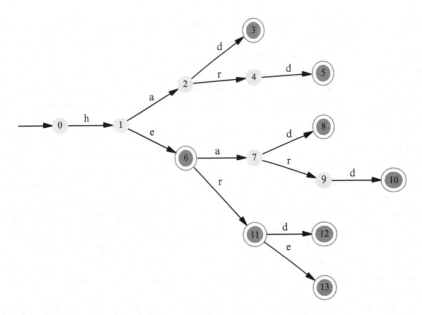

Fig. 7.2 Trie example

Again, taking a few examples from Fig. 7.2: $\delta^*(0, \epsilon) = 0, \delta^*(0, h) = 1$, $\delta^*(0, hea) = 7, \delta^*(6, ard) = 10, \delta^*(6, ab) = \perp$, etc. Thus, $\delta^*(p, w)$ returns the state in which we land (if any) if we recursively apply δ to the members of the string w, starting from state p.

Definition 7.2.8 (Right language of a state). The right language of a state p, denoted $\mathcal{L}(p)$, is defined by $\mathcal{L}(p) = \{w | \delta^*(p, w) \in F\}$.

In words, $\mathcal{L}(p)$ is the set of strings associated with all the paths from state p to any final state. For example, in Fig. 7.2, $\mathcal{L}(6) = \{\epsilon, ad, ard, rd, re\}$. The example shows that if $p \in F$, (which is true of state 6 in the figure) then $\epsilon \in \mathcal{L}(p)$. On the other hand, if $p = s$, the start state of ADFA M, then clearly $\mathcal{L}(s) = L(M)$.

Definition 7.2.9 (The w-path from state p). For state p and $w \in \Sigma^*$, $[p \overset{w}{\rightsquigarrow}]$ is the sequence of states $p, \ldots, \delta^*(p, v)$ where v is the longest prefix of w such that $\delta^*(p, v) \neq \perp$.

Here are a few examples from Fig. 7.2 of w-paths from various states:

$$[0 \overset{had}{\rightsquigarrow}] = \langle 0.1.2.3 \rangle$$

$$[0 \overset{ha}{\rightsquigarrow}] = \langle 0.1.2 \rangle$$

$$[0 \overset{hat}{\rightsquigarrow}] = \langle 0.1.2 \rangle$$

$$[6 \overset{\text{ere}}{\leadsto}] = \langle 6 \rangle$$

$$[6 \overset{\text{re}}{\leadsto}] = \langle 6.11.13 \rangle$$

In some contexts, we may pass a path argument $[p \overset{w}{\leadsto}]$ to a predicate or function which expects a *set* argument, thereby implicitly treating the path as a set of states.

We also need to denote the set of states that are on paths leading out from some other set of states.

Notation 7.2.10 (Successors of states in X). *If $X \subseteq Q$ then $Succ^*(X)$ denotes the set:*

$$\{p \in Q \mid \exists q, w : (q \in X \wedge w \in \Sigma^*) \cdot \delta^*(q, w) = p\}.$$

For example, the successor states of all final nodes in the ADFA in Fig. 7.2 is given by $Succ^*(F) = \{3, 5, 6, 7, 8, 9, 10, 11, 12, 13\}$. Note that state 6 is included in the set, because $\delta(6, \epsilon) = 6$.

Note that in a trie, there is only one path from the start state, s to any other state. This is clearly visible in the example trie of Fig. 7.2. However, in general there may be more than one path from the start state to another state in an ADFA. For example, in Fig. 7.1 there are two paths from state 0 to state 3. This means that we cannot characterise a state p by distance from the start state. Instead, we have to talk about the minimum path length from the start state. This leads to the following notation and definition.

Notation 7.2.11 (Minimum path length). *Let $minpath(p)$ denote the minimum path length over all paths from the start state of ADFA M to state p.*

This allows us to define the notion of depth in an ADFA

Definition 7.2.12 (Depth levels). In ADFA M, for each $k \in \mathbb{N}$ we denote the set of states at depth level k by DL_k, defined as follows:

$$DL_k = \{p \mid (p \in Q) \wedge (minpath(p) = k)\}.$$

The depth levels form a partition of Q, i.e., on the assumption that the depth level of states are in the range $[0, n)$, we have that $Q = DL_0 \cup DL_1 \cup \cdots DL_{n-1}$ and $\forall i, j : [0, n) \cdot (i \neq j \Rightarrow DL_i \cap DL_j = \varnothing)$. We also allow range specification as part of our depth level notation. For example, $DL_{\geq k}$ refers to the set of states $DL_k \cup \cdots DL_{n-1}$, and $DL_{<k}$ refers to the set of states $DL_0 \cup \cdots DL_{k-1}$.

Notation 7.2.13 (Shortest word length of an ADFA). *Function $minlen(M)$ (or simply $minlen$) is the length of the shortest word accepted by M.*

Clearly, *minlen* is the depth of a final state closest (in terms of path-length) to start state s.

In principle, words in $\mathcal{L}$ can be ordered in many ways: by length, by number of vowels, by the number of zeros in their ascii representation, etc. One specific ordering will be designated the lexicographic ordering. In a natural language context, this would typically be the alphabetically-based lexicographic ordering used in dictionaries. At least one of the words in $\mathcal{L}$ will be the lexicographically greatest word.

Notation 7.2.14 (Lexicographically greatest word). *Let lexmax denote the lexicographically greatest word in $\mathcal{L}$.*

It is worth emphasising that in the discussion to follow, a set of words W will be provided as input for various algorithms to be considered. M will change over time as the algorithm under discussion runs along. Any reference to *lexmax* in such a context should be construed to be in reference to the language $\mathcal{L}(M)$, as determined by the description of M at that stage of the algorithm—i.e., *lexmax* is *not* the lexicographically greatest word in the set of words W that is provided at input.

In order to minimize an automaton, one has to identify all so-called equivalent states, and merge them. The notion of state equivalence is neatly defined as follows:

Definition 7.2.15 (State equivalence). Define E as an equivalence relation on states where

$$E(p, q) \equiv (\mathcal{L}(p) = \mathcal{L}(q)).$$

In other words, states p and q are equivalent if and only if they have the same right-languages. Equivalent states p and q can be merged. This entails selecting one of them, say p, redirecting all inbound transitions that go into q into p instead, and removing q from the set of states. The result will be a smaller automaton but with $\mathcal{L}$ the same as before. We assume that procedure *merge* is available to do this.

Once all equivalent states have been merged, the resulting ADFA will in fact be a MADFA, i.e., MIN will hold.

It is handy to have notation for expressing the pairwise inequivalence of elements *within* a given set of states.

Definition 7.2.16 (Pairwise inequivalent states). Let *Inequiv*(X) be a predicate asserting that no pair of states in the set of states, X, is equivalent, i.e.,

$$Inequiv(X) \equiv \forall p, q : X \cdot ((p \neq q) \Rightarrow \neg E(p, q)).$$

Using this notation, the key characteristic of a MADFA—that no pair of its states are equivalent—can now be expressed symbolically:

$$MIN \equiv Inequiv(Q).$$

It is also handy to be able to assert that the elements *between* two states are pairwise inequivalent.

Definition 7.2.17 (Pairwise inequivalent sets of states). Assuming X and Y are two sets of states, let *Pairwise_inequiv*(X, Y) be a predicate asserting that no pairing of a state in X and a state in Y is equivalent, i.e.,

$$Pairwise\_inequiv(X, Y) \equiv \forall (p, q) : (X \times Y) \cdot \neg E(p, q).$$

It will be seen that the following equivalence relationship between the two foregoing definitions serves as an important basis for classifying some of the minimising strategies used in various algorithms.

Property 7.2.18.

$$Inequiv(X \cup Y) \equiv Inequiv(X) \wedge Inequiv(Y) \wedge Pairwise\_inequiv(X, Y)$$

Equipped with the foregoing notation and concept definitions we are now in a position to provide a basis for systematically classifying MADFA construction algorithms.

7.3 An Abstract MADFA Construction Algorithm

The task of constructing a MADFA can be specified as follows:

$$Q, \delta, F : [W \subset \Sigma^*, \text{Min} \wedge \mathcal{L} = W].$$

It is assumed that $M = (Q, \Sigma, \delta, s, F)$ starts off with known and fixed Σ. This specification is then refined to a general algorithm skeleton for constructing a MADFA from a set of words. We skip the detailed refinement steps because they are fairly obvious, and will distract from the main theme at hand.

An abstract type, *State*, is assumed that characterises the elements of Q. A function, *create*( ), is also assumed that creates and returns a new object of type *State*. The function is used to create the start state, s. The remaining components of M (namely Q, δ and F) are then minimally initialised. The algorithm thereafter adds the words from W one-by-one to $\mathcal{L}$, ensuring that at each step, Q, δ and F are changed appropriately.

In some cases, the order in which the words are added is important—and so we assume some partial order $\leq$ on the words. In the remaining cases, $\leq$ should be regarded as degenerate in the sense that it renders all words incommensurate—i.e., for no two words, say w and v is it the case that $w \leq v$ or $v \leq w$. In these cases words are selected in any order.

In the skeleton algorithm, a number of matters will be left in abstract form. In subsequent discussions we will show how particular instantiations of these abstractions lead to different algorithmic solutions to the general problem of deriving a MADFA from a set of words. The following lists the abstractions at issue:

1. A structural invariant, *Struct(D)* (for the set of words *D* already processed), is maintained on the ADFA; that is, *Struct(D)* holds both before and after a word *w* is added to the ADFA. Subsequent instantiations of this abstract invariant are: *the ADFA has a trie structure*, *the ADFA is minimal*, etc.
2. The body of a procedure, *add_word*, to add individual words is not given in the skeleton algorithm.
3. The nature of the partial order $\leq$ on the words is not specified in the skeleton algorithm.
4. A cleanup procedure, *cleanup*, is applied to the ADFA after the words have been added, yielding the desired MADFA. However, its body is not specified.

All of these are, in some sense, meta-parameters of the skeleton algorithm, and are instantiated in various ways by existing (in some cases, recently invented) concrete algorithms.

With some of the *add_word* procedures, the intermediate automaton derived after adding all the words in *W* may not yet be minimal. Consequently, a *cleanup* procedure is specified to transform the ADFA into a MADFA. For this reason, in the body of the algorithm, *M* is assumed to be an ADFA, but not necessarily a MADFA.

The algorithm partitions $W \subset \Sigma^*$ into *D* (for "*Done*") and *T* (for "*To-do*"). The boundary of this partition is constantly shifted. It is also assumed that word set *W* and ADFA *M* are global variables:

> **Algorithm 7.3.1.**
> $[\![$ **var** D, T : **set of** Σ^*
> $|$ $\{ W \subset \Sigma^* \}$
> $\quad s := create();$
> $\quad (Q, \delta, s, F) := (\{s\}, \varnothing, s, \varnothing);$
> $\quad D, T := \varnothing, W;$
> $\quad \{ \text{ invariant } :Struct(D)$
> $\qquad variant :|T| \}$
> $\quad \textbf{do } T \neq \varnothing \rightarrow [\![\textbf{var } w : \Sigma^*$
> $\qquad\qquad\qquad | \textbf{ let } w : w \text{ is any minimal element of } T \text{ under } \leq;$
> $\qquad\qquad\qquad\quad \{ \text{ Struct}(D) \}$
> $\qquad\qquad\qquad\qquad Q, \delta, F : add\_word(w);$
> $\qquad\qquad\qquad\quad \{ \text{ Struct}(D \cup \{w\}) \}$
> $\qquad\qquad\qquad\qquad D, T := D \cup \{w\}, T - \{w\}$
> $\qquad\qquad\qquad\quad \{ \text{ Struct}(D) \}$
> $\qquad\qquad\qquad]\!]$
> $\quad \textbf{od};$
> $\quad \{ \text{ Struct}(W) \}$
> $\qquad Q, \delta, F : cleanup()$
> $\quad \{ \text{ Min} \wedge \mathcal{L} = W \}$
> $]\!]$

Known MADFA construction algorithm can be derived by refining specific versions of *add_word* and *cleanup*, based on specific instantiations of *Struct(D)* and $\leq$. The general process is outlined in the following subsections.

7.3.1 Structural Invariant Instantiations

The way in which the structural invariant, $Struct(D)$, is instantiated neatly exposes various possible ways of constructing the MADFA. The following instantiations lead to known (sometimes recently invented) MADFA algorithms:

1. $Struct_T(D) \equiv Is\_Trie \wedge \mathcal{L} = D$.

   This leads to the trie-based algorithms which will be discussed in Sect. 7.4 on page 242. These are characterised as non-incremental because they first build an ADFA, then minimize afterwards—i.e., they do not incrementally minimize the evolving ADFA.

2. $Struct_N(D) \equiv \mathcal{L} = D$

   This leads to non-incremental algorithms in which the evolving ADFA is not constrained to be a trie. These algorithms are briefly discussed in Sect. 7.5 on page 250. Note that $Struct_T(D) \Rightarrow Struct_N(D)$.

3. $Struct_I(D) \equiv Min \wedge \mathcal{L} = D$

   Here the invariant requires that every instantiation of M after a word has been added to its language, $\mathcal{L}$, results in a MADFA—the generated ADFA is minimal. Thus, an implicit invariant requirement is that $Inequiv(Q)$ should hold. However, because $Min \equiv Inequiv(Q)$, including $Inequiv(Q)$ as a conjunct in the invariant is superfluous. Again, note that $Struct_I(D) \Rightarrow Struct_N(D)$. These incrementally minimizing algorithms will not be discussed further in this text. Readers seeking further details may refer to [43].

4. $Struct_R(D) \equiv Is\_Trie \wedge \mathcal{L} = D^R$

   The superscript R on the set D indicates that all elements of D are reversed. Thus, in add_word, an ADFA is built of words that are the reverse of the words provided in W. The ADFA is built as a trie. The $clean\_up$ operation then flips around this trie (in effect, it changes the direction of the arrows in the transition graph) and provides the resulting structure with a new start state. Although the resulting transition graph's acyclic nature is retained by this operation, it will no longer represent a DFA (for technical reasons not discussed here). The transition graph represents a so-called *non-deterministic* finite automaton (an NFA). A known general algorithm is then used that converts NFAs to DFAs. What renders this approach particularly elegant is that the outcome of this known determinising algorithm, in this particular case, is not just a DFA, but an ADFA. Even more elegant is the fact that this ADFA is already minimised—it is a MADFA. The algorithm is related to Brzozowski's minimization algorithm [45, 47] and given in alternative forms in [44, 46]. We will not give it further attention in this text.

5. $Struct_S(D) \equiv Inequiv(Q - [s \overset{lexmax}{\leadsto}]) \wedge Confl\_free([s \overset{lexmax}{\leadsto}]) \wedge \mathcal{L} = D$.

   This leads to the algorithm by Daciuk, Mihov and others, in which words are added in lexicographic order. We will provide a little more information about this algorithm, as well as those compliant with the next two structural invariants in Sect. 7.6 on page 255.

6. $Struct_D(D) \equiv Inequiv(D_{>minlen}) \wedge Confl\text{-}free(DL_{\leq minlen}) \wedge \mathcal{L} = D$.
   This leads to a new algorithm where words are added in order of decreasing length. The idea is briefly described in Sect. 7.6 on page 255.
7. $Struct_W(D) \equiv Inequiv(Succ^*(F)) \wedge Confl\text{-}free(Q - Succ^*(F)) \wedge \mathcal{L} = D$.
   This leads an alternative algorithm for adding words in order of decreasing length. It, too, is briefly described in Sect. 7.6 page 255.

Each of these structural invariants can be cast into the general form:

$$Struct_X(D) \equiv Inequiv(Y) \wedge Confl\text{-}free(Z) \wedge \mathcal{L} = f(D)$$

where:

X is one of the seven structural variants (i.e., $X \in \{T, N, I, R, S, D, W\}$);
Y and Z are subsets of Q; and
$f(D) = D^R$ when $X = R$ and $f(D) = D$ otherwise.

The matter is summarised in Table 7.1. Clearly in degenerate cases where $Y = \varnothing$ then $Inequiv(Y) = \text{true}$ and when $Z = \varnothing$ then $Confl\text{-}free(Z) = \text{true}$. Moreover, because $Is\text{-}trie \equiv Confl\text{-}free(Q)$ (per definition of a trie), the table contains Q in the column for confluence-free states wherever the original invariant had a conjunct $Is\text{-}trie$.

The table shows that in all but one case (the case in the second row of the table), Q, Z and Y are related by the equation $Y = Q - Z$. In other words, in six of the seven cases, $add\text{-}word$ conforms to a generic invariant that requires a subset of the states to be held inequivalent, while the rest of the states are rendered confluence free.

Rows 1 and 4 (i.e., where $X \in \{T, R\}$) are associated with $add\text{-}word$ variants which ensure a trie at each iteration without paying any attention minimization opportunities. In these cases $clean\text{-}up$ does the minimization afterwards. Row 3 is associated with an $add\text{-}word$ variant that ignores the matter of confluence-free states entirely, focussing on retaining a minimized structure throughout. In this case, $clean\text{-}up$ is not required. Row 2 represents a "degenerate" case, which also ignores the matter of confluence-free states entirely.

Table 7.1 Invariant summary: $Struct_X(D) \equiv Inequiv(Y) \wedge Confl\text{-}free(Z) \wedge \mathcal{L} = f(D)$

	X	Y: Inequivalent states	Z: Confluence-free states	Y	$f(D)$
1	T	$\varnothing$	Q	$(Q - Z)$	D
2	N	$\varnothing$	$\varnothing$	$\varnothing$	D
3	I	Q	$\varnothing$	$(Q - Z)$	D
4	R	$\varnothing$	Q	$(Q - Z)$	D^R
5	S	$Q - [s \overset{lexmax}{\rightsquigarrow}]$	$[s \overset{lexmax}{\rightsquigarrow}]$	$(Q - Z)$	D
6	D	$DL_{>minlen}$	$DL_{\leq minlen}$	$(Q - Z)$	D
7	W	$Succ^*(F)$	$Q - Succ^*(F)$	$(Q - Z)$	D

The rows 5, 6 and 7 point to *add_word* versions that partition Q in somewhat less extreme ways than those relating to rows 1, 3 and 4. We shall discuss these partitions in slightly more detail in Sect. 7.6.

7.3.2   The Procedures to be Instantiated

The general specification for *add_word* is:

Algorithm 7.3.2.
{ *Struct(D)* }
   $Q, \delta, F : add\_word(w)$
{ *Struct(D* $\cup$ {*w*}) }

The various instances of *Struct* given above lead to different versions of *add_word*. These versions will be given names of the form add_word_X where X is the corresponding subscript of *Struct* as per one of the above instances.

Note, however, that in the general structure of Algorithm 7.3.1, *add_word* is invoked within a loop that first acquires some w as "any minimal element of T". Hence, there is an implicit conjunct in the precondition of *add_word* asserting that w is a minimal element of T. In the case of the first four versions of *Struct*, all elements in W (and therefore in T) are considered equally minimal, and so this requirement plays no role in the elaboration of the corresponding version of *add_word*—it can just as well be left out. In the case of the last three versions of *Struct*, however, different notions of minimality are used in each respective case, leading to different versions of *add_word*. In these cases, the requirement that w should be a minimal of T is therefore an important consideration, and is made an explicit conjunct in the precondition.

For each version of *Struct*, we also have a corresponding specification for *cleanup*, whose general specification is:

Algorithm 7.3.3.
{ *Struct(W)* }
   $Q, \delta, F : cleanup$
{ Min $\wedge \mathcal{L} = W$ }

The versions of *cleanup* will be given names of the form $cleanup_X$ where X is the corresponding subscript of *Struct*.

7.3.3   The Importance of the Skeleton-Based Taxonomy

The common algorithm skeleton is a key aspect of the algorithm presentation in this text. All of the presently known algorithms have been successfully cast into this framework, and there is every reason to believe that newly discovered algorithms will also fit within this or a similar taxonomy.

Moreover, the framework serves to spark fresh ideas about how the task of MADFA construction might be approached. For example, [43] notes that the loop in which *add_word* is embedded is premised on the selection and insertion of one word at a time. This exposes questions like:

- Could *add_wordset* algorithms perhaps be developed that added a *set* of words at a time to the currently developed ADFA? What might these properties be?
- Could we envisage a multi-threaded parallel execution of the body of the loop, each thread handling a different word or set of words? What synchronisation mechanisms would be needed? On what basis should such thread assignment take place?

In this sense, taxonomisation and classification not only support comprehension, but also act as a stimulus for research ideas.

In the next two sections, we will refine the first two *Struct* variants to corresponding versions of *add_word*. Additionally, the next section will also refine *cleanup* to a level where possibilities for "bifurcation" into different refinement paths becomes clearly visible. However, tracing the refinements down each path to fully implementable algorithms is considered outside the scope of the present text, whose principal concern is to illustrate how correctness by construction supports taxonomisation within a domain.

7.4 Trie Intermediate ADFA

In this section, we maintain M as a trie during the construction of the ADFA, and use the associated structural invariant:

$$Struct_T(D) \equiv Is\_Trie \wedge \mathcal{L} = D.$$

Following the construction of the trie using add_word_T, procedure $cleanup_T$ merges equivalent states yielding the sought-after MADFA.

7.4.1 Procedure add_word_T

For add_word_T, we get specification. We use $\mathcal{L}_0$ to represent the initial value of $\mathcal{L}$.

$$
\begin{aligned}
&\textbf{proc } add\_word_T(\textbf{in } w : \Sigma^*) \rightarrow \\
&\qquad \{ \textbf{ pre } Is\_Trie \wedge \mathcal{L} = \mathcal{L}_0 \} \\
&\qquad S_{7.4.1} \\
&\qquad \{ \textbf{ post } Is\_Trie \wedge \mathcal{L} = \mathcal{L}_0 \cup \{w\} \} \\
&\textbf{corp}
\end{aligned}
$$

It is convenient to weaken both the pre- and postcondition of $S_{7.4.1}$ in such a way that it can be reused as part of the *add_word* implementations in some of the other instantiations of *Struct*.

In both cases, we weaken the *Is_Trie* conjunct to *Confl_free*($[s \overset{w}{\leadsto}]$). This is indeed a weakening, because no state in a trie may be a confluence, whereas the weakened conjunct only forbids states in the set $[s \overset{w}{\leadsto}]$ to be a confluence. Recall that $[s \overset{w}{\leadsto}]$ refers to the sequence of states in the existing structure whose transitions will spell out the longest possible prefix of w, as it were—i.e., it is meaningful to refer to $[s \overset{w}{\leadsto}]$ in an ADFA (trie in this case), even if w is not yet part of its language.

Note that in terms of the refinement rules, weakening the precondition constitutes a true refinement, but weakening the postcondition is not! However, with this postcondition weakening, we will still obtain a trie after all words W are added, provided that when adding a new word, say w', we do not disturb the confluence-free status of $[s \overset{w}{\leadsto}]$ with respect to a previously added word, w. This will indeed be the case.

The simplest way to proceed in refining $S_{7.4.1}$ is to introduce a new state variable q, establish $q = \delta^*(s, w) \wedge q \neq \perp$ and then make q a final state (so that the ADFA accepts w), as in the following example. Assume we initially have the ADFA accepting herd, as in Fig. 7.3a. We wish to add the word her, which is a prefix of herd. This results in state 3 becoming a final one, as in Fig. 7.3b.

We therefore have the following procedure

$$\textbf{proc } \textit{add\_word}_T \, (\textbf{in } w : \Sigma^*) \rightarrow$$
$$\left\{ \textbf{pre } \textit{Confl\_free}([s \overset{w}{\leadsto}]) \wedge \mathcal{L} = \mathcal{L}_0 \right\}$$
$$\lVert \; \textbf{var } q : State$$
$$\mid \; S'_{7.4.1};$$
$$\{ \; q = \delta^*(s, w) \wedge q \neq \perp \; \}$$
$$F := F \cup \{q\}$$
$$\rVert$$
$$\left\{ \textbf{post } \textit{Confl\_free}([s \overset{w}{\leadsto}]) \wedge \mathcal{L} = \mathcal{L}_0 \cup \{w\} \right\}$$

$$\textbf{corp}$$

We can continue our derivation with $S'_{7.4.1}$.

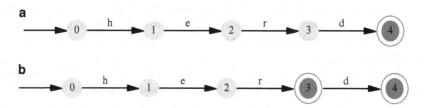

Fig. 7.3 Adding a prefix word. (**a**) ADFA for herd. (**b**) ADFA for her and herd

7.4.2   *Adding Only Prefix Words*

In this subsection only, we assume that w is a prefix of a word already accepted by (Q, δ, s, F)—that is $\delta^*(s, w) \neq \bot$. Clearly, this is an unrealistic assumption—it is rarely applicable—but it forms a good starting point for a simple algorithm. We also introduce two additional variables $l, r : w = lr$ and maintain invariant $q = \delta^*(s, l)$, giving the following for $S'_{7.4.1}$.

$$\vdots$$

$$\{ \ \delta^*(s, w) \neq \bot \ \}$$
$$\| [\ \mathbf{var} \ l, r : \Sigma^*$$
$$| \ l, r, q := \epsilon, w, s;$$
$$\quad \{ \ \text{invariant: } w = lr \wedge q = \delta^*(s, l)$$
$$\quad \quad \text{variant: } |r| \ \}$$
$$\quad \mathbf{do} \ r \neq \epsilon \rightarrow$$
$$\quad \quad l, r, q := l \cdot head(r), tail(r), \delta(q, head(r))$$
$$\quad \mathbf{od}$$
$$] |$$
$$\{ \ q = \delta^*(s, w) \wedge q \neq \bot \ \}$$

$$\vdots$$

The precondition $\delta^*(s, w) \neq \bot$ sometimes becomes established just by adding the words in a certain order (i.e., by the choice of $\leq$). However, for the version of *Struct* which we are currently considering, no ordering relationship is assumed— any $w \in W$ may be the next word to be added. We therefore may not rely on any such ordering advantages, and therefore generalise the algorithm in the next section.

7.4.3   *Adding a Non-prefix Word in a Trie*

In the case where $\delta^*(s, w) = \bot$, we begin by finding the longest prefix l of w which is recognised by the existing ADFA—i.e., the longest l such that $\delta(s, l) \neq \bot$. We then build additional states and transitions if required, to cater for recognising the suffix of w that follows on l. The matter is illustrated in the following example.

Initially, we have the ADFA in Fig. 7.4a accepting her. We wish to add the word had. The (longest common) prefix h (of had and her) lies on a path to state 1, at which point we are stuck and new states 4 and 5 must be created, eventually giving the ADFA in Fig. 7.4b.

Recall that we are assuming that $w = lr$. To express that "l is the longest prefix on a path reachable from s," we use the following (using the invariant $q = \delta^*(s, l)$)

$$\delta^*(s, l) \neq \bot \wedge (r = \epsilon \ \mathbf{cor} \ \delta(q, head(r)) = \bot)$$

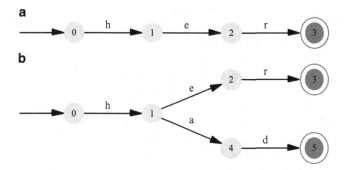

Fig. 7.4 Adding a non-prefix word (**a**) ADFA for her. (**b**) ADFA for her and had

Intuitively, this means that there is a full l-path from the start state s, and that either we have run out of symbols to consider (i.e., $r = \epsilon$) or no further transitions are possible.

Instead of our previous refinement of $S'_{7.4.1}$, we obtain

$$\vdots$$
$$\begin{aligned}
&\lvert\lbrack\ \textbf{var}\ l, r : \Sigma^* \\
&\lvert\ S''_{7.4.1}; \\
&\quad \{\ q = \delta^*(s, l) \wedge \delta^*(s, l) \neq \bot \wedge (r = \epsilon\ \textbf{cor}\ \delta(q, head(r)) = \bot)\ \} \\
&\quad S'''_{7.4.1} \\
&\rbrack\rvert \\
&\{\ q = \delta^*(s, w) \wedge q \neq \bot\ \}
\end{aligned}$$
$$\vdots$$

Statement $S''_{7.4.1}$ simply follows the w-path through M until no further transition is possible, then statement $S'''_{7.4.1}$ extends M as necessary with new states and transitions.

The final procedure is given below. It uses function *create*( ) that creates a new object of type *State*, inserts it into Q and returns a reference to this object.

$$\begin{aligned}
&\textbf{proc}\ \textit{add\_word}_T\,(\textbf{in}\ w : \Sigma^*) \rightarrow \\
&\qquad \Big\{\ \textbf{pre}\ \textit{confl\_free}([s \overset{w}{\leadsto}]) \wedge \mathcal{L} = \mathcal{L}_0\ \Big\} \\
&\qquad \lvert\lbrack\ \textbf{var}\ q : \textit{State} \\
&\qquad \lvert\ \ \lvert\lbrack\ \textbf{var}\ l, r : \Sigma^* \\
&\qquad \lvert\ \ \ \ l, r, q := \epsilon, w, s; \\
&\qquad\qquad \{\ \text{invariant:}\ w = lr \wedge q = \delta^*(s, l) \\
&\qquad\qquad \ \ \text{variant:}\ |r|\ \} \\
&\qquad\qquad \textbf{do}\ r \neq \epsilon\ \textbf{cand}\ \delta(q, head(r)) \neq \bot \rightarrow \\
&\qquad\qquad\qquad l, r, q := l \cdot head(r), tail(r), \delta(q, head(r)) \\
&\qquad\qquad \textbf{od}; \\
&\qquad\qquad \{\ q = \delta^*(s, l) \wedge \delta^*(s, l) \neq \bot \wedge (r = \epsilon\ \textbf{cor}\ \delta(q, head(r)) = \bot)\ \}
\end{aligned}$$

$$\{ \text{ invariant: } w = lr \wedge q = \delta^*(s, l)$$
$$\quad \text{variant: } |r| \ \}$$
$$\textbf{do } r \neq \epsilon \rightarrow [\![\ \textbf{var} \ p : State$$
$$\quad | \ p := create();$$
$$\quad\quad \delta(q, head(r)), q := p, p;$$
$$\quad\quad l, r := l \cdot head(r), tail(r)$$
$$\quad]\!]$$
$$\textbf{od}$$
$$]\!];$$
$$\{ \ q = \delta^*(s, w) \wedge q \neq \perp \ \}$$
$$F := F \cup \{q\}$$
$$]\!]$$
$$\left\{ \ \textbf{post } \ confl\_free([s \overset{w}{\rightsquigarrow}]) \wedge \mathcal{L} = \mathcal{L}_0 \cup \{w\} \right\}$$

corp

This algorithm corresponds closely to most trie-construction algorithms—including that sketched by Fredkin, the inventor of tries [16]. An example of its output is given on page 249 in Sect. 7.4.5.

7.4.4 Procedure cleanup$_T$

In this section, we briefly consider minimization procedures with the following specification:

$$\textbf{proc } cleanup_T() \rightarrow$$
$$\quad \{ \ \textbf{pre } \ Is\_Trie \wedge \mathcal{L} = \mathcal{L}_0 \ \}$$
$$\quad S_{7.4.4}$$
$$\quad \{ \ \textbf{post } Min \wedge \mathcal{L} = \mathcal{L}_0 \ \}$$
$$\textbf{corp}$$

Our objective is to outline the broad structure of commonly used minimizing algorithms, without fully elaborating them. We avoid a full elaboration, because the current concern is to show how correctness by construction can serve as a means of classifying algorithms. While minimization of ADFAs (and indeed of DFAs in general) is of great importance, we would loose focus of our major objective if we attended to the details here. Instead the reader is referred to other sources, where [43] would be an excellent starting point.

The minimisation algorithms that we allude to in this text do not insist on starting off with a trie. We therefore relax the precondition to $\mathcal{L} = \mathcal{L}_0$—i.e., we drop the first conjunct Is_Trie, and allowing M to have confluence states.

A partition of "done" and "to-do" states of Q is maintained, namely D, T. D is "done" in the sense that it is a set of pairwise inequivalent states—that is $Inequiv(D)$ holds. T is the set of states still to be processed. A loop is envisaged in which each iteration sees the selection of a non-empty set of states N from T. N is then modified to ensure that each pair of states taken respectively from $D \cup N$ and D are inequivalent. When this is achieved, N is added into D.

The loop thus guarantees that T shrinks at every iteration. However, while D is guaranteed not to shrink in any iteration, it cannot be guaranteed to grow: it may in fact remain the same size for many iterations when equivalent states are being merged. The algorithm outline is therefore:

Algorithm 7.4.1.

proc $cleanup_T() \rightarrow$
    $\{$ **pre** $\mathcal{L} = \mathcal{L}_0 \}$
    $\lbrack\!\lbrack$ **var** D, T : **set of** *State*
    $|$ $D, T := \varnothing, Q;$
      $\{$ *invariant* :*Inequiv*$(D) \wedge \mathcal{L} = \mathcal{L}_0$
        variant :$|T|$ $\}$
      do $T \neq \varnothing \rightarrow \lbrack\!\lbrack$ **var** N : **set of** *State*
                 $|$ **let** $N : N \subseteq T \wedge N \neq \varnothing;$
                  $T := T - N;$
                  $\{$ $N \neq \varnothing$ $\}$
                  $N : S'_{7.4.4};$
                  $\{$ *Inequiv*$(D \cup N)$ $\}$
                  $D := D \cup N$
                  $\{$ *Inequiv*(D) $\}$
                $\rbrack\!\rbrack$
    od
    $\rbrack\!\rbrack$
    $\{$ **post** Min $\wedge \mathcal{L} = \mathcal{L}_0$ $\}$
corp

This gives a specification for statement $S'_{7.4.4}$: establish *Inequiv*$(D \cup N)$ while changing only N (and implicitly M).

To map out the refinement paths of $S'_{7.4.4}$ that flow from this skeletal form of $cleanup_T$, note that because of Property 7.2.18, the postcondition of $S'_{7.4.4}$ conforms to the following equivalence relationship:

$$Inequiv(D \cup N) \equiv Inequiv(D) \wedge Inequiv(N) \wedge Pairwise\_inequiv(D, N)$$

Thus the postcondition of $S'_{7.4.4}$ may be replaced by the right hand side of the above equivalence relationship. Since conjunct *Inequiv*(D) is in the loop invariant, D should be left intact when refining $S'_{7.4.4}$. The remaining two conjuncts can serve as the basis for two different refinement paths of $S'_{7.4.4}$. In each of these cases, one of the conjuncts is "moved" into the **let** statement which selects N in the first place, thereby simplifying $S'_{7.4.4}$ because that conjunct now becomes a conjunct to the precondition to $S'_{7.4.4}$.

7.4.4.1   First Refinement Path

In the first refinement path, we select N in the **let** statement so that $Inequiv(N)$ holds but not necessarily $Pairwise\_inequiv(D, N)$. The task in $S'_{7.4.4}$ is therefore to ensure that $Pairwise\_inequiv(D, N)$ holds. In the second refinement path, the opposite strategy is followed: N is selected so that $Pairwise\_inequiv(D, N)$ holds, and $S'_{7.4.4}$ is designed to ensure that $Inequiv(N)$ is holds.

The first refinement path in turn leads to at least two further possibilities.

- The easiest is to select N as a single state, $p \in T$, in which case $Inequiv(\{p\})$ holds trivially. This leads to the following refined code extract as one particular version of $clean\_up_T$:

$$\vdots$$

```
{ invariant: Inequiv(D) ∧ L = L₀
  variant: |T| }
do T ≠ ∅ → ⟦ var  p : State
            | let  p : p ∈ T;
              T := T − {p};
              { Inequiv({p}) }
              if ∃q : D · Equiv(p, q) →
                  let  q : q ∈ D ∧ Equiv(p, q);
                  merge(p, q)
              ⫾ ∄q : D · Equiv(p, q) →
                  { Inequiv(D ∪ {p}) }
                  D := D ∪ {p}
              fi
              { Inequiv(D) }
            ⟧
od
```

$$\vdots$$

Note that the existence of a procedure $merge(p, q)$ is assumed. It changes δ and Q by merging the two states, p and q. Viewed from the perspective of the associated transition graph, this means redirecting all in-transitions of node q into node p instead, removing all out-transitions from node q, and indeed removing node q itself.

There are several further refinements related to this code segment whose details we omit. Essentially they relate to the functions needed to establish the predicate $Equiv(p, q)$, as well as various strategies to select the next p from T.

- An alternative way of selecting N in the skeleton Algorithm 7.4.1 that ensures $Inequiv(N)$, is to choose a path of states $[r, \overset{x}{\rightsquigarrow}] \subseteq T$ for some state r and string x. This is based on a property whose proof we omit, but which is intuitively clear, namely that $Inequiv([r, \overset{x}{\leadsto}])$ for arbitrarily chosen r and x. Again, we omit full details of how $S'_{7.4.4}$ could be refined in this case.

7.4.4.2 Second Refinement Path

In the second refinement path that flowed from a consideration of Property 7.2.18, we pointed out that algorithms could be developed whereby N is chosen at each step such that

$Pairwise\_inequiv(D, N)$ provably holds. Equivalent nodes in N are then merged and the resulting N is added to D. We will skip a detailed discussion of the theoretical considerations that show how such an N can be selected, and that result in an alternative version of $clean\_up_T$ based on this idea. Instead, we present in the next section an example to illustrate the general idea.

7.4.5 An Example

Figure 7.5a shows the trie resulting from using iteratively add_word_T to add the words had, hard, head, heard, herd, here, her, he. In applying $cleanup_T$, D starts off as $\varnothing$ and T is the set of all the nodes.

In the first iteration, we select N as all the leaf final states, namely $\{3, 5, 8, 10, 12, 13\}$. Since $D = \varnothing$, $Pairwise\_inequiv(D, N)$ holds trivially. Since the right languages of all states in N are all the same, (namely $\{\epsilon\}$) these states are equivalent. They are therefore merged into a state called 3, as shown in Fig. 7.5b. At this point, therefore, $D = \{3\}$.

In the next step, we let N be the set of all the states one level 'back' from the merged state 3, namely $N = \{4, 9, 11\}$. Theory which has not been covered above guarantees that they will be pairwise inequivalent to D. This is also evident if one examines the right languages of the relevant states. However, these right languages will also reveal that 9 and 4 are equivalent. They are therefore merged into 4. (Of course the merging could have occurred vice-versa, with 4 merged into 9.) State 11 is not merged since it is final and the other two are not (i.e., the right languages of the respective states differ because ϵ is in the right language 11 but not in that of 4 or 9). The resulting automaton is shown in Fig. 7.6a. At this stage, $D = \{3, 4, 11\}$.

Moving one step back from state 4, we consider $N = \{2, 7\}$. Again, note that each of these states are pairwise inequivalent with all the states in D. The right languages of these two states also turn out to be the same, so that they may be merged. The result is shown in Fig. 7.6b, at which point $D = \{2, 3, 4, 11\}$. The remaining states $\{6\}, \{1\}, \{0\}$ are easily seen to be inequivalent, and are also pairwise inequivalent with the states in D, so that the ADFA in Fig. 7.6b is minimal.

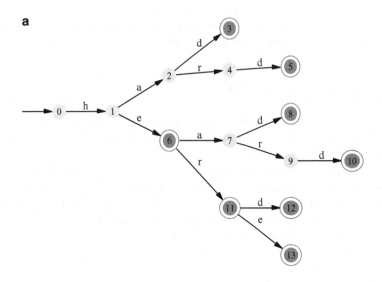

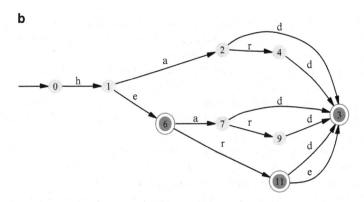

Fig. 7.5 First minimization step. (**a**) Initial trie: $D = \varnothing$. (**b**) Merge final states: $D = \{3\}$

7.5 Arbitrary Intermediate ADFA

In this section, we reflect on how to add a word to an *arbitrary* ADFA—one in which confluences may be encountered (when adding word w) on the w-path. We will, however, make use of the fact that s (the start state) cannot be a confluence due to acyclicity. The structural predicate is simply

$$Struct_N(D) \equiv \mathcal{L} = D.$$

a

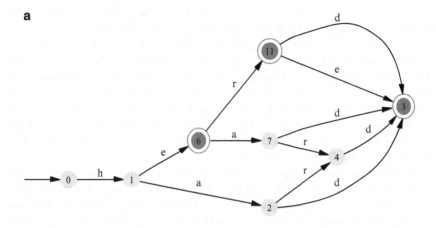

b

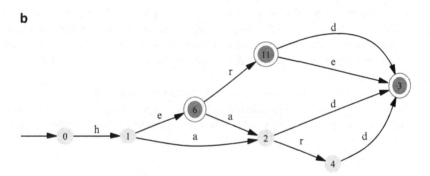

Fig. 7.6 Second and final minimisation steps. (**a**) Merge states 4 and 9: $D = \{3, 4, 11\}$. (**b**) Merge states 2 and 7: $D = \{2, 3, 4, 11\}$

Following construction, procedure $cleanup_N$ merges states in the same way as any of the variants of $cleanup_T$ discussed in Sect. 7.4.4.

7.5.1 Procedure add_word$_N$

Without modification, the algorithms of Chap. 7.4 (add_word_T and variants) may add words accidentally if a confluence state is encountered. Consider the following example.

Initially, we have the ADFA shown in Fig. 7.7a that accepts hard and herd, but is not confluence-free. While adding the new word head, we arrive at the confluence state 2. From state 2, there is no a out-transition and so we naïvely extend the automaton as in Fig. 7.7b to accept the new word head. An unintended side-effect of is that the ADFA now incorrectly also accepts haad!

A "cloning" operation is required at the confluence state. By this, we mean that an additional state should be created, and out transitions to the new state should be inserted that match out transitions from the confluence state both in alphabet and in destination states. We will assume that a function *clone(p)* returns such a new state, which is a 'clone' of its argument *p*. We assume that *clone(p)* adds the cloned state into *Q* and the cloned out transitions to *δ*. The transition to the confluence state that is traversed by the new word to be added should then be moved to this cloned state. The next example illustrates the point.

As in the previous example, we begin with the MADFA accepting hard and herd shown in Fig. 7.7a. While adding the new word head, we arrive at confluence state 2 which is cloned, yielding new state 5. As shown in Fig. 7.8a the transition on e from state 1 to state 2 is changed to end in state 5. Note that the languages of the ADFAs in Figs. 7.7a and 7.8a are the same. Two additional states are then added, as shown in Fig. 7.8b, giving the final automaton.

Recall that procedure *add_word*$_T$ (in Sect. 7.4 on page 242) contains two repeat loops. The first visits states in the transition graph, ending in the state that identifies in the graph the longest matching prefix of the word to be added. The second repeat loop then creates new states from that point onwards to cater for the suffix that remains of the word.

In modifying *add_word*$_T$ to *add_word*$_N$, the modified algorithm needs to clone confluence states that are encountered in the first repeat loop (i.e., the loop that identifies the longest matching prefix). The second repetition need not be changed,

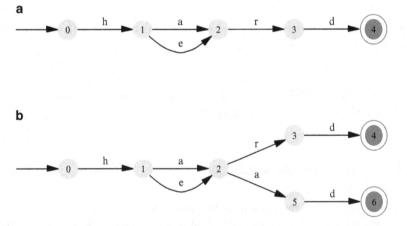

Fig. 7.7 Naïve extension of an automaton. (a) ADFA accepting hard and herd. (b) ADFA accepting hard, herd, head and haad

a

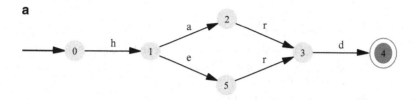

b

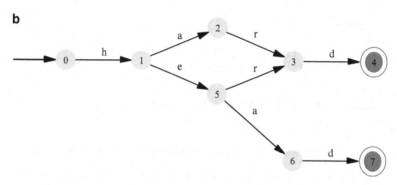

Fig. 7.8 Second and final minimisation steps. (**a**) Confluent state 2 in Fig. 7.7a produces cloned state 5. (**b**) ADFA accepting hard, herd and head

since it is only creating new states, *none* of which can be a confluence state. We can modify the first repetition accordingly yielding the procedure body:

proc add_word_N (**in** $w : \Sigma^*$) →
 { **pre** $\mathcal{L} = \mathcal{L}_0$ }
 |[**var** q : *State*
 | |[**var** $l, r : \Sigma^*$; p : *State*
 | $l, r, q := \epsilon, w, s$;
   { invariant: $w = lr \wedge q = \delta^*(s, l) \wedge \mathit{Confl\_free}([s \overset{l}{\leadsto}])$
   variant: $|r|$ }
  do $r \neq \epsilon$ **cand** $\delta(q, head(r)) \neq \perp$ →
   $p := \delta(q, head(r))$;
   as $\mathit{Is\_Confl}(p)$ →
    $p := clone(p)$;
    $\delta(q, head(r)) := p$
  sa;
  $q := p$;
  $l, r := l \cdot head(r), tail(r)$

```
    od;
    { Confl_free([s ↝ᵂ]) }
    { q = δ*(s, l) ∧ δ*(s, l) ≠ ⊥ ∧ (r = ε cor δ(q, head(r)) = ⊥) }
    { invariant: w = lr ∧ q = δ*(s, l)
      variant: |r| }
    do r ≠ ε → [[ var p : State
              | p := create();
                δ(q, head(r)), q := p, p;
                l, r := l · head(r), tail(r)
              ]]
    od
  ]];
  { q = δ*(s, w) ∧ q ≠ ⊥ }
  F := F ∪ {q}
]]
{ post Confl_free([s ↝ᵂ]) ∧ L = L₀ ∪ {w} }
```

corp

This, however, is also subject to improvement thanks to another observation:

Once a confluence state has been cloned, further states in the w path (other than newly created ones) will also have to be cloned.

For this reason, we can again split the first of the above repetitions into two sequentially composed repetitions, in our final algorithm:

proc $add\_word'_N$ (**in** $w : \Sigma^*$) →
```
  { pre L = L₀ }
  [[ var q : State
  | [[ var l, r : Σ*; p : State
  | l, r, q := ε, w, s;
        { invariant: w = lr ∧ q = δ*(s, l) ∧ Confl_free([s ↝ˡ]) 
          variant: |r| }
        do r ≠ ε cand δ(q, head(r)) ≠ ⊥ cand ¬Is_Confl(δ(q, head(r))) →
           l, r, q := l · head(r), tail(r), δ(q, head(r))
        od;
        { invariant: w = lr ∧ q = δ*(s, l) ∧ Confl_free([s ↝ˡ]) 
          variant: |r| }
        do r ≠ ε cand δ(q, head(r)) ≠ ⊥ →
           { Is_Confl(δ(q, head(r))) }
           p := δ(q, head(r));
           { Is_Confl(p) }
           p := clone(p);
           δ(q, head(r)), q := p, p;
           l, r := l · head(r), tail(r)
```

od;

$$\left\{ \, \textit{Confl\_free}([s \overset{w}{\rightsquigarrow}]) \, \right\}$$
$$\{ \; q = \delta^*(s,l) \land \delta^*(s,l) \neq \perp \land (r = \epsilon \textbf{ cor } \delta(q, head(r)) = \perp) \; \}$$
$$\{ \; \text{invariant: } w = lr \land q = \delta^*(s,l)$$
$$\quad \text{variant: } |r| \; \}$$
$$\textbf{do } \; r \neq \epsilon \rightarrow p := \textit{create}();$$
$$\delta(q, head(r)), q := p, p;$$
$$l, r := l \cdot head(r), tail(r)$$
$$\textbf{od}$$
$$]\!];$$
$$\{ \; q = \delta^*(s,w) \land q \neq \perp \; \}$$
$$F := F \cup \{q\}$$
$$]\!]$$
$$\left\{ \, \textbf{post } \; \textit{Confl\_free}([s \overset{w}{\rightsquigarrow}]) \land \mathcal{L} = \mathcal{L}_0 \cup \{w\} \, \right\}$$

corp

This algorithm always clones confluences, which proves to be inefficient if they are subsequently found to be equivalent (and therefore merged). High-performance implementations of this algorithm perform a "lazy cloning" (also known as "virtual cloning") operation, substantially improving the performance [10].

7.5.2   Procedure cleanup$_N$

For *cleanup$_N$* we can use any one of the general minimization algorithms from [44] or a version of *cleanup$_T$* from Sect. 7.4.4.

7.5.3   Commentary

If the MADFA is to be built from scratch, *add_word$_N$* is uninteresting since the initial ADFA will be a trie in which no confluences occur. Procedure *add_word$_N$* is primarily interesting for adding words to an ADFA in which some confluences already occur from previous minimization steps. Interestingly, *add_word$_N$* also works on cyclic DFA's.

7.6   Word Adding Based on a Partial Order

There are two *add_word* variants that allow confluent states to be constructed— those associated with the *Struct* variants in rows 2 and 3 of Table 7.1 (i.e., *Struct$_N$* and *Struct$_I$*). In Sect. 7.5's review of the *add_word$_N$* algorithm, we saw that if a confluence state is encountered on the prefix path of the new word to be inserted, then that confluence state has to be cloned. Such cloning is also required when encountering a confluence state in add_word_I, whose form has not been discussed here.

Performance profiling of implementations of the algorithms partially presented in Sect. 7.5, as well as of algorithms derived from $Struct_I(D)$ shows that most of the execution time is spent on two operations:

- Cloning confluence states.
- Merging states found to be equivalent.

(Creating new states is a cheap operation in practice.) While the merging operation is generally unavoidable in constructing a MADFA, some MADFA research has focussed on performance improvement by limiting, if not quite eliminating, the need for cloning.

The structural invariants in rows 5, 6 and 7 of Table 7.1 have their origin in a quest to limit cloning. Each of the three associated add_word algorithms avoid cloning by ensuring that in adding the next word, only a confluence-free path needs to be investigated. Since cloning only has to be applied to confluence states, the expense of cloning is thereby avoided.

At the same time these three add_word variants guarantee that all states not on this confluence-free path are retained as inequivalent. (Recall that these variants are designated add_word_S, add_word_D and add_word_W corresponding to the structural invariants in rows 5, 6 and 7 of the table, respectively.)

Each variant of add_word therefore consists of a loop that selects and inserts the next word into the ADFA to generated date. The bodies of the respective loops all conform to the following general pattern:

$$\{\ P(w) \wedge Inequiv(Q - Z) \wedge Confl\_free(Z) \wedge \mathcal{L} = \mathcal{L}_0\ \}$$
$$\quad add\_word_T(w);$$
$$\{\ R'(w) \wedge Inequiv(Q - Z') \wedge Confl\_free(Z') \wedge \mathcal{L} = \mathcal{L}_0 \cup \{w\}\ \}$$
$$\quad S_{7.6}$$
$$\{\ R(w) \wedge Inequiv(Q - Z) \wedge Confl\_free(Z) \wedge \mathcal{L} = \mathcal{L}_0 \cup \{w\}\ \}$$

Here Q, Z, Z', $P(w)$, $R'(w)$ and $R(w)$ assume values according to the algorithm under consideration. Q and Z assume the values shown in rows 5, 6 and 7 of Table 7.1.

$P(w)$ is an assertion indicating how w must be ordered in relation to the words already incorporated into $\mathcal{L}$. $R'(w)$ and $R(w)$ are revised assertions about the ordering relationship of words in $\mathcal{L}$. In overview, the following holds:

- In the case of add_word_S, $P(w)$ requires that the next word, w, to be added must be lexicographically greater than all words already in $\mathcal{L}$. Both $R'(w)$ and $R(w)$ simply state that w is now the lexicographically largest word in $\mathcal{L}$, i.e., $w = lexmax$. By implication, words are to be submitted to add_word_T in increasing lexicographic order.

- In the case of add_word_D, $P(w)$ requires that the *length* of the next word to be added, $|w|$, must be less or equal to *minlin*—the shortest word length in $\mathcal{L}$ to date. In this case, $R'(w)$ and $R(w)$ state that w is now smallest length word in $\mathcal{L}$, i.e., $w = minlen$. By implication, words are to be submitted to add_word_T in decreasing order of word length.

- In the case of add_word_W, $P(w)$ and $R(w)$ are the same as in add_word_D. However, $R'(w)$ has a somewhat more complicated form, namely that $F = F_0 \cup \{\delta^*(s, w)\} \wedge \delta^*(s, w) \notin F_0$. Elaborating on the meaning of this requirement is beyond the scope of this present discussion. However, note that again, words are to be submitted to add_word_T in decreasing order of word length.

The general form given above uses Z' to indicate that the call to add_word_T modifies the set of states that are now inequivalent, and, accordingly, the set of states that are confluence free. In order to reestablish the invariants that apply in each of the three respective cases, commands generically denoted above by $S_{7.6}$ need to be carried out. The detailed form of these commands are beyond the scope of this discussion. However, in general, these commands reestablish a the partition of inequivalent states and confluence-free states, in preparation for the next iteration of the loop.

Once all words have been added, a residual *cleanup* needs to be carried out to ensure inequivalence of states that remain at the end of the loop's final iteration. Again, the commands relevant to each will differ slightly, and will not be discussed here.

The intention here has been to illustrate that a correctness by construction approach to understanding related algorithms provides deep insight into the commonalities and differences between the algorithms. We have also claimed that the process of uncovering and articulating these commonalities and differences often results in new insights into alternative ways of solving the problem concerned. This is precisely the case in the three algorithms overviewed above: in seeking a correctness by construction understanding of pre-existing algorithms add_word_S and add_word_W, the algorithm add_word_D suggested itself as an entirely new algorithm, which was published for the first time in [43].

References

1. A. Aho, M. Lam, R. Sethi, J. Ullman, *Compilers: Principles, Techniques and Tools*, 2nd edn. (Pearson Education, 2007), ISBN-10: 0321491696, ISBN-13: 9780321491695
2. A. Alexandrescu, *Modern C++ Design: Generic Programming and Design Patterns Applied* (Addison-Wesley, Boston, Massachusetts, 2001), ISBN 978-0201704310
3. G. Arévalo, in *Proceedings of LMO 2003: Langages et Modeles à Objets*, Understanding behavioral dependencies in class hierarchies using concept analysis, Hermes, Paris, January 2003. pp 47–59
4. G. Birkhoff, *Lattice Theory* (Amer. Math. Soc. Coll. Publ., Providence, R.I., 1973)
5. C.L. Blake, C.J. Merz, UCI repository of machine learning databases. University of California, Irvine, Dept. of Information and Computer Sciences, 1998
6. J.P. Bordat, Calcul pratique du treillis de Galois d'une correspondance. Math. Sci. Hum. **23**(2), 243–250 (1978)
7. J. Bresenham, A linear algorithm for incremental digital display of circular arcs. Commun. ACM **20**(2), 100–106 (1977)
8. C. Carpineto, G. Romano, *Concept Data Analysis: Theory and Applications* (John Wiley & Sons Ltd, New York, 2004)
9. C. Carpineto, G. Romano, A lattice conceptual clustering system and its application to browsing retrieval. Mach. Learn. **24**(2), 95–122 (1996)
10. J. Daciuk, S. Mihov, B.W. Watson, R.E. Watson, Incremental construction of minimal acyclic finite state automata. Comput. Linguist. **26**(1), 3–16 (2000)
11. B. Davey, H. Priestley, *Introduction to Lattices and Order*, 2nd edn. (Cambridge University Press, Cambridge, 2002)
12. U. Dekel, Applications of concept lattices to code inspection and review. Technical report, Department of Computer Science, Technion (2002)
13. E.W. Dijkstra, On the cruelty of really teaching computer science. Commun. ACM **32**(12), 1414 (1989)
14. J.D. Foley, A. van Dam, S.K. Feiner, J.F. Hughes, *Computer Graphics: Principles and Practice in C*, 2nd edn. (Pearson, New York, 1995)
15. F.P. Brooks Jr., in *The Mythical Man-Month: Essays on Software Engineering*, No silver bullet (Addison-Wesley, New York, 1995), ISBN 0-201-83595-9
16. E. Fredkin, Trie memory. Commun. ACM **3**(9), 490–499 (1960)
17. L.C. Freeman, D.R. White, Using Galois lattices to represent network data. Sociol. Methodol. **23**, 127–146 (1993)
18. B. Ganter. Two basic algorithms in concept analysis, FB4-Preprint No. 831 (Technische Hochschule Darmstadt, June 1984)

D.G. Kourie and B.W. Watson, *The Correctness-by-Construction Approach to Programming*, DOI 10.1007/978-3-642-27919-5,
© Springer-Verlag Berlin Heidelberg 2012

19. B. Ganter, R. Wille, *Formal Concept Analysis: Mathematical Foundations* (Springer, Berlin, 1999)
20. R. Godin, R. Missaoui, H. Alaoui. Incremental concept formation algorithms based on Galois lattices. Comput. Intell. **11**(2), 243–250 (1995)
21. R. Godin, H. Mili, in *Proceedings of the OOPSLA '93 Conference on Object-oriented Programming Systems, Languages and Applications*, Building and maintaining analysis-level class hierarchies using Galois lattices. (1993), pp. 394–410
22. P.A. Grigoriev, S.A. Yevtushenko, in *Concept Lattices: Proc. of the 2nd Int. Conf. on Formal Concept Analysis*, ed. by P. Eklund. Quda: applying formal concept analysis in a data mining environment, vol 2961/2004 (Springer, Berlin/Heidelberg, 2004), pp. 386–393
23. J. Gutknecht, Pulling rabbits out of a hat. South African Comput. J. **3**, 1–4 (1990)
24. M. Huchard, H. Dicky, H. Leblanc, Galois lattice as a framework to specify algorithms building class hierarchies. Theor. Inform. Appl. **34**, 521–548 (2000)
25. A Kaldewaij, *Programming: Derivation of Algorithms* (Prentice Hall International Ltd, New York, 1990)
26. D.G. Kourie, S. Obiedkov, B.W. Watson, F.D. van der Merwe, An incremental algorithm to construct a lattice of set intersections. Sci. Comput. Program. **74**(3), 128–142 (2009)
27. D.G. Kourie, An approach to defining abstractions, refinements and enrichments. Quæst. Inf. **6**(4), 174–178 (1989)
28. S. Kuznetsov, S. Obiedkov, Comparing performance of algorithms for generating concept lattices. J. Exp. Theor. Artif. Intell. **14**(2/3), 189–216 (2002)
29. S. Kuznetsov, in *Concept Lattices: Proceedings of the 2nd International Conference on Formal Concept Analysis*, ed. by P. Eklund. Machine learning and formal concept analysis. LNCS, vol. 2961 (Springer-Verlag, Berlin, Heidelberg, 2004), pp. 287–312
30. C. Lindig, G. Snelting, in *Proceedings of the 1997 International Conference on Software Engineering (ICSE '97)*, Assessing modular structure of legacy code based on mathematical concept analysis, Boston, MA, May 1997. pp. 349–359
31. B. Meyer, *Touch of Class: Learning to Program Well with Objects and Contracts* (Springer-Verlag, Berlin, Heidelberg, 2009)
32. C. Morgan, Programming from specifications (1998), http://web2.comlab.ox.ac.uk/oucl/publications/books/PfS/
33. E.M. Norris, An algorithm for computing the maximal rectangles in a binary relation. Rev. Roum. Math. Pures A. **23**(2), 243–250 (1978)
34. L. Nourine, O. Raynaud, A fast algorithm for building lattices. Inform. Process. Lett. **71**, 199–204 (1999)
35. U. Priss, in *Formal Concept Analysis, Foundations and Applications*, ed. by B. Ganter, G. Stumme, R. Wille. Linguistic applications of formal concept analysis. LNAI, vol. 3626 (Springer-Verlag, Berlin, Heidelberg, 2005), pp. 149–160
36. C. Roth, S. Obiedkov, D.G. Kourie, in *Proceedings of the 4th International Conference on Concept Lattices and Their Applications*, ed. by S.B. Yahia, E.M. Nguifo. Towards concise representation for taxonomies of epistemic communities, Faculté des Sciences de Tunis, Université Centrale, Hammamet, Tunisia, 2006, pp. 205–218
37. G. Snelting, F. Tip, Reengineering class hierarchies using concept analysis. SIGSOFT Softw. Eng. Notes **23**(6), 99–110 (1998)
38. G. Stumme, A. Mädche, in *Proceedings of the17th International Conference on Artificial Intelligence (IJCAI '01)*, ed. by B. Nebel. FCA-merge: Bottom-up merging of ontologies, Seattle, WA, USA, 2001. pp. 225–230
39. T. Tilley, R. Cole, P. Becker, P. Eklund, in *Formal Concept Analysis, Foundations and Applications*, ed. by Bernhard Ganter, Robert Godin, A survey of formal concept analysis support for software engineering activities. Lecture Notes in Computer Science, vol. 3626, July 2005, pp. 250–271
40. P. Valtchev, R. Missaoui, R. Godin, in *Concept Lattices: Proceedings of the 2nd International Conference on Formal Concept Analysis*, ed. by P. Eklund. Formal concept analysis for knowledge discovery and data mining: The new challenges. LNCS, vol. 2961 (Springer-Verlag, Berlin, Heidelberg, 2004), pp. 352–371

41. F.J. van der Merwe, Constructing concept lattices and compressed pseudo-lattices, Master's thesis, University of Pretoria, 2003

42. F.J. van der Merwe, S. Obiedkov, D.G. Kourie, in *Concept Lattices: Proc. of the 2nd Int. Conf. on Formal Concept Analysis*, ed. by P. Eklund. AddIntent: A new incremental algorithm for constructing concept lattices. LNCS, vol. 2961 (Springer-Verlag, Berlin, Heidelberg, 2004), p. 411

43. B.W. Watson, *Minimizing acyclic deterministic finite automata*, Ph.D., FASTAR Research Group, Department of Computer Science, University of Pretoria, South Africa, 2011

44. B.W. Watson, *Taxonomies and Toolkits of Regular Language Algorithms*, Ph.D. thesis, Eindhoven University of Technology, Faculty of Computing Science, September 1995

45. B.W. Watson, in *CIAA 2000*, ed. by Yu, Păun. Directly constructing minimal DFAs: Combining two algorithms by Brzozowski (2000), pp. 242–249

46. B.W. Watson, in *CIAA 2000*, ed. by Yu, Păun. A history of Brzozowski's DFA minimization algorithm (2000)

47. B.W. Watson, Directly constructing minimal DFAs: Combining two algorithms by Brzozowski. South African Comput. J. **29**, 17–23 (2002)

48. R. Wille, in *ICFCA '09: Proceedings of the 7th International Conference on Formal Concept Analysis*, ed. by Sébastien Ferré, Sebastian Rudolph, Restructuring lattice theory: An approach based on hierarchies of concepts (Springer-Verlag, Berlin, Heidelberg, 2009), pp. 314–339

49. S.A. Yevtushenko, in *Proceedings of the 7th national conference on Artificial Intelligence KII-2000*. System of data analysis "concept explorer" (in Russian), Russia (2000), pp. 127–134

Index

D.G. Kourie and B.W. Watson, *The Correctness-by-Construction Approach*
to Programming, DOI 10.1007/978-3-642-27919-5,
© Springer-Verlag Berlin Heidelberg 2012